Managerial Ec

Now in its fifth edition, Ivan Png's *Managerial Economics* has been extensively revised with

- an introductory chapter emphasizing decision-making and behavioral biases,
- an intensive application to recent business decisions, as well as
- a streamlined presentation focusing on the economics that managers need to know.

As always, the text presents the key concepts of microeconomics intuitively, without sophisticated mathematics. Throughout, it emphasizes actual management applications, and links to other functions including marketing and finance.

The new fifth edition is updated with fresh up-to-date discussion questions from all over the world and enhanced with detailed instructor supplements. It is an ideal text for any course focusing on the practical application of microeconomic principles to management.

Truly useful economics for managers. In the words of one professor, "I can use your book for serious conversation with adult students."

Ivan Png is a Distinguished Professor in the School of Business and Department of Economics at the National University of Singapore. Previously, Dr Png was a faculty member at the Anderson School, University of California, Los Angeles (1985–1996) and the Hong Kong University of Science and Technology (1993–1996), and Visiting Professor at the Tuck School of Business, Dartmouth College (2011–12). His book, *Managerial Economics*, has been published in multiple editions and adapted into Chinese (traditional and simplified characters), Korean, and Polish. He received the NUS-UCLA Executive MBA Teaching Excellence Award in 2008 and 2011. Dr Png was a nominated MP (10th Parliament of Singapore), 2005–2006, a member of the Trustworthy Computing Academic Advisory Board, Microsoft Corporation, 2006–10, and an independent director of Healthway Medical Corporation, 2008–2011.

"I often use this book in my MBA-level Managerial Economics classes. It provides clear and rigorous explanations of major microeconomic theories and supports them with a large number of relevant examples from around the world. I find this book well-written, concise, and interesting."

Annamaria Conti, *Assistant Professor, Scheller College of Business, Georgia Institute of Technology, USA*

"Ivan Png's *Managerial Economics* is a concise and effective textbook that makes use of endless real-life examples not only to illustrate a point, but rather to motivate it, explain it, and convince students of its relevance. The wide range of situations, industries, and historical events covered make this book quite an enriching read. In my opinion, *Managerial Economics* is an excellent tool when used to teach MBAs and students without much economics background. Economics majors will benefit from reading it as they will gain valuable practical knowledge of the use of their tools."

Eugenio J. Miravete, *Rex G. Baker Jr. Professor of Political Economy, University of Texas at Austin, USA*

"Ivan Png's *Managerial Economics* has made my life easy as a lecturer! It is a fantastic integration of theory, real life examples, and case studies, which makes both teaching and learning a joy. The chapters are well organized and highly relevant – keeping in mind business and management students' needs. I have thoroughly enjoyed using this book as the main text for my postgraduate management economics class."

Abhijit Sengupta, *Lecturer, Essex Business School, University of Essex, UK*

"I have been using this text for teaching the EMBA Global Asia program (a joint program of Columbia Business School, HKU Business School, and London Business School) in the last six years. Students like the text very much as it offers possibly the simplest and most concise explanation of economic concepts and principles that are applicable for business decision making."

Tao Zhigang, *Professor of Economics and Strategy, Faculty of Business and Economics, University of Hong Kong*

Managerial Economics

Fifth Edition

Ivan Png

Routledge
Taylor & Francis Group

LONDON AND NEW YORK

First published 2016
by Routledge
2 Park Square, Milton Park, Abingdon, Oxon OX14 4RN

and by Routledge
711 Third Avenue, New York, NY 10017

Routledge is an imprint of the Taylor & Francis Group, an informa business

British Library Cataloguing-in-Publication Data
A catalogue record for this book is available from the British Library

Library of Congress Cataloging-in-Publication Data
Png, Ivan, 1957-
    Managerial economics / Ivan Png. – 5th edition.
    1. Managerial economics. I. Title.
    HD30.22.P62 2015
    338.5024'658–dc23   2014049719

ISBN: 978-1-138-81025-9 (hbk)
ISBN: 978-1-138-81026-6 (pbk)
ISBN: 978-1-315-74964-8 (ebk)

Typeset in Times
by Sunrise Setting Ltd, Paignton, UK

For my parents and three Cs – CW, CY, CH

Tables

Preface

Managerial economics is the science of directing scarce resources in the management of a business or other organization. This book presents tools and concepts from managerial economics that practicing managers can and do use. It

- emphasizes simple, practical ideas,
- focuses on application to business decision-making,
- integrates global business issues and practice,
- provides conceptual rigor without mathematical complexity.

This book is aimed at business students as well as practitioners. Accordingly, it is deliberately written in a simple and accessible style. It presents a minimum of technical jargon, complicated figures, and highbrow mathematics. It starts with the very basics and does not presume any prior knowledge of economics. While the mathematics is minimal, the economics is rigorous. The application of economic concepts to business practice will challenge even readers with some background in economics.

Managerial economics is unique in integrating the various functions of management. In addition to presenting the essentials of managerial economics, this book includes many links to other management functions. Some examples are accounting (transfer pricing), finance (opportunity cost of capital and takeover strategies), human resource management (incentives and organization), and marketing (advertising and pricing).

In addition to the managerial focus, two features are worth emphasizing. First, the same principles of managerial economics apply globally. Reflecting this unity, the book includes examples and cases from throughout the world. Second, the book uses examples from both consumer and industrial markets. The reasons are simple: a customer is as likely to be another business as a human being, and likewise for suppliers.

For most readers, this may be their only formal book on economics. Accordingly, the book eschews sophisticated theories and models, such as indifference curves and production functions, which are more useful in advanced economics courses. Further, the book recognizes that many topics traditionally covered by managerial economics textbooks are now the domain of other basic management courses. Accordingly, the book omits linear programming and capital budgeting.

Regarding language, this book refers to businesses rather than firms. Realistically, many firms are involved in a wide range of businesses. In economics, the usual unit of analysis is a business, industry, or market rather than a firm. Also, the book refers to buyers and sellers rather than consumers and firms, since in most real markets, demand and supply do not neatly divide among households and businesses. To cite just two examples, in the market for telecommunications, the demand side consists of businesses and households, while in the market for human resources the supply side comprises households and businesses. Outsourcing has reinforced this diversity of suppliers.

Managerial economics is a practical science. Just as no one learns swimming or tennis simply by watching a professional, so no one can learn managerial economics merely by reading this book. Every chapter of this book includes progress checks, and review and discussion questions. The progress checks and review questions are to help the reader check and reinforce the chapter material.

Readers must practice their new-found skills on these checks and questions. The discussion questions are intended to challenge, provoke, and stretch. They will be useful for class and group discussions.

Key Features

- Simple, practical ideas for business decision-making
- Integrates managerial economics into finance, accounting, human resources, and other management functions
- Mini-cases and examples from around the world
- Every chapter is reinforced with progress checks, review questions, and discussion questions
- Easy to read, with minimal technical jargon, figures, and mathematics
- Complete instructor's supplements – transparency masters, answers to discussion questions, casebank, and testbank.

Organization

This book is organized into three parts. Following the Introduction, Part I presents the framework of perfectly competitive markets. Chapters 2–6 are the basic starting point of managerial economics. These are presented at a very gradual pace, accessible to readers with no prior background in economics.

The book gathers pace in Parts II and III. These are relatively self-contained, so the reader may skip Part II and go directly to Part III. Part II broadens the perspective to situations of market power, while Part III focuses on the issues of management in imperfect markets. Chapter 15 on regulation is the only chapter in Part III that depends on understanding Part II.

A complete course in managerial economics would cover the entire book. For shorter courses, there are three alternatives. One is a course focusing on the managerial economics of strategy, which would comprise Chapters 1–11. Another alternative focuses on the managerial economics of organization, comprising Chapters 1–7 and 12–14. The third alternative focuses on modern managerial economics – strategy and organization – and would comprise Chapters 1–4 and 7–14.

Website

Online support for this book can be found at https://sites.google.com/site/pngecon/. The site contains additional cases and applications, as well as updates and corrections to the book. The site also contains a link to resources for instructors, including transparencies, answers to discussion questions, a testbank, and a casebank.

Acknowledgments

In preparing the fifth edition, I gratefully acknowledge advice and suggestions from Nicholas Snowden, Richard Leigh, and Joy Cheng. Finally, I thank generations of students at NUS, HKUST, and UCLA for their enthusiastic support and encouragement.

About the Author

Ivan Png is a Distinguished Professor in the School of Business and Department of Economics at the National University of Singapore. He was a Visiting Professor at the Tuck School of Business, Dartmouth College (2011–2012). Previously, he was a faculty member at the Anderson School, University of California, Los Angeles (1985–1996) and the Hong Kong University of Science and Technology (1993–1996).

Dr Png attended the Anglo-Chinese School, Singapore, and graduated with first class honors in economics from the University of Cambridge (1978) and a PhD from the Stanford Graduate School of Business (1985).

His research has been published in leading management and economics journals including *Management Science*, *American Economic Review*, and *Journal of Political Economy*. He received the NUS-UCLA Executive MBA Teaching Excellence Award in 2008 and again in 2011.

Dr Png was a nominated MP in the 10th Parliament of Singapore (2005–2006), member of the Trustworthy Computing Academic Advisory Board, Microsoft Corporation (2006–2010), and an independent director of Hyflux Water Trust Management Pte Ltd (2007–2011) and Healthway Medical Corporation (2008–2011).

Dr Png speaks English and Chinese (Mandarin). He is married to Ms Joy Cheng. They have two sons, Max and Lucas.

Introduction to Managerial Economics

LEARNING OBJECTIVES

- Appreciate the objective of managerial economics.
- Understand value added and economic profit.
- Apply total benefit and total cost to decide participation.
- Apply marginal benefit and marginal cost to decide extent.
- Appreciate the effect of bounded rationality on decision-making.
- Apply net present value to evaluate benefits and costs that flow over time.
- Understand the vertical and horizontal boundaries of an organization.
- Distinguish competitive markets, market power, and imperfect markets.

1. What Is Managerial Economics?

Airbus and Boeing dominate the manufacturing of large commercial jet aircraft (with 150 or more seats).[1] Boeing's most successful and profitable plane is the Boeing 737, a twin-engine, single-aisle, medium-range jet. First flown in 1967, the Boeing 737 has been developed into nine models. As of December 2010, Boeing had delivered 6,687 units of the 737, with a further 2,186 on order. The Boeing 737 competes with Airbus's A320 family, comprising five models – the A318, A319, A320, A321, and ACJ business jet. According to Boeing forecasts, airlines would buy 23,370 new single-aisle planes in the next 20 years.

However, at the Paris Air Show in June 2011, Jim Albaugh, CEO of Boeing Commercial Airplanes, conceded: "The days of the duopoly with Airbus are over." Manufacturers, from China, Canada, Russia, and Brazil, have developed, launched, or are poised to launch new aircraft to compete with Boeing's 737 and Airbus's A320 family.

In November 2010, the Commercial Aircraft Corporation of China (COMAC) announced that it had booked 100 orders for the C919, a new 150-seat single-aisle plane, the leading customers being Air China, China Southern Airlines, and China Eastern Airlines. By September 2014, COMAC reported an increase to 400 orders from 16 customers. The maiden flight of the C919 is scheduled for late 2015.

Bombardier, headquartered in Canada, had long manufactured regional jets, which are smaller short-range planes with up to 100 seats. It aspired to expand into larger aircraft, but only began development in 2008, upon securing a letter of interest for 60 planes from Deutsche Lufthansa. The new CSeries, a family of 100- to 149-seat aircraft, is scheduled to enter service in 2015. The CSeries will reduce fuel consumption by 20% through use of advanced materials and a more fuel-efficient engine, the PW1000G from Pratt & Whitney. As of September 2014, Bombardier had 203 orders.

The Russian manufacturer of military aircraft, Irkut, is diversifying into commercial jets and launched the MC-21 in 2007. By February 2014, Irkut had secured 170 orders, all from Russian airlines. The MC-21 will reduce fuel consumption through lower weight, better aerodynamics, and more efficient engines. It is scheduled to enter service around 2016.

Like Bombardier, the Brazilian manufacturer, Embraer, is an established manufacturer of regional jets. However, as of June 2011, it had not secured any orders and had deferred a decision on whether to commence development. CEO Frederico Curado remarked: "Going up against Boeing and Airbus in head-to-head competition is really tough, not only because of their size, but because of their existing product line and industrial capacity . . . . They can have a very quick response and literally flood the market." Moreover, Tom Enders, CEO of Airbus, cautioned that there might not be sufficient room for six manufacturers.

In December 2010, Airbus announced that it would develop a new version of the A320 – the A320neo ("new engine option"). The A320neo would be powered by either CFM International's LEAP-X engine or the engine in the Bombardier's CSeries, Pratt & Whitney's PW1000G. In March 2011, Airbus announced that it would raise production of the A320 family from 34 to 36 units per month.

Boeing's Jim Albaugh acknowledged that the CSeries 300 appeared to target customers of the Boeing 737. He insisted that Boeing would respond: "I look at the 737 business that we have and it is one of the cornerstones of Boeing Commercial and it is a marketplace we are going to defend." Just before the Paris Air Show, Boeing announced an increase in production of the Boeing 737 from 31.5 units to 42 units per month.

Why did Bombardier wait until securing orders from Lufthansa before launching the CSeries? Why does Bombardier emphasize the fuel efficiency of its CSeries? Who among the new entrants that have commenced development – Bombardier,

COMAC, and Irkut – has the best chance of succeeding in competition with Boeing and Airbus? Should Embraer stay out of the market?

What about Boeing? How should it respond to the new entry? Should it launch a new product or, like Airbus, modify its existing plane? Did it make sense to expand production of the 737? Why did Airbus respond to the entry of Bombardier and COMAC with a new version of the A320 rather than a totally new plane?

All of these are questions of *managerial economics*. **Managerial economics** is the science of cost-effective management of scarce resources. Wherever resources are scarce, managers can make more cost-effective decisions by applying the discipline of managerial economics. The decisions may regard customers, suppliers, competitors, or the internal workings of the organization. Whether the organization is a profit-oriented business, non-profit organization, or household, managers must make the best use of scarce resources.

> **Managerial economics:** The science of cost-effective management of scarce resources.

Boeing has limited financial, human, and physical resources. Boeing managers seek to maximize the financial return from these limited resources. The same is true of Airbus. While Boeing is a publicly traded company with diversified shareholders, Airbus is controlled by French, German, and Spanish corporate shareholders. Despite the differences in organization, the principles of managerial economics apply to both Airbus and Boeing. Each must compete effectively against the other and against Bombardier, COMAC, and Irkut, each must allocate resources to research and development (R&D), each must manage demand and costs, and each must set prices.

Managerial economics consists of three branches: competitive markets, market power, and imperfect markets. Accordingly, this book is organized into three parts. Before introducing the three branches of managerial economics, let us first develop some background.

2. Value Added

For the most part, this book takes the viewpoint of a profit-oriented business, while also considering the management of non-profit organizations and households. The primary goal of a profit-oriented business is to maximize profit. Indeed, the aim of competitive strategy is to deliver sustained profit above the competitive level.

Accordingly, an essential concept for managerial decision-making is *economic profit*. To appreciate the concept of economic profit, consider the basic equation of managerial economics:

Value added = Buyer benefit − Seller cost

$$= \text{Buyer surplus} + \text{Seller economic profit.} \qquad (1.1)$$

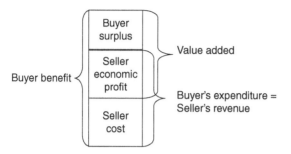

FIGURE 1.1 Value added.

Note: Value added=Buyer benefit–Seller cost=Buyer surplus+Seller economic profit.

Source: adapted from Luke M. Froeb and Brian T. McCann, *Managerial Economics: A Problem-Solving Approach*, Mason, OH: South-Western, 2010, p. 127.

This equation states that **value added** is the difference between buyer benefit and seller cost. It is only to the extent that businesses deliver benefit to buyers that exceeds the cost of production that they *create* value. Equation (1.1) is basic to all organizations – whether profit-oriented, non-profits, or households. To create value, they must deliver benefit that exceeds cost. Anyone who delivers benefit which is less than the cost of production is destroying value.

> **Value added:** Buyer benefit less seller cost. Comprises buyer surplus and economic profit.

Referring to Figure 1.1, value added is shared by buyer and seller. The buyer gets some part of the value added in *buyer surplus*, which is the difference between the buyer's benefit and their expenditure. The seller gets the other part of the value added in *economic profit*, which is the difference between the revenue that the seller receives (equal to the buyer's expenditure) and the cost of production.

The larger is the value added, the larger is the amount to be shared by buyer and seller. For profit-oriented businesses, that means the potential for economic profit is greater!

The concept of value added applies to governments and non-profits as well. Suppose that the government provides free healthcare. Since the healthcare is free, the government receives no revenue. While the healthcare service makes a financial "loss," that does not mean that the service is a mistake. The healthcare provides a benefit. Referring to Figure 1.1, the value added is the buyer benefit minus the cost of provision. So long as the benefit exceeds the cost, the service adds value.

PROGRESS CHECK 1A

Explain the relation among the following: buyer benefit, seller cost, value added, buyer surplus, and economic profit.

---

3. Decision-Making

The two fundamental decisions in business can be stated simply as participation ("which") and extent ("how much"). Which market to enter? How much to invest? Which products to sell? How much to produce? Which R&D strategy to follow? How much to spend on R&D? Which job to take? How many hours to work?

Here, we present fundamental techniques to decide on participation and extent. Then we discuss psychological limitations in individual decision-making. All organizations – whether businesses, non-profits, or households – are managed by individual human beings. To the extent that those individuals are subject to biases, the biases affect the organizations.

Which and How Much?

The decisions on participation (which) and extent (how much) resolve into analyzing the total and marginal benefits and costs. Let us use the following example to introduce the concepts of *total* and *marginal*, and then relate them to the decisions of *which* and *how much*.

Annabel must decide how to invest $10,000. Her bank pays 2% interest on savings accounts of any amount. The bank also offers a fund in units of $10,000 with an interest rate of 3%.

If Annabel were to deposit the money in a savings account, her interest income would be 2% × $10,000 = $200. If Annabel were to deposit the money in the fund, her interest income would be 3% × $10,000 = $300. So, to maximize her interest income, Annabel should invest in the fund.

In deciding *which* investment to make, Annabel should choose according to the *total* interest income. She should invest in the fund.

Closely related to the total is the concept of *average*. Generally, the **average value** of a variable with respect to some measure is the total value of the variable divided by the total quantity of the measure. Annabel could also choose the investment according to the average interest income. Her average interest income would be 2% from the savings account and 3% from the fund.

> **Average value:** The total value of the variable divided by the total quantity of the measure.

Now, suppose that Annabel's uncle gives her $1,000. How should she invest the gift? For incremental decisions such as how to invest the additional $1,000, or generally, how *much* to invest, the decision-maker should consider the marginal benefits and costs.

The **marginal value** of a variable with respect to some measure is the change in the variable associated with a unit increase in the measure. If Annabel were to deposit the gift in the savings account, her interest income would be 2% × $1,000 = $20. Hence, her marginal interest income from a deposit of $1,000 in the savings account would be $20.

> **Marginal value:** The change in the variable associated with a unit increase in a measure.

Annabel cannot deposit the gift in the fund because the fund is sold in units of $10,000. So, the marginal interest income from a deposit of $1,000 in the money market fund is zero. Thus, to maximize her interest income, Annabel should deposit the gift in the savings account.

Generally, the marginal value of a variable may be less than, equal to, or greater than the average value. The relation between the marginal and average values with respect to some measure depends on whether the average value is decreasing, constant, or increasing with respect to the measure.

PROGRESS CHECK 1B

What would be Annabel's marginal interest income from deposits of $1,000, $2,000, . . ., $9,000, $10,000 in the fund?

Here is another example of using total and marginal benefits and costs to decide on participation and extent. Max is working as an associate in a management consulting firm for after-tax earnings of $30,000 per year. Should he get an MBA, forgoing two years of earnings and possibly securing a higher-paid job after graduation? After the MBA, having secured a job, how many hours should he work?

In deciding *which* career path to follow – whether to continue with his current job or get an MBA – Max should consider the *total* earnings (and *total* costs) of each alternative. To be precise, since these earnings and costs flow over time, Max should consider the net present value of the total earnings and total costs of each alternative. (The next section explains the concept of net present value.) He should choose the alternative that maximizes the net present value of the total earnings and total costs.

Having secured a job, Max must decide how many hours to work. In deciding *how much* to work, Max should consider the *marginal* earnings and *marginal* cost of each additional hour.

He should work up to the point that the marginal earnings per hour equal the marginal cost per hour. If the marginal earnings exceed the marginal cost, then he should work more. The additional earnings would exceed the additional cost. By contrast, if the marginal earnings are less than the marginal cost, then he should work less. The reduction in earnings would be less than the reduction in cost.

Generally,

- in decisions on participation – which market, which product, which job – the manager should compare the total benefit with the total cost;
- in decisions on extent – how much to invest, how much to produce, how many hours to work – the manager should compare the marginal benefit with the marginal cost.

With regard to vertical boundaries, a cable TV provider that produces movies is more vertically integrated than a cable TV provider that buys movies from others. With regard to horizontal boundaries, a cable TV provider that also provides broadband service is operating with a larger scope than one that specializes in just cable TV.

Outsourcing

Outsourcing is the purchase of services or supplies from external sources. It is the opposite of vertical integration, and affects the vertical boundaries of the organization. If an aircraft manufacturer outsources the production of wings and landing gear, then it is shrinking its vertical boundaries. Similarly, if a cable TV provider outsources the production of movies, it is shrinking its vertical boundaries.

> **Outsourcing:** The purchase of services or supplies from external sources.

Owing to declining costs of transport and communications, and falling barriers to trade and investment, international outsourcing has grown rapidly. Chapter 14 on incentives and organizations discusses outsourcing in detail.

PROGRESS CHECK 1D

Explain the difference between the vertical and horizontal boundaries of an organization.

NEW BUSINESS ORGANIZATION: PEER-TO-PEER

Some of the fastest-growing businesses challenge conventional thinking about business organization. Janus Friis and Niklas Zennstrom applied peer-to-peer technology to develop Skype, software for voice calls over the Internet. They remarked: "The telephony market is characterized both by what we think is rip-off pricing and a reliance on heavily centralized infrastructure. We just couldn't resist the opportunity to help shake this up a bit."

Unlike conventional businesses, Skype is located nowhere and everywhere. It operates from the computers of over 300 million worldwide users and through the Internet. As for organization, its vertical chain is short, while its horizontal boundaries are large in terms of scale but, with just one product, narrow in terms of scope. In May 2011, software publisher Microsoft acquired Skype for $8.5 billion.

Sources: CNET, "Kazaa founders tout PTP VoIP," October 19, 2004; Wired, "Microsoft Buys Skype for $8.5 billion. Why, Exactly?" May 10, 2011.

6. Markets

One concept of managerial economics – the market – is so fundamental that it appears in the names of each branch of the discipline. A **market** consists of buyers and sellers who communicate with one another for voluntary exchange. In this sense, a market is not limited to any physical structure or particular location. The market extends as far as there are buyers or sellers who can communicate and trade at relatively low cost.

> **Market:** Buyers and sellers who communicate with one another for voluntary exchange.

Consider, for instance, the market for cotton. This extends beyond the Intercontinental Exchange in New York to growers in Texas and textile manufacturers in East Asia. If the price on the Intercontinental Exchange increases, then that price increase will affect Texas growers and Asian textile manufacturers. Likewise, if the demand for cotton in Asia increases, this will be reflected in the price on the Exchange.

In markets for consumer products, the buyers are households and sellers are businesses. In markets for industrial products, both buyers and sellers are businesses. Finally, in markets for human resources, the buyers are businesses and sellers are households.

By contrast with a market, an **industry** consists of businesses engaged in the production or delivery of the same or similar items. For instance, the clothing industry consists of all clothing manufacturers, and the textile industry consists of all textile manufacturers. Members of an industry can be buyers in one market and sellers in another. The clothing industry is a buyer in the textile market and a seller in the clothing market.

> **Industry:** Businesses engaged in production or delivery of the same or similar items.

Competitive Markets

The global cotton market includes many competing producers and buyers. How should a producer respond to an increase in the price of water, a drop in the price of cotton, or a change in labor laws? How will these changes affect buyers?

The basic starting point of managerial economics is the model of competitive markets. This applies to markets with many buyers and many sellers. The market for cotton is an example of a competitive market. In a competitive market, buyers provide the demand and sellers provide the supply. Accordingly, the model is also called the *demand–supply model*.

The model describes the systematic effect of changes in prices and other economic variables on buyers and sellers. Further, the model describes the interaction of these changes. In the cotton example, the model can describe how the cotton producer should adjust prices when the price of water increases, the price of cotton drops, and labor laws change. These changes affect all cotton producers. The model also describes the interaction among the adjustments of the various cotton producers and how these affect buyers.

Part I of this book presents the model of competitive markets. We begin with the demand side, considering how buyers respond to changes in prices and income (Chapter 2). Next, we develop a set of quantitative methods that support precise estimates of changes in economic behavior (Chapter 3). Then we look at the supply side of the market, considering how sellers respond to changes in the prices of products and inputs (Chapter 4). We bring demand and supply together and analyze their interaction in Chapter 5, then show that the outcome of market competition is efficient (Chapter 6).

THE EXTENT OF E-COMMERCE MARKETS

A conventional bricks-and-mortar retail store serves a geographical area defined by a reasonable traveling time. By contrast, an Internet retailer serves a much larger market – defined by the reach of telecommunications and the cost of shipping.

Founded in 1994, Amazon.com began by retailing books. Twenty years later, by November 2014, its market capitalization of US$141.27 billion was over 100 times greater than that of the leading conventional bookstore, Barnes and Noble. The vast disparity reflects the stock market's assessment of the difference in the long-term profitability of the two companies.

Besides serving a much larger geographical market, an e-commerce business can more readily expand into other product lines. Not having to maintain physical stores, the e-commerce business may achieve lower costs.

Market Power

In a competitive market, an individual manager may have little freedom of action. Key variables such as prices, scale of operations, and input mix are determined by market forces. The role of a manager is simply to follow the market and survive. Not all markets, however, have so many buyers and sellers to be competitive.

Market power is the ability of a buyer or seller to influence market conditions. A seller with market power will have relatively more freedom to choose suppliers, set prices, and use advertising to influence demand. A buyer with market power will be able to influence the supply of products that it purchases.

> **Market power:** The ability of a buyer or seller to influence market conditions.

A business with market power must determine its horizontal boundaries. These depend on how its costs vary with the scale and scope of operations. Accordingly, businesses with market power – whether buyers or sellers – need to understand and manage their costs.

In addition to managing costs, sellers with market power need to manage their demand. Three key tools in managing demand are price, advertising, and policy toward competitors. What price maximizes profit? A lower price boosts sales, while a higher price brings in higher margins. What is the best way to compete with other businesses?

Part II of this book addresses all of these issues. We begin by analyzing costs (Chapter 7), then consider management in the extreme case of market power, where there is only one seller or only one buyer (Chapter 8). Next, we discuss pricing policy (Chapter 9), and strategic thinking in general (Chapter 10) and in the context of competition among several sellers or buyers in particular (Chapter 11).

Imperfect Markets

Businesses with market power have relatively more freedom of action than those in competitive markets. Managers will also have relatively more freedom of action in markets that are subject to imperfections. A market may be **imperfect** in two ways: when one party directly conveys a benefit or cost to others, or when one party has better information than others. The challenge for managers operating in imperfect markets is to resolve the imperfection and so enable the cost-effective provision of their products.

> **Imperfect market:** One party directly conveys a benefit or cost to others, or one party has better information than others.

Consider the market for residential mortgages. Applicants for mortgages have better knowledge of their ability and willingness to repay than potential lenders. In this case, the market is imperfect owing to differences in information. The challenge for lenders is how to resolve the informational differences so that they can provide loans in a cost-effective way.

Managers of businesses in imperfect markets need to think strategically. For instance, a residential mortgage lender may require all loan applicants to pay for a credit evaluation, with the lender refunding the cost if the credit evaluation is favorable. The lender might reason that bad borrowers would not be willing to pay for a credit evaluation because they would fail the check. Good borrowers, however, would pay for the evaluation because they would get their money back from the lender. Hence, the credit evaluation requirement will screen out the bad borrowers. This is an example of strategic thinking in an imperfect market.

Differences in information and conflicts of interest can cause a market to be imperfect. The same imperfection can arise within an organization, where some members have better information than others and interests diverge. Accordingly, another issue is how to structure incentives and organization.

Part III of this book addresses all of these issues. We begin by considering the sources of market imperfections – where one party directly conveys a benefit or cost to others (Chapter 12) and where one party has better information than others (Chapter 13). Then we study the appropriate structure of incentives and organization (Chapter 14). Finally, we discuss how government regulation can resolve market imperfections (Chapter 15).

PROGRESS CHECK 1E

Distinguish the three branches of managerial economics.

KEY TAKEAWAYS

- Managerial economics is the science of cost-effective management of scarce resources.
- Value added is the difference between buyer benefit and seller cost, and comprises buyer surplus and economic profit.
- In decisions on participation, compare the total benefit and total cost.
- In decisions on extent, compare the marginal benefit and marginal cost.
- In decision-making, take care to avoid systematic biases, including the sunk-cost fallacy, status quo bias, and anchoring.
- When evaluating benefits and costs that flow over time, use net present value with the appropriate discount rate.
- The vertical boundaries of an organization delineate activities closer to or further from the end user.
- The horizontal boundaries of an organization are defined by the scale and scope of operations.
- Businesses with market power must manage their costs, pricing, advertising, and relations with competitors.
- Businesses in imperfect markets should act strategically to resolve the imperfection.

REVIEW QUESTIONS

1. Explain the difference between value added and economic profit.
2. Consider a charity that gives free mosquito nets to poor people. Since the charity receives no revenue while mosquito nets are costly, does the free distribution mean that the charity is destroying value?
3. Give an example in which the marginal exceeds the average value.
4. Give an example in which the marginal is less than the average value.
5. Why do individuals act with bounded rationality?
6. Explain why an employer expecting $1 million of future pension costs need not provide $1 million today in order to meet the pension fund's future obligations.
7. Referring to the net present value example in Section 4 above on timing, under what circumstances, if any, could the NPV be positive?
8. Describe the vertical boundaries of your local cable television provider. In what ways could the vertical boundaries be expanded or reduced?
9. Describe the horizontal boundaries of your university. In what ways could the horizontal boundaries be expanded or reduced?
10. In the context of manufacturing Apple iPhones, explain the difference between outsourcing and vertical integration.

11. Explain the difference between: (a) the market for electricity; and (b) the electricity industry.
12. True or false?
    (a) In every market, all buyers are consumers.
    (b) In every market, all sellers are businesses.
13. What is another name for the model of competitive markets?
14. What distinguishes a manufacturer with market power from one without market power?
15. Should managers operating in an imperfect market: (a) set high prices to make up for the imperfection; or (b) act strategically to resolve the imperfection?

DISCUSSION QUESTIONS

1. Mercy Hospital provides healthcare at subsidized prices and is so popular that patients wait in long queues. Revenue is $75 million a year, while the cost of providing service is $100 million a year. A government subsidy covers the difference. Some critics argue that, since Mercy Hospital is losing money, it should be shut down. The management of Mercy Hospital argues that the long waiting times justify a larger government subsidy to expand staff and facilities.
    (a) What is Mercy Hospital's economic profit?
    (b) What is the minimum benefit that Mercy Hospital must provide to add value?
    (c) Do you agree that Mercy Hospital should be shut down?
    (d) What information do you need to decide whether Mercy Hospital should expand or reduce service?
2. Alan and Hilda are clerks at a department store. The store pays each clerk $10 per hour for a basic eight-hour day, $15 per hour for overtime of up to four hours, and $20 for overtime exceeding four hours a day.
    (a) Alan works 10 hours a day. What are his: (i) marginal pay; and (ii) average pay?
    (b) Hilda works 14 hours a day. What are her: (i) marginal pay; and (ii) average pay?
    (c) Under what pay structure would the marginal pay be less than the average pay?
3. Ford offers a three-year or 36,0000-mile warranty on the Explorer car. Consumers must pay for extended warranties beyond the manufacturer's warranty period. The Auto Club offers an extended warranty for a Ford Explorer in Hanover, New Hampshire, at a price of $1,259. This would cover years 4 and 5, after the expiry of manufacturer's warranty.
    (a) Explain the role of discounting in your decision whether or not to purchase the extended warranty.
    (b) Suppose that the expected cost of repair is $800 in each of years 4 and 5. If your discount rate is 6% per year, should you purchase the extended warranty?
    (c) Would your decision be different if your discount rate were 1% per year?

4. In each of the following instances, discuss whether horizontal or vertical boundaries have been changed, and whether they were extended or shrunk.
    (a) The Canadian manufacturer of regional jets, Bombardier, launched the CSeries, a family of 100- to 149-seat, long-range jets.
    (b) Software publisher Microsoft acquired Skype, a provider of Internet telephony services.
    (c) Conglomerate General Electric divested its subsidiary, NBC Universal, which merged with cable TV provider, Comcast.
    (d) Dutch financial services group ING divested its insurance and investment management businesses as NN Group.
5. Referring to the definition of a market, answer the following questions:
    (a) Opponents of the Iraqi government periodically sabotage the pipelines through which Iraq exports oil to the rest of the world. Is Iraq part of the world market for oil?
    (b) Prisoners cannot freely work outside jail. How would changes in prisoners' wages affect the national labor market?
    (c) The Australian national electricity transmission grid links eastern states including New South Wales, South Australia, and Victoria, but not Western Australia. How would price changes in Western Australia affect the other states?
    (d) By executive order, President Barack Obama will allow illegal immigrants to work legally in the United States. How would that affect US wages?

You are the consultant!

In your organization or personal experience, identify and explain any decisions that have been systematically biased by: (a) the sunk-cost fallacy, (b) status quo bias, or (c) anchoring. Explain how the organization or you could have achieved a better outcome by controlling the bias.

Notes

1   This discussion is based, in part, on Richard Tortoriello, "Aerospace & defense," *Standard & Poor's Industry Surveys*, February 10, 2011; "Boeing likely to boost 737, 777 production rates," *ATWOnline*, March 18, 2010; "Airbus and Boeing call end to 'duopoly'," *Financial Times*, June 21, 2011; "Airbus-Boeing duopoly holds narrow-body startups at bay at Paris Air Show," *Bloomberg*, June 23, 2011; "Comac's C919 jet to complete assembly by September 2015," *South China Morning Post*, September 25, 2014; "Bombardier C Series said to be favourite for Austrian fleet revamp," *Bloomberg*, October 15, 2014.

Competitive Markets

CHAPTER 2

Demand

LEARNING OBJECTIVES

- Appreciate why consumers and business buyers buy more at lower prices.
- Distinguish consumer demand for normal products and inferior products.
- Appreciate the impact on demand of changes in the prices of substitutes and complements.
- Understand differences between consumer and business demand.
- Appreciate the concept of buyer surplus.
- Apply package deals and two-part pricing to extract buyer surplus.

1. Introduction

China Mobile is the world's largest mobile telephone service provider. As of September 2014, China Mobile served 799 million customers, of which 40.95 million and 244.5 million subscribed to 4G and 3G services, respectively. The company employed 170,030 persons at the end of 2013.

In his letter to shareholders for the year 2010, Chairman Wang Jianzhou reported that the company had added 62 million new customers, "a large part of whom continued to come from rural and migrant markets." Analysis of the company's operational data reveals that, while the company has continued to grow its customer base, the rate of growth declined from 24% in 2008 to 14% in 2009, and to 12% in 2010.

Chairman Wang also credited the company with achieving average revenue per user (ARPU) of 73 yuan per month and "a slowdown in decline." The company's ARPU declined by 7% in 2008 and 2009, and by 5% in 2010.

In discussing the outlook for the company, he stressed the "vast potential for sustainable development." Further, he reiterated that "Our commitment is unwavering – we will strive to create value for our shareholders."

Facing saturation in the demand for mobile service in urban areas, China Mobile has sought growth among rural and migrant consumers. Yet, amidst the growth, the company faces the perplexing challenge of declining ARPU. Is the growth of rural and migrant subscribers somehow related to the decline in ARPU?

Like mobile service providers throughout the world, China Mobile offers subscribers a choice of multiple price plans in each market. Plans with higher monthly fixed charges offer more "free minutes." How do consumers choose among these plans, and how should China Mobile price the plans?

This chapter introduces the concept of a demand curve, which describes the quantity demanded of an item as a function of its price and other factors. Next, we consider how demand depends on income, the prices of complementary and substitute products, and advertising. Businesses can use the model of demand to influence their sales. China Mobile can use the model to understand how the growth of rural and migrant consumers is systematically related to the decline in ARPU.

Using the individual buyer's demand curve, a seller can determine the maximum that the buyer is willing to pay for any specified quantity, and thereby extract the highest possible price. We apply this approach to explain how China Mobile should set prices for mobile service plans.

Finally, we extend from the individual demand to the demand curve of the entire market. The principles of consumer demand for final goods and services apply, with suitable adjustments, to business demand for inputs.

2. Individual Demand

To understand how a price cut will affect sales, we need to know how the cut in price will affect the purchases of the individual buyers and, generally, how an individual's purchases depend on the price of the item. The *individual demand curve* provides this information: it is a graph that shows the quantity that the buyer will purchase at every possible price.

Construction

Let us construct Joy's demand for movies. We must ask Joy a series of questions that elicit her responses to changes in price. We first ask: "How many movies would you attend a month at a price of $20 per movie?" Suppose that Joy's answer is: "None." (Strictly, we pose the question holding "other things equal," because Joy's decision may depend on other factors, such as her income.)

We then pose similar questions to Joy for other possible prices for a movie: $19, $18, ..., $1, and $0. For each price, Joy says how many movies she would attend a month. Table 2.1 presents this information and represents Joy's demand for movies. (Assuming that the consumer's demand curve is a straight line, we can draw the demand without filling all the rows of the table.)

Next we graph the information from Table 2.1 as shown in Figure 2.1. We represent the price of movies on the vertical axis and the quantity in movies a month on the horizontal axis. (Note that demand and supply curves do not follow the scientific convention of representing the independent variable on the horizontal axis and the dependent variable on the vertical axis.)

At a price of $20, Joy says that she would not go to any movies, so mark the point with the price equal to $20 and quantity of movies equal to zero. Continuing with the information from Table 2.1, mark every pair of price and quantity that Joy reports. Joining these points then yields Joy's demand curve for movies.

Table 2.1 Individual demand

Price ($ per movie)	Quantity (movies per month)
20	0
19	1
18	2
. . .	. . .
0	20

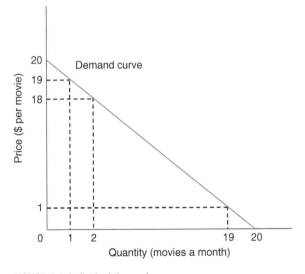

FIGURE 2.1 Individual demand curve.

Notes: The individual demand curve shows, for every possible price, the quantity of movies that Joy will buy. It also shows how much Joy would be willing to pay for various quantities.

Knowing Joy's demand curve, a movie theater can predict how Joy will respond to changes in its price. For instance, if presently the theater charges $12 per movie, Joy will buy eight movies a month. If the theater reduces its price to $11, it knows that Joy will increase consumption to nine movies a month. By contrast, if the theater raises its price to $13 per movie, Joy would cut back to seven movies a month.

Marginal Benefit

The individual demand curve shows the quantity that the buyer will purchase at every possible price. Let us now consider the individual demand curve from another perspective.

Referring to Joy's demand curve in Figure 2.1, we can use the curve to determine how much Joy would be willing to pay for various quantities of movies. Specifically, the curve shows that she is willing to pay $19 per movie for one movie a month. Further, it shows that Joy is willing to pay $18 per movie for two movies a month, and so on.

Generally, if the number of movies is larger, the price that Joy is willing to pay is lower. Equivalently, at a lower price, Joy is willing to buy a larger quantity. These two related properties of a demand curve reflect the principle of diminishing marginal benefit.

Any item that a consumer is willing to buy must provide some benefit. We measure the benefit in monetary terms. The **marginal benefit** is the benefit provided by an additional unit of the item. The marginal benefit of the first movie is the benefit from one movie a month. Similarly, the marginal benefit of the second movie is the additional benefit from seeing a second movie each month.

> **Marginal benefit:** The benefit provided by an additional unit.

> **Diminishing marginal benefit:** Each additional unit provides less benefit than the preceding unit.

By the **principle of diminishing marginal benefit**, each additional unit of consumption provides less benefit than the preceding unit. In Joy's case, this means that the marginal benefit of the second movie is less than the marginal benefit of the first movie, the marginal benefit of the third movie is less than the marginal benefit of the second movie, and so on.

Accordingly, the price that an individual is willing to pay will decrease with the quantity purchased. Hence, the demand curve will slope downward. This is a general property of all demand curves: the lower the price, the larger will be the quantity demanded. The fundamental reason for the downward slope is diminishing marginal benefit.

PROGRESS CHECK 2A

Suppose that the theater presently charges $11 per movie. By how much must the theater cut its price for Joy to increase her consumption by three movies a month?

Preferences

The procedure for constructing a demand curve relies completely on the consumer's individual preferences. The individual decides how much he or she wants to buy at each possible price. The demand curve then displays information in a graphical way.

Consumers may have different preferences and hence different demand curves. One consumer may like red meat while another is a vegetarian. Further, demand curves will change with changes in the consumer's preferences. As a person grows older, her demand for rock videos and athletic events will decline, while her demand for healthcare and will increase.

GASOLINE PRICES AND DRIVING

Brittany and Danny Schulz live in Murfreesboro, Tennessee. Early in November 2014, Ms Schulz was pleasantly surprised to fill up her Nissan Altima for only $45, substantially less than the usual $55.

With the average price of gasoline falling below $3 per gallon, American households will spend more on electronics, holiday gifts, and other discretionary items. And buy more gasoline. Chris Christopher, director of consumer markets at market researcher, IHS, predicts: "People are more likely to drive – and drive longer distances – this season". Indeed, Mr and Mrs Shulz are planning a 300-mile road trip to visit friends in Columbus, Georgia.

Source: "Why Americans don't trust lower gas prices," *Washington Post*, November 4, 2014.

3. Demand and Income

Joy's demand for movies may vary not only with the price of such movies, but also with her income. If she gets a raise, how would that affect her demand for movies?

Income Changes

Suppose that Joy's income is presently $50,000 a year. Table 2.1 and Figure 2.1 represent Joy's demand for movies with an income of $50,000 a year.

We then ask Joy a series of questions. These questions probe the effect of changes in income as well as price: "Suppose that your income is $40,000 a year. How many movies would you buy a month at a price of $20 per movie?" We then repeat the question with other possible prices and tabulate the information.

Suppose that Table 2.2 represents Joy's answers. We also represent this information in Figure 2.2. Marking the pairs of prices and quantities, and joining the points, we have Joy's demand curve with an income of $40,000 a year.

Table 2.2 Individual demand with lower income

Price ($ per movie)	Quantity (movies per month)
20	0
19	0
. . .	0
10	0
9	2
8	4
. . .	. . .
0	20

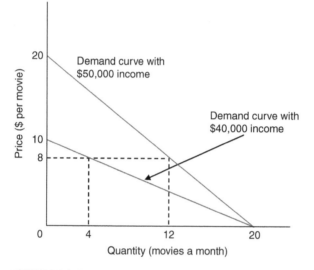

FIGURE 2.2 Individual demand curve with lower income.

Note: As Joy's income falls from $50,000 to $40,000, her entire demand curve shifts toward the left.

Joy's demand curve for movies with $40,000 income lies to the left of her demand curve with $50,000 income. At every price, the quantity demanded with $40,000 income is less than or equal to the quantity demanded with $50,000 income.

Referring to Figure 2.1, if the price of movies drops from $8 to $7 per movie, while Joy's income remains unchanged at $50,000 a year, we trace Joy's response by moving *along* her demand curve from the $8 level to the $7 level. By contrast, referring to Figure 2.2, if her income falls from $50,000 to $40,000, while the price remains at $8 per movie, we represent Joy's response by *shifting* the entire demand curve to the left. The essential reason for this difference is that the figure, having just two axes, does not explicitly represent the buyer's income.

Let us understand the difference in graphical representation between a change in price and a change in income in another way. On Figure 2.2, at the $8 level, mark two quantities: a quantity of 12 movies a month when Joy's income is $50,000, and another quantity of four movies a month when Joy's income is $40,000.

Can we join these points to form a demand curve? The answer is definitely "no," because each point corresponds to a different income and different demand curve. A demand curve shows how a buyer's purchases depend on changes in the price of some item, holding income and other factors unchanged. Accordingly, for each of the points, there is a separate demand curve.

In general, we represent a change in the price of the item by a movement *along* the demand curve. By contrast, we represent a change in income or any factor other than the price of the item by a *shift* in the entire demand curve.

Normal and Inferior Products

When Joy's income drops from $50,000 to $40,000 a year, her demand for movies shifts to the left. As Joy's income falls, her demand for movies also falls. By contrast, if her income were to rise, her demand would increase.

Let us compare Joy's demand for movies in general with her demand for afternoon matinees. If Joy's income falls, it is quite possible that she will substitute cheaper forms of entertainment for more expensive ones. In particular, the drop in her income may lead to an increase in her demand for afternoon matinees.

By contrast, when Joy's income increases, we can expect her to switch away from cheaper forms of entertainment and toward more expensive alternatives. So, as her income rises, Joy's demand for afternoon matinees will fall.

Goods and services can be categorized according to the effect of changes in income on demand. If the demand for an item increases as the buyer's income increases, while the demand falls as the buyer's income falls, then the item is a *normal product*. Equivalently, the demand for a **normal product** is positively related to the buyer's income.

> **Normal product:** Demand is positively related to buyer's income.

By contrast, the demand for an **inferior product** is negatively related to the buyer's income. This means that the demand falls as the buyer's income increases, while the demand increases as the buyer's income falls.

> **Inferior product:** Demand is negatively related to buyer's income.

For Joy, movies are a normal product, while afternoon matinees are an inferior product. Generally, broad categories of products tend to be normal, while particular products within the categories may be inferior.

Consider, for instance, consumer electronics. While consumer electronics as a category are a normal product, particular products such as all-in-one stereos may be inferior. In passenger transport services, the entire category is probably a normal product. Within the category, taxis are a normal product while buses may be an inferior product.

The distinction between normal and inferior products is important for business strategy. When the economy is growing and incomes are rising, the demand for normal products will rise, while the demand for inferior products will fall. By contrast, when the economy is in recession and incomes are falling, the demand for normal products will fall, while the demand for inferior products will rise.

The distinction is also useful in international business. The demand for normal products is relatively higher in richer countries, while the demand for inferior products is relatively higher in poorer countries. For instance, in developed countries, relatively more people commute to work by car than bicycle. The reverse is true in very poor countries.

PROGRESS CHECK 2B

Draw a curve to represent an individual consumer's demand for all-in-one stereos. (a) Explain why it slopes downward. (b) How will a drop in the consumer's income affect the demand curve?

CHINA MOBILE: GROWING SUBSCRIBERS, SHRINKING ARPU

With prepaid mobile service, subscribers pay for specific quantities of air-time in advance. By contrast, with contract (also called "post-paid") service, subscribers enter into an agreement for a minimum period, and may use any quantity of air-time subject to paying the monthly bill.

Prepaid service and contract service cater to different market segments. Typical subscribers to prepaid service include consumers with lower income, such as rural people, migrant workers, and students.

Analysts estimate that, in 2011, over 90% of China Mobile's subscribers bought prepaid service. By contrast, 10 years earlier, the prepaid proportion was 48%. The growth in prepaid customers is consistent with China Mobile's push to rural and migrant consumers.

People with lower income typically spend less on consumer goods. China Mobile would derive lower ARPU from rural and migrant consumers. As a result, the company's quest for growth among rural and migrant consumers is unavoidably associated with lower ARPU.

Sources: Business Monitor International, *China Telecommunications Report – Q2 2011*; China Mobile Ltd.

4. Other Factors in Demand

The individual demand may depend on other factors besides the price of the item and the buyer's income. The other factors may include the prices of related products, advertising, durability, season, and location. Here, we focus on the prices of related products and advertising.

Complements and Substitutes

Assume that Joy always eats popcorn when she goes to the movies. How will an increase in the price of popcorn affect Joy's demand for movies? A change in the price of popcorn will affect Joy's purchases of movies at all movie prices. Hence, it will cause a shift in the entire demand curve.

Suppose that presently the price of popcorn is $1. Figure 2.3 represents Joy's demand curve for movies when the price of popcorn is $1. We next construct Joy's demand when the price of popcorn is $2. To do so, we ask Joy how many movies she would see at various movie prices if the price of popcorn were $2. Figure 2.3 shows the demand curve: when the price of popcorn is higher, the demand curve for movies is further to the left.

In general, related products can be classified as either complements or substitutes according to the effect of a price increase in one product on the demand for the other. Two products are **complements** if an increase in the price of one causes the demand for the other to fall. By contrast, two products are **substitutes** if an increase in the price of one causes the demand for the other to increase.

> **Complements:** An increase in the price of one causes a fall in the demand for the other.

For Joy, popcorn and movies are complements. The more movies she sees, the more popcorn she will want. Hence, if the price of popcorn is higher, the price of the overall movie experience will be higher, and she will go to fewer movies.

> **Substitutes:** An increase in the price of one causes an increase in the demand for the other.

How will an increase in the price of online movies affect Joy's demand for movies in the theater? Instead of going to the theater, Joy could watch an online movie. Accordingly, these two products are substitutes. If there is an increase in the price of online movies, Joy's demand for theater movies will increase.

Generally, a demand curve will shift to the left if there is either an increase in the price of a complement or a fall in the price of a substitute. By contrast,

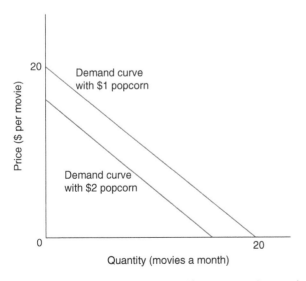

FIGURE 2.3 Individual demand curve with more expensive complement.

Note: As the price of popcorn increases, Joy's entire demand curve shifts toward the left.

a demand curve will shift to the right if there is either a fall in the price of a complement or an increase in the price of a substitute.

PROGRESS CHECK 2C

Referring to Figure 2.1, how would a fall in the price of online movies affect the original demand curve?

GASOLINE PRICES AND THE DEMAND FOR SUVS AND COMPACT CARS

Sport-utility vehicles (SUVs) like the Cadillac Escalade, Chevrolet Tahoe, and Lincoln Navigator consume more fuel than compact cars like the Chevrolet Aveo. Gasoline is a complement to motor vehicles, while compact cars are a substitute for SUVs.

With gasoline prices falling, the American demand for SUVs and trucks has increased. J.D. Power and Associates survey consumers on factors that influence their car buying. Between June 2013 and 2014, fuel economy dropped from third to seventh in the list, behind reliability, styling, brand preference, ride and handling, reputation, and price.

Nevertheless, taking a long-term view, Ford redesigned its popular F-series truck, replacing steel with aluminum to reduce the vehicle weight by 700 pounds. CEO Mark Fields remarked that consumers know that oil prices can go up as quickly as down and want fuel economy.

Source: "Cheap gas won't let us off the hook: Ford CEO," *CNBC*, November 12, 2014.

Advertising

Advertising expenditure is another factor in demand. For instance, Joy's demand for movies may depend on advertising by the theater. Generally, an increase in the seller's advertising will increase the buyer's demand. We represent this by shifting the buyer's demand curve to the right.

Advertising may be informative or persuasive. Informative advertising communicates information to potential buyers and sellers. For instance, movie theaters list the movies that they are showing and their show times in the daily newspapers. These listings inform potential customers. Persuasive advertising aims to influence consumer choice. Manufacturers of cigarettes and cosmetics, for instance, use advertising to retain the loyalty of existing consumers and attract others to switch brands.

5. Business Demand

Movies and mobile telephone service are consumer goods. By contrast, TV advertisements and excavators are industrial goods – they are bought by businesses rather than consumers. In any economy, the majority of economic transactions are business-to-business sales. Accordingly, managers must understand the principles of business demand.

Inputs

Consumers buy goods and services for final consumption or usage. By contrast, businesses buy goods and services not for their own sake but to use them as inputs in the production of other goods and services. Chapter 4 will provide a detailed analysis of business operations. Here, we will review only the essentials necessary to understand the business demand for inputs.

The inputs purchased by a business can be classified into materials, energy, labor, and capital. Businesses use these inputs to produce goods and services for sale to consumers or other businesses. For example, an express delivery service uses human resources, equipment, and energy to deliver documents and packages for consumers and businesses.

The inputs may be substitutes or complements. For the express delivery service, trucks and drivers are complements: a truck without a driver is quite useless, as is a driver without a truck. Other inputs may be substitutes: the service can use workers or machines to sort packages and to load shipments.

Demand

A business produces items for sale to consumers or other businesses. The business earns revenues from sales. By increasing inputs, the business can produce a larger output and raise revenue. Accordingly, the business can measure its marginal benefit from an input as the increase in revenue arising from an additional unit of the input.

Using the marginal benefit of an input, we can construct the individual demand curve of a business. This shows the quantity of the input that the business will purchase at every possible price. A business should buy an input up to the quantity that its marginal benefit from the input exactly balances the price.

Suppose that, with a larger quantity of an input, each additional unit of the input generates a smaller increase in revenue. This means that the input provides a diminishing marginal benefit to the business.

Hence, when the price is lower, the business will buy a larger quantity, and conversely, when the price is higher, the business will buy a smaller quantity. Thus, the demand curve for the input slopes downward.

Demand Factors

A change in the price of an input is represented by a movement along the demand curve. By contrast, changes in other factors will lead to a shift of the entire demand curve. Business demand does not depend on income but rather on the output of the item being produced. If the output is larger, then the business will increase its demand for inputs. If, however, the output is lower, then the demand for inputs will be lower.

The business demand for an input also depends on the prices of complements and substitutes in the production of the output. For instance, delivery trucks and drivers are complements, hence an increase in drivers' wages will reduce the demand for trucks.

6. Buyer Surplus

The individual demand curve shows the quantity that the buyer will purchase at every possible price. The demand curve also shows the maximum amount that a buyer is willing to pay for each unit of the item.

The perspective of "willingness to pay" is important for pricing policy as it shows the maximum that the buyer can be charged. We will explain two pricing schemes to extract the maximum that the buyer is willing to pay, and so maximize the seller's profit.

Benefit

The demand curve shows the buyer's marginal benefit from each unit. Using this

> **Total benefit:** The benefit provided by all the units that the buyer consumes.

information, we can calculate the buyer's **total benefit**, which is the benefit provided by all the units that the buyer consumes. The total benefit is the marginal benefit from the first unit plus the marginal benefit from the second unit, and so on, up to and including marginal benefit from the last unit that the buyer purchases.

A buyer's total benefit is the maximum that the buyer is willing to pay. Graphically, the total benefit is represented by the area under the buyer's demand curve up to and including the last unit consumed.

Let us calculate Joy's total benefit from eight movies a month. Her total benefit is the area under her demand curve up to and including eight movies a month. In Figure 2.4, this is area $0bcd = \frac{1}{2}(\$8 \times 8) + \$12 \times 8 = \$128$. So, the maximum that Joy would be willing to pay for eight movies a month is $128.

Benefit and Expenditure

Suppose that the price of a movie is $12. Then Joy buys eight movies a month. As already calculated, her total benefit would be $128. Joy, however, needs to pay only $12 \times 8 = \$96$, which is less than her total benefit.

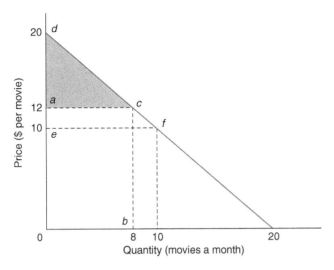

FIGURE 2.4 Individual buyer surplus.

Notes: The individual buyer surplus is the buyer's total benefit from some quantity of purchases less the actual expenditure. At a price of $12, Joy's buyer surplus is the shaded area *acd* between the demand curve and the $12 line.

The difference between a buyer's total benefit from some consumption and her actual expenditure is the **buyer surplus**. At the price of $12 per movie, Joy's buyer surplus is $128 − $96 = $32.

Referring to Figure 2.4, at the price of $12, her expenditure on eight movies a month is represented by the area *0bcad* under the $12 line up to and including eight movies a month. Hence, Joy's buyer surplus is the difference between the area *0bcad* which represents total benefit and the area *0bca* which represents expenditure, or the area *acd* between her demand curve and the $12 line.

> **Buyer surplus:** The difference between the buyer's total benefit from some consumption and actual expenditure.

Generally, provided that purchases are voluntary, a buyer must get some surplus. If not, he or she would not buy. The maximum that a seller can charge is the buyer's total benefit. If a seller tries to charge more, then the buyer will walk away.

PROGRESS CHECK 2D

Suppose that the price of movies is $8. On Figure 2.4, mark Joy's buyer surplus.

Price Changes

Referring to Joy's demand for movies, at the price of $12, Joy goes to eight movies a month, and her buyer surplus is area *acd*. Now suppose that the price drops to $10. Then Joy will raise her attendance from eight to ten movies a month. Her buyer surplus will increase by area *efca*: she gets the eight original movies at a lower price, and she goes to more movies.

Generally, a buyer gains from a price reduction in two ways. First, the buyer gets a lower price on the quantity that they would have purchased at the original higher price. Second, she will buy more, gaining buyer surplus on each of the additional purchases. The extent of the second effect depends on the buyer's sensitivity to the price reduction. The greater the increase in purchases, the larger will be the buyer's gain from the price reduction.

Similarly, a buyer loses from a price increase in two ways – the buyer must pay a higher price, and will buy less.

Package Deals and Two-Part Pricing

A seller who has complete flexibility over pricing maximizes profit by charging each buyer just a little less than total benefit. Practically, this can be implemented in two ways – through package-deal pricing and two-part pricing.

Let us explain these pricing policies in the context of Jania's demand for mobile telephone calls, shown in Figure 2.5. If the mobile telephone provider charges a price of 10 cents per minute, Jania will make 100 minutes of calls a month. The provider would earn revenue of 100×10 cents $= \$10$. Jania would get a buyer surplus of $\frac{1}{2} \times 40 \times 100$ cents $= \$20$.

Jania's total benefit from 100 minutes of calls a month is the area under her demand curve from 0 to 100 minutes, or $100 \times \frac{1}{2} \times (50+10) = \$30$. Suppose that the mobile provider offers Jania a package deal of 100 minutes of calls at $29 with

> **Package deal:** A pricing scheme comprising a fixed payment for a fixed quantity of consumption.

no other alternative. A **package deal** is a pricing scheme comprising a fixed payment for a fixed quantity of consumption. The package deal will give Jania a buyer surplus of $30 – $29 = $1. Since there is no other alternative, Jania will buy this package.

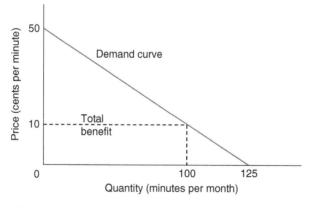

FIGURE 2.5 Package deal.

Note: Jania will buy a package deal of 100 minutes of calls for any price not exceeding her total benefit of $30.

The mobile provider would earn $29 in revenue, which is almost three times the revenue from the 10-cent pricing policy. The package deal enables the service to soak up almost all of Jania's buyer surplus. Since Jania's consumption is the same under 10-cent and package-deal pricing, the provider's cost would be the same. So, its profit would definitely be higher.

The mobile provider could also extract Jania's buyer surplus through two-part pricing. A **two-part price** is a pricing scheme comprising a fixed payment and a charge based on consumption.

> **Two-part price:** A pricing scheme comprising a fixed payment and a charge based on consumption.

Suppose that the mobile provider offers a two-part plan comprising a $19 monthly charge and an airtime charge of 10 cents a minute. Referring to Figure 2.5, under this plan, Jania would buy 100 minutes of calls a month. Her total benefit would be the area under her demand curve from 0 to 100 minutes, which we earlier calculated to be $30. She would pay a $19 monthly charge and 100×10 cents = $10 in airtime charges. Hence, her buyer surplus would be $30 - $19 - $10 = $1.

Just like the package deal, the two-part price enables the service provider to soak up most of the consumer's buyer surplus. The mobile provider would earn $29 in revenue and the cost would be the same as under 10-cent pricing.

Providers of many services, including banking, car rentals, telecommunications, and Internet access, make use of package deals and two-part pricing. They also combine the two pricing techniques so that the monthly charge covers a specified quantity of "free" usage while the user must pay a usage charge beyond the free quantity.

CHINA MOBILE: "WORLDWIDE CONNECT" SERVICE

China Mobile offers nine price plans for its "Worldwide Connect" service in the city of Nanjing. The cheapest plan provides 350 "free minutes" of calls for 68 yuan per month. The price of additional calls is 0.29 yuan per minute.

Suppose that Figure 2.6 depicts Lin Jun's demand curve for mobile telephone service. The 68 yuan per month plan involves two-part pricing. The plan provides 350 free minutes. At the 351th minute, her marginal benefit exceeds 0.29 yuan per minute. Accordingly, she would consume beyond 350 minutes. Specifically, she would consume more minutes up to the quantity where her marginal benefit is exactly 0.29 yuan per minute. That quantity is 400 minutes per month.

At that level of consumption, Lin Jun's total benefit would be $(0.29 \times 400 + 0.5 \times 1.00 \times 400) = 116 + 200 = 316$ yuan per month. Her buyer surplus would be her total benefit less the monthly fee and less the airtime charge, or $316 - 68 - 0.29 \times 50 = 233.50$ yuan per month.

Realistically, Lin Jun can choose among the various plans offered by China Mobile and other service providers. Suppose, however, that China Mobile is the only provider and offers only the plan with 350 free minutes. Then China Mobile could raise the monthly charge by 233 yuan. Lin Jun would still subscribe and get a buyer surplus of 0.50 yuan per month.

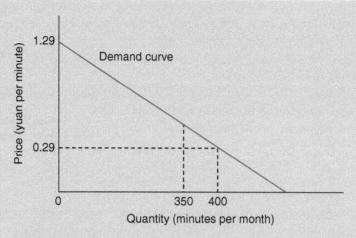

FIGURE 2.6 Demand curve for mobile telephone service.

Notes: The 68 yuan per month plan provides 350 free minutes. Lin Jun would consume beyond the free minutes up to the quantity where her marginal benefit is exactly 0.29 yuan per minute.

7. Market Demand

For strategy, marketing, and other purposes, businesses may plan on the basis of the entire market rather than individual customers. They must then understand the demand of the entire market.

The **market demand curve** is a graph that shows the quantity that all buyers will purchase at every possible price. The market demand curve is constructed in a similar way to the individual demand curve. To construct the market demand for an item, ask each potential buyer the quantity that they would buy at every possible price. Then, at each price, add the reported individual quantities to get the quantity that the market as a whole will demand. (The appendix to this chapter explains how to construct the market demand curve by *horizontal summation* of the individual demand curves.)

> **Market demand curve:** A graph showing the quantity that all buyers will purchase at every possible price.

The properties of the market demand curve are similar to those of the individual demand curve. As each buyer's marginal benefit diminishes with the quantity of consumption, the market demand curve slopes downward. Equivalently, at a lower price, the market as a whole will buy a larger quantity.

The market demand depends on other factors that affect individual demand. The market demand for a consumer good depends on buyers' incomes, the prices of related products, and advertising. The market demand for a business input depends on output of the business and the prices of related products.

The market buyer surplus is the difference between the buyers' total benefit from consumption and the buyers' actual expenditure. Graphically, it is the area between the market demand curve and the price line.

BOMBARDIER CSERIES

In the 1990s, with the price of oil around US$20 per barrel, the cost of fuel amounted to less than 20% of an airline's operating costs. By 2010, the price climbed above US$100 per barrel, and airline fuel costs ballooned to as high as 40% of operating costs, exceeding the cost of labor. However, with the expansion of US oil production and weakening growth in demand, the price of oil has since moderated to around US$50 per barrel.

Depending on their expectations about the future price of oil, airlines may be willing to pay for new aircraft that provide greater fuel efficiency. Bombardier's new CSeries promises to reduce fuel consumption by 20% through two innovations. One is use of advanced materials – comprising 46% lightweight composites and 24% aluminium lithium – in construction of the airframe. The other innovation is a more fuel-efficient engine, Pratt & Whitney's PW1000G.

Sources: Zubin Jelveh, "Flying on empty," Portfolio.com, June 4, 2008; Bombardier Incorporated.

KEY TAKEAWAYS

- Owing to diminishing marginal benefit, consumers and business buyers buy more at lower prices.
- Consumer demand for normal products increases with income, while consumer demand for inferior products decreases with income.
- The demand for a product increases with the price of a substitute, and decreases with the price of a complement.
- Business demand increases with the output of the item being produced.
- Buyer surplus is the difference between the buyers' total benefit from consumption and the buyers' actual expenditure.
- A seller can extract the buyers' surplus and raise profit by selling through package deals and two-part pricing.

REVIEW QUESTIONS

1. Think of a good or service that you bought recently. Would you have bought less of the item if the price had been lower? Explain why or why not.
2. Define (a) normal product, and (b) inferior product, and give examples to illustrate your definition.

3. Think of a good or service that you bought recently. Would you have bought more or less of the item if your income had been lower? Explain why or why not.

4. Define what is meant by (a) a substitute, and (b) a complement, and give examples to illustrate your definition.

5. A new birth-control device protects women against pregnancy but not sexually transmitted diseases. How will this new product affect the demand for: (a) male condoms; (b) birth-control pills?

6. How does Pepsi advertising affect the demand for: (a) Pepsi; and (b) Coca-Cola?

7. A key component of mobile phones is the microprocessor. Explain how changes in consumer incomes affect Apple's demand for microprocessors.

8. Why are automated teller machines (ATMs) relatively more common in countries with higher labor costs?

9. Explain the meaning of buyer surplus.

10. Buyer surplus applies to consumer demand but not business demand. True or false?

11. Passengers on a London to Sydney flight compared fares and discovered that they had paid different prices for the same flight. Explain how this illustrates that the market demand curve is downward-sloping.

12. The price of mobile telephone calls is 10 cents a minute. Antonella buys 200 minutes a month. Illustrate her demand curve and identify her buyer surplus.

13. "Summer sale: the more you buy, the more you save." Comment.

14. What is a package deal? How can a broadband service provider use package deals to increase profit?

15. What is two-part pricing? How can a broadband service provider use two-part pricing to increase profit?

DISCUSSION QUESTIONS

1. An important issue in economic development is the relationship between fertility and female literacy. With data from 110 countries, the following linear relationship between the female literacy rate and the number of births per woman (fertility rate) was estimated: when the literacy rate is 0%, the fertility rate is 7.63 per woman; and when the literacy rate is 100%, the fertility rate is 2.42 per woman.

   (a) On a figure with female literacy on the vertical axis and fertility on the horizontal axis, draw a graph of the linear relationship. Referring to the linear relationship, if the literacy rate is 60%, what would be the fertility rate (approximately)?

   (b) A large cost of having a baby is the time that the mother must invest in bearing and rearing the child. For a more educated woman, is the value of this time higher or lower?

   (c) In the chart, mark "cost of child" on the vertical axis. Does the trend line have any relation to a demand curve? Explain.

   (d) Give an alternative explanation of the figure: use the fertility rate to explain female literacy.

2. Sprint is one of the largest mobile service providers in the USA. In March 2011, Sprint had 13.1 million prepaid customers, and 33 million post-paid

customers. Sprint's prepaid brands include Virgin Mobile USA, Boost Mobile, and Assurance Wireless. Sprint's ARPU from prepaid customers was $28 per month, as compared with $56 per month from post-paid customers.

    (a) Explain the meaning of normal and inferior products.

    (b) Apply the concepts of normal and inferior products to prepaid and post-paid mobile telephone service.

    (c) Refer to Sprint's ARPU from prepaid and post-paid customers. Are the data consistent with your answer to (b)?

3. In fall 2005, an ABC News poll reported that 46% of lower-income Americans (earning less than $100,000 a year) were angry about gasoline prices, while just 32% of higher-income people were angry. Despite higher gasoline bills, just 22% of survey respondents said that they had reduced driving. However, 63% said that they would cut back on driving if gasoline prices rose above $3 per gallon.

    (a) Use a demand curve to explain why the proportion of people who would reduce driving is higher when the price of gasoline is higher. (*Hint*: You are free to assume any data necessary to draw the demand.)

    (b) Explain how people can adjust to higher gasoline prices by replacing their cars rather than driving less.

    (c) Why were relatively fewer higher-income people "angry" about high gasoline prices?

4. The Coca-Cola Company markets the Coke brand and manufactures concentrate for sale to regional bottlers. Coke bottlers mix concentrate with sweetener and water to produce the soft drink for supermarkets, restaurants, and other retail outlets. Possible sweeteners include corn syrup and sugar. Owing to federal restrictions against imports, sugar is relatively more expensive in the United States than in the rest of the world.

    (a) Why do US soft drink bottlers use relatively more corn syrup than bottlers elsewhere in the world?

    (b) Draw a US Coke bottler's demand for corn syrup. (*Hint*: You are free to assume any data necessary to draw the demand.)

    (c) Use your figure to explain how the following changes would affect the Coke bottler's demand for corn syrup: (i) removal of the federal restrictions against sugar imports; (ii) a fall in the price of corn syrup; and (iii) an increase in the sales of Pepsi.

    (d) Who benefits and who loses from the federal restrictions against sugar imports?

5. Historically, Bombardier specialized in producing regional jets, which are smaller short-range jets with up to 100 seats. In 2008, it secured a launch customer for the new CSeries, a family of 100- to 149-seat mid-range aircraft, which is scheduled to enter service in late 2015. The CSeries will reduce fuel consumption by 20% through use of advanced materials and a more fuel-efficient engine, the Pratt & Whitney PW1000G.

    (a) Draw the market demand for jet aircraft. (*Hint*: You are free to assume any data necessary to draw the demand.)

    (b) Use your figure to explain how changes in the consumer demand for air travel affect the airline demand for jet aircraft.

(c) If travelers are less sensitive to fare increases, how would that affect the demand for fuel-efficient aircraft?

(d) How does the price of oil affect the demand for advanced materials?

6. More than half of all residential water connections in Britain are not metered. Residential customers pay a flat fee regardless of usage. Scottish Water, which supplies water in Scotland, says that it has no evidence that "installation of meters encourages lower than normal usage of water." (Source: "Will switching to a water meter save money?" *Guardian*, July 8, 2014.)

(a) Suppose that the Salmond home water supply is not metered, and the family consumes 10,000 gallons a month. Illustrate the family's monthly demand curve for water, assuming that the demand curve is a straight line, and, if the price is £ 50 per 1,000 gallons, the Salmond family would consume nothing.

(b) Calculate the total benefit and marginal benefit from water when the Salmond family consumes 10,000 gallons a month. What is the family's buyer surplus?

(c) Suppose that Scottish Water installs a water meter at the Salmond home and charges a price of £ 5 per 1,000 gallons. How much water would the family buy and how much would it spend each month?

(d) What is the maximum that Scottish Water could charge the Salmond family for the consumption in (c)?

(e) Suppose that, with metering, the Salmonds' neighbors spend more than the Salmond family on water each month. Does this imply that the neighbors get more benefit from water?

7. Students at the University of California, Los Angeles, enjoy several privileges. One is a good education at a low price. Another is California's unbeatable weather, and a third is access to discounted movie tickets. Suppose that Alan buys 12 tickets a year at $7 rather than the full price of $10. By how much does he gain from the discount scheme?

(a) One answer is that Alan "saves" $10 – $7 = $3 on each ticket, which sums to a total of $3 × 12 = $36. Explain why this overestimates Alan's gain.

(b) Using a suitable diagram and the concept of buyer surplus, explain how much Alan gains from the discount scheme.

(c) Taking account of the discount movie scheme, by how much could the University raise Alan's tuition fees?

8. Suppose that the typical buyer of a packaging machine has a straight-line individual demand curve for packaging materials. At a price of $5 per kilogram of materials, she would buy zero, while at a price of $1 per kilogram, she would buy 100,000 kg per year. The buyer plans to use the machine for one year. Production costs $150,000 for the machine and $1 per kilogram of materials.

(a) On a figure with price per kilogram of materials on the vertical axis and quantity per year on the horizontal axis, draw the demand curve.

(b) Suppose that the manufacturer sells the machine bundled with 100,000 kg of material. What is the maximum that the manufacturer can charge for the bundle? What would be the manufacturer's profit per customer?

(c) Suppose that the manufacturer sets a two-part pricing policy, comprising a price for the machine and a price of $2 per kilogram of materials. What is the maximum price, F, that the manufacturer can charge for the machine? What would be the manufacturer's profit per customer?

(d) Suppose that the manufacturer sets a two-part pricing policy, with price, F, for the machine and a price of $2 per kilogram of materials. After buying the machine, the customer is influenced by sunk costs and her demand curve shifts up by $1 at all levels of consumption. On the figure in (a), draw the new demand curve. What would be the manufacturer's profit?

9. China Mobile offers nine price plans for its "Worldwide Connect" service in the city of Nanjing. The cheapest plan provides 350 "free minutes" of calls for 68 yuan per month, while the next cheapest plan provides 450 "free minutes" of calls for 88 yuan per month. Under both plans, the price of additional calls is 0.29 yuan per minute.

(a) Lin Jun's demand curve for mobile calling is a straight line. Two points on her demand curve are: (i) at a price of 1.29 yuan per minute, a quantity of 0 minutes; and (ii) at a price of 0.29 yuan per minute, a quantity of 400 minutes. Draw her demand curve.

(b) Suppose that Lin Jun subscribes to the 88 yuan per month plan. (i) How much calling time would she consume? (ii) What would be her total benefit? (iii) What would be her buyer surplus (benefit less charges)?

(c) Replicate (b) assuming that Lin Jun subscribes to the 68 yuan per month plan. Note that she might decide to buy additional minutes beyond the free minutes.

(d) Which plan should she choose to maximize buyer surplus?

You are the consultant!

Consider a product that your organization sells.
(a) What customer segments buy the product?
(b) Describe the current pricing policy.
(c) Under the current pricing policy, do any of the customer segments enjoy buyer surplus?
(d) Explain how you could use the techniques of package-deal or two-part pricing to extract the buyer surplus and raise profit.

Appendix: Constructing Market Demand by Horizontal Summation

This chapter introduces the concept of market demand, which shows the quantity that all buyers will buy at every possible price. One way to construct the market demand is to ask each potential consumer the quantity that they would buy at every

Table 2.3 Market demand

Price ($) (per movie)	Joy	Max	Lucas	Market
20	0	0	0	0
19	1	0	0	1
18	2	0	0	2
. . .	. . .	0	0	. . .
10	10	10	0	20
8	12	14	2	28
. . .	. . .	. . .	. . .	. . .
0	20	30	10	60

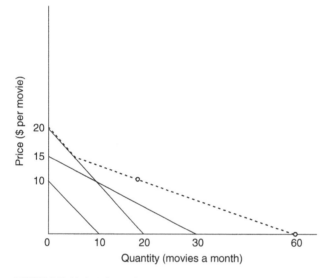

FIGURE 2.7 Market demand curve.

Notes: The market demand curve is the horizantal summation of the individual demand curves. At every price, the market quantity demanded is the sum of the individual quantities demanded.

possible price. Then, at each price, sum the reported individual quantities to get the quantity that the market as a whole will buy. Table 2.3 reports the market demand.

Another way to construct the market demand is by *horizontal summation* of the individual demand curves. In Figure 2.7, we draw the individual demand curves of the three potential consumers – Joy, Max, and Lucas. Horizontal summation means adding the curves in the horizontal direction.

Each individual demand curve shows the number of movies that the consumer would buy at every possible price. So, at every price, add the quantities that the three consumers would buy to obtain the quantity that the market as a whole will buy. Figure 2.7 depicts the market demand as a dashed line.

Elasticity

1. Introduction

In 2005, the online retailer Amazon launched its "Prime" service, which provides free two-day shipping with no requirement of a minimum purchase, unlimited photo storage, and exclusive access to movies, music and Kindle books for a fixed annual fee of $79. In January 2014, when reporting its fourth quarter financial results, Amazon revealed that it was considering raising the price of the Prime service by between $20 and $40.[1]

The investment bank UBS surveyed Amazon Prime subscribers: 58% said that they would renew if Amazon raised the price by $20, while 24% would renew if the price rose by $40. On February 12, UBS reduced its rating of Amazon shares from "Buy" to "Neutral," and the price of Amazon shares fell.

Separately, stockbroker Piper Jaffray surveyed 500 Amazon Prime subscribers, asking how likely they would be to renew their subscription if the price were raised to $109. Although 66% of respondents answered that they would be unlikely or highly unlikely to renew, analyst Gene Munster argued that, at most, the highly unlikely group or about a quarter of subscribers would not renew. Projecting from prior increases in prices by Netflix and Redbox, Mr Munster concluded that "the two comparable price increases point to a mid single digit percent decrease in Prime customers if Amazon were to raise prices."

In March 2014, Amazon announced a $20 increase for the Prime service. On the day of the announcement, the price of Amazon shares rose by 87 cents or 0.2%. Wedbush Securities analyst Michael Patcher remarked: "A lot of people say they would quit, but the truth is most people get used to the convenience . . . . It's like higher fees on credit cards. People complain about them bitterly when they go up, but most never get around to actually changing their service." Wedbush Securities estimated that Amazon had 25 million Prime subscribers and that the price increase would add about $500 million in revenue and operating profit per year.

How would a price increase affect the demand for Amazon's Prime service? How would the price increase affect Amazon's revenues? By how much should Amazon adjust the price of the Prime service?

To address these questions, we apply the concept of *elasticity*. The elasticity of demand measures the responsiveness of demand to changes in an underlying factor, such as the price of the item, the prices of complementary or substitute products, buyers' income, and advertising expenditure. There is an elasticity corresponding to every factor that affects demand.

The *own-price elasticity* of demand measures the responsiveness of the quantity demanded to changes in the price of the item. With the own-price elasticity, a seller can estimate the impact of an increase or reduction in price on quantity demanded. The seller can then estimate the impact on buyers' expenditure and its own revenue.

Using the own-price elasticity of the demand for the Prime service, Amazon could estimate the impact of the March 2014 price increase on demand and revenues. A price increase will always reduce the quantity demanded. We show that a price increase will raise consumers' expenditure and sellers' revenue if demand is price inelastic, but reduce consumers' expenditure and sellers' revenue if demand is price elastic.

Next, we introduce the concepts of income, cross-price, and advertising elasticities of demand. Then we discuss how elasticities vary with the time for adjustment, and, finally, how behavioral biases affect elasticities.

The concept of elasticity is essential to gauging the impact of changes in prices, incomes, and other factors on demand, consumers' expenditure, and sellers' revenue. It is fundamental to the management of both profit-oriented businesses and non-profit organizations. For instance, just like online retailers Amazon and Alibaba, hospitals and city transport systems need the own-price elasticity to gauge the impact of price increases on demand, revenue, and profit.

2. Own-Price Elasticity

To gauge the impact of changes in price on quantity demanded, we need a measure of buyers' sensitivity to price changes – the own-price elasticity of demand. The concept of own-price elasticity of demand is so basic that it is often called simply the *price elasticity* or *demand elasticity*.

The **own-price elasticity of demand** is the percentage by which the quantity demanded will change if the price of the item rises by 1%. Equivalently, the own-price elasticity is the ratio

> **Own-price elasticity of demand:** The percentage by which quantity demanded will change if price of the item rises by 1%.

$$\frac{\text{Proportionate change in quantity demanded}}{\text{Proportionate change in price}} \tag{3.1}$$

or

$$\frac{\text{Percentage change in quantity demanded}}{\text{Percentage change in price}}. \tag{3.2}$$

Estimation

To estimate the own-price elasticity of demand, collect records of price changes and the corresponding changes in quantity demanded. Then calculate the own-price elasticity as the ratio of the proportionate (percentage) change in quantity demanded to the proportionate (percentage) change in price.

To illustrate, Figure 3.1 represents the demand for cigarettes. Presently, the price of cigarettes is $1 a pack and the quantity demanded is 1.5 billion packs a month. According to Figure 3.1, if the price rises to $1.10 per pack, the quantity demanded would drop to 1.44 billion packs.

The proportionate change in quantity demanded is the change in quantity demanded divided by the initial quantity demanded. The change in quantity demanded is 1.44 − 1.5 = −0.06 billion packs, and the initial quantity demanded is 1.5 billion packs. Hence, the proportionate change in quantity demanded is −0.06/1.5 = −0.04.

Similarly, the proportionate change in price is the change in price divided by the initial price. The change in price is $1.10 − $1 = $0.10 per pack, while the initial price is $1 per pack. Hence, the proportionate change in price is 0.1/1 = 0.1.

Thus, by equation (3.1), the own-price elasticity of the demand for cigarettes is −0.04/0.1 = −0.4. Equivalently, in this example, the percentage change in quantity demanded was −4%, while the percentage change in price was 10%. By equation (3.2), the own-price elasticity is −4/10 = −0.4.

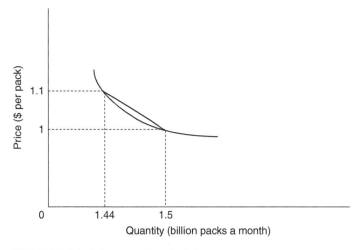

FIGURE 3.1 Calculating own-price elasticity.

Note: The own-price elasticity of the demand for cigarettes is the proportionate change in quantity demanded divided by the proportionate change in price = $-0.04 \div 0.1 = -0.4$.

Properties

The cigarette example illustrates several properties of the own-price elasticity of demand. First, as discussed in Chapter 2, demand curves generally slope downward: if the price of an item rises, the quantity demanded will fall. Hence, the own-price elasticity is a negative number. For ease of interpretation, some analysts report own-price elasticities as an absolute value, that is, without the negative sign. When applying the concept, note that the own-price elasticity is a negative number.

Second, the own-price elasticity is a pure number, independent of the units of measurement. The quantity demanded of cigarettes is measured in billion packs per month. The proportionate change in quantity demanded, however, is the change in quantity demanded divided by the initial quantity demanded. Hence, it is a pure number that does not depend on any units of measurement: the proportionate change would be the same whether we measure quantity demanded in billions, millions, or thousands of packs. Likewise, the proportionate change in price is a pure number.

Since the own-price elasticity is the proportionate change in quantity demanded divided by the proportionate change in price, it is also a pure number. Thus, the own-price elasticity of demand provides a handy way of characterizing price sensitivity that does not depend on units of measurement. Hence, it can be used to compare the price sensitivity of the demand for different goods and services.

Third, recall from equation (3.1) that the own-price elasticity is the ratio of the proportionate change in quantity demanded to the proportionate change in price. If a very large proportionate change in price causes no change in quantity demanded, then the elasticity will be 0. By contrast, if an infinitesimal percentage change in price causes a large change in quantity demanded, then the elasticity will be negative infinity. Accordingly, the own-price elasticity ranges from 0 to negative infinity.

Accuracy

The estimate of the own-price elasticity depends on the calculation of the proportionate change, and specifically the denominator of the proportionate change. Equation (3.1) uses the initial prices and quantities as the denominator, but the calculation could also use the average or final prices and quantities. As we consider smaller and smaller price changes, the estimate of the own-price elasticity will converge to a single number, which is called the "point estimate" of the elasticity.

Evidently, from equation (3.1), the formula using the initial price/quantity as the denominator of the proportionate change in price/quantity is not workable if the initial price/quantity is zero. In that case, we should use either the average or final price/quantity as the denominator.

Also, note that the own-price elasticity is a measure that depends on all factors that affect demand – including price, income, prices of complementary and substitute products, and sellers' advertising. So, changes in any of these may lead to a change in the own-price elasticity.

In particular, the own-price elasticity may vary along the demand curve, and so vary with changes in the price itself. Hence, strictly, the own-price elasticity is accurate only for small changes in the price.

PROGRESS CHECK 3A

Referring to Figure 3.1, suppose that, initially, the price of cigarettes is $1.10 a pack and the quantity demanded is 1.44 billion packs a month. Then the price falls to $1 per pack and the quantity demanded rises to 1.5 billion packs. Calculate the own-price elasticity.

AMAZON PRIME: EFFECT OF PRICE INCREASE

Wedbush Securities estimated that, at the original price of $79 a year, Amazon Prime had 25 million subscribers. According to the UBS survey, if Amazon raised the price by $20, subscriptions would fall by 42% to 14.5 million. The $20 increase amounts to a change in price of 20/79 = 25.3%. So, the predicted change in demand implies that the own-price elasticity of demand is –42/25.3 = –1.66.

Also according to UBS survey, if Amazon raised the price by $40, subscriptions would fall by 76% to 6 million. Hence, between the prices, $99 and $119, an increase of 20/99 = 20.2%, subscriptions would fall from 14.5 to 6 million, that is, by 58.6%. Thus, over this range, the predicted change in demand implies that the own-price elasticity of demand is –58.6/20.2 = –2.90.

Sources: "Will Amazon Prime customers accept price hike? Maybe not," *Forbes*, February 12, 2004; Wedbush Securities, "Quick note: Amazon.com (AMZN – NEUTRAL)," March 13, 2014.

3. Elastic/Inelastic Demand

The demand for an item is described as **price elastic** or elastic with respect to price if a 1% increase in price leads to more than a 1% drop in quantity demanded. Equivalently, demand is price elastic if a price increase causes a proportionately *larger* reduction in quantity demanded.

> **Price elastic:** A price increase causes a proportionately larger reduction in quantity demanded.

If the demand is elastic, the elasticity is less than -1. This means that the absolute value (that is, without the negative sign) of the elasticity exceeds 1.

By contrast, the demand is described as **price inelastic** or inelastic with respect to price if a 1% price increase causes less than a 1% drop in quantity demanded. Equivalently, demand is price inelastic if a price increase causes a proportionately *smaller* reduction in quantity demanded.

> **Price inelastic:** A price increase causes a proportionately smaller reduction in quantity demanded.

If the demand is inelastic, the elasticity exceeds -1. This means that the absolute value (that is, without the negative sign) of the elasticity is less than 1.

Intuitive Factors

To estimate the own-price elasticity requires information on a change in price and the corresponding change in quantity demanded. However, changing the price to estimate the elasticity may be too costly or not practical. As an alternative, managers can consider several intuitive factors to gauge the own-price elasticity of demand.

- *Availability of direct or indirect substitutes.* The fewer substitutes that are available, the less elastic will be the demand. People who are dependent on alcoholic drinks or cigarettes feel that there is no other way to satisfy their needs. Hence, the demand for these items is relatively inelastic.

  There are fewer substitutes for a product category than for specific products within a category. Consider, for instance, the demand for beer compared with the demand for a particular brand. The particular brand has many more substitutes than the category as a whole. Accordingly, the demand for the brand will tend to be more elastic than the demand for the category. This means that, if beer manufacturers can collectively raise prices by 10%, their sales will fall by a smaller percentage than if a single manufacturer increases its price by 10%.

- *Buyer's prior commitments.* A person who has bought a particular car becomes a captive customer for spare parts. Automobile manufacturers understand this very well. They set relatively higher prices on spare parts than on new cars. The same applies as well in the software business. Once users have invested time and effort to learn one program, they become "locked in" for future upgrades. Whenever there is such a lock-in, demand is less elastic.

Typically, commitments unwind over time. For instance, subscribers to 24-month mobile service contracts will be free to switch after 24 months. Accordingly, the effect of buyer commitments on the own-price elasticity of demand will diminish over time.

* *Benefits/costs of economizing.* Buyers have limited time to spend on searching for better prices, so they focus attention on items that account for relatively larger expenditures. Parents, for instance, spend more time economizing on diapers than on cotton buds. Similarly, office managers focus attention on copying paper rather than on paper clips. Marketing practitioners have given the name "low involvement" to products that get relatively little attention from buyers.

The balance between the benefit and cost of economizing also depends on a possible split between the person who incurs the cost of economizing and the person who benefits. If you bring a damaged car for repair, the repair manager will surely ask: "Are you covered by insurance?" Car owners who are covered by insurance care less about price. They get the benefit of the repair work, while the insurer pays most or all the costs. A car owner who bargains over the repairs must spend his or her own time, while the insurer will enjoy most of the saving.

PROGRESS CHECK 3B

What are the intuitive factors that influence the own-price elasticity of demand?

SHARED COSTS: FREQUENT FLYER PROGRAMS

Whenever there is a split between the person who pays and the person who chooses the product, the demand will be less elastic. In 1981, American Airlines established its AAdvantage program for frequent flyers. This program gives free flights and other awards according to the member's travel on American Airlines.

The AAdvantage program does not give mileage credit for travel on competing airlines such as United or Delta. So, it provides members with a strong incentive to concentrate travel on American Airlines.

The AAdvantage program is especially attractive to travelers, such as business executives, who fly at the expense of others. Such travelers are relatively less price sensitive than those who pay for their own tickets. AAdvantage gives them an incentive to choose American Airlines even if the fare is higher. Among customers who fly at the expense of others, the program makes demand relatively less elastic.

AAdvantage was a brilliant marketing strategy, and the other major airlines soon established their own frequent flyer programs.

4. Forecasting

The own-price elasticity of demand can be applied to forecast the effect of price changes on quantity demanded and buyers' expenditure. Expenditure is related to the quantity demanded, since expenditure equals the quantity demanded multiplied by the price. (In Chapter 9 on pricing, we consider the possibility of price discrimination. With price discrimination, different buyers pay different prices, so expenditure is not simply quantity demanded multiplied by price.)

The own-price elasticity concept can be applied at the level of an entire market as well as for individual sellers. From the standpoint of an individual seller, the quantity demanded is sales, while buyers' expenditure is revenue. Hence, using the own-price elasticity of demand, the seller can forecast the effect of price changes on sales and revenue.

Quantity Demanded

Let us first consider how to use the own-price elasticity of demand to forecast the effect of price changes on the quantity demanded. Refer to the demand for cigarettes in Figure 3.1. Suppose that the price is $1 a pack and the quantity demanded is 1.5 billion packs a month. How would a 5% increase in the price affect the quantity of cigarettes that buyers demand?

Above, we calculated the own-price elasticity of demand at the $1 price to be −0.4. By definition, the own-price elasticity is the percentage by which the quantity demanded will change if the price rises by 1%. Hence, if the price of cigarettes increases by 5%, then the quantity demanded will change by −0.4 × 5 = −2%, that is, the quantity demanded will fall by 2%.

To forecast the change in quantity demanded in terms of cigarettes, multiply the percentage change of −2% by the quantity demanded before the price change. Accordingly, the 5% price increase would change the quantity demanded by −2% × 1.5 billion = 30 million packs a month.

As the cigarette example illustrates, the rule for estimating the impact of prices changes on buyers' quantity demanded is:

Proportionate change in quantity demanded

= Proportionate change in price × Own-price elasticity of demand.   (3.3)

We can also use the above rule to estimate the effect of a reduction in the price on the quantity demanded. Suppose that the price of cigarettes is initially $1 a pack and then falls by 5%. The quantity demanded will change by −0.4 × (−5%) = 2%, that is, it will increase by 2%. This example shows that it is important to keep track of the signs of the own-price elasticity and the price change.

Expenditure

Next, let us see how to use the own-price elasticity of demand to estimate the effect of changes in price on buyers' expenditure. Buyers' expenditure equals the quantity demanded multiplied by the price. Hence, a change in price will affect expenditure through the price itself as well as through the related effect on quantity demanded.

Generally, the rule for estimating the impact of prices changes on buyers' expenditure is:

Proportionate change in expenditure = Proportionate change in price

+ Proportionate change in quantity demanded. (3.4)

Consider the effect of an increase in price. By itself, the price increase will tend to raise the expenditure. The price increase, however, will reduce the quantity that buyers demand, which would tend to reduce the expenditure. Hence, the net effect on expenditure depends on which effect is relatively larger.

The concept of own-price elasticity helps to determine whether the price or quantity effect is relatively larger. Recall that demand is elastic with respect to price if an increase in price causes a proportionately larger fall in quantity demanded, while demand is inelastic if a price increase causes a proportionately smaller fall in quantity demanded. The own-price elasticity enables us to compare the relative magnitude of changes in price and quantity demanded.

If the demand is price elastic, then the drop in the quantity demanded will be proportionately larger than the increase in price, and hence, the price increase will reduce expenditure. Generally, if demand is price elastic, a price increase will reduce expenditure while a price reduction will increase expenditure.

By contrast, if the demand is price inelastic, the drop in quantity demanded will be proportionately smaller than the increase in price, and then the price increase will increase expenditure. Generally, if demand is price inelastic, a price increase will increase expenditure while a price reduction will reduce expenditure.

To clarify further, substitute from equation (3.3) for the proportionate change in quantity demanded in (3.4). Then the rule for estimating the impact of prices changes on buyers' expenditure simplifies to:

Proportionate change in expenditure

= Proportionate change in price × (1 + Own-price elasticity of demand). (3.5)

Pricing Strategy

Whenever sales managers are asked to raise prices, their most frequent response is: "But my sales would drop!" Since demand curves slope downward, it certainly is true that a higher price will reduce sales. The real issue is the *extent* to which the price increase will reduce sales. Sales managers ought to be thinking about the own-price elasticity of demand.

To explain, suppose that a manufacturer's demand is price inelastic at the current price. What if the manufacturer raises the price? Since demand is price inelastic, the price increase will lead to a proportionately smaller reduction in the quantity demanded. The buyers' expenditure will increase, which means that the manufacturer's revenue will increase.

Meanwhile, owing to the reduction in quantity demanded, the manufacturer can reduce production, cutting its costs. Since revenues will be higher and costs will be lower, the manufacturer's profits definitely will be higher. Accordingly, if demand is price inelastic, a seller can increase profit by raising price.

As this discussion shows, under the right conditions (inelastic demand), a price increase can raise profits even though it may cause sales to drop. Therefore, when setting the price for an item, managers should focus on the own-price elasticity of demand. Generally, the price should be raised until the demand becomes price elastic. We will develop this idea further in Chapter 9 on pricing.

PROGRESS CHECK 3C

Suppose that the own-price elasticity of the demand for a particular mobile phone service provider is −2.5. If the service provider raises price by 7%, what would be the proportionate effect on quantity demanded and buyers' expenditure?

NEW YORK TIMES: MAY 2009 PRICE INCREASES

In 2008, the New York Times Media Group earned revenues of $668 million from circulation, $1.077 billion from advertising, and $181 million from other sources. Facing competition from new media and free newspapers, the Group management decided on a strategy to raise circulation prices and trim less profitable readership. In May 2009, the *New York Times* planned to raise its weekday cover price from $1.50 to $2, and its Sunday cover price from $5 to $6. The price increase was estimated to raise revenue by $40 million.

How reasonable is the estimate of the impact on revenue? We can address this question by using the rule for calculating the impact of a price increase on buyers' expenditure, equation (3.5).

At the current circulation of 1.04 million and price of $1.50, and assuming 300 weekdays a year, the current annual revenue from weekday sales of the *Times* is 1.04 × $1.50 × 300 million = $468 million. So, the price increase was estimated to raise revenue by 40/468 = 8.5%.

Focusing on the price increase for weekday papers from $1.50 to $2, the percentage change in price would be (2.00 − 1.50)/1.50 = 0.50/1.50 = 33%. Using equation (3.5), the proportionate change in revenue is 0.085 = 0.33 × (1 + Own-price elasticity of demand). Hence, the own-price elasticity of demand is 0.085/0.33 − 1 = 0.26 − 1 = −0.74.

For the *Times* price increase to raise revenue by $40 million, the own-price elasticity of demand must be −0.74. This assumption on the elasticity seems quite reasonable.

However, commentators on the price increases did not mention the impact on advertising revenues. The demand for advertising depends on the circulation of the newspaper. Assuming that the own-price elasticity of demand is −0.74, the 33% price increase would have changed circulation by 33% × −0.74 = −24%. The 24% reduction in circulation would have substantially reduced advertising revenue.

Sources: "New York Times set to increase price," *Financial Times*, May 2, 2009; New York Times Company, Annual Reports 2008 and 2009.

5. Other Elasticities

In addition to price, the demand for an item also depends on buyers' incomes, the prices of complementary and substitute items, and sellers' advertising. Changes in any of these factors shift the demand curve.

There is an elasticity to measure the responsiveness of demand to changes in each factor. Managers can use these elasticities to forecast the effect of changes in these factors. In particular, the elasticities can be used to forecast the effect of changes in multiple factors that occur at the same time.

The analysis of elasticities of demand with respect to income, the prices of complementary and substitute items, and sellers' advertising is quite similar to that for the own-price elasticity. Accordingly, we will focus on the differences for the other elasticities.

Income Elasticity

The income elasticity of demand measures the sensitivity of demand to changes in buyers' incomes. By definition, the **income elasticity** of demand is the percentage by which the demand will change if the buyers' incomes rise by 1%. Equivalently, the income elasticity is the ratio

> **Income elasticity:** The percentage by which demand will change if buyers' incomes rise by 1%.

$$\frac{\text{Percentage change in demand}}{\text{Percentage change in buyers' income}}.$$ (3.6)

For a normal product, if buyers' incomes rise, the demand will rise, so the income elasticity will be positive. By contrast, for an inferior product, if incomes rise, demand will fall, so the income elasticity will be negative. Thus the sign of the income elasticity will depend on whether the product is normal or inferior. Hence, it is important to note the sign of the income elasticity. The income elasticity can range in value from negative infinity to positive infinity.

Demand is described as *income elastic* or elastic with respect to income if a 1% increase in income causes more than a 1% change in demand. Demand is described as *income inelastic* or inelastic with respect to income if a 1% increase in income causes less than a 1% change in demand.

The demand for necessities tends to be relatively less income elastic than the demand for discretionary items. Consider, for instance, the demand for raw food as compared with restaurant meals. Eating in a restaurant is more of a discretionary item as compared to cooking at home. Accordingly, the demand for raw food is relatively less income elastic than the demand for restaurant meals.

Cross-Price Elasticity

Cross-price elasticity:
The percentage by which demand will change if the price of a related item rises by 1%.

Just as the income elasticity of demand measures the sensitivity of demand to changes in income, the cross-price elasticity measures the sensitivity of demand to changes in the prices of related products. By definition, the **cross-price elasticity** of demand with respect to another item is the percentage by which the demand will change if the price of the related item rises by 1%. Equivalently, the cross-price elasticity is the ratio

$$\frac{\text{Percentage change in demand}}{\text{Percentage change in price of related item}}. \tag{3.7}$$

If two products are substitutes, an increase in the price of one will increase the demand for the other, so the cross-price elasticity will be positive. The more substitutable are two items, the higher their cross-price elasticity will be. By contrast, if two products are complements, an increase in the price of one will reduce demand for the other, and so the cross-price elasticity will be negative. The cross-price elasticity can range from negative infinity to positive infinity.

Advertising elasticity:
The percentage by which demand will change if sellers' advertising expenditure rises by 1%.

Advertising Elasticity

The advertising elasticity measures the sensitivity of demand to changes in the sellers' advertising expenditure. By definition, the **advertising elasticity** of demand is the percentage by which the demand will change if the sellers' advertising expenditure rises by 1%. Equivalently, the advertising elasticity is the ratio

$$\frac{\text{Percentage change in demand}}{\text{Percentage change in sellers' advertising expenditure}}. \qquad (3.8)$$

Generally, an increase in advertising will raise the demand, and so the elasticity will be positive. Most advertising is undertaken by individual sellers to promote their own business. By drawing buyers away from competitors, advertising has a much stronger effect on the sales of an individual seller than on the market demand. Accordingly, the advertising elasticity of the demand faced by an individual seller tends to be larger than the advertising elasticity of the market demand.

Forecasting Multiple Factors

The business environment will often change in conflicting ways. For instance, incomes may rise, while the prices of substitutes and complements rise as well. For a normal product, the higher income would raise demand, the higher price of substitutes would also raise demand, but the higher price of complements would reduce demand.

What is the net effect on demand? This question can be addressed using the elasticities with respect to each of the factors affecting demand. Generally, the percentage change in demand due to changes in multiple factors is the sum of the percentage changes due to each separate factor.

To illustrate, suppose that the price of cigarettes is $1 per pack and sales are 1.5 billion packs a month. Then the price increases by 5%, while buyers' incomes rise by 3%. What would be the net impact on demand?

Suppose that the own-price elasticity of the demand for cigarettes is −0.4 and the income elasticity of demand is 0.1. Then the 5% increase in price would change the quantity demanded by $-0.4 \times 5\% = -2\%$. Further, the 3% increase in incomes would change demand by $0.1 \times 3\% = 0.3\%$. Hence, the net effect of the increases in price and incomes is to change demand by $-2\% + 0.3\% = -1.7\%$.

Originally, the quantity demanded of cigarette services was 1.5 billion packs per month. After the increases in price and incomes, the quantity demanded will be 0.983×1.5 billion $= 1.475$ billion packs per month. A similar approach can be used to forecast the effects of changes in other factors, including the prices of related products and sellers' advertising expenditures.

PROGRESS CHECK 3D

Refer to Section 2 of this chapter for the properties of own-price elasticity. What are the corresponding properties of the income elasticity?

GASOLINE PRICES AND CAR CHOICE

With gasoline prices falling below $3 a gallon, Americans are buying more SUVs (sport-utility vehicles) and pick-up trucks. Mike Jackson, chief executive of auto retailer AutoNation, remarked: "Americans just love big."

Falling gasoline prices have reinforced an existing trend of buying larger vehicles. Between October 2014 and 2015, the percentage of SUVs and trucks rose from 68.5% to 72% of Ford's sales.

Brian Johnson, auto analyst at investment bank Barclays, emphasized that buying a new SUV could save gasoline: "A new Ford Escape [crossover SUV] is more fuel efficient than a 10-year-old Camry".

Indeed, in the United States between 1997 and 2005, consumers adjusted to higher gasoline prices by scrapping less fuel-efficient cars and buying more fuel-efficient ones. The cross-price elasticity for fuel economy with respect to gasoline prices was 0.02 in the short run and 0.20 in the long run.

Source: Shanjun Li, Christopher Timmins, and Roger H. von Haefen, "How do gasoline prices affect fleet fuel economy?" *American Economic Journal: Economic Policy*, Vol. 1, No. 2, August 2009, pp. 113–137.

6. Adjustment Time

We have analyzed the elasticities of demand with respect to changes in price, income, the prices of related products, and advertising expenditures. In addition, another factor affects all elasticities: the time available for buyers to adjust.

Short run: Time horizon within which buyers cannot adjust at least one item of consumption.

With regard to adjustment time, it is important to distinguish the short run from the long run. The **short run** is a time horizon within which a buyer cannot adjust at least one item of consumption. By contrast, the **long run** is a time horizon long enough for buyers to adjust all items of consumption.

Long run: Time horizon long enough for buyers to adjust all items of consumption.

To illustrate the distinction, consider how Fred commutes into Chicago. He does not have a car, so he takes the train. To switch from the train to a car, he needs time to buy or lease a car. Accordingly, with regard to Fred's choice of transport, the short run is any period of time shorter than that which he needs to get a car. The long run is any period of time longer than that which he needs to get a car.

Let us now discuss the effect of adjustment time on the elasticities of demand, and how the effect depends on whether the item is durable or non-durable.

Non-durables

Consider an everyday item such as commuter train services. Suppose that one Monday morning, the train operator announces a permanent 10% increase in fares. Many commuters may have already made plans for that day, so the response to the higher fare may be quite weak on that day. Over time, however, the response will be stronger: as more commuters acquire cars, the demand for train services will drop.

Generally, for a **non-durable good**, the longer the time that buyers have to adjust, the bigger will be the response to a price change. Accordingly, the demand for such items will be more elastic in the long run than in the short run. This applies to all non-durable items, including both goods and services.

> **Non-durable good:** Demand is more elastic in long run than short run.

Figure 3.2 illustrates the short- and long-run demand for a non-durable item. Suppose that the current price is $5 and quantity demanded is 1.5 million units. If the price drops to $4.50, the quantity demanded will rise to 1.6 million units in the short run and 1.75 million units in the long run.

At the price of $5 and quantity demanded of 1.5 million units, the proportionate change in the price is ($4.50 − $5)/$5 = −$0.50/$5 = −0.1. In the short run, the proportionate change in the quantity demanded is (1.6 − 1.5)/1.5 = 0.1/1.5 = 0.067. Accordingly, the short-run own-price elasticity is 0.067/(0.1) = −0.67.

In the long run, the proportionate change in the quantity demanded is (1.75 − 1.5)/1.5 = 0.25/1.5 = 0.167. Thus, the long-run own-price elasticity is 0.167/(−0.1) = −1.67. This confirms that the demand is more elastic in the long run than in the short run.

Durables

The effect of adjustment time on the demand for durable goods such as cars is somewhat different. For both durables and non-durables, buyers need time to adjust, which causes demand to be relatively more elastic in the long run.

However, for durables only, a countervailing effect causes demand to be relatively more elastic in the short run. This countervailing effect is especially strong with respect to changes in income.

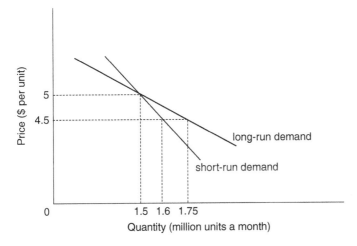

FIGURE 3.2 Short- and long-run demand for a non-durable item.

Note: If the price drops from $5 to $4.50, the quantity demanded will rise to 1.6 million units in the short run and 1.75 million units in the long run.

Consider, for instance, the demand for cars. Most drivers buy cars at intervals of several years. Suppose that there is a drop in incomes. Then drivers will plan to keep their cars longer. Some drivers, who were just about to replace their cars, will put off the decision to do so. So the drop in incomes will cause purchases to dry up until sufficient time passes that these drivers want to replace their cars at the new lower income.

However, in the long run, the effect on sales will be more muted: eventually, all drivers will replace their cars, but less frequently. Thus, the drop in income will cause demand to fall more sharply in the short run than in the long run.

Similarly, if income rises, drivers will replace their cars more frequently. Some drivers will find that they want to replace their cars immediately, causing a boom in purchases. This boom, however, will last only as long as it takes all such drivers to adjust to their new replacement frequency. Thus, the increase in income will tend to cause demand to increase more sharply in the short run than in the long run.

Durable good: Demand may be more or less elastic in long run than short run, depending on the balance between time for adjustment and replacement frequency.

Accordingly, for a **durable good**, the difference between short- and long-run elasticities of demand depends on a balance between the need for time to adjust and the replacement frequency effect.

PROGRESS CHECK 3E

For a non-durable good, explain why the long-run demand is more elastic than the short-run demand.

DEMAND FOR GASOLINE AND CARS: EFFECT OF TIME

People buy gasoline to fuel their cars. So the demand for gasoline depends on the ownership of cars and their fuel efficiency. As households change their cars over time, their demand for gasoline will also change.

A Canadian study estimated the demand for gasoline as measured by the fuel consumption per unit of distance. The own-price elasticity was -0.029 in the short run and -0.089 in the long run. Apparently, taking into consideration the long-run impact of gasoline on car ownership, the demand was three times more price elastic in the long run than in the short run.

The same study also estimated the demand for car ownership. The income elasticity of the demand for cars was 0.285 in the short run and 0.391 in the long run. Among Canadians, the long-run demand for cars was 37% more income elastic than in the short run. The estimates suggest that the effect of adjustment time outweighed the replacement frequency.

Source: Philippe Barla, Bernard Lamonde, Luis F. Miranda-Moreno, and Nathalie Boucher, "Traveled distance, stock and fuel efficiency of private vehicles in Canada: price elasticities and rebound effect," *Transportation*, Vol. 36, No. 4, 2009, pp. 389–402.

7. Bounded Rationality

Owing to cognitive limitations and difficulties in self-control, individuals behave with bounded rationality. Bounded rationality leads to systematic biases in decision-making that affect the elasticity of demand.

*   *Sunk-cost fallacy.* Once a person has incurred a sunk cost, she may feel mentally obliged to justify the sunk cost and that mental obligation will affect her subsequent choices. For instance, having paid the annual subscription fee for unlimited shipping, a consumer may feel that she must make more purchases to justify the annual fee. If the subscription fee is higher, the consumer will feel obliged to spend even more and her demand for shopping will be less price elastic.
*   *Anchoring.* Facing uncertainty, individuals need information and may use cues, even irrelevant cues, to guide their choices. Consumers may be imprecise about their benefit from consumer products. Appreciating this uncertainty, retailers set list prices to anchor consumer perceptions of the benefit. To the extent of such anchoring, consumers perceive that prices above the list price exceed their benefit, while prices below the list price yield buyer surplus. Accordingly, the consumer demand is price elastic at prices above the list price and price inelastic at prices below the list price.

KEY TAKEAWAYS

*   The own-price elasticity of demand is the percentage by which the quantity demanded will change if the price of the item rises by 1%.
*   The demand for an item is price elastic if a 1% increase in price leads to more than a 1% drop in quantity demanded, and price inelastic if a 1% increase in price leads to less than a 1% drop in quantity demanded.
*   The demand for an item will be more elastic to the extent that: (i) it has more direct or indirect substitutes; (ii) the buyer has fewer prior commitments to the item; and (iii) the benefits of economizing are larger than the costs.
*   If demand is inelastic, the seller can increase profit by raising the price.
*   The income elasticity of demand is the percentage by which the demand will change if buyers' incomes rise by 1%.
*   The cross-price elasticity of demand is the percentage by which the demand will change if the price of a related item rises by 1%.
*   The advertising elasticity of demand is the percentage by which the demand will change if sellers increase advertising expenditure by 1%.
*   For non-durables, the demand is more elastic in the long run than in the short run. For durables, the demand may be more or less elastic in the long run than in the short run, depending on the balance between time for adjustment and replacement frequency.

- Incurring a sunk cost causes demand to be less price elastic.
- Demand is price elastic above the anchor price, and price inelastic below the anchor price.

REVIEW QUESTIONS

1. Consider a service that you buy frequently. (a) Suppose that the price is 5% lower. How much more would you buy each year? (b) Calculate the own-price elasticity of your demand.
2. Explain why the own-price elasticity is a pure number with no units and is negative.
3. Under what conditions is demand price elastic or price inelastic?
4. Consider the intuitive factors that influence the own-price elasticity of demand. Apply the factors to gauge the own-price elasticity of demand for air travel among executives traveling at the expense of their employers.
5. Suppose that the own-price elasticity of the market demand for food is −0.7 and that, as a result of a severe drought, the price of food rises by 10%. Will expenditure on food rise or fall?
6. The own-price elasticity of the demand for one brand of frozen vegetables is −1.5. Suppose that the manufacturer reduces price by 5%. What would be the percentage effect on the volume of sales?
7. Consider a good that you buy frequently. (a) Suppose that your income is 10% higher. How much more would you buy each year? (b) Calculate the income elasticity of your demand.
8. Changes in the price of an item may affect the income elasticity of demand. True or false?
9. Tire manufacturers use both natural and synthetic rubber to produce tires. Suppose that the cross-price elasticity of demand for natural rubber with respect to changes in the price of synthetic rubber is negative. Are the two types of rubber substitutes or complements?
10. Explain why the advertising elasticity of the market demand for beer may be less than the advertising elasticity of the demand for one particular brand.
11. Suppose that the advertising elasticity of the demand for one brand of cigarettes is 1.3. If the manufacturer raises advertising expenditure by 5%, by how much will the demand change?
12. Consider the effect of changes in fares on the quantity demanded of taxi services. Do you expect demand to be more elastic with respect to fare changes in the short run or in the long run?
13. Suppose that the income elasticity of the demand for cars is 0.285 in the short run and 0.391 in the long run. Compare the effect of a 10% rise in incomes on the demand for cars in the short and long run.
14. How does the sunk-cost fallacy affect the elasticity of demand?
15. Compare the own-price elasticity of the demand for a particular brand of inkjet cartridges: (a) before the user has bought an inkjet printer; and (b) after the user has bought the printer.

DISCUSSION QUESTIONS

1. At a major French food retailer, the own-price elasticities of the demand for various brands of pasta were: –1.36 for national brands, –2.16 for private labels, and –1.85 for low-price brands. At the same retailer, the own-price elasticities of the demand for various brands of biscuits were: –1.00 for national brands, –1.14 for private labels, and –0.50 for low-price brands. (Source: Fabian Berges, Daniel Hassan, and Sylvette Monier-Dilhan, "Are consumers more loyal to national brands than to private labels?" Working Paper, Toulouse School of Economics, 2009.)
   (a) Compare the elasticities of the demand for national brands and private labels of pasta. Does the difference make sense?
   (b) Do national brands or private labels or low-price brands command more brand loyalty? (*Hint*: Interpret brand loyalty by the own-price elasticity.)
   (c) Which is more elastic? The demand for pasta or biscuits?
   (d) Based on the own-price elasticities, can you make any recommendations on pricing?
2. Between 1995 and 2005, the own-price elasticity of the demand for water among urban residential users ranged between a high of –0.20 in October and a low of –0.06 in December. Among urban commercial users, the own-price elasticity of demand ranged from a high of –0.17 in December to a low of –0.08 in January. (Source: David R. Bell and Ronald C. Griffin, "Urban water demand with periodic error correction," *Land Economics*, Vol. 87, No. 3, August 2011, pp. 528–544.)
   (a) Are the residential and commercial demands for water price elastic or inelastic?
   (b) Do you expect the elasticities of the residential and commercial demands to be similar or different?
   (c) Explain why the own-price elasticity of the demand varies by season.
   (d) If urban suppliers of water were to raise their prices by 10%, what would be the effect on residential and commercial expenditures?
3. In 2008, the New York Times Media Group earned revenues of $668 million from circulation, $1.077 billion from advertising, and $181 million from other sources. The Group decided to raise circulation prices and trim less profitable readership. In May 2009, the *New York Times* planned to raise its weekday cover price from $1.50 to $2. The previous year, the *Times* had raised the price from $1.25 to $1.50, and circulation fell 3.6% to 1.04 million.
   (a) Using the 2008 price and circulation information, calculate the own-price elasticity of demand for the *New York Times* weekday edition.
   (b) At the current price of $1.50, and assuming 300 weekdays a year, what is the annual revenue from weekday sales?
   (c) Consider the expected 2009 price increase from $1.50 to $2. What is the percentage change in price?

(d) Suppose that the expected 2009 price increase from $1.50 to $2 does indeed yield $40 million in incremental revenue. What is the percentage change in revenue?

(e) Calculate the price elasticity of demand which would imply the $40 million increase in revenue. (*Hint*: Use equation (3.5).)

(f) Compare the elasticities in (a) and (e). Does the difference make intuitive sense?

4. In the US market for four prescription medicines (analgesic/musculoskeletal, antilipidemics, gastrointestinal acid reducers, and insomnia remedies), the elasticity of demand with respect to consumer advertising ranged between 0.13 and 0.19, while the elasticity of demand with respect to physician advertising was 0.51. The own-price elasticity was –0.67 for drugs advertised to consumers and –0.73 for drugs not advertised to consumers. (Source: Dhaval Dave and Henry Saffer, "Impact of direct-to-consumer advertising on pharmaceutical prices and demand," *Southern Economic Journal*, Vol. 79, No. 1, 2012, pp. 97–126.)

(a) How would a 5% increase in expenditure on advertising to consumers affect the demand for the four prescription medicines?

(b) What about a 5% increase in expenditure on advertising to physicians?

(c) Do you expect the same difference between advertising to consumers *vis-à-vis* physicians in the demand for over-the-counter (non-prescription) medicines?

(d) Suppose that a drug manufacturer were to increase advertising. Explain why it should also raise the price of its drugs.

5. At an Asian mobile service provider, the demand for voice calls had an own-price elasticity of –0.085 and cross-price elasticity with respect to the price of short message service (SMS) of –0.078. The demand for SMS had an own-price elasticity of –0.03 and cross-price elasticity with respect to the price of voice calls of –0.03. (Source: Youngsoo Kim, Rahul Telang, William B. Vogt, and Ramayya Krishnan, "An empirical analysis of mobile voice service and SMS: A structural model," *Management Science*, Vol. 56, No. 2, February 2010, pp. 234–252.)

(a) For which service was the demand more price inelastic?

(b) How would you describe the relation between the demand for voice calls and for SMS? Are they (i) complements, or (ii) substitutes?

(c) Which is the relatively stronger complement/substitute? (i) SMS for voice calls, or (ii) voice calls for SMS?

(d) Describe the impact on revenues from (i) voice and (ii) SMS if the provider were to raise the price of voice calls by 5%.

6. Electric power producers have a choice of various fuels, including oil, natural gas, coal, and uranium, as well as solar and wind energy. Once an electric power plant has been built, however, the scope to switch fuels may be very limited. Since power plants last for 30 years or more, producers must consider

the relative prices of the alternative fuels well into the future when choosing a generating plant.

   (a) Do you expect the cross-price elasticity between the demand for wind power plants and the price of coal to be positive or negative?

   (b) Will the cross-price elasticity between the demand for oil-fired power plants and the price of coal be positive or negative?

   (c) Would the demand for fuel be more or less elastic in the long run as compared to the short run?

7. The demand for automobile travel (measured in total number of miles driven) depends on the price of gasoline and travel time. The cross-price elasticity of the demand for automobile travel with respect to the price of gasoline is estimated to be −0.10 in the short run and −0.29 in the long run. The elasticity of the demand for automobile travel with respect to travel time is −0.27 in the short run and −0.57 in the long run. (Source: Victoria Transport Policy Institute, www.vtpi.org/elasticities.pdf.)

   (a) Explain why the demand for automobile travel is more elastic in the long run than in the short run.

   (b) Suppose that the price of gasoline rises by 20% and construction of new roads reduces travel time by 10%. Calculate the percentage change in the total number of miles driven in the (i) short run, and (ii) long run.

8. According to a study of US cigarette sales, when the price of cigarettes was 1% higher, consumption would be 0.4% lower in the short run and 0.75% lower in the long run. (Source: Gary Becker, Michael Grossman, and Kevin Murphy, "An empirical analysis of cigarette addiction," *American Economic Review*, Vol. 84, No. 3, June 1994, pp. 396–418.)

   (a) Calculate the short- and long-run own-price elasticities of the demand for cigarettes.

   (b) Explain why the demand for cigarettes is more elastic in the long run than in the short run.

   (c) If the government were to impose a tax that raised the price of cigarettes by 5%, what would be the effect on consumer expenditure on cigarettes in the (i) short run, and (ii) long run?

9. In the following scenarios, it may (not necessarily) help to consider biases in individual decision-making.

   (a) Your mobile service provider requires a cash deposit of $100 from every customer. A competing provider does not require any deposit. Both providers raise the prices of their calling plans by 10%. Which would experience a larger drop in sales?

   (b) The local fitness club prices in two ways. It charges $5 per two-hour visit. It also offers a membership for $240 a year which includes 80 free visits. (i) What is the break-even between the annual membership and per-visit price? (ii) Why do many people buy the membership yet use the club fewer than 48 times a year?

(c) One supermarket sets a regular price of €5 for a six-pack of Coca-Cola and discounts to €3. Another supermarket sets a regular price of €4 for a six-pack of Coca-Cola and discounts to €3. Which supermarket would experience a larger increase in sales?

You are the consultant!

Identify a product that your organization sells for which the demand is price inelastic. Write a memorandum to the chief financial officer of your organization to recommend an increase in price.

Note

1   The following discussion is based in part on "Will Amazon Prime customers accept price hike? Maybe not," *Forbes*, February 12, 2004; "Piper Jaffray reduces churn estimates for potential Amazon Prime price hike," *Tech Trader Daily*, March 7, 2014; Wedbush Securities, "Quick note: Amazon.com (AMZN – NEUTRAL)," March 13, 2014.

Supply

LEARNING OBJECTIVES

- Appreciate why producers supply more at higher prices.
- Appreciate how to decide, in the short run, whether to continue in business, and if so, the scale of production.
- Distinguish fixed and variable costs in the short run.
- Understand the concepts of marginal cost and marginal revenue.
- Appreciate how to decide, in the long run, whether to continue in business, and if so, the scale of production.
- Appreciate that, in the long run, businesses can adjust by entering or exiting the industry.
- Appreciate the concept of seller surplus and apply it in purchasing.
- Apply the concept of price elasticity of supply.

1. Introduction

Founded in Durham, Ontario, in 1899, Durham Furniture produces bedroom furniture. In 2003, the company completed a new plant at Chesley, Ontario, to manufacture dining room furniture. The total cost was C$38 million, comprising C$8 million for the 147,500 square foot factory and C$30 million on equipment. The new plant included eight modern kilns capable of drying 70,000 board feet of hardwood every 11 days.[1]

However, the opening of the Chesley plant coincided with increased competition from Asia and the appreciation of the Canadian dollar against the US dollar. Then, the Great Recession struck, crimping US demand. In 2008, Durham decided to exit the dining room category and mothball the plant.

Later in the year, Durham Furniture filed for protection under the Companies' Creditors Arrangement Act. The company had a net worth of between C\$3.5 and C\$6.3 million, excluding the Chesley plant and equipment, while owing C\$37 million in secured borrowings to the Royal Bank of Canada. The Royal Bank of Canada agreed to the restructuring of the loans provided that Durham found new investors.

In January 2012, GRS Wood Products, a Chinese-owned company with two manufacturing plants in China, purchased the Chesley plant. Mayor Paul Eagleson of the municipality understood that GRS would use the plant to produce hardwood flooring and employ 50 workers.

Ready access to lumber products gives an advantage to Canadian manufacturers of furniture. However, the manufacturing of furniture is also fairly labor-intensive. Furniture manufacturers in Asia benefit from lower labor costs. With falling trade barriers and costs of transportation, Asian furniture manufacturers can increase their exports to the United States.

How do changes in the prices of inputs such as lumber affect the furniture industry? How would the increase in exports of furniture from Asian competitors affect Canadian manufacturers like Durham? Should new investors put money into Durham?

To address these questions, we need to understand two key decisions of a business: first, whether to continue in operation; and, second, the scale at which to operate. The first is a decision on participation and depends on whether the business would break even, and, in turn, on the total revenue and total (relevant) cost. The second is a decision on extent and depends on the marginal revenue and marginal cost.

In this chapter, we study the two key decisions in the short run, when businesses are restricted in the extent to which they can adjust inputs, and in the long run, when businesses can freely adjust all inputs and possibly enter or exit. We can analyze whether new investors should invest in Durham.

The analyses of whether to remain in business and, if so, the scale of business provide the foundation for the concepts of the supply curve. The supply curve is the seller-side counterpart to the demand curve. Applying the market supply curve, we can explain the impact of Asian manufacturers on the US market for furniture and the prospects for Durham and other Canadian manufacturers. Further, we can explain the impact of lumber and steel prices on the furniture industry.

This chapter also presents the concepts of seller surplus and elasticity of supply. Seller surplus is the seller-side counterpart to buyer surplus. By extracting seller surplus, managers can reduce the cost of purchasing and raise profit. The own-price elasticity of supply measures the responsiveness of quantity supplied to changes in the price of the item. This will tell managers how much of a price increase will be necessary to meet any desired increase in purchases.

The decision-making techniques and concepts presented here apply to any industry which is characterized by competition among many small suppliers, each of which can sell as much as it would like at the market price. They obviously apply to mining, farming, and fisheries, and also to small-scale manufacturing and service industries.

2. Short-Run Costs

The two key decisions of a business – whether to continue in operation and the scale at which to operate – both depend on the time horizon. In Chapter 3, we introduced the concepts of short run and long run in relation to buyers. The same concepts apply to sellers as well.

The **short run** is a time horizon in which a seller cannot adjust at least one input. In the short run, the business must work within the constraints of past commitments such as employment contracts and investment in facilities and equipment. Over time, however, these commitments expire. The **long run** is a time horizon long enough for the seller to adjust all inputs, including possibly entering or exiting the industry.

> **Short run:** A time horizon in which a seller cannot adjust at least one input.

> **Long run:** A time horizon long enough for the seller to adjust all inputs, including possibly entering or exiting the industry.

The difference between the short run and long run depends on the circumstances. Consider a factory that has just engaged 50 workers on 12-month contracts. The employment of these workers cannot be adjusted until the expiration of the contracts. Hence, the factory's short run is at least 12 months long. By contrast, a factory that hires all workers on a daily basis can adjust its workforce every day. Similarly, a factory that has purchased manufacturing equipment has committed to a relatively longer horizon than one that has leased the equipment on a yearly contract.

Fixed and Variable Costs

To determine its scale or rate of production, a business needs to know the cost of delivering an additional unit of product (for convenience, we use "scale" and "rate" of production interchangeably). To decide whether to continue in operation, a business needs to know how shutting down will affect its total costs.

An important factor in both decisions is the distinction between fixed and variable costs. The **fixed cost** is the cost of inputs that do not change with the production rate. By contrast, the **variable cost** is the cost of inputs that do change with the production rate.

> **Fixed cost:** The cost of inputs that do not change with the production rate.

> **Variable cost:** The cost of inputs that do change with the production rate.

Let us consider the distinction between fixed and variable costs in the context of Luna Plywood, which produces plywood. Like those of most businesses, Luna's accounting records do not classify expenses into fixed and variable. Rather, the records organize expenses according to the type

Table 4.1 Short-run weekly expenses

Weekly production rate	Rent ($)	Equipment leasing ($)	Salaries ($)	Wages ($)	Cost of supplies ($)	Total ($)
0	2,000	10,000	8,000	2,000	0	22,000
1,000	2,000	10,000	8,000	5,290	1,000	26,290
2,000	2,000	10,000	8,000	8,360	2,000	30,360
3,000	2,000	10,000	8,000	12,160	3,000	35,160
4,000	2,000	10,000	8,000	16,970	4,000	40,970
5,000	2,000	10,000	8,000	22,930	5,000	47,930
6,000	2,000	10,000	8,000	30,150	6,000	56,150
7,000	2,000	10,000	8,000	38,700	7,000	65,700
8,000	2,000	10,000	8,000	48,620	8,000	76,620
9,000	2,000	10,000	8,000	59,960	9,000	88,960

Table 4.2 Analysis of short-run costs

Weekly production rate	Fixed cost ($)	Variable cost ($)	Total cost ($)	Marginal cost ($)	Average fixed cost ($)	Average variable cost ($)	Average cost ($)
0	22,000	0	22,000				
1,000	22,000	4,290	26,290	4.29	22.00	4.29	26.29
2,000	22,000	8,360	30,360	4.07	11.00	4.18	15.18
3,000	22,000	13,160	35,160	4.80	7.33	4.39	11.72
4,000	22,000	18,970	40,970	5.81	5.50	4.74	10.24
5,000	22,000	25,930	47,930	6.96	4.40	5.19	9.59
6,000	22,000	34,150	56,150	8.22	3.67	5.69	9.36
7,000	22,000	43,700	65,700	9.55	3.14	6.24	9.39
8,000	22,000	54,620	76,620	10.92	2.75	6.83	9.58
9,000	22,000	66,960	88,960	12.34	2.44	7.44	9.88

of input: rent, equipment lease, salaries, wages, and payments for supplies. By interviewing Luna's management, we can learn the costs required for alternative short-run production rates. Table 4.1 presents this information.

To distinguish between fixed and variable costs, a business must analyze how each category of expense varies with changes in the scale of operations. Referring to Table 4.1, we can perform this analysis for Luna. In the short run, Luna cannot adjust the size of its facility, equipment or managers' salaries, so the rent and equipment leasing do not vary with the production rate. The rent is $2,000, equipment leasing is $10,000 and managers' salaries are $8,000 whether Luna produces nothing or 9,000 sheets of plywood a week; hence, they are a fixed cost. Workers' wages vary with the production rate, but even when Luna produces nothing, it incurs wages of $2,000. Hence, the wages include a fixed component of $2,000, while the remainder is variable. Finally, the cost of supplies is completely variable.

In Table 4.2, we assign Luna's expenses – rent, managers' salaries, wages, and cost of supplies – into the two categories of fixed costs and variable costs. As the production rate increases from nothing to 9,000 sheets of plywood a week, the

fixed cost is always $22,000. By contrast, the variable cost increases from nothing
for no production to $66,960 for 9,000 sheets a week.

Total cost is the sum of fixed cost and variable cost. If we
represent total cost by C, fixed cost by F, and variable cost
by V, then

> **Total cost:** The sum of fixed cost and variable cost.

$$C = F + V. \tag{4.1}$$

Provided that there are some variable costs, the total cost will increase with operations. In Luna's case, referring to Table 4.2, the total cost is $22,000 for no pro-
duction, and rises to $88,960 for production of 9,000 sheets a week.

It is helpful to illustrate the concepts of total, fixed, and variable costs graphically. In Figure 4.1, the vertical axis represents cost, while the horizontal axis represents the scale of production. We draw a curve representing variable cost. The
total cost curve is the variable cost curve, shifted up everywhere by the amount of
the fixed cost. In particular, the fixed cost is represented by the height of the total
cost curve at the production rate of zero.

By analyzing its costs as fixed and variable, the management of a business can
understand which cost elements will be affected by changes in the scale of operations. The distinction between fixed and variable costs is important whether the
business is growing or shrinking. For instance, suppose that management is planning to reduce costs by downsizing the scale of operations. Downsizing will have
no effect on fixed costs and will only reduce the variable costs. Hence, in a business
whose costs are mostly fixed, downsizing may have relatively little effect on costs.

PROGRESS CHECK 4A

In Figure 4.1, if the fixed cost were higher, how would that affect the total and
variable cost curves?

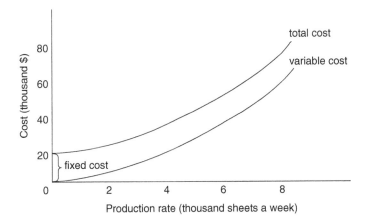

FIGURE 4.1 Short-run total cost.

Note: The total cost is the variable cost curve shifted up by the amount of the fixed cost.

Marginal Cost

To determine the scale at which it should operate, a business needs to know the cost of making an additional unit of product. Then the business can see whether selling the additional unit will add to or subtract from its total profit. The change in total cost due to the production of an additional unit is the **marginal cost**. The marginal cost can be derived from the analysis of fixed and variable costs.

> **Marginal cost:** The change in total cost due to the production of an additional unit.

Let us derive the marginal cost in the case of Luna Plywood. Referring to Table 4.2, as the production rate increases from zero to 1,000 sheets of plywood a week, the total cost increases from $22,000 to $26,290. The increment of $26,290 – $22,000 = $4,290 is the additional cost of producing the 1,000 sheets. Hence, the marginal cost is $4,290/1,000 = $4.29 per sheet.

Notice that, as the production rate increases from zero to 1,000 sheets a week, the fixed cost remains unchanged; only the variable cost increases. Hence, we can also calculate the marginal cost from the increase in variable cost. Using this approach, as the production rate increases from zero to 1,000 sheets a week, the variable cost increases from $0 to $4,290. Therefore, the marginal cost is $4,290/1,000 = $4.29 per sheet.

Similarly, as the production rate increases from 1,000 to 2,000 sheets a week, the variable cost increases from $4,290 to $8,360. The marginal cost is now $4,070 for 1,000 sheets, or $4.07 per sheet. With each increase in the production rate, the marginal cost increases, reaching $12.34 at the rate of 9,000 sheets a week.

In Luna's case, each additional sheet requires more variable cost than the one before. We display this information in Table 4.2.

Average Cost

The marginal cost is the cost of producing an additional unit. A related concept is the **average cost**, which is the total cost divided by the production rate. The average cost is also called the *unit cost*. Given the scale of operations, the average cost reflects the cost of producing a typical unit.

> **Average cost** (unit cost): The total cost divided by the production rate.

Let us derive the average cost in the case of Luna Plywood. Referring to Table 4.2, we can obtain the average cost as the total cost divided by the production rate. At 1,000 sheets a week, the average cost is $26,290/1,000 = $26.29 per sheet, while at 2,000 sheets a week, the average cost is $30,360/2,000 = $15.18 per sheet. The average cost continues to fall with increases in the production rate until it reaches a minimum of $9.36 at 6,000 sheets a week. Thereafter, it increases with the production rate. At 9,000 sheets a week, the average cost is $9.88 per sheet.

To understand why the average cost first drops with increases in the production rate and then rises, recall that the total cost is the sum of the fixed cost and the variable cost. Let q represent the production rate. Then dividing equation (4.1) throughout by q, we have

$$\frac{C}{q} = \frac{F}{q} + \frac{V}{q}. \tag{4.2}$$

In words, the average cost is the average fixed cost plus the average variable cost. The average fixed cost is fixed cost divided by the production rate. So, if the production rate is higher, the fixed cost will be spread over more units; hence, the average fixed cost will be lower. This factor causes the average cost to fall with increases in the production rate.

The other element in average cost is the average variable cost, which is the variable cost divided by the production rate. In the short run, at least one input is fixed; hence, to raise the production rate, the business must combine increasing quantities of the variable inputs with an unchanged quantity of the fixed input.

The increase in output arising from an additional unit of an input is called the **marginal product** from that input. At low production rates, there is a mismatch between the variable inputs and the fixed input. Owing to the mismatch, the marginal product is low and the average variable cost is high. With a higher production rate, the variable inputs match the fixed input relatively better, and the average variable cost is lower.

> **Marginal product:** The increase in output arising from an additional unit of an input.

As more of the variable inputs are added in combination with the fixed input, there will be a mismatch again. Eventually, there will be a *diminishing marginal product* from the variable inputs. This means that the marginal product becomes smaller with each increase in the quantity of the variable inputs. With a diminishing marginal product from the variable inputs, the average variable cost will increase with the production rate.

In Luna's case, Table 4.2 shows that the average variable cost first drops from $4.29 to $4.18 per sheet as the production increases from 1,000 to 2,000 sheets a week. Then the average variable cost rises from $4.18 to $7.44 per sheet as the production increases from 2,000 to 9,000 sheets a week.

Recall that the average cost is the average fixed cost plus the average variable cost. While the average fixed cost falls with the production rate, the average variable cost falls and then increases. Accordingly, where the average variable cost is increasing, the relationship between the average cost and the production rate depends on the balance between the declining average fixed cost and the increasing average variable cost.

If the fixed cost is not too large and the average variable cost increases sufficiently, the average cost will first decline with the production rate and then increase. As Table 4.2 shows, this is the case for Luna.

Figure 4.2 graphs the marginal, average, and average variable costs against the production rate. The vertical axis represents cost per unit of production, while the

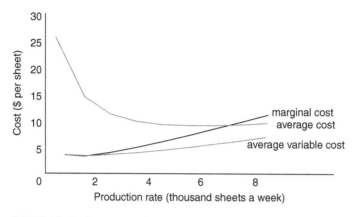

FIGURE 4.2 Short-run marginal, average variable, and average costs.

Notes: The marginal, average variable, and average cost curves are U-shaped. The curves decrease at low production rates, reach a minimum, and then increase for high production rates.

horizontal axis represents the production rate. The marginal cost curve falls from $4.29 per sheet at 1,000 sheets a week, to reach a minimum of $4.07 at 2,000 sheets a week, and rises thereafter. The average variable cost curve falls from $4.29 per sheet at 1,000 sheets a week, to a minimum of $4.18 per sheet at 2,000 sheets a week, and then rises. Similarly, the average cost curve falls from $26.29 per sheet at 1,000 sheets a week, to a minimum of $9.36 at 6,000 sheets a week, and then rises. The graphs of the marginal, average variable, and average cost curves are each U-shaped.

PROGRESS CHECK 4B

In Figure 4.2, if the fixed cost were higher, how would that affect the average cost, average variable cost, and marginal cost curves?

Production Technology

In the preceding analysis, we derived the information about costs by asking the seller for the cost of producing at various rates. Accordingly, at every production level, the total, average, and marginal costs depend on the seller's production technology.

This approach has two implications. First, the curves will change with adjustments in the seller's technology. A manufacturer that discovers a technology involving a lower fixed cost will lower its average cost curve. A manufacturer that uses a technology with a lower variable cost will lower its average, average variable, and marginal cost curves.

Second, sellers may use different technologies, and hence have different cost curves. They may differ in the structure of fixed and variable costs. Some may have better technologies and hence lower overall costs than others.

FAME: FROM WASTE TO ENERGY

With stocks of fossil fuel depleting and emissions exacerbating global warming, the worldwide demand for renewable, low-emissions sources of energy is growing. Fatty acid methyl ester (FAME) is a biodiesel fuel that is aromatic-free, highly biodegradable, and generates low emissions.

FAME is an attractive source of energy as it can be manufactured from waste cooking oil. The challenge in producing FAME is that the manufacturing process requires large quantities of water to remove impurities.

A recent study compared four batch processing methods, using different catalysts and processes, to produce FAME from waste cooking oil. For a production scale of 7,269 tons a year, the method with the lowest variable cost, $391 per ton, required a fixed investment in plant of $8.3 million. The method with the highest variable cost, $416 per ton, required a relatively lower fixed investment of $7.99 million.

Source: Tsutomu Sakai, Ayato Kawashima, and Tetsuya Koshikawa, "Economic assessment of batch biodiesel production processes using homogeneous and heterogeneous alkali catalysts," *Bioresource Technology*, Vol. 100, No. 13, July 2009, pp. 3268–3276.

3. Short-Run Individual Supply

Costs are one aspect of the short-run decisions whether to continue in operation and how much to produce. The other side to these decisions is revenue. We now consider the revenues of a business.

In analyzing revenues, we shall assume that the business aims to maximize profit and that the business is so small relative to the market that it can sell as much as it would like at the market price. We need the assumption of smallness to construct individual and market supply, which are the counterparts to individual and market demand.

Production Rate

Supposing that the price of plywood is $7 per sheet, how much should Luna produce? Generally, the profit of a business is its total revenue less its total cost, and in turn, total revenue is the price multiplied by sales.[2]

In Table 4.3, we show Luna's cost and revenue at various production rates, with the assumption that the price is $7. For instance, if sales are 1,000 sheets a week, then Luna's total revenue will be $7 × 1,000 = $7,000. If sales are 2,000 sheets a week, then Luna's total revenue will be $7 × 2,000 = $14,000. Similarly, we can calculate the total revenue at other production rates.

Table 4.3 Short-run profit

Weekly production rate	Variable cost ($)	Total cost ($)	Total revenue ($)	Accounting profit ($)	Economic profit ($)	Marginal cost ($)	Marginal revenue ($)
0	0	22,000	0	(22,000)	0		
1,000	4,290	26,290	7,000	(19,290)	2,710	4.29	7.00
2,000	8,360	30,360	14,000	(16,360)	5,640	4.07	7.00
3,000	13,160	35,160	21,000	(14,160)	7,840	4.80	7.00
4,000	18,970	40,970	28,000	(12,970)	9,030	5.81	7.00
5,000	25,930	47,930	35,000	(12,930)	9,070	6.96	7.00
6,000	34,150	56,150	42,000	(14,150)	7,850	8.22	7.00
7,000	43,700	65,700	49,000	(16,700)	5,300	9.55	7.00
8,000	54,620	76,620	56,000	(20,620)	1,380	10.92	7.00
9,000	66,960	88,960	63,000	(25,960)	(3,960)	12.34	7.00

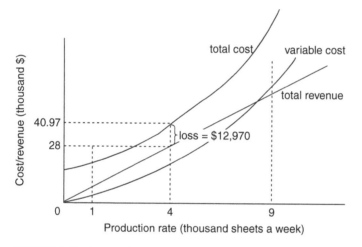

FIGURE 4.3 Short-run profit.

Notes: At a production rate of 4,000 sheets a week, the total revenue is $28,000 and the total cost is $40,970; hence, the vertical difference between total revenue and total cost is a loss of $12,970. Marginal revenue is represented by the slope of the total revenue line, while marginal cost is represented by the slope of the total cost curve.

From Table 4.3, the highest accounting profit is a loss of $12,930, which comes from producing at a rate of 5,000 sheets a week. (Below, we discuss why it makes sense for Luna to produce "at a loss.")

We can derive a general rule for the profit-maximizing production rate by illustrating cost and revenue with a diagram. Figure 4.3 shows the cost curves from Figure 4.1, and includes a line to represent Luna's total revenue at a price of $7. The line rises at a rate of $7,000 for every increase of 1,000 sheets in the production rate. Equivalently, the slope of the line is $7. For instance, one point on the total revenue line is a production rate of 4,000 sheets a week and revenue of $7 × 4,000 = $28,000.

Using Figure 4.3, we can measure the difference between the total revenue and the total cost at any production rate. In the figure, the vertical difference between the total revenue line and the total cost curve represents the accounting profit. For instance, at a production rate of 4,000 sheets a week, the height of the total revenue line is $28,000, while the height of the total cost curve is $40,970. Hence, the vertical difference is a loss of $12,970.

Generally, to maximize profit, a business should produce at that rate where its marginal revenue equals its marginal cost. The **marginal revenue** is the change in total revenue arising from selling an additional unit.

> **Marginal revenue:** The change in total revenue arising from selling an additional unit.

To explain the rule for maximizing profit, consider Figure 4.3. Graphically, the marginal revenue is represented by the slope of the total revenue line. Similarly, since marginal cost is the change in total cost due to the production of an additional unit, the marginal cost is represented by the slope of the total cost curve.

At a production rate of 1,000 sheets a week, the total revenue line climbs faster than the total cost curve, or equivalently, the marginal revenue exceeds the marginal cost. Then an increase in production will raise the profit. Wherever the marginal revenue exceeds the marginal cost, Luna can raise profit by increasing production.

By contrast, at a production rate of 9,000 sheets a week, the total revenue climbs more slowly than the total cost curve, or equivalently, the marginal revenue is less than the marginal cost. Then a reduction in production will increase profit. Wherever the marginal revenue is less than the marginal cost, Luna can raise profit by reducing production.

Thus, Luna will *maximize profit at the production rate where its marginal revenue equals marginal cost*. At that point, the total revenue line and the total cost curve climb at exactly the same rate. Hence, a small change in production (either increase or reduction) will affect both total revenue and total cost to the same extent. Accordingly, it is not possible to increase profit any further.

For a small seller, which can sell as much as it would like at the market price, the rule for **profit-maximizing production** can be expressed in another way. By definition, the marginal revenue is the change in total revenue arising from selling an additional unit. For a business that can sell as much as it would like at the market price, the change in total revenue arising from selling an additional unit is exactly equal to the price. Hence, the marginal revenue equals the price of the output.

> **Profit-maximizing scale of production:** The scale where marginal revenue equals marginal cost.

In Figure 4.4, we draw the marginal and average cost curves from Figure 4.2 and also include a line representing the marginal revenue and the price. Where the price exceeds the marginal cost, Luna can increase profit by raising production. By contrast, where the price is less than the marginal cost, Luna can increase

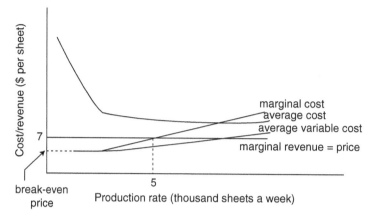

FIGURE 4.4 Short-run production rate.

Note: Given the price of $7, the seller maximizes profit by producing at the rate of 5,000 sheets a week, where marginal cost equals the price.

profit by cutting production. Therefore, Luna will maximize profit by producing at 5,000 sheets a week, a rate at which its marginal cost just balances the price.

Break-Even Analysis

Should the business continue in operation? To make this decision, the business needs to compare the profit from continuing in production with the profit from shutting down. An essential consideration in this comparison is the structure of fixed and variable costs.

Suppose that a business continues production. Let the total revenue from the profit-maximizing production rate be R, while the fixed cost is F and the variable cost is V. Then the maximum profit is $R - F - V$.

Now suppose that the business shuts down. Clearly, this will reduce its total revenue to 0. How will the shutdown affect its costs? We assume that the entire fixed cost, F, of the business is also sunk in the short run. A **sunk cost** is one that has been committed and cannot be avoided. Costs which are not sunk are *avoidable*.

> **Sunk cost:** A cost that has been committed and cannot be avoided.

By assumption, the entire fixed cost, F, is also sunk. This means that, even if the business shuts down, it must still pay the fixed cost, F. In contrast to the fixed cost, the variable cost is avoidable. Hence, if the business shuts down, it need not incur any variable cost. Thus, if it shuts down, the profit will be the zero revenue minus the fixed cost, that is, $-F$.

The business should continue in production if the maximum profit from continuing in production is at least as large as the profit from shutting down. Algebraically, this break-even condition is

$$R - V - F \geq -F. \tag{4.3}$$

which simplifies to

$$R \geq V. \tag{4.4}$$

The business should continue in production so long as its total revenue covers the variable cost.

Given that the fixed cost is sunk, it is *not relevant* to the decision whether to continue in production. Hence, as generally outlined in Chapter 1, the short-run decision whether to continue in production resolves into comparing the total revenue with the total (relevant) cost. Since sunk costs are not relevant, the total relevant cost is just the variable cost.

Recall that total revenue is the price multiplied by sales, $R = p \times q$. Divide the break-even condition (4.4) throughout by sales (which is also the production rate) to obtain

$$p \geq \frac{V}{q}. \tag{4.5}$$

Hence an equivalent way of stating the **short-run break-even** condition is that the price must cover the average variable cost.

> **Short-run break-even:** Total revenue covers variable cost, or price covers average variable cost.

To summarize, in the short run, a business (which can sell as much as it would like at the market price) maximizes profit by:

- if the total revenue covers the variable cost, producing at the rate where the marginal cost equals the price;
- if the total revenue does not cover the variable cost, shutting down.

How does the short-run break-even analysis apply to Luna Plywood? Suppose that Luna continues in production. Then, from Table 4.3, by producing at a rate of 5,000 sheets a week, Luna will operate at a loss of $12,930. By assumption, Luna's entire $22,000 fixed cost is also sunk. Thus, if Luna shuts down, its profit will be the zero revenue minus the $22,000 fixed cost, that is, a loss of $22,000. Clearly, Luna is better off continuing in production.

Another way to make this decision simply ignores the fixed cost – because it is sunk and thus not relevant. Table 4.3 shows the variable cost and total revenue. If Luna produces 5,000 sheets a week, it will earn a total revenue of $35,000, while its variable cost would be $25,930. Since the total revenue exceeds the variable cost, Luna should continue in production. Thus, it makes sense for Luna to produce "at a loss" – the reason is that the "loss" includes a sunk cost that should not be considered in the decision-making.

Using the concept of economic profit, the correct break-even analysis is obvious. In calculating economic profit, sunk costs should be ignored. So, the economic profit from producing 5,000 sheets a week is the total revenue of $35,000 less the variable cost of $25,930. Hence, the economic profit is $9,070, which is positive, hence Luna should continue in operation.

ALASKA MARINE HIGHWAY SYSTEM: $22 MILLION BAILOUT

In Alaska, the state ferry service, officially called the Alaska Marine Highway System, provides ferry transport for passengers and vehicles within the state as well as to Canada and the lower United States. In 2005, owing to financial losses, the state ferry service required a government bailout of $22 million.

Governor Frank Murkowski blamed the ferry's losses in part on increases in scheduled sailings, particularly in winter. The director of the Alaska Marine Highway System, Robin Taylor, disagreed: "Even when a vessel is tied up, expenses are still incurred as a captain and crew must be on board and line handlers must be available. When those expenses are coupled with the loss of revenue, the more economical choice would be to operate the vessel rather than to tie it up."

Sources: Alaska State Senate Finance Committee hearing, March 2, 2006; Alaska Public Radio, October 17, 2005.

Individual Supply Curve

Using the rule for profit-maximizing production, we can determine how much a business (which can sell as much as it would like at the price) should produce at various prices for its output. The rule is that it should produce at the rate that balances its marginal cost with the price, provided that the price covers the average variable cost.

Referring to Figure 4.4, if the price of the plywood is $8 rather than $7 a sheet, Luna should expand production to the rate where the new price equals the marginal cost. Indeed, by varying the price, we can trace out the quantity that Luna should supply at every possible price. This is the information needed to construct Luna's individual supply curve. The **individual supply curve** is a graph showing the quantity that a seller will supply at every possible price.

> **Individual supply curve:** A graph showing the quantity that a seller will supply at every possible price.

The individual supply curve is identical with the portion of the seller's marginal cost curve that lies above the average variable cost curve. To expand production, the seller must incur a higher marginal cost. So the seller will expand production only if it receives a higher price. Accordingly, the individual supply curve slopes upward.

The individual supply curve shows how a seller should adjust its production in response to changes in the price of its output. Hence, the effect of any

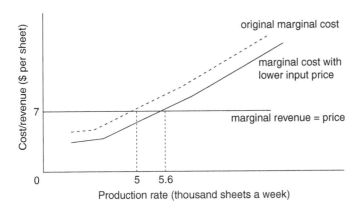

FIGURE 4.5 Lower input price.

Note: With a lower input price, the marginal cost curve will shift downward; hence the seller will increase the production rate from 5,000 to 5,600 sheets.

change in the output price will be represented by a movement along the supply curve.

PROGRESS CHECK 4C

Using Figure 4.4, show the quantity that Luna should produce at a price of $7.50 per sheet.

Input Demand

We can now explain the individual seller's demand for inputs. We derived the seller's marginal cost from its total cost, which in turn was derived from the estimates of the expenses on rent, salaries, wages, and other supplies needed at various production rates. These estimates depend on the prices of the various inputs.

Suppose, for instance, that Table 4.1 assumes a wage of $10 per hour. Then the calculations in Tables 4.2 and 4.3 and Figures 4.3 and 4.4 are based on a wage of $10 per hour. What if the wage is $9 per hour? Then we must go back to adjust Tables 4.1–4.3 and Figures 4.3 and 4.4 using the new wage rate.

Intuitively, as we show in Figure 4.5, the marginal cost curve will shift downward. The profit-maximizing production rate increases from 5,000 to 5,600 sheets a week. From the new production rate of 5,600 sheets, we can go back to determine the corresponding quantity of the labor input. With a higher rate of production, the quantity of labor demanded will also be higher.

By varying the wage rate, we can determine the quantity of labor demanded at every possible wage rate. This provides the individual seller's demand for labor. As just shown, the quantity demanded will be higher at a lower wage; hence, the demand curve for labor will slope downward. The same method can be used to derive the individual seller's demand for every other input.

OIL: TO PRODUCE OR NOT TO PRODUCE?

In the oil industry, production is the activity of extracting crude oil from the ground. As the price of oil fluctuates on world markets, oil producers must consider whether to enter into production, continue in production, suspend production, or exit the industry.

Following the Great Recession, the price of West Texas Intermediate crude oil fell from $100 per barrel in 2008 to $62 per barrel in 2009. With the economic recovery, the price of oil climbed steady to over $98 per barrel in 2013.

The high price of oil and improvements in production technology have boosted US production of oil, particularly from shale deposits. Between 2008 and 2013, US production rose by almost half from 302.3 to 446.2 million tonnes. Owing to this increase in US production, coupled with slowing economic growth, energy conservation, and greater use of renewable energy, the price of oil peaked in 2014 and fell to around $50 per barrel.

In parallel, the number of active rotary production rigs in the United States fell from a peak of over 1,700 in late 2008 to a low of below 1,200 in mid-2009. The number of active rigs then rose steadily to over 2,000 in 2011 and then fluctuated between 1,800 and 2,000 thereafter.

Sources: *BP Statistical Review of World Energy*, 63rd edition, June 2014; Baker Hughes, North America Rotary Rig Count, November 7, 2014.

4. Long-Run Individual Supply

In the short run, a business must work within the constraints of past commitments such as employment contracts and investment in facilities and equipment. Over time, however, contracts expire and investments wear out. With sufficient time, all inputs become avoidable. A *long-run* planning horizon is a time frame far enough into the future that all inputs can be freely adjusted. Then the business will have complete flexibility in deciding on inputs and production.

How should a business make two key decisions – whether to continue in operation and how much to produce – in the long run? To address these decisions, we first analyze the long-run costs and then look at the revenue.

Long-Run Costs

Let us analyze long-run costs in the context of Luna Plywood. We ask the management to estimate the costs of producing at various rates when all inputs are avoidable. Suppose that Table 4.4 presents the expenses classified into rent, salaries, wages, and cost of supplies.

In the long run, Luna can adjust the managers' employment according to the production rate, and so their salaries vary from $2,500 a week at zero production up to

Table 4.4 Long-run weekly expenses

Weekly production rate	Rent ($)	Equipment leasing ($)	Salaries ($)	Wages ($)	Cost of supplies ($)	Total ($)
0	1,000	1,000	2,500	0	0	4,500
1,000	1,000	1,000	5,000	790	1,000	8,790
2,000	1,000	1,000	7,500	2,610	2,000	14,110
3,000	1,000	1,000	10,000	5,570	3,000	20,570
4,000	1,000	1,000	12,500	9,760	4,000	28,260
5,000	1,000	1,000	15,000	15,220	5,000	37,220
6,000	1,000	1,000	17,500	22,030	6,000	47,530
7,000	1,000	1,000	20,000	30,210	7,000	59,210
8,000	1,000	1,000	22,500	39,820	8,000	72,320
9,000	1,000	1,000	25,000	50,890	9,000	86,890

Table 4.5 Analysis of long-run costs

Weekly production rate	Total cost ($)	Marginal cost ($)	Average cost ($)
0	4,500		
1,000	8,790	4.29	8.79
2,000	14,110	5.32	7.06
3,000	20,570	6.46	6.86
4,000	28,260	7.69	7.07
5,000	37,220	8.96	7.44
6,000	47,530	10.31	7.92
7,000	59,210	11.68	8.46
8,000	72,320	13.11	9.04
9,000	86,890	14.57	9.65

$25,000 at a production rate of 9,000 sheets a week. Similarly, the wages are nothing at zero production and rise to $50,890 at a production rate of 9,000. The cost of supplies rises from nothing at zero production to $9,000 at a production rate of 9,000.

Extracting the relevant information from Table 4.4, we can compile the long-run marginal and average costs in Table 4.5 and graph them in Figure 4.6. As this example shows, even in the long run, there may be fixed costs (but these are not sunk).

Production Rate

How much should the business produce in the long run? The general rule that we derived for short-run production also applies. To maximize profit, a business should produce at that rate where its marginal cost equals the marginal revenue. In the long run, we use the long-run marginal cost. For a business that can sell as much as it would like at the market price, the marginal revenue equals the price

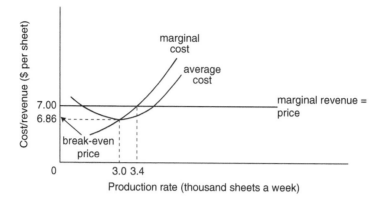

FIGURE 4.6 Long-run production rate.

Note: Given a price of $7, the seller maximizes profit by producing at the rate of 3,400 sheets a week, where the long-run marginal cost equals the price.

Table 4.6 Long-run profit

Weekly production rate	Total cost ($)	Total revenue ($)	Economic profit ($)	Marginal cost ($)	Marginal revenue ($)
0	4,500	0	(4,500)		
1,000	8,790	7,000	(1,790)	4.29	7.00
2,000	14,110	14,000	(110)	5.32	7.00
3,000	20,570	21,000	430	6.46	7.00
4,000	28,260	28,000	(260)	7.69	7.00
5,000	37,220	35,000	(2,220)	8.96	7.00
6,000	47,530	42,000	(5,530)	10.31	7.00
7,000	59,210	49,000	(10,210)	11.68	7.00
8,000	72,320	56,000	(16,320)	13.11	7.00
9,000	86,890	63,000	(23,890)	14.57	7.00

of its output. Hence, the rule to maximize profit is to produce at that rate where marginal cost equals the price.

For Luna Plywood, Table 4.6 shows the long-run cost, revenue, and profit. The column for economic profit shows that profit reaches a maximum at a production rate of around 3,000 sheets a week. Referring to Figure 4.6, the precise profit-maximizing production rate is 3,400. The marginal cost at a production rate of 3,400 is $7 per sheet. Since the price is $7 per sheet, this confirms that the production rate of 3,400 maximizes profit.

Break-Even Analysis

Should the business continue in operation? In the long run, a business should continue in production if the maximum profit from continuing in production is at least as large as the profit from shutting down. In the long run, all costs are avoidable. Hence, if the business shuts down, it will incur no costs and so its profit from shutting down would be zero.

Let $R - C$ represent the maximum profit from continuing in production. Then the business should continue in production if

$$R - C \geq 0, \tag{4.6}$$

which simplifies to

$$R \geq C. \tag{4.7}$$

This break-even condition says that the business should continue in production so long as total revenue covers total cost.

Since total revenue is price multiplied by sales, $R = p \times q$, we can divide the break-even condition by sales (equal to the production rate) to obtain

$$p \geq \frac{C}{q}. \tag{4.8}$$

Thus, an equivalent way of stating the **long-run break-even** condition is that the price must cover the average cost.

> **Long-run break-even:**
> Total revenue covers total cost, or price covers average cost.

To summarize, in the long run, a business (which can sell as much as it would like at the market price) maximizes profit by:

- if the total revenue covers the total cost, producing at the rate where the marginal cost equals the price;
- if the total revenue does not cover the total cost, shutting down.

Referring to Table 4.5, Luna's lowest average cost is $6.86. It attains this cost at a production rate of 3,000 sheets a week. Hence, if the price of plywood falls below $6.86, then Luna should go out of business.

Individual Supply Curve

A seller maximizes profit by producing at the rate where its long-run marginal cost equals the price of the output. By varying the price, we can determine the quantity that the seller will supply at every possible price of the output. Further, the seller should remain in business only if the price covers the average cost. Thus, the seller's long-run individual supply curve is that part of its long-run marginal cost curve which lies above its long-run average cost curve.

Short and Long Run

Referring to Tables 4.2 and 4.5, the average cost of production is higher in the short run than in the long run. The reason is that, in the long run, the seller has more flexibility in optimizing inputs to changes in the production rate. Accordingly, it can produce at a relatively lower cost than in the short run, when one or more inputs cannot be adjusted.

Note, however, that the short-run average cost includes the average fixed cost, which, being sunk, is not relevant. So, to compare the short- and long-run break-even conditions, the relevant comparison is between the short-run *average variable cost* and the long-run *average cost*.

PROGRESS CHECK 4D

Referring to Table 4.5, if the long-run market price of plywood is $10.31 per sheet, how much should Luna produce?

DURHAM: CONTINUE IN BUSINESS?

Durham Furniture produces bedroom furniture at Durham, Ontario, Canada. In 2003, the company invested C$38 million in a new plant at Chesley, Ontario, to manufacture dining room furniture. However, the initiative coincided with increased competition from Asia and the appreciation of the Canadian dollar against the US dollar, followed by the US economic downturn.

In 2008, Durham mothballed the Chesley plant and filed for protection under the Companies' Creditors Arrangement Act. The company had a net worth of between C$3.5 and C$6.3 million, excluding the Chesley plant and equipment. However, the company owed C$37 million in secured borrowings to the Royal Bank of Canada. The Bank supported a restructuring provided that new investors invested in the company.

Why would new investors put money in Durham Furniture? The long-run break-even condition for a business is that the (long-run) price covers the average cost. The new investors must expect that, in the long run, demand would recover and that growth in supply from Asia and elsewhere would not outstrip the growth in demand. Then the long-run price would appreciate to cover the average cost.

Source: "Durham Furniture plant may be sold," *Sun Media*, January 30, 2009.

5. Seller Surplus

We derived the individual supply curve by asking the seller how much it would supply at every possible price. Another way to interpret the supply curve is that it

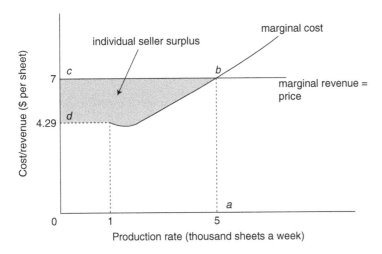

FIGURE 4.7 Individual seller surplus.

Notes: The marginal cost of producing 1,000 sheets is $4.29. At a price of $7, the seller receives a surplus of ($7 – $4.29) × 1,000 = $2,710 for that production. At the $7 price, the seller will produce 5,000 sheets a week. The individual seller surplus is the shaded area *dbc* between the price line and the marginal cost curve.

shows the minimum price that the seller will accept for each unit of production. Using this approach, we can explain how sellers benefit or suffer from changes in the price of output. This also motivates a concept that is essential to effective management of purchasing.

In the case of Luna, referring to Figure 4.7, the marginal cost of producing 1,000 sheets a week is $4.29. This is the minimum price that Luna will accept for the first 1,000 sheets. At a market price of $7, however, Luna receives $7 for each sheet produced. The difference of (7 – 4.29) × 1,000 = $2,710 is a *surplus* for the seller. Indeed, the seller will get a surplus on every unit up to the marginal unit produced.

Generally, the **seller surplus** is the difference between a seller's total revenue from some quantity of production and the seller's avoidable cost of producing that quantity. To illustrate, consider Luna's short-run seller surplus at the price of $7.

> **Seller surplus:** The difference between a seller's total revenue from some quantity of production and the seller's avoidable cost of producing that quantity.

Referring to Figure 4.7, the total revenue is represented by the area of the rectangle 0*abc* under the price line up to the production of 5,000 sheets a week. The variable cost is the area 0*abd* under Luna's marginal cost curve up to 5,000 sheets. The shaded area *dbc* between the price line and the marginal cost curve represents the seller surplus.

In the short run, the seller surplus equals total revenue less variable cost (assuming that the fixed cost is sunk). In the long run, the seller surplus equals total revenue less total cost (assuming that the fixed cost is avoidable).

The concept of seller surplus is central to the management of purchasing. Note that the minimum that a seller would be willing to accept for some quantity of

production is the avoidable cost. Any extra payment would yield seller surplus. So the ideal for a purchasing manager is to pay each supplier just the avoidable cost, leaving the supplier with zero surplus. Essentially, the ideal would be to buy up the seller's marginal cost curve.

PROGRESS CHECK 4E

In Figure 4.7, show how an increase in the price of plywood to $9 per sheet would affect Luna's seller surplus.

---

6. Elasticity of Supply

Consider a typical issue for an industry analyst. If the price of plywood and wages increase by 5% and 10% respectively, what would be the effect on the supply of plywood? The analyst could answer this question with the supply curve. In practice, however, analysts seldom have sufficient information to construct the entire supply curve.

Another response to the question applies the elasticities of supply, which measure the responsiveness of supply to changes in underlying factors such as the prices of the item and inputs. The elasticities of supply are the supply-side counterparts to the elasticities of demand, introduced in Chapter 3.

The price elasticity is a handy way of comparing the sensitivity of the sellers of different items to changes in price. For instance, a food manufacturer that processes fruits and vegetables will want to know how sensitive suppliers of the fruits and vegetables are to changes in prices. The manufacturer can address this question by comparing the price elasticities of the supplies.

Price Elasticity

Price elasticity of supply: The percentage by which the quantity supplied will change if the price of the item rises by 1%.

The price elasticity of supply measures the responsiveness of the quantity supplied to changes in the price of the item. By definition, the **price elasticity of supply** is the percentage by which the quantity supplied will change if the price of the item rises by 1%. Equivalently, the price elasticity is the ratio

$$\frac{\text{Percentage change in quantity supplied}}{\text{Percentage change in price}}. \tag{4.9}$$

Let us calculate the price elasticity of Luna's supply of plywood. Referring to Figure 4.8, at a price of $7, Luna produces 5,000 sheets a week. If the price increases to $8, Luna would increase production to 5,800 sheets. The percentage change in quantity supplied is the change in quantity supplied divided by the

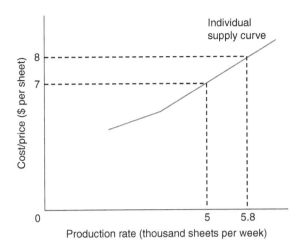

FIGURE 4.8 Price elasticity of supply.

Notes: The percentage change in quantity supplied is 16%, while the percentage change in price is 14.3%. Hence, the price elasticity of supply is 16/14.3 = 1.12.

initial quantity supplied. The change in quantity supplied is 5,800 – 5,000 = 800 sheets, hence the percentage change in quantity supplied is 800/5,000 = 16%.

Similarly, the percentage change in price is the change in price divided by the initial price. The change in price is $8 – $7 = $1, hence, the percentage change in price is 1/7 = 14.3%. Accordingly, the price elasticity of Luna's short-run supply is 16/14.3 = 1.12.

Intuitive Factors

To estimate the price elasticity requires information on a change in price and the corresponding change in quantity supplied. However, changing the price to estimate the elasticity may be too costly or not practical. As an alternative, managers can consider two intuitive factors to gauge the price elasticity of supply.

- *Available production capacity.* One factor is the available production capacity. A seller with considerable excess capacity will step up production in response to even a small increase in price. So supply will be relatively elastic. On the other hand, if capacity is tight, the seller may not increase production by much for even a substantial price increase. Then supply will be relatively inelastic.
- *Adjustment time.* In the short run, some inputs may be costly or impossible to change. Consequently, the marginal cost of production will be high. For instance, a factory wishing to step up production quickly may have to pay overtime rates to workers. Since overtime rates are higher than regular wage rates, the marginal cost of expanding production will be relatively high. With sufficient time, however, the factory could hire more workers at the regular

wage. Accordingly, in the long run, the marginal cost will increase more gently. So, generally, the long-run supply will be more elastic than the short-run supply.

> **PROGRESS CHECK 4F**
> Under what intuitive conditions would supply be inelastic?

7. Market Supply

To address questions such as the impact of entry of new manufacturers and changes in the prices of wood on the furniture market, we need to understand the *market supply*. The **market supply curve** of an item is a graph showing the quantity that all sellers will supply at every possible price. The market supply is the seller-side counterpart to the market demand, introduced in Chapter 2. Together, the supply and demand constitute a market.

Market supply curve: A graph showing the quantity that all sellers will supply at every possible price.

The market supply curve is constructed in a similar way to the individual supply curve. To construct the market supply for an item, ask each potential seller for the quantity that it would supply at every possible price. Then, at each price, add the reported individual quantities to get the quantity that the market as a whole will supply.[3]

Short and Long Run

The long-run market supply differs from the short-run market supply in one essential way. In the long run, every business will have complete flexibility in deciding on inputs and production. This flexibility implies that existing sellers can leave the industry, and new sellers can enter. The freedom of entry and exit is the essential difference between the short and long run.

For a seller to break even in the long run, its total revenue must cover its total cost. If a seller's total revenue does not cover the total cost, then the seller should leave the industry. Hence, the seller's individual supply will fall to zero. This departure will reduce the market supply, hence raise the market price and the profits of the other sellers. Sellers that cannot cover their total costs will leave the industry until all the remaining sellers break even.

By contrast, an industry where businesses can make (economic) profits, in the sense that total revenue exceeds total cost, will attract new entrants. Each of the new entrants will contribute its individual supply and so add to the market supply. The increase in the market supply will push down the market price and hence reduce the profits of all the existing sellers.

Accordingly, in the long run, when there is a change in the market price, the quantity supplied will adjust in two ways: first, all existing sellers will adjust their quantities supplied along their individual supply curves; and second, some sellers may enter or leave the market. Therefore, for any change in price, the long-run market supply is more elastic than the short-run market supply.

Properties

The properties of the market supply curve are similar to those of the individual supply curve. As each seller's marginal cost increases with production, the market supply curve slopes upward. Equivalently, at a higher price, the market as a whole will supply a larger quantity.

The market supply depends on other factors that affect individual demand – in particular, the prices of inputs. So, for instance, the market supply of furniture depends on the price of wood. If the price of wood is higher, the marginal cost of producing furniture will be higher, and so sellers will produce less. This implies that the market supply curve will shift to the left.

The market supply curve also depends on the sellers in existence. If Asian furniture manufacturers enter the US furniture market, then, at every possible price, there will be a larger quantity supplied. This means that the market supply curve will shift to the right.

The market seller surplus is the difference between the sellers' total revenue and the sellers' avoidable cost. Graphically, it is the area between the price line and the market supply curve.

In general, the effect of a change in the price of the output is represented by a movement along the market supply curve. By contrast, a change in the price of any input will cause a shift of the entire market supply curve.

US FURNITURE SUPPLY

The US supply of furniture combines supply by domestic, Canadian, and Asian manufacturers. Furniture manufacturing is relatively intensive in wood and labor. Canada's ample forests give it a natural advantage in the furniture industry.

With the advantage of substantially lower labor costs, Asian manufacturers pose direct and indirect challenges to Canadian furniture. Asian manufacturers can directly challenge the Canadian industry in both fully assembled and ready-to-assemble furniture. In this regard, the Asian manufacturers have increased US supply at the lower-cost end of the supply curves for fully assembled and ready-to-assemble furniture.

Moreover, Asian manufacturers pose an indirect challenge to Canadian and US domestic manufacturers of ready-to-assemble furniture. Fully assembled furniture from Asia is cheap enough to compete with ready-to-assemble furniture made in Canada and the United States.

KEY TAKEAWAYS

- To the extent that marginal costs increase with production, sellers will only increase production for higher prices.
- In the short run, a business (which can sell as much as it would like at the market price) maximizes profit by: if the total revenue covers the variable cost, producing at the rate where the marginal cost equals the price; if the total revenue does not cover the variable cost, shutting down.
- Fixed cost is the cost of inputs that do not change with the production rate, while variable cost is the cost of inputs that do change with the production rate.
- Marginal cost is the change in total cost due to the production of an additional unit, while marginal revenue is the change in total revenue arising from selling an additional unit.
- In the long run, a business (which can sell as much as it would like at the market price) maximizes profit by: if the total revenue covers the total cost, producing at the rate where the marginal cost equals the price; if the total revenue does not cover the total cost, shutting down.
- In the long run, businesses can adjust by entering or exiting the industry.
- Seller surplus is the difference between the seller's total revenue from some quantity of production and the seller's avoidable cost of producing that quantity.
- Managers can raise the profit from purchasing by extracting the sellers' surplus.
- The price elasticity of supply is the percentage by which quantity supplied will change if price of the item rises by 1%.

REVIEW QUESTIONS

1. Explain the distinction between the short run and long run. How is this related to the distinction between fixed and variable costs?
2. Comment on the following statement: "It costs our factory an average of $5 to produce a shirt. I cannot accept any order for less than $5 per shirt."
3. Farmer Axel's fixed cost of growing corn is higher than that of Farmer Julia. What, if anything, does this imply for the difference in their marginal costs of growing corn?
4. Advertising is an important input into the marketing of shampoo. Explain the meaning of the marginal product of advertising for a manufacturer of shampoos.
5. Under what conditions would a seller's marginal revenue equal the market price of its product?
6. Presently, Jupiter Oil is producing 2,000 barrels of crude oil a day. The market price is $15 per barrel. Its marginal cost is $20 per barrel. Explain how the company can increase its profit.
7. Does the following analysis under- or overestimate the change in profit? The price of eggs is 60 cents per dozen and Farmer Luke produces 10,000 dozen eggs a month. If the price of eggs rises to 70 cents a dozen, Luke's profit will increase by $1,000.
8. Explain why the following two conditions for short-run break-even are equivalent: (i) revenue covers variable cost; and (ii) price covers average variable cost.
9. Some companies continue in business even though they are losing money. Are they making a mistake?

10. Explain why the following two conditions for long-run break-even are equivalent: (i) revenue covers total cost; and (ii) price covers average cost.

11. Explain the differences between the short-run and long-run decisions to continue in business.

12. How would (a) a higher price of lumber, and (b) lower wages affect the supply of furniture?

13. For a given increase in price of the product, will the increase in seller surplus be smaller or larger if the supply is more elastic? (*Hint*: Draw two supply curves, one more elastic than the other.)

14. If the supply curve slopes upward, the price elasticity of supply will be positive. True or false?

15. Consider the price elasticity of the market supply of taxi service. Do you expect supply to be relatively more elastic with respect to the fare in the short run or long run?

DISCUSSION QUESTIONS

1. A retail bank's sources of funds include savings, time, and checking (current) deposits. In June 2011, Hang Seng Bank, a leading Hong Kong bank, quoted interest rates of 0.01% on savings accounts, 0.15% on a 12-month time deposit, and nothing on checking accounts.

    (a) Suppose that the bank incurs an additional 0.2% cost to administer checking accounts, and 0.1% cost for savings accounts and time deposits. List the three sources of funds in ascending order of annual cost per dollar of funds.

    (b) Suppose that the bank has $2 billion of savings deposits, $5 billion of time deposits, and $3 billion of checking deposits. On a diagram with amount of funds in billions of dollars (from 0 to 10 billion) on the horizontal axis and cost in millions of dollars on the vertical axis, illustrate the (i) average variable cost of funds, and (ii) marginal cost of funds.

2. Table 4.1 shows the weekly expenses of Luna Plywood. Suppose that wages are 5% higher, increasing the cost of labor by 5%.

    (a) By recalculating Table 4.1, explain how the increase in wages will affect the (i) average variable cost, and (ii) average cost.

    (b) Luna's management says that the wage increase has raised its break-even price by 5%. Do you agree?

    (c) Supposing that the market price remains at $7, how should Luna adjust production?

3. Ole Kirk Kristiansen, founder of the Lego Group in Billund, Denmark, invented the Lego brick, made from acrylonitrile butadinese styrene. In 2005, Lego outsourced the production of Duplo bricks to Flextronics, a contract manufacturer with a plant in Hungary. Then, in 2006, Lego sold its Lego brick factory at Kladno, Czech Republic, to Flextronics. Lego retained production of only the more complicated Technic and Bionicles products in Billund.

    (a) Wages are higher in Denmark than in Hungary. Compare the equipment and labor costs of producing Duplo bricks in Denmark and Hungary.

(b) How did the sale of the Kladno factory affect Lego's fixed relative to variable costs of producing Lego bricks?

(c) How did the sale of the Kladno factory affect Lego's short- and long-run break-even for Lego bricks? (*Hint*: State any assumption on the price which Flextronics charges to manufacture Lego bricks.)

4. Barrick Gold's two most productive gold mines are Cortez and Goldstrike in Nevada, USA. Table 4.7 reports the selling prices and costs for the two mines. The "average cash cost" includes operating cost, royalties, and taxes, while the "average cost" includes the cash cost as well as amortization.

(a) Suppose that Barrick Gold operates each mine at the scale where the (upward-sloping) marginal cost equals the price of gold. The marginal cost curve shifts with past production, the prices of inputs, and production technology. Using the data from Table 4.7, illustrate the shifts in Goldstrike's marginal cost curve, selling price, and profit-maximizing scale of production between 2010 and 2012. (*Hint*: Barrick Gold reports only one point on each marginal cost curve. You are free to assume any other data necessary to draw the figures.)

(b) Use Barrick's 2012 data to compare the (i) short-run break-even conditions for Cortez and Goldstrike; and (ii) the long-run break-even conditions for the two mines.

(c) If the price of gold falls to $600 per ounce, how should Barrick adjust production at the two mines?

5. In Alaska, the state ferry system transports passengers and vehicles. With the ferry system incurring a financial deficit, Governor Frank Murkowski blamed losses in part on increased winter sailings. However, management's view was that: "Even when a vessel is tied up, expenses are still incurred as a captain and crew must be on board and line handlers must be available." In 2005, the ferry system raised fares by 17%, and revenue fell. However, the following year, the system cut fares and registered an 18% increase in winter revenue. (Sources: Alaska State Senate Finance Committee hearing, March 2, 2006; Alaska Public Radio, October 17, 2005.)

Table 4.7 Barrick Gold

	Cortez			Goldstrike		
	2010	2011	2012	2010	2011	2012
Production (thousand ounces)	1,141	1,421	1,370	1,239	1,088	1,174
Selling price ($ per ounce)	1,228	1,578	1,669	1,228	1,578	1,669
Average cash cost ($ per ounce)	244	245	282	475	511	541
Average cost ($ per ounce)	452	426	503	569	593	629

Source: Barrick Gold Corporation, year-end reports and year-end mine statistics.

   (a) Categorize the following as fixed or variable costs in the short run: (i) depreciation of ships; (ii) salaries and wages; (iii) fuel expenses.

   (b) How can you infer that the demand for ferry service is elastic?

   (c) Supposing that the ferry system aims to minimize losses, under what condition should the system increase winter sailings?

6. Japanese researchers compared various methods, using different catalysts and processes, of producing fatty acid methyl ester (FAME) from waste cooking oil at a scale of 7,269 tons a year. With the CaO-D method, the average fixed cost is $232 per ton and average variable cost is $391 per ton (including the cost of 3,226 kilograms of methanol). With the KOH-D method, the average fixed cost is $225 per ton and average variable cost of $416 per ton (including the cost of 3,970 kilograms of methanol).

   (a) The price of FAME will fluctuate in the future according to demand and supply. Which method has the lower break-even price in the: (i) short run; (ii) long run?

   (b) You are setting up a factory to produce FAME. Explain how to use the technique of net present value to choose between the CaO-D and KOH-D methods.

   (c) The original estimates assumed that the price of methanol is $0.455 per kilogram. How would an increase in the price of methanol affect the choice between the two methods?

7. The US supply of furniture combines supply by domestic, Canadian, and Asian manufacturers. Furniture is sold in two formats – fully assembled, and ready-to-assemble in kits which the consumer must assemble at home. Manufacturing of furniture is relatively labor-intensive.

   (a) How do wages affect the relative cost of manufacturing fully assembled compared to ready-to-assemble furniture?

   (b) Asian manufacturers benefit from lower wages. Using suitable diagrams, illustrate how the entry of Asian manufacturers would affect the US supply of: (i) fully assembled; and (ii) ready-to-assemble furniture.

   (c) Using either of your diagrams for (b), show how a reduction in the cost of shipping would affect the supply of furniture.

   (d) Which do lower shipping costs affect relatively more: Asian exports of fully assembled or ready-to-assemble furniture?

8. In July 2012, Johnson Service Group decided to close 100 of its 460 dry cleaning shops in Britain. At the outlets targeted for closure, sales had declined by 2.7% in the first half of the year. However, Johnson did not know whether the fall in demand for dry cleaning was due to continued weakness in the macroeconomy or consumers switching to machine-washable suits. (Source: "Johnson closing 100 shops as dry cleaning feels the pinch," *The Independent*, July 5, 2012.)

   (a) What is the long-run break-even condition for a dry cleaner?

   (b) Which of the following affects the long-run price of dry cleaning relatively more: (i) macroeconomic weakness; or (ii) a shift in consumer preference toward machine-washable suits?

(c) Using a suitable figure, illustrate how the Johnson Service Group's decision affected the supply of dry cleaning services. (*Hint*: You are free to assume any data necessary to draw the figures.)

    (d) For a competing dry cleaner, was the Johnson Service Group's decision good or bad news?

9. A controversial issue in managing climate change is the effect of taxes on gasoline. Higher taxes would reduce the after-tax price received by gasoline producers. The price elasticity of the supply of gasoline has been estimated to be 2.0. (Source: David Austin and Terry Dinan, "Clearing the air: The costs and consequences of higher CAFE standards and increased gasoline taxes," *Journal of Environmental Economics and Management*, Vol. 50, No. 3, November 2005, pp. 562–582.)

    (a) Explain why the elasticity of supply with respect to price is positive.

    (b) Suppose that a tax on gasoline reduces the after-tax price of gasoline by 5%. By how much would suppliers reduce gasoline production?

    (c) Do you expect the impact of the tax on the production of gasoline to be smaller or larger in the short run as compared to the long run? Explain your answer.

You are the consultant!

Consider the various products that your organization sells. Identify products for which your organization is planning to reduce production.

(a) Compare the assumptions about the market underlying the original production plan and the actual outcomes.

(b) Are the key differences in (a) of a short- or long-run nature?

(c) Should your organization immediately cut production or gradually reduce production over time?

Appendix: Constructing Market Supply

This chapter has introduced the concept of market supply, which shows the quantity that all sellers will supply at every possible price. Here, we discuss in detail the method by which to construct the market supply curve from the individual supply curves of the various sellers.

Generally, the market supply curve is the horizontal sum of the individual supply curves. At any particular price, each seller's individual supply curve shows the quantity that the seller will supply. The sum of these quantities is the quantity supplied by the market as a whole. By varying the price, we can get the information needed to construct the market supply curve.

Short Run

The short-run supply curve of an individual seller is the portion of its marginal cost curve that lies above its average variable cost curve. Hence, the market supply

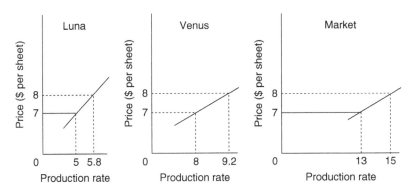

FIGURE 4.9 Market supply.

Notes: The market supply curve is the horizontal summation of the individual supply curves. At a price of $7 per sheet, the market quantity supplied is 5,000 + 8,000 = 13,000 sheets. At a price of $8 per sheet, the market quantity supplied is 5,800 + 9,200 = 15,000 sheets.

curve begins with the seller that has the lowest average variable cost. The market supply curve then gradually blends in sellers with higher average variable cost.

In Figure 4.9, we assume that there are just two producers of plywood: Luna Plywood and Venus Manufacturing. We draw the individual supply curves of the two producers and sum these horizontally to obtain the market supply curve. For instance, at a price of $7, the market as a whole will supply 5,000 + 8,000 = 13,000 sheets a week. At a price of $8, the market will supply 5,800 + 9,200 = 15,000 sheets.

Long Run

The long-run supply curve of an individual seller is the portion of its marginal cost curve that lies above its average cost curve. Hence, the market supply curve begins with the seller that has the lowest average cost. The market supply curve then gradually blends in sellers with higher average cost.

Notes

1   The following analysis is based, in part, on "Durham Furniture plant may be sold," *Sun Media*, January 30, 2009; "Chesley wood plant to reopen," *Homegoodsonline*, January 30, 2012.
2   Here, we assume that every unit is sold at the same price – a policy of *uniform pricing*. In Chapter 9, we consider the possibility of *price discrimination*, where various units are sold at different prices. With price discrimination, total revenue is not simply price multiplied by sales.
3   The appendix to this chapter discusses in detail the method by which to construct the market supply curve from the individual supply curves of the various sellers.

5 CHAPTER

Market Equilibrium

LEARNING OBJECTIVES

- Appreciate the impact of excess supply on the market price.
- Appreciate the impact of excess demand on the market price.
- Apply the price elasticities of demand and supply to predict the impact of shifts in supply on market price and production.
- Apply the price elasticities of demand and supply to predict the impact of shifts in demand on market price and production.
- Appreciate the short- and long-run effects of shifts in demand on market price.
- Appreciate the short- and long-run effects of shifts in demand on production.

1. Introduction

As the leading source of energy, oil underpins economic growth throughout the world. Oil from major exporting countries in the Middle East, West Africa, and the Gulf of Mexico is shipped by tankers to consumers in the West and Asia.

With the Great Recession, the demand for oil, and consequently the demand for tanker services, fell precipitously. In just 12 months, between 2008 and 2009, freight rates for very large crude carriers (VLCCs), with capacities of around 300,000 tons, collapsed from a record high of $88,400 to $28,000 a day. Rates for Suezmax tankers, with capacities of around 160,000 tons, fell from $67,200 to $25,900 a day. In tandem, the utilization rate of the overall tanker fleet, including VLCCs, Suezmax, and smaller tankers, fell from 91% to 84%. The industry analysts Platou remarked: "This indicates an overcapacity not seen since the 1980s."[1]

In 2010, following the economic recovery led by China and other Asian economies, the demand for tanker services began to recover. VLCC rates increased to $34,800 a day, while Suezmax rates rose to $28,000 a day. Utilization of the overall tanker fleet rose to 86%.

The tanker industry is a global industry but quite fragmented. It includes the fleets of integrated oil producers such as BP, ExxonMobil, and Saudi Aramco, as well as independent owner-operators. In December 2010, total tonnage of the industry amounted to 451 million deadweight tons (dwt).

The shipping tycoon John Fredriksen controls Frontline, a large independent owner-operator, with a fleet of 17.6 million dwt comprising 44 VLCCs and 21 Suezmaxes. Frontline owns 12 VLCCs and 12 Suezmaxes, and operates the other vessels under charter, spot rentals, and other contractual arrangements. The average age of its tankers is 11 years, compared to the industry average of 9 years.

Frontline emphasized in its 2010 Annual Report: "The tanker industry is highly cyclical, experiencing volatility in profitability, vessel values and freight rates. Freight rates are strongly influenced by the supply of tanker vessels and the demand for oil transportation."

Nevertheless, the company must plan for the future. When facing declining freight rates and falling utilization, it must decide whether to lay up or scrap vessels. When facing rising freight rates and increasing utilization, it must decide whether to charter new vessels and/or to place orders with shipyards for new vessels. Frontline must also respond to changes in wages, interest rates, and the costs of other inputs.

Looking into the future, Frontline's management must make short- and long-run decisions – whether to remain in business, and the scale of operations (how many vessels to operate). To address each of these decisions, management must understand demand, supply, and the interaction between the two sides of the market.

At first glance, the need to understand both demand and supply may seem surprising. Worldwide economic recession and recovery affect the demand for oil and thus the demand for tanker services. They do not affect the supply of tanker services.

Yet, as we shall see, management cannot make correct decisions unless they consider both sides of the market. The same applies to many other managerial issues. Although the initial change affects only one side of a market, it is necessary to consider the interaction with the other side to make the best decisions.

This chapter combines the earlier analyses of demand and supply to understand how they interact in competitive markets. The central concepts are the role of price in communicating information to buyers and sellers, and market equilibrium of demand and supply.

Within the demand–supply framework, we can explain the effects of global economic recession and recovery on the market for tanker service. When demand falls, the market will be in excess supply and price will fall. When demand rises, the market will be in excess demand and price will increase. For Frontline, with global economic recovery, the key to investment decisions is the increase in demand and the short- and long-run elasticities of supply.

The demand–supply framework is the core of managerial economics. It can be applied to address managerial decision-making in a wide range of markets, including both goods and services, consumer as well as industrial products, and domestic and international markets.

2. Perfect Competition

Generally, demand–supply analysis applies to markets in which competition is very keen in the particular sense of *perfect competition*. The following conditions define perfect competition:

* The product is homogeneous.
* There are many buyers, each of whom purchases a quantity that is small relative to the market supply.
* There are many sellers, each of whom supplies a quantity that is small relative to the market demand.
* New buyers and sellers can enter freely, and existing buyers and sellers can exit freely.
* All buyers and all sellers have symmetric information about market conditions.

In practice, very few markets exactly satisfy the conditions for perfect competition. This means that demand–supply analysis does not precisely apply. Nevertheless, this method of analysis is still useful: many of the managerial implications are similar even if a market is not perfectly competitive.

Homogeneous Product

Competition in a market where products are differentiated is not as keen as that in a market where products are homogeneous. Gold is a homogeneous commodity. Gold mined in Canada is a perfect substitute for gold from Australia, Brazil, and South Africa. If a Canadian gold producer tried to sell its gold at even 1% above the prevailing world market price, absolutely no one would buy. By the same token, if the Canadian producer offered its gold at 1% less than the market price, it would be swamped with orders. The price of gold from any source is exactly the same.

In contrast, mineral water is not homogeneous. Water from different sources has different chemical composition and hence different taste and therapeutic effect. A mineral water producer can raise its price by 1% without worrying that all of its consumers would switch to other brands. Likewise, if it reduced its price by 1%, its sales would increase, but by only a limited degree. Consequently, there is no uniform price for mineral water: different manufacturers may charge different prices. In general, competition among manufacturers of mineral water is relatively weaker than competition among gold mines.

Many Small Buyers

The second condition for perfect competition is that there are many buyers, each of whom purchases a quantity that is small relative to the market supply. In such a market, no buyer can get a lower price than others; hence, all buyers face the same price and all buyers compete on the same level playing field.

In a market where some buyers have market power, the buyers pay different prices, and the same buyer might even pay different prices for different units of the same product. Thus, when some buyers have market power, it is not possible to construct a market demand curve. (This is because constructing the demand curve requires an assumption that each buyer can buy as much as they would like at the market price.)

In the market for cotton, there are countless buyers of cotton, ranging from Indian villagers to Paris designers. Each buyer's purchases are very small relative to the world supply. Every buyer pays the same world price.

By contrast, the demand for the Chinese star anise herb is dominated by the pharmaceutical manufacturer, Roche, which uses it to produce the flu vaccine, Tamiflu. Roche has market power in the demand for the herb. As a result, it can buy at better prices than smaller buyers.

Many Small Sellers

The third condition for perfect competition is that there are many sellers, each of whom supplies a quantity that is small relative to the market demand. In such a market, no seller can get a higher price than others; hence, they all face the same price and compete on the same level playing field.

By contrast, when some sellers have market power, they receive different prices. Then it would not be possible to construct a market supply curve. (This is because constructing the supply curve requires an assumption that each seller can supply as much as they would like at the market price.)

Compare the markets for dry cleaning and cable television. In any city, there are many dry cleaners, none of which has market power. By contrast, there would be one or two providers of cable television, each of which has substantial market power. Accordingly, the market for dry cleaning is more competitive than that for cable television.

Free Entry and Exit

The fourth condition for perfect competition is that new buyers and sellers can enter freely, and existing buyers and sellers can exit freely. In particular, this means that no technological, legal, or regulatory barriers constrain entry or exit. To explain this condition, let us focus on free entry by new sellers and free exit by existing sellers. The logic for free entry and exit among buyers is quite similar.

Consider a market with free entry and exit. As we saw in Chapter 4 on market supply, if the market price rises above a seller's average cost, then new sellers will be attracted to enter. This will add to the market supply and bring down the price.

Hence, with free entry and exit, the market price cannot stay above a seller's average cost for very long. The market will be very competitive.

To illustrate, compare the markets for telephone service and telemarketing. Telephone service providers must make huge investments to build networks. By contrast, a telemarketer can set up with a few telephone lines and staff. As a result, there is much more competition among telemarketers.

The degree of competition also depends on barriers to exit. Suppose that a telephone service provider must pay the government a compensation fee to cease service. It must consider this exit cost when deciding whether to enter the market. Therefore, the higher the exit costs, the less likely new providers are to enter the market; hence, the less competitive the market will be.

Symmetric Information

The fifth condition for perfect competition is that all buyers and all sellers have symmetric information about market conditions such as prices, available substitutes, and technology. With symmetric information, every seller or buyer will be subject to intense competition. If, for instance, a new supplier offers a key input at a lower price, then every producer will immediately get the same lower price. No seller can enjoy the privilege of secret information.

Dry cleaning service is a mature industry. Information about service quality is transparent and evenly available among buyers and sellers.

By contrast, information is not symmetric in the market for medical services. Patients rely on their doctors for advice. In this market, sellers (doctors) have better information than buyers (patients). There may be differences in information on the supply side as well as between the two sides of the market. Doctors who attend continuing education and follow the latest journals may provide better advice and treatment than others.

Markets where there are differences in information among buyers, or among sellers, or between buyers and sellers are not as competitive as those where all buyers and all sellers have symmetric information.

PROGRESS CHECK 5A

What are the conditions for a market to be in perfect competition?

---

3. Market Equilibrium

Market equilibrium: The price at which the quantity demanded equals the quantity supplied.

For markets that meet the conditions for perfect competition, we can apply the *demand–supply framework*. In this framework, the concept of *market equilibrium* unifies demand and supply. **Market equilibrium** is the price at which the quantity demanded equals the quantity supplied.

Market equilibrium is the basis for all analyses of how changes in demand or supply affect market outcomes.

Demand and Supply

To introduce the concept of market equilibrium, consider the market for tanker services. Shippers generate the demand, and tanker lines provide the supply. On a graph with the price of tanker service in dollars per ton-mile on the vertical axis and the quantity of tanker service in billions of ton-miles a year on the horizontal axis, we can draw the demand for and the supply of tanker service. (One ton-mile represents the carriage of one ton over a distance of one mile.)

Suppose that the equilibrium in the market for tanker service is at a price of $200 per ton-mile and quantity of 10 billion ton-miles a year. Referring to Figure 5.1, the demand curve shows that, at the price of $200, buyers want to purchase a total of 10 billion ton-miles a year. The supply curve shows that, at the price of $200, sellers want to supply a total of 10 billion ton-miles a year. The quantity that buyers want to purchase exactly balances the quantity that sellers want to supply.

At the market equilibrium, there is no tendency for price, purchases, or sales to change. The price will not tend to change because the quantity demanded of 10 billion ton-miles just balances the quantity supplied of 10 billion ton-miles. Purchases will not tend to change because, at the price of $200, buyers (shippers) maximize benefits less expenditure by purchasing 10 billion ton-miles. Further, sales will not tend to change because, at the price of $200, sellers (tanker lines) maximize profits by supplying 10 billion ton-miles.

For a market to be in equilibrium, both the quantity demanded and the quantity supplied must be the result of voluntary choices by buyers and sellers, respectively. Neither buyers nor sellers may face rationing or other restrictions.

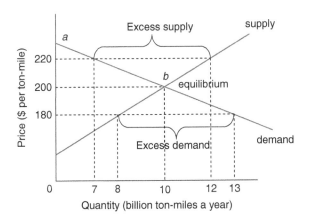

FIGURE 5.1 Market equilibrium.

Notes: At the price of $200 per ton-mile, the quantity demanded is 10 billion ton-miles a year and the quantity supplied is the same. When the price is $220 per ton-mile, the excess supply is 5 billion ton-miles a year. When the price is $180 per ton-mile, the excess demand is 5 billion ton-miles a year.

What happens when the market is not in equilibrium? Then, generally, the market price will tend to change in such a way as to restore equilibrium. The price signals information and provides an incentive for buyers and sellers to converge to equilibrium.

Excess Supply

One way in which the market can be out of equilibrium is when the price exceeds the equilibrium level. Suppose that the market price is $220 per ton-mile. Then, referring to the demand curve in Figure 5.1, buyers would cut back purchases to 7 billion ton-miles a year. Referring to the supply curve, sellers would increase quantity supplied to 12 billion ton-miles a year.

Hence, at a price of $220 per ton-mile, the quantity supplied would exceed the quantity demanded by 12 − 7 = 5 billion ton-miles a year. In more colorful terms, there would be too many ships chasing too few customers. The amount by which the quantity supplied exceeds the quantity demanded is the

> **Excess supply:** The amount by which the quantity supplied exceeds the quantity demanded.

excess supply. So, at a price of $220, there would be an excess supply of 5 billion ton-miles a year.

In a situation of excess supply, the market price will tend to fall. Tanker lines would compete to clear their extra capacity and the market price would drop back toward the equilibrium level of $200.

From Figure 5.1 it is clear that, if the price were even higher, at $250 per ton-mile, the excess supply would be even larger than the excess supply at a price of $220. Generally, the higher is the price above the equilibrium level, the larger will be the excess supply.

Excess Demand

Another way in which the market can be out of equilibrium is when the price is below the equilibrium level. Then the market price will tend to rise. In the market for tanker service, suppose that the price is $180 per ton-mile, and that, at the price of $180, buyers would purchase 13 billion ton-miles a year, and sellers would supply 8 billion ton-miles a year. Then the quantity demanded would exceed the quantity supplied by 13 − 8 = 5 billion ton-miles a year.

> **Excess demand:** The amount by which the quantity demanded exceeds the quantity supplied.

The amount by which the quantity demanded exceeds the quantity supplied is the **excess demand**. At a price of $180 per ton-mile, there would be excess demand of 5 billion ton-miles a year. Faced with this excess demand, buyers would compete for the limited capacity and the market price would rise toward the equilibrium level of $200. Generally, the lower is the price below the equilibrium level, the greater will be the excess demand.

PROGRESS CHECK 5B

In Figure 5.1, illustrate the excess demand if the price is $160 per ton-mile. Mark the quantities demanded and supplied.

---

4. Supply Shift

In general, changes in wages, interest rates, and the cost of other inputs, or government policies will shift the demand, supply, or both. Even if the change superficially appears to affect only one side of the market, it is essential to analyze the effects on the other side as well. Any analysis that ignores the other side of the market could be seriously incomplete.

In this section, we consider the effect of a change that shifts the supply curve. Specifically, how would a reduction in wages affect the price of tanker service?

Let us apply the demand–supply framework to address this question. We start from the equilibrium before the change in wages. Suppose that, before the change in wages, the price of tanker service was $200 per ton-mile and the quantity purchased was 10 billion ton-miles a year.

Equilibrium Change

The supply curve of tanker service does not explicitly show wages. Accordingly, any change in wages will shift the entire supply curve. Suppose that the reduction in wages causes the entire supply curve of tanker service to shift downward by $6 per ton-mile. We represent this shift in Figure 5.2.

The entire supply curve shifts down because the reduction in wages affects sellers' marginal costs whatever the quantity that they supply. Another way of looking at the impact of the change in wages is that it shifts the supply curve to the right: at every possible price, sellers want to supply more.

The change in wages, however, does not affect the demand for tanker service. Referring to Figure 5.2, the new supply curve crosses the unchanged demand curve at a new equilibrium point d, where the price is $196 per ton-mile. The fall in price from $200 to $196 increases the quantity demanded from 10 to 10.4 billion ton-miles a year. On the new supply curve, at the price of $196, the quantity supplied is 10.4 billion ton-miles a year. The price of $196 is the new market equilibrium.

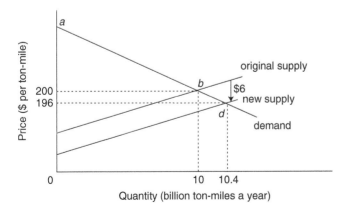

FIGURE 5.2 Supply shift.

Notes: When wages fall, the entire supply curve shifts downward by $6. At the new equilibrium, the price is $196 per ton-mile and the quantity is 10.4 billion ton-miles per year.

When the supply curve shifts down by $6, the equilibrium price falls by only $4. Generally, a shift in the supply curve will change the equilibrium price by no more than the amount of the supply shift. What determines the change in price? It depends on the price elasticities of demand and supply.

Price Elasticity of Demand

Intuitively, on the demand side, if buyers are extremely insensitive to price, then they will not buy more; hence, the price will fall by the entire $6. If, however, they are very sensitive to price, then the shift in supply would result in no change to the equilibrium price.

To illustrate, consider Figure 5.3(a), which depicts an *extremely inelastic demand*. This means that buyers are completely insensitive to the price: they purchase the

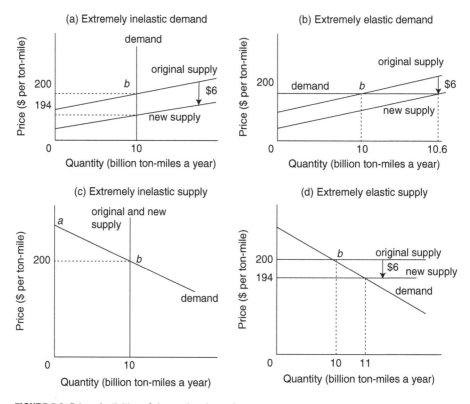

FIGURE 5.3 Price elasticities of demand and supply.

Notes:
(a) When demand is extremely inelastic, the supply curve shift reduces the price by exactly $6 but does not affect quantity.
(b) When demand is extremely elastic, the supply curve shift does not affect the price but raises the quantity to 10.6 billion.
(c) When supply is extremely inelastic, the supply curve does not shift.
(d) When supply is extremely elastic, the supply curve shift reduces the price by exactly $6 and raises the quantity to 11 billion.

same quantity regardless of the price. Accordingly, when the supply curve shifts, the buyers do not change their behavior – they continue to purchase exactly the same quantity. In Figure 5.3(a), when the supply curve shifts down by $6, the equilibrium price drops by exactly $6 to $194 per ton-mile.

Figure 5.3(b) depicts the other extreme, which is an *extremely elastic demand*. This means that buyers are extremely sensitive to price. When the supply curve shifts, the buyers soak up all the additional quantity supplied. Consequently, the equilibrium price does not change at all. In Figure 5.3(b), when the supply shifts down by $6, the equilibrium price remains unchanged at $200 per ton-mile. The new equilibrium quantity is 10.6 billion.

Comparing Figures 5.3(a) and (b), we see the relationship between the price elasticity of demand and the outcome of a shift in supply. Generally, if the demand is more elastic, then the change in the equilibrium price resulting from a shift in supply will be smaller.

Price Elasticity of Supply

Intuitively, on the supply side, if sellers are very insensitive to price, then the reduction in cost will not induce them to sell more; hence, the price of tanker service will not change at all. If, however, sellers are very sensitive to price, then the shift in supply would cause the price to fall by the entire $6.

To illustrate, consider Figure 5.3(c), which depicts an *extremely inelastic supply*. This means that sellers are completely insensitive to the price: they provide the same quantity regardless of the price. In particular, if their costs change, they will not change the quantity supplied. In Figure 5.3(c), tanker lines supply 10 billion ton-miles a year whatever the market price. Consequently, the change in fuel cost does not change the equilibrium price.

Figure 5.3(d) depicts the other extreme, which is an *extremely elastic supply*. This means that, essentially, the marginal cost of production is constant. Accordingly, if the cost of an input changes, the marginal cost changes by the same amount at all production levels. Then the equilibrium price changes by exactly the same amount. In Figure 5.3(d), when the supply curve shifts down by $6, the equilibrium price drops by exactly $6 per ton-mile. The quantity supplied rises to 11 billion ton-miles a year.

Comparing Figures 5.3(c) and (d), we see the relationship between the price elasticity of supply and the outcome of a shift in supply. Generally, if the supply is more elastic, then the change in the equilibrium price resulting from a shift in supply will be larger.

PROGRESS CHECK 5C

Which of (a) and (b) is true? For a given downward shift of the market supply curve, the drop in the equilibrium price will be larger if: (a) the demand is more price elastic; or (b) the supply is more price elastic.

THE DEMAND FOR FRENCH PRODUCTS: FOIE GRAS AND BUTTER

France exports foie gras and butter. The supplies of French products to world markets depend on the exchange rate between the euro and other world currencies. If the euro becomes more expensive, the supply curves of French products to world markets will be higher. If, however, the euro becomes cheaper, then the supply curves will be lower.

Suppose that the euro becomes 10% more expensive, causing the supply curves of French foie gras and butter to shift up by 10%. How will these shifts affect the prices of foie gras and butter on world markets?

There are few substitutes for French foie gras; hence, the demand is relatively inelastic. The upward shift of the supply curve will result in a relatively large increase in the world price. By contrast, there are many close substitutes for French butter, so that the demand is relatively elastic. Accordingly, the upward supply shift curve will result in a relatively small increase in the world price.

TANKERS AND INTEREST RATES

As tankers cost up to $100 million and operate for 20 years or more, the demand for tankers depends on financing. So the demand for tankers and, in turn, the supply of tanker services are sensitive to interest rates.

In the wake of the Great Recession, national central banks boosted the money supply, leading to lower interest rates. To the extent that they also reduced long-run interest rates, the supply of tanker services would have shifted downward. This would have further depressed the rates for tanker services.

5. Demand Shift

We have just shown that, to understand the impact of a shift in supply, it is crucial to consider the interaction between supply and demand. Our next application begins with a change that shifts demand. For a complete understanding of the outcome, however, it is necessary to consider the supply side as well.

How would an increase in oil shipments affect the price and quantity of tanker service? Figure 5.4 shows the original equilibrium at point b, with a price of $200 and quantity of 10 billion ton-miles a year.

Suppose that the demand rises by 1 billion ton-miles at all price levels. Accordingly, in Figure 5.4, the entire demand curve shifts to the right by 1 billion ton-miles. The increase in oil shipments, however, does not directly affect the supply of tanker service. So the supply curve does not change.

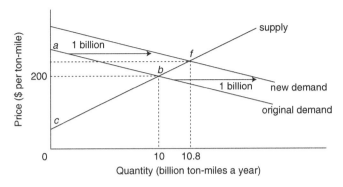

FIGURE 5.4 Demand shift.

Note: A 1 billion ton-mile increase in demand shifts the demand curve to the right and results in a higher price and larger quantity.

Referring to Figure 5.4, the new demand curve crosses the unchanged supply curve at a new market equilibrium (point f). The new equilibrium has a higher price and a larger quantity of tanker service. By how much will the price rise and by how much will the quantity of tanker service increase? They depend on the price elasticities of both demand and supply.

PROGRESS CHECK 5D

In Figure 5.4, show how a 2 billion ton-mile reduction in demand would affect the supply curve and the equilibrium price.

DEMAND AND SUPPLY ON VALENTINE'S DAY

People buy greeting cards and roses throughout the year. As Valentine's Day approaches, the demand for both cards and roses increases. Applying demand–supply analysis, we expect the prices of both products to rise. The price of roses, however, always increases much more sharply than the price of greeting cards. Why?

Consider the price elasticities of supply in the two markets. The supply of greeting cards on Valentine's Day is much more elastic than the supply of roses. Greeting cards can be stored, so manufacturers can easily step up production and prepare larger stocks ahead of Valentine's Day. This means that the supply of cards is relatively elastic; hence, an increase in demand has little effect on price.

By contrast, roses are perishable. Only roses maturing around Valentine's Day will be suitable for that day. It is relatively costly to increase the quantity supplied just for Valentine's Day. This means that the supply is relatively inelastic, and consequently, the increase in demand causes the price to increase sharply.

Source: B. Peter Pashigian, "Demand and supply on Valentine's Day," in *Price Theory and Applications*, New York: McGraw-Hill, 1995, p. 19.

6. Adjustment Time

The impact of shifts in demand and supply on the market equilibrium depends on the price elasticities of demand and supply. The elasticities vary with the time horizon. Accordingly, shifts in demand and supply may have different short-run and long-run effects.

To illustrate these differences, suppose that, originally, the market for tanker service was in short- and long-run equilibrium, with a price of $200 per ton-mile and quantity of 10 billion ton-miles. What are the short-run and long-run effects of an increase in demand by 1 billion ton-miles?

Short-Run Equilibrium

Figure 5.5 depicts the *short-run market equilibrium* at a price of $200 per ton-mile. Figure 5.5(a) shows the cost and demand curves of an individual seller. The short-run supply curve of any individual seller is that portion of its short-run marginal cost curve that lies above its short-run average variable cost curve.

By the assumption of perfect competition, each seller supplies a quantity that is small relative to the market. Equivalently, it has a small market share. Hence, the demand facing the seller is extremely elastic at the $200 market price. In the short run, the seller maximizes profit by operating at the point where its short-run marginal cost equals the market price. In Figure 5.5(a), the profit-maximizing scale is 100 million ton-miles a year.

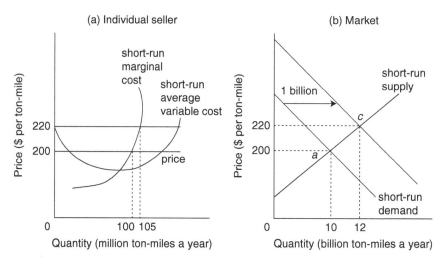

FIGURE 5.5 Short-run market equilibrium.

Notes:

(a) An individual seller operates at 100 million ton-miles a year, where the short-run marginal cost equals the market price.

(b) The market is in equilibrium at a price of $200, where the short-run demand crosses the short-run supply.

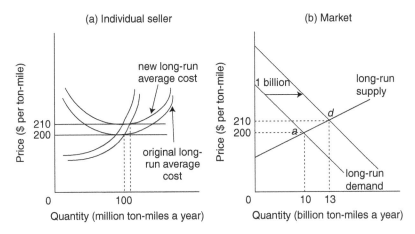

FIGURE 5.6 Long-run market equilibrium.

Notes:

(a) An individual seller operates at 100 million ton-miles a year, where the long-run marginal cost equals the market price.
(b) The market is in equilibrium at a price of $200, where the long-run demand crosses the long-run supply.

Figure 5.5(b) shows the short-run market equilibrium at point *a*. At the $200 equilibrium price, the short-run market demand curve crosses the short-run market supply curve.

Long-Run Equilibrium

Figure 5.6 depicts the *long-run market equilibrium* at a price of $200 per ton-mile. Figure 5.6(a) shows the cost and demand curves of an individual seller. The long-run supply curve of any individual seller is that portion of its long-run marginal cost curve that lies above its long-run average cost curve.

As each seller has a small market share, it faces a demand that is extremely elastic at the $200 market price. In the long run, it maximizes profit by operating at the point where its long-run marginal cost equals the market price. By Figure 5.6(a), the profit-maximizing scale is 100 million ton-miles a year.

Figure 5.6(b) shows the long-run market equilibrium at point *a*. At the $200 equilibrium price, the long-run market demand curve crosses the long-run market supply curve.

Demand Increase

Starting from the short- and long-run equilibria, we suppose that the demand curve shifts to the right by 1 billion ton-miles. For simplicity, we assume that the short- and long-run demand curves are the same.

First consider the new short-run equilibrium. Referring to Figure 5.5(b), the shift in demand will move the short-run market equilibrium to point *c*, with a higher price of $220. At the same time, referring to Figure 5.5(a), every seller expands its operations to the scale of 105 million ton-miles, where its short-run marginal cost equals the new market price of $220. This means operating service capacity more intensively – for instance, by delaying routine maintenance on ships and postponing the crews' annual vacations.

Generally, the extent to which a seller expands its operations depends on the slope of its short-run marginal cost curve. If the short-run marginal cost curve is steep, then the price increase will not lead the seller to expand operations by very much. By contrast, if the short-run marginal cost curve is gentle, then the price increase will induce a large expansion in operations. The slope of the short-run marginal cost curve depends on such factors as the availability of excess production capacity and the cost of overtime relative to standard wage rates.

Next consider the new long-run equilibrium. In a long-run horizon, there is enough time for all costs to become avoidable, for new sellers to enter the market, and for existing sellers to leave. Accordingly, as shown in Chapter 4, the market supply tends to be more elastic in the long run than in the short run.

In the tanker service market, the increase in demand raises the market price and hence each seller's profits. Over the long run, this will induce existing sellers to expand – acquire new ships and hire more crew – and also will attract new sellers to enter the market. The industry will expand along the long-run market supply curve. Referring to Figure 5.6(b), the shift in demand will move the long-run market equilibrium to point d with a price of $210.

Figure 5.6(a) shows the new long-run equilibrium for an individual seller. Although the price is higher than in the original equilibrium, higher input prices result in higher marginal and average cost curves. Accordingly, in the new long-run equilibrium, each individual seller just breaks even. No other sellers will wish to enter the industry, and no seller will wish to leave.

Figure 5.7 depicts both the short- and long-run market equilibria. The original equilibrium is point a, the new short-run equilibrium is point c, and the new long-run equilibrium is point d. The price in the new long-run equilibrium is lower than in the new short-run equilibrium but higher than in the original equilibrium. The quantity in the new long-run equilibrium is higher than in the new short-run equilibrium, which in turn is higher than in the original equilibrium. The basic reason for these differences is that the supply is more elastic in the long run than the short run.

In the new long-run equilibrium, there will be more sellers than in the new short-run equilibrium or the original equilibrium. The higher price attracts new sellers to enter and supports a larger number of sellers; hence, the industry becomes larger.

Demand Reduction

We have considered the short- and long-run impacts of an increase in demand. We can apply the same approach to study the effects of a reduction in demand. Figure 5.8 illustrates a 1 billion ton-mile reduction in the demand for tanker service. The original equilibrium is at point a.

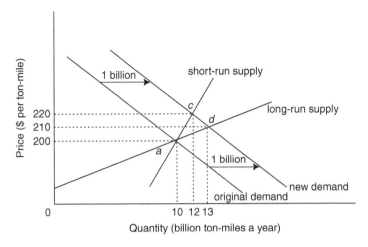

FIGURE 5.7 Demand increase: short and long run.

Notes: Following an increase in demand, the new short-run equilibrium is at point *c* and the long-run equilibrium is at point *d*. The price rises more in the short run than in the long run. The quantity increases less in the short run than in the long run.

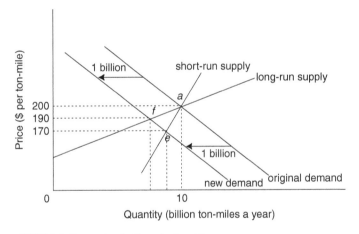

FIGURE 5.8 Demand reduction: short and long run.

Notes: Following a reduction in demand, the new short-run equilibrium is at point *e* and the long-run equilibrium is at point *f*. The price falls more in the short run than in the long run. The quantity drops less in the short run than in the long run.

The reduction in demand will move the short-run market equilibrium to point *e*, with a lower price of $170. Those sellers whose average variable cost exceeds the price will shut down. In the tanker market, this means laying up their ships. Those sellers for whom the price covers their average variable cost will continue in business. Each will cut back operations to the scale where its short-run marginal cost equals the new market price of $170.

The extent of the cutback depends on two factors. One factor is the extent of sunk costs. If a seller has many prior commitments, most costs are sunk. It will continue to produce so long as the price covers its average variable cost. In this case, the price reduction will lead to a relatively minor cutback in operations. Generally, in an industry where production involves substantial sunk costs, the reduction in demand will translate into a relatively large drop in price and a small reduction in quantity.

The second factor is the slope of the seller's short-run marginal cost curve. If the short-run marginal cost curve is steep, then the price reduction will not induce the seller to cut back operations by very much. By contrast, if the short-run marginal cost curve is gentle, then the price reduction will have a relatively larger impact on quantity.

In the long run, there is enough time for all costs to become avoidable, for new sellers to enter the market, and for existing sellers to leave. Referring to Figure 5.8, the shift in demand will move the long-run market equilibrium to point f, with a price of $190. For some sellers, the long-run price is below their average total cost. These will exit the industry, which means scrapping their ships and dismissing all workers. The entire industry will shrink along the long-run market supply curve. In the new long-run equilibrium, there will be a smaller number of sellers, and each will exactly break even with average total cost equal to the market price.

Referring to Figure 5.8, the price in the new long-run equilibrium is higher than in the new short-run equilibrium but lower than in the original equilibrium. Further, the quantity in the new long-run equilibrium is less than in the new short-run equilibrium, which in turn is less than in the original equilibrium. The basic reason for these differences is that the market supply is more elastic in the long run than in the short run.

Short and Long Run

In the short run, some costs are sunk, and, with less adjustment time, supply is less price elastic. By contrast, in the long run, all costs are avoidable and, with more adjustment time, supply is more price elastic.

Generally, in response to shifts in demand:

- The market price will change more in the short run than the long run. Specifically, if there is an increase in demand, the market price will increase more in the short run than in the long run. By contrast, if there is a reduction in demand, then the market price will fall more in the short run than in the long run. Generally, the market price tends to overshoot – adjusting relatively more in the short run and then *reversing* toward the initial price in the long run.
- Production will adjust more over the long run than in the short run. If there is an increase in demand, production will increase somewhat in the short run and more in the long run. Likewise, if there is a reduction in demand, production will fall somewhat in the short run and more in the long run. Generally, the long-run adjustment in production *amplifies* the short-run adjustment.

We can apply the same approach to consider the short- and long-run effects of shifts in supply. Note that demand is less price elastic in the short run than in the long run (except possibly for durables).

PROGRESS CHECK 5E

In Figure 5.8, suppose that the short-run supply is less elastic and the long-run supply is more elastic. How would that affect the difference between short- and long-run prices?

FRONTLINE

Frontline is a large independent owner-operator of tankers, with a fleet of 17.6 million dwt comprising 44 VLCCs and 21 Suezmaxes. Frontline owns 12 VLCCs and 12 Suezmaxes, and operates the other vessels under charter, spot rentals, and other contractual arrangements.

With the Great Recession, the demand for tanker services fell sharply. Between 2008 and 2009, freight rates for VLCCs collapsed from a record high of $88,400 to $28,000 a day. Rates for Suezmax tankers fell from $67,200 to $25,900 a day. The utilization rate of the overall tanker fleet fell from 91% to 84%.

How should Frontline adjust its fleet to the fall in freight rates? Suppose that the fall in demand was permanent (which it was not).

Over time, fleet operators would lay up vessels and others would even scrap their ships. So, at every price, there would be less capacity. Referring to Figure 5.8, the long-run supply would be more elastic than the short-run supply. Hence, in the long run, freight rates would recover. Indeed, by 2010, VLCC rates increased to $34,800 a day, while Suezmax rates rose to $28,000 a day.

For long-run decisions whether to scrap vessels or acquire new ships, management should distinguish short-run from long-run freight rates. It is the long-run rates that matter.

KEY TAKEAWAYS

- If the market price exceeds equilibrium, there will be excess supply and the price will tend to fall.
- If the market price falls below equilibrium, there will be excess demand and the price will tend to rise.
- A shift in supply will affect the market price and quantity to an extent that depends on the elasticities of both demand and supply.
- A shift in demand will affect the market price and quantity to an extent that depends on the elasticities of both demand and supply.

- A shift in demand will lead to a larger change in price in the short run than in the long run.
- A shift in demand will lead to a smaller change in production in the short run than in the long run.

REVIEW QUESTIONS

1. To what extent does the market for dry cleaning meet the conditions for perfect competition?
2. To what extent does the market for plywood meet the conditions for perfect competition?
3. How would the requirement for a government license affect the competitiveness of an industry?
4. If the market is in excess supply, what will happen to the price?
5. If the market is in excess demand, what will happen to the price?
6. Explain why the effect of an increase in consumer incomes on the market price of clothing depends on the price elasticity of supply.
7. Under what conditions of the price elasticities of demand and supply would an upward shift in demand (due to buyers getting more benefit) have a larger effect on the price?
8. Under what conditions of the price elasticities of demand and supply would an upward shift in demand (due to buyers getting more benefit) have a larger effect on the quantity consumed?
9. Consider an increase in consumer incomes that shifts the demand to the right (at every price, consumers want to buy more). Explain why the effect on the production of cars depends on the price elasticity of demand.
10. Under what conditions on the price elasticities of demand and supply would a reduction of supply (shift in supply curve to the left) have a larger effect on the price?
11. Under what conditions on the price elasticities of demand and supply would a reduction of supply (shift in supply curve to the left) have a larger effect on the quantity produced?
12. Explain why the effect of an increase in wages of waiters and kitchen staff on the market price of restaurant meals depends on the price elasticity of demand.
13. Suppose that demand increases. Why does the price increase more in the short run than in the long run?
14. Suppose that demand increases. Why does production increase more in the long run than in the short run?
15. How does the difference in short- and long-run effects of an increase in demand depend on the difference between short- and long-run price elasticities?

DISCUSSION QUESTIONS

1. Between 2008 and 2009, freight rates for VLCCs collapsed from $88,400 to $28,000 a day. The utilization rate of the overall tanker fleet fell from 91% to

84%. Between 2009 and 2010, as the world economy recovered, VLCC rates rose to $34,800 a day, and utilization of the overall tanker fleet rose to 86%.

    (a) Using relevant demand and supply curves, illustrate the shift in short-run equilibrium in tanker services between 2008 and 2009.

    (b) Using relevant demand and supply curves, illustrate the shift in short-run equilibrium between 2009 and 2010.

    (c) Comment on the price elasticity of the short-run supply of tanker services.

2. Producers of television sets outsource production to contract manufacturers in China and elsewhere. As of November 2014, the exchange rate of the Chinese yuan to the US dollar was 16 US cents to 1 yuan.

    (a) Explain how the appreciation of the Chinese yuan from 16 to 18 US cents would affect the cost of supplying TVs to the United States.

    (b) Suppose that the Chinese yuan rises by 10% against the US dollar. Which of the following are plausible explanations of why the US retail price of Chinese-made TVs will rise by less than 10%: (i) the wholesale cost accounts for only part of retailers' costs; (ii) American retail demand for Chinese-made TVs is inelastic; (iii) American retail supply of Chinese-made TVs is inelastic?

3. Seasonal changes can affect demand and supply. In the market for fresh fruit and vegetables, the supply varies with the season. By contrast, in the market for heating oil, the demand varies with the season.

    (a) Using suitable demand and supply curves, explain how prices of fruit and vegetables would vary over the four seasons of the year.

    (b) Using suitable demand and supply curves, explain how the price of heating oil would vary through the seasons.

4. Using Figure 5.3 as a basis, construct a set of four diagrams to show the effect of an increase in the demand for tanker service on the market price when: (a) demand is extremely inelastic; (b) demand is extremely elastic; (c) supply is extremely inelastic; and (d) supply is extremely elastic.

5. Manufacturers of packaging use inputs of wood pulp and wastepaper. In Sweden, the estimated price elasticity of the demand for wastepaper is -0.8 in the short run and -1.7 in the long run. The estimated price elasticity of the supply is 0.6 in the short run and 0.4 in the long run. (Source: Anna Mansikkasalo, Robert Lundmark, and Patrik Söderholm, "Market behavior and policy in the recycled paper industry: A critical survey of price elasticity research," *Forest Policy and Economics*, Vol. 38, January 2014, pp. 17–29.)

    (a) Consider a government policy that reduces the price of wastepaper to manufacturers by 5%. How will this affect the quantity demanded in the short and long run?

    (b) Consider a government policy that increases the price of wastepaper to sellers by 5%. How will this affect the quantity supplied in the short and long run?

    (c) Are price incentives an effective way of increasing the recycling of wastepaper?

6. The Japanese consume relatively more fish and less meat than people in other developed countries. In 1995, Worldwatch Institute President Lester R. Brown

pronounced: "[I]f the Chinese were to consume seafood at the same rate as the Japanese do, China would need the annual world fish catch." (Source: Lester R. Brown, *Who Will Feed China?*, New York: Norton, 1995, p. 30.)

(a) On a single figure, draw the world demand and supply of fish. (*Hint:* You are free to assume any data necessary to draw the curves.)

(b) Using your figure, explain how increases in the Chinese demand for fish would affect the world market.

(c) How would increases in the Chinese demand for fish affect Japanese consumption of fish?

(d) Is it likely that China would consume the entire world fish catch?

7. The Kurdistan region of Iraq, estimated to have 45 billion barrels of oil reserves, has been exporting crude oil by truck through Turkey. In late 2013, the regional government completed a 20-inch diameter connection to the main Iraq–Turkey pipeline. The connection can convey 125,000 barrels of oil per day to the port of Ceyhan in Turkey. (Source: "Iraqi Kurds, Turkey to double oil export pipeline capacity," *Bloomberg*, August 20, 2014.)

(a) Compare the fixed and marginal costs of transporting oil by (i) truck and (ii) pipeline.

(b) Which involves more sunk cost: supply by truck or pipeline?

(c) Draw the short-run supply curve of crude oil from Kurdistan through Turkey. On the supply curve, mark the supplies by truck and pipeline. (*Hint:* Consider whether the pipeline or trucks supply oil more inelastically.)

(d) Suppose that the Kurdistan government levies a tax on oil transported by the pipeline to pay for security. How would the tax affect the supply curve?

(e) The demand for Kurdistan oil fluctuates with global market conditions. Would the price of Kurdistan oil be more volatile if supplied by truck or pipeline?

8. With January 1, 2000 heralding a new millennium, many predicted shortages of lobsters. New England and Canadian wholesalers amassed stockpiles. Boston dealer James Hook ordered 675,000 kilograms, 50% more than the previous year. The anticipated shortages, however, did not materialize. In early December, with just weeks to the New Year, the wholesale price of lobster sank 12% to $11.70 per kilogram (Source: "Lobster dealers net meager sales on New Year celebration stockpile," *Asian Wall Street Journal*, December 29, 1999, pp. 1 and 7.)

(a) On a suitable diagram, draw the long-run supply of lobster for New Year's Eve. In gauging the price elasticity of supply, note that lobster can be stockpiled for over 6 months.

(b) Illustrate the effect of an increase in demand from 1998 to 1999. How would the increase in demand affect the price? How would the price effect depend on the price elasticity of supply?

(c) Processors have developed a method to freeze whole lobsters in a plastic sleeve of brine that provides a quality almost equal to the fresh animal. How would this new technology affect the elasticity of long-run supply?

9. In January 2009, Vaughan-Bassett, a manufacturer of bedroom furniture, suspended work at its Elkin, North Carolina, plant, laying off 400 workers. Eight months later, with sales up by 10%, the company reopened part of the Elkin plant

to finish furniture produced at its main plant at Galax, Virginia. Vaughan-Bassett easily found workers to staff the reopened plant. (Source: "Vaughan-Bassett reopens part of Elkin factory," *Time Warner Cable News*, November 16, 2014.)

(a) How do sales of new and existing residential housing affect the demand for furniture?

(b) How would the appreciation of the Chinese yuan against the US dollar affect the North Carolina furniture industry?

(c) In the face of falling demand, how should Vaughan-Bassett decide between suspending ("mothballing") a plant and closing it permanently?

(d) Using suitable short-run demand and supply curves, illustrate the shifts in the market equilibrium between January and September 2009.

You are the consultant!

Consider some good or service that your organization supplies in a competitive market. You have experienced a surge in demand, which is expected to be permanent. Prices have risen sharply and senior management is proposing new investment to capitalize on the higher prices. Write a memorandum analyzing the business case for the new investment, focusing on the short- and long-run increase in prices.

Note

1   The following discussion is based in part on data from Frontline Ltd, Annual Report 2010; and *Platou Report*, 2011.

6 CHAPTER

Economic Efficiency

LEARNING OBJECTIVES

- Appreciate economic efficiency as a benchmark for maximizing value.
- Apply the conditions for economic efficiency.
- Appreciate the invisible-hand role of price in competitive markets.
- Apply transfer pricing and outsourcing in decentralization of an organization.
- Appreciate the incidence of changes in demand or supply on buyers and sellers.
- Appreciate the incidence of intermediation on buyers and sellers.

1. Introduction

The Port Authority of New York and New Jersey manages John F. Kennedy International, Newark Liberty International, and LaGuardia airports. In 2008, Newark served 35.4 million passengers, as compared with 47.8 million at Kennedy and 23.1 million at LaGuardia.

Continental Airlines, with 72% of takeoff and landing slots, dominates flights at Newark. The remaining 28% of slots are spread among other US and international carriers. By contrast, LaGuardia (where the largest carrier is US Airways with 32%) and Kennedy (where the largest carrier is Delta Airlines with 31%) are less concentrated.

The Port Authority charges airlines landing fees based on aircraft weight. Larger aircraft pay higher fees than smaller planes for the same slot. The fees are an average of $6 per passenger and do not vary with the time of day.

During peak hours, the demand for takeoffs and landings at Newark exceeds capacity.[1] With two closely-spaced parallel runways, Newark is particularly susceptible to increased delays when weather conditions reduce visibility.

Between 2000 and 2007, average daily operations (landings and takeoffs) at Newark decreased by 3% from 1,253 to 1,219. However, on-time arrivals fell from 71% to 62%, and delays in arrival of one hour or more rose from 54 to 93 per day. In 2007, the proportion of flights arriving on time at Newark was the second worst among the top 35 US airports.

In October 2008, the Federal Aviation Administration (FAA) presented a 10-year plan limiting scheduled takeoffs and landings to 81 per hour and establishing an auction for landing and takeoff slots. Carriers with 20 or fewer daily slots would be assigned the same number of slots for 10 years. Carriers with more than 20 daily slots would be assigned 20 slots plus 90% of slots in excess of 20 for 10 years, but had to return the remaining 10% to the FAA. The FAA expected that it would take back 96 slots out of a total of 1,219. It planned to auction them over 5 years.

The FAA estimated that the plan would reduce the average delay by 23% and increase buyer and seller surplus by $839 million over the 10-year period 2009–2019. However, the Port Authority, airline associations, Continental Airlines, and US Airways resisted the FAA plan. Finally, in May 2009, by order of the US Court of Appeals, the FAA abandoned the plan and sought other ways to relieve congestion at Newark.

This chapter introduces the concept of *economic efficiency* and explains how to identify inefficiency. Understanding economic inefficiency is fundamental to every manager because it points to opportunities to increase value added and profit. Wherever the allocation of resources is not economically efficient, there is a way to add value and make money by resolving the inefficiency. This is a simple yet very powerful rule.

Next, we show that competitive markets allocate scarce resources in an economically efficient way. Market prices communicate information and provide incentives for users and suppliers to maximize the value added from scarce resources.

Takeoff and landing slots at an airport with limited runway capacity are a scarce resource. However, if the slots are allocated by administrative rule, the allocation of resources might not be economically efficient. Indeed, the FAA estimated that a reallocation could increase buyer and seller surplus by $839 million over 10 years.

This chapter presents two important applications of economic efficiency. One is to decentralization within an organization and the use of transfer pricing. The other is intermediation in the context of competitive markets. The analysis of intermediation explains the impact of transportation costs, brokerage fees, and taxes on buyers and sellers.

Economic efficiency is an important benchmark in settings of market power and imperfect markets as well as competitive markets. Chapters 9, 12, 13, and 14 apply economic efficiency to pricing, externalities, asymmetric information, and internal organization, respectively. In all of these contexts, the concept of economic efficiency helps managers to identify and exploit opportunities to increase value added and profit.

2. Benchmark

An allocation of resources is economically efficient if no reallocation of resources can make one person better off without making another person worse off. To appreciate economic efficiency as a benchmark, consider a situation that is not economically efficient. Then, by some reallocation of resources, it is possible to add value – specifically, to make one person better off without making another person worse off. Clearly, the original situation should be avoided.

From the viewpoint of a manager, if a situation is not economically efficient, then there will be some way to add value, that is, increase benefit by more than cost. There will also be some way to take some of the value added in profit. So, economic efficiency is a very useful benchmark for management in profit-oriented and non-profit organizations.

Conditions for Economic Efficiency

Economic efficiency:

- Same marginal benefit for all users.
- Same marginal cost for all suppliers.
- Marginal benefit equals marginal cost.

The concept of **economic efficiency** is a useful benchmark. The definition, however, is difficult to apply in practice. In practice, it is much easier to use a set of three conditions that are based on users' benefits and suppliers' costs. An allocation of resources is economically efficient if: all users achieve the same marginal benefit; all suppliers operate at the same marginal cost; and marginal benefit equals marginal cost.

Let us review these three conditions in the context of passenger airlines providing a service between Hong Kong and New York. Suppose that the route from Hong Kong is served by several airlines.

- *Equal marginal benefit.* The first condition for economic efficiency is that all users receive the same marginal benefit. Compare two passengers on a Hong Kong–New York flight. Max, whose father is a pilot, gets unlimited free travel, while Maria must pay for her flight. Max flies until his marginal benefit is zero, while Maria's marginal benefit equals the fare that she pays. If society reallocated a seat from Max to Maria, Max's loss would be less than Maria's gain, so society as a whole would be better off. This shows that an allocation of resources is economically efficient only if all users achieve the same marginal benefit.
- *Equal marginal cost.* The second condition for efficiency is that all suppliers must operate at the same marginal cost. Suppose that, owing to better

management, lower labor costs, and higher fuel efficiency, one airline provides the service at a marginal cost which is 10% lower than the other airlines. Society as a whole could reduce the overall cost of airline travel while maintaining the number of flights by expanding the services of the lower-cost airline and shrinking the services of the other airlines. This shows that an allocation of resources is economically efficient only if all suppliers operate at the same marginal cost.

• *Marginal benefit equals marginal cost.* The final condition for efficiency links users with suppliers: for a resource allocation to be economically efficient, the users' marginal benefit must equal the suppliers' marginal cost. If the marginal benefit is less than the marginal cost, society overall could add value by reducing the number of flights. Likewise, if the marginal benefit exceeds the marginal cost, then society could add value by increasing the number of flights. Thus, an allocation of resources is economically efficient only if the users' marginal benefit equals the suppliers' marginal cost.

Consumer Sovereignty

The concept of economic efficiency assesses resource allocations in terms of each individual user's evaluation of their benefit. The principle of taking individual users' evaluations as given is that of consumer sovereignty. For instance, if some people like heavy metal, while others like opera, the concept of economic efficiency takes these preferences as a given in assessing the efficiency of resource allocation. So, an economy in which some consumers like heavy metal but which produces only opera is not efficient, while an economy in which some consumers like opera but which produces only heavy metal is also inefficient.

Technical Efficiency

Technical efficiency means providing an item at the minimum possible cost. Technical efficiency alone, however, does not imply that scarce resources are being well used. For instance, an airline may be providing service at the minimum possible cost. But these may be flights that no one wants.

> **Technical efficiency:** Provision of an item at minimum cost.

The concept of economic efficiency extends beyond technical efficiency. For economic efficiency, the production of the item must be such that the marginal benefit equals the marginal cost.

PROGRESS CHECK 6A

Explain the difference between economic efficiency and technical efficiency.

FREE STORAGE, UNLIMITED SERVICE – FOR HOW LONG?

Many Web portals offer a limited quantity of free service to entice consumers. Initially, Google's Gmail offered 1 gigabyte of free storage. In competition with Microsoft's Hotmail and Yahoo! mail, Gmail increased its free storage to over 7.5 gigabytes. Not to be outdone, in April 2012, Microsoft's OneDrive expanded its free offering to 25 gigabytes.

However, these free services are costly to provide. In 2013, the data centers that support computing services and storage consumed an estimated 910 million megawatt-hours of electricity.

So how do service providers control the cost of free services? One way is to close accounts that have been dormant for specified periods of time. In its terms of service, Gmail clearly states that: "Google may terminate your account ... if you fail to login to your account for a period of nine months."

Source: "America's data centers consuming and wasting growing amounts of energy," National Resources Defense Council, December 4, 2014.

3. Adam Smith's Invisible Hand

[H]e intends only his own gain, and he is ... led by an invisible hand to promote an end which was no part of his intention.[2]

> **Invisible hand:** Market price guides buyers and sellers, acting independently and selfishly, to channel scarce resources into economically efficient uses.

Although published over 200 years ago, Adam Smith's insight is no less valid today. In a competitive market, buyers and sellers, each acting independently and selfishly, will channel scarce resources into economically efficient uses. The **invisible hand** that guides the multitude of buyers and sellers is the market price. This invisible hand is a simple and practical way of achieving economic efficiency.

Competitive Market

Consider how the invisible hand works in the market for airline services between Hong Kong and New York. Demand comes from travelers and supply from airlines. Figure 6.1 shows the market equilibrium with a price of $2,000 and quantity of 1.1 million seats a year.

On the demand side, as explained in Chapter 2, each person will buy up to the quantity such that their marginal benefit equals the price of travel, $2,000, and this is true for every buyer. In a perfectly competitive market, all buyers face the same $2,000 price; hence, their respective marginal benefits will be equal. This is the first condition for economic efficiency.

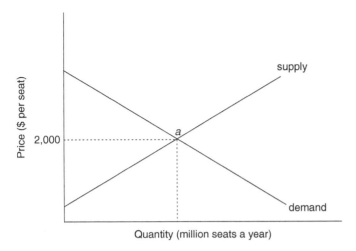

FIGURE 6.1 Air travel market.

Notes: In equilibrium, the demand crosses the supply at a price of $2,000. Each consumer purchases up to the quantity where the marginal benefit is $2,000. Each provider supplies the quantity where marginal cost is $2,000.

What about the airlines? On the supply side, as shown in Chapter 4, each airline will expand up to the scale where the marginal cost equals the price, $2,000. This scale of operations maximizes profit. Again, in a perfectly competitive market, all airlines face the same $2,000 price. Thus, with each airline selfishly maximizing profits, every airline will operate at the same marginal cost. This is the second condition for economic efficiency.

So all buyers balance marginal benefit with price and all airlines balance marginal cost with price. But, in market equilibrium, all buyers and all airlines face the same $2,000 price. Therefore, marginal benefit and marginal cost must be equal. This is the third condition for economic efficiency. Thus, a perfectly competitive market satisfies all three requirements for economic efficiency.

This example illustrates the power of Adam Smith's invisible hand. The market price guides multiple buyers and sellers, each acting independently and selfishly, to achieve economic efficiency.

Market System

The market price performs two roles to achieve economic efficiency:

- The price communicates the necessary information. It tells buyers how much to purchase and tells sellers how much to supply.
- The price provides a concrete incentive for each buyer to purchase the quantity that balances marginal benefit with the market price: by purchasing this quantity, the buyer achieves the maximum net benefit. Similarly, the price provides a concrete incentive for every seller to supply the quantity that

balances marginal cost with the market price: by supplying this quantity, the seller maximizes its profit.

The term **market system** or **price system** describes an economic system in which freely moving prices guide the allocation of resources. The term recognizes the key role of prices in a market system. The role of the invisible hand in achieving economic efficiency is the intellectual foundation of the market system.

> **Market (price) system:**
> An economic system in which freely moving prices guide the allocation of resources.

PROGRESS CHECK 6B

Explain the two functions of price in a market system.

NEWARK LIBERTY: INVISIBLE HAND DISABLED

The Federal Aviation Administration regulates air services in the United States. A major issue for the FAA is delays in airline operations. In 2007, the proportion of flights arriving on time at Newark Liberty International Airport was the second worst among the top 35 US airports.

In October 2008, the FAA presented a 10-year plan to limit scheduled operations to 81 per hour and establish an auction for landing and takeoff slots. Given limited takeoff and landing slots, it is economically efficient to allocate the slots to the users with the highest marginal benefit. Indeed, the FAA estimated that the plan would reduce the average delay by 23% and increase buyer and seller surplus by $839 million over the 10-year period 2009–2019.

By contrast with administrative fiat (or historical legacy), an auction is more likely to assign slots to the airlines serving travelers with the highest marginal benefit. The airlines whose passengers were willing to pay the most for the flights would bid the highest. These airlines would win the auction and get the slots.

However, the Port Authority of New York and New Jersey, which manages the airport, Continental, the dominant airline at Newark, and others opposed the FAA. By court order, the FAA was forced to abandon its plan. The invisible hand was disabled even before it could get to work.

Source: "Congestion management rule for John F. Kennedy International Airport and Newark Liberty International Airport: Final regulatory evaluation," US Federal Aviation Administration, Office of Aviation Policy and Plans, Aircraft Regulatory Analysis Branch, October 10, 2008.

4. Decentralized Management

The concept of economic efficiency applies not only across the economy but also within an organization. Consider a bank with two divisions – commercial banking and personal banking. Each division takes deposits and makes loans. The bank must decide how to allocate funds across the two divisions.

The concept of economic efficiency guides the bank in the use of its limited funds. Applying the concept, the allocation of funds will be efficient if all users achieve the same marginal benefit, all suppliers operate at the same marginal cost, and every user's marginal benefit balances every supplier's marginal cost.

In the context of the bank and its limited funds, the users are the lending units and the suppliers are the deposit-taking units of the two divisions. The first condition for efficiency is that all users receive the same marginal benefit. This means that each of the bank's lending units must get the same profit from an additional dollar of funds. If one lending unit could get more profit than another, the bank should switch some funds to the lending unit that gets the higher profit. Then the bank's overall profit will be higher.

The second condition for efficiency is that all suppliers must operate at the same marginal cost. If one deposit-taking unit can produce funds at a lower marginal cost than another, then the bank should direct the lower-cost unit to produce more and the higher-cost unit to produce less. This would increase the bank's overall profit.

The final condition for efficiency is that the marginal benefit must balance the marginal cost. If the marginal benefit of funds to the lending unit is less than the marginal cost of producing the funds, then the bank should cut back deposit-taking. The reduction in cost would be greater than the reduction in benefit, so overall profit would rise. By contrast, if the marginal benefit of funds is greater than the marginal cost, then the bank should increase deposit-taking. The bank will maximize profit when the marginal benefit equals the marginal cost.

Internal Market

Just as the invisible hand works to achieve economic efficiency across the entire economy, it can also work within an individual organization. How should the bank organize the production and use of funds?

One approach is central planning: the bank headquarters can collect information about deposit-taking and lending unit costs and revenues from all lending units, and then decide the level of funds each unit should accept and how much each lending unit should lend.

Suppose that there is a competitive market for funds. Then an alternative is for the bank to decentralize management of deposit-taking in the following way. The bank can direct the managers of every deposit-taking unit to maximize profit and sell funds at the market price, whether to the company's own lending units or outside buyers. Similarly, the bank can direct every lending unit to maximize profit and allow them the freedom to procure funds from any source, whether it be one of the bank's own deposit-taking units or external to the bank.

As these sales are a transfer within the same organization, the corresponding price is called a **transfer price**. The bank

> **Transfer price:** The sale price of an item within an organization.

should set the transfer price for funds equal to the market price. With the decentralized policy, each lending unit will buy funds up to the point that its marginal benefit balances the market price.

Since all lending units face the same market price, their marginal benefits will be equal. Similarly, each deposit-taking unit will produce up to the point that its marginal cost balances the market price. As all deposit-taking units face the same market price, their marginal costs will be equal.

Since the deposit-taking and lending units face the same market price, marginal benefit will be equal to marginal cost. Thus, the decentralized policy achieves the three conditions for economic efficiency within the same organization. Essentially, by decentralizing the management of funds, the bank is establishing an internal market that is integrated with the external market.

Outsourcing

An organization should follow two general rules when decentralizing control over an internal resource. First, if there is a competitive market for the item, the transfer price should be set equal to the market price. If there is no competitive market for the item, then the appropriate transfer price is more complicated. We discuss transfer pricing more generally in Chapter 7.

The second general rule is that producing units should be allowed to sell the product to outside buyers and consuming units should be allowed to buy the product from external sources. Recall from Chapter 1 that *outsourcing* is the purchase of services or supplies from external sources.

To explain why the right to outsource is crucial, suppose that the bank requires all lending units to source funds internally. Then the bank's deposit-taking units would have market power, and as Chapter 8 explains, they would charge a price above the competitive market level. As a result, the lending units would no longer secure the economically efficient quantity of funds. A similar argument shows why it is necessary to allow producing units to sell the product to outside buyers.

Any organization that uses resources or products for which there are competitive markets can apply decentralization to achieve internal economic efficiency. Energy producers can apply the technique to manage the production and use of crude oil and natural gas, and automobile manufacturers can apply it to manage production and use of components.

PROGRESS CHECK 6C

Jupiter Electronics manufactures semiconductors and consumer electronics. Its semiconductors are inputs into the production of electronics. Explain how the company can use decentralization to ensure that its consumer electronics division will make efficient use of semiconductors produced by the semiconductor division.

SINOPEC: TRANSFER PRICING

China Petroleum & Chemical Corporation (Sinopec) is a vertically integrated producer of oil and chemicals. It operates in four lines of business: exploration and production, refining, marketing and distribution, and chemicals. The company's policy is to set inter-segment transfer prices according to "the market price or cost plus an appropriate margin."

With a network of over 30,000 stations, Sinopec's marketing and distribution division is China's largest and the world's second largest. In 2013, the division earned operating income of 35 billion yuan on revenues of 1486 billion yuan and assets of 274 billion yuan.

In early 2014, Sinopec announced that it would restructure the marketing and distribution division and open it to private investment. A key concern for investors is the transfer prices for supplies of refined petroleum. If Sinopec refineries set high transfer prices, the marketing and distribution division may be uncompetitive in the retail market. However, if the investors bargain hard to reduce transfer prices, then Sinopec refineries may incur losses.

Source: Sinopec, Annual Report, 2014.

5. Intermediation

An important application of the demand–supply framework is to understand the impact of the costs of retailing, distribution, transportation, brokerage, and other forms of intermediation on the market for the final good or service.

For instance, manufacturers of industrial products must decide whether to include the cost of shipment in the price to the customer. One approach is to set an *ex-works* or *free on board* (FOB) price and leave the customer to pay the freight, while the alternative is to charge a price including freight. Using the demand–supply framework, we will show that both pricing methods have exactly the same impact on the manufacturer and customer.

Freight-Inclusive Pricing

We begin by considering the cement market with freight-inclusive pricing. A price that includes freight is called **cost including freight** (CF).

> **CF price:** Includes the cost of delivery to the buyer.

In the market for cement, the buyers are building contractors and the sellers are cement manufacturers. Suppose that all manufacturers set CF prices that include a freight cost of 25 cents per bag. The market price is $4.50 per bag and buyers purchase 1 billion bags a year. Figure 6.2 illustrates the market equilibrium at point *a*. In this equilibrium, the marginal

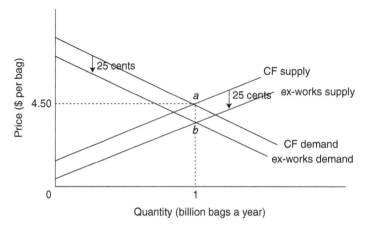

FIGURE 6.2 Pricing and freight cost.

Notes: If all manufacturers switch to ex-works pricing, the supply curve shifts down by 25 cents and the demand also shifts down by 25 cents. The equilibrium quantity remains unchanged at 1 billion bags.

benefit of cement is $4.50 per bag and the marginal cost (inclusive of freight) is also $4.50 per bag.

Free on Board Pricing

FOB price: Does not include the cost of delivery to the buyer.

Next, suppose that all cement manufacturers switch to FOB pricing. An **FOB price** does not include the freight cost: it literally means "the price at the gate to the works."

Since manufacturers no longer incur the freight cost of 25 cents, the switch will shift the entire supply curve of cement down by 25 cents. In Figure 6.2, the entire supply curve shifts down because each manufacturer's marginal cost of supplying cement is reduced whatever the quantity that it actually supplies.

The switch to FOB pricing also affects the market demand. With FOB pricing, each buyer must pay 25 cents a bag to obtain the cement. In Figure 6.2, this can be represented by shifting the entire retail demand curve down by 25 cents. Since each buyer must pay 25 cents in freight for every bag, the buyer's willingness to pay will be 25 cents lower at all quantities. This means that the entire demand curve will shift down by 25 cents.

There is another way to confirm that the switch to FOB pricing will shift down the demand curve. Consider the buyer of the 1 billionth bag. By the original demand curve, that buyer would be willing to pay exactly $4.50 for that bag. If, however, the buyer must incur a 25-cent freight cost, it will now be willing to pay $4.50 − $0.25 = $4.25 for the 1 billionth bag. The same 25 cent reduction in willingness to pay applies to all the inframarginal units as well. Hence, the entire demand curve shifts down by 25 cents.

In Figure 6.2, the new demand and supply curves cross at point b. Relative to the original equilibrium at point a, the price is lower. The new demand curve is the original demand curve shifted down by 25 cents. Likewise, the new supply curve is the original supply curve shifted down by 25 cents. Hence, the new equilibrium point b must be vertically below the original equilibrium point a, and the vertical distance a must be 25 cents.

Thus, in the new equilibrium, each buyer pays $4.25 to the seller and $0.25 in freight, making a "total price" of $4.25 + $0.25 = $4.50, which is exactly the price under freight-inclusive pricing. Further, the quantity of sales is exactly the same in the old and new equilibria. Generally, the price and sales are the same whether the sellers do or do not include the freight cost in their prices.

Further, in the new equilibrium, the marginal benefit of cement is $4.50 per bag, while the marginal cost (inclusive of freight) is also $4.50 per bag. Accordingly, from the viewpoint of economic efficiency, the new and old equilibria are identical.

ONLINE RETAIL: FREE(?) SHIPPING

Some online retailers include free shipping while others charge for shipping. In November 2014, R.T. Edwards offered the Samsung UA65HU9000 65-inch high definition LED TV for A$4,238 with free shipping, while Exeltek offered the same TV for $4,095 with a shipping charge of $145 to Perth, Western Australia.

Demand–supply analysis predicts that, whether online retailers charge for shipping or provide free shipping, the net price to consumers would be the same. Indeed, Exeltek's price plus shipping was A$4,240, which is almost identical to R.T. Edwards's price.

Source: getprice.com.au (accessed November 17, 2014).

6. Incidence

When demand or supply shifts, the consequent change in the price for a buyer or seller is called the **incidence** on that party. In the freight example, when manufacturers switch from freight-inclusive to FOB pricing, the market price drops by 25 cents to $4.25; hence, the net effect on buyers is zero.

> **Incidence:** The change in price for a buyer or seller resulting from a shift in demand or supply.

This shows that, although the switch in pricing method requires buyers to "pay" the freight cost, there is no net effect after we consider adjustments in both demand and supply. Equivalently, whether manufacturers set prices that do or do not include the freight cost, the incidence is the same. The incidence does not depend on which side – buyer or seller – initially pays the freight cost.

In fact, the incidence of the freight cost depends only on the price elasticities of demand and supply. This analysis reflects common sense. If sellers pay the freight cost, the buyers will be willing to pay a higher price. By contrast, buyers that must pay the freight cost will insist on paying less to sellers.

The distinction between receiving or paying an amount of money and the incidence of the receipt or payment is a fundamental economic concept. We have applied this distinction in the decision whether to include freight in pricing. The distinction is also important for understanding the effect of retailing and distribution costs, brokerage fees, and government taxes.

Consider, for instance, the impact of free shipping in e-commerce. Does it matter whether the vendor offers free shipping or the consumer pays for shipping? Using similar demand–supply analysis to that applied to freight costs, we can show that, regardless of whether vendors or consumers pay the shipping costs, the market price and quantity will be the same.

The analysis of incidence must be qualified if buyers or sellers are subject to biases in decision-making. The behavioral biases due to sunk costs, status quo, and anchoring may affect the incidence of receipts or payments. For instance, with regard to free shipping, consumers might anchor on the free shipping, and so demand for vendors that offer free shipping would be higher. On the other hand, consumers might anchor on the price of the product (and give insufficient attention to shipping charges), and then demand for vendors that charge separately for shipping would be higher.

PROGRESS CHECK 6D

In Figure 6.2, draw a more elastic supply curve passing through equilibrium *a*. How does this affect the difference between freight-inclusive and FOB pricing?

---

7. Taxes

Governments depend on tax revenues to support public services such as national defense, administration of justice, and public health. Some taxes are levied on consumers, others on businesses, and some are levied on both. For instance, the US government imposes an air travel tax on airlines. By contrast, some Asian governments impose the air travel tax on the passenger. What difference does this make?

From the viewpoint of demand and supply, taxes are like a cost of intermediation. So, we can apply the analysis above to understand the effect of taxes on market price and quantity. Specifically, suppose that the US government levies a $10 tax on air travel between Chicago and Paris.

Buyer's and Seller's Price

We assume that the market is perfectly competitive. The demand comes from business and leisure travelers, while American and foreign airlines provide the supply.

Since this market is subject to a tax, it is necessary to make one change to the usual demand–supply analysis. We must distinguish the price that the buyer pays (buyer's price) from the price that the seller receives (seller's price). The seller's price is the buyer's price minus the amount of the tax.

We can draw the demand and supply curves as in Figure 6.3. Suppose that, initially, there is no tax on airline tickets and the equilibrium is at point *b*, with a price of $800. Since there is no tax, $800 is the buyer's price as well as the seller's price. At the price of $800, airlines sell 920,000 tickets a year.

Now the federal government requires airlines to pay a tax of $10 on each ticket. Referring to Figure 6.3, we can represent this graphically in one of three equivalent ways: (a) shift the supply curve vertically up by $10, showing the market from buyers' point of view; (b) shift the demand curve vertically down by $10, showing the market from airlines' point of view; or (c) shift neither demand nor supply, but show the $10 tax as a wedge between the demand and supply curves.

As a result of the tax, there will be a new equilibrium at point *e* in each diagram, with a price of $804 and quantity of 900,000 tickets a year. The price is higher and the quantity of travel is smaller.

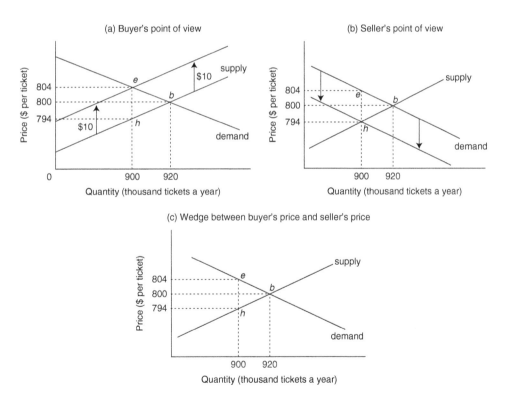

FIGURE 6.3 Air travel tax.

Notes: The tax of $10 per ticket (a) raises the marginal cost of supplying air travel, (b) reduces the willingness to pay by $10, or (c) drives a $10 wedge between buyers' willingness to pay and the marginal cost of air travel. In all these cases the buyers end up paying $804, the sellers keep $794, and the quantity is reduced to 900,000 tickets a year.

Now that there is a tax, the buyer's price differs from the seller's price. The buyer's price is $804, while the seller's price is the buyer's price less the $10 tax, or $794. In the new equilibrium, the seller's price of $794 is lower than the original seller's price with no tax, which was $800.

Tax Incidence

So what is the difference between levying a tax on airlines and a tax on travelers? Obviously, there may be administrative and perhaps psychological differences. Since there are relatively fewer airlines than passengers, it may be less costly to collect the tax from airlines. A tax on passengers may be more salient to travelers, and may have a larger effect when they vote in elections.

Aside from administrative and psychological differences, however, we claim that the effect of a tax will be the same whether it is collected from the buyers or the sellers. Incidence depends only on the price elasticities of demand and supply. The side of the market that is relatively less sensitive to price changes will bear the relatively larger portion of the tax. Incidence is the same whether it is collected from the buyers or the sellers.

PROGRESS CHECK 6E

In Figure 6.3, draw in a more inelastic demand curve. How does this affect the incidence of tax on travelers relative to airlines?

MIGRANT WORKERS – EARN MORE, PAY MORE

The government of Singapore levies a tax on the employment of foreign workers. Some have called for the government to convert the tax into a contribution to a savings fund. The savings would benefit the foreign workers at the end of their employment in Singapore when they return to their home country.

Let us use demand and supply to analyze the likely effects of the proposed savings fund. Wages in Singapore are substantially higher than in the foreign workers' home countries, creating a huge excess supply. In market equilibrium, foreign workers pay intermediaries to secure Singapore jobs. Among Bangladeshi construction workers, the average fee was S$7,256.

With millions of people keen to work in Singapore, it is reasonable to stipulate that the supply of foreign labor is fairly elastic. Hence, the conversion of the tax into a savings fund would just add to the excess supply of foreign workers. How would the market equilibrate? Through workers paying more in placement fees to intermediaries. The workers themselves might not benefit at all.

Source: Transient Workers Count Too, "Worse off for working?" Singapore, August 12, 2012.

KEY TAKEAWAYS

- Resource allocation is economically efficient if: (a) all users achieve the same marginal benefit; (b) all suppliers operate at the same marginal cost; and (c) marginal benefit equals marginal cost.
- In competitive markets, the invisible hand (price) leads to economic efficiency by communicating information and providing incentives.
- For economic efficiency within an organization, set the transfer price equal to the market price and allow outsourcing.
- The incidence of changes in demand or supply on buyers and sellers depends only on the price elasticities of demand and supply.
- Whether the buyer or seller pays for the cost of intermediation does not affect the incidence of the cost.

REVIEW QUESTIONS

1. The government of the Soviet Union subsidized bread. In 1987, the Soviet leader Mikhail Gorbachev complained that children were kicking bread in football games. Comment on the economic efficiency of the production and consumption of bread.
2. The external auditor of the local school system has found that some schools pay 20% more for cleaning services than other schools. Which condition of economic efficiency is being violated?
3. In a World War II camp, every prisoner of war received an identical parcel containing cigarettes, chocolate, pen, and writing paper. Comment in terms of economic efficiency.
4. In some countries, self-employed people can evade income tax while people employed by the government and large organizations must pay income tax in full. Comment on the economic efficiency of the labor market.
5. Consider a competitive finance market. Explain how the invisible hand ensures that the allocation of investment funds is economically efficient.
6. To limit inflation, some governments impose controls on increases in the prices of rice and other essential foods. Explain the impact on economic efficiency in the market for rice.
7. Explain the meaning of outsourcing. What is the opposite of outsourcing?
8. An integrated oil producer both produces crude oil and refines the oil for sale as gasoline, diesel, and other products in the retail market. In this context, explain the concept of a transfer price.
9. A real estate group operates a chain of department stores using its own buildings. Why should the group charge rent to the department store?
10. Explain the difference between CF pricing and FOB pricing.
11. Buyers of residential property must pay a percentage of the house price as a commission to the agent. In this context, explain the difference between the payment and incidence of the brokerage fee.
12. Consider two otherwise identical e-commerce retail markets. In one, vendors offer free shipping, while in the other, vendors charge for shipping. What is the difference for the price (including shipping charges) that buyers pay?

13. Referring to Figure 6.3(a), under what condition of the price elasticity of demand would the incidence of the tax on consumers be the lowest?
14. Travelers can reduce costs for airlines by booking tickets through online channels rather than travel agents. How would you assess whether airlines or consumers benefit from the lower cost?
15. Free Duty offers tax-free sales of liquor and tobacco products at Hong Kong International Airport. Do you expect any difference in the *pre-tax* prices of liquor and cigarettes between the airport and the city?

DISCUSSION QUESTIONS

1. Tickets to popular sporting events, such as the FIFA World Cup and the Super Bowl, often sell out. Devoted fans must either spend long hours waiting in line for a limited supply of tickets or pay a premium price to scalpers or touts. Scalpers buy tickets to resell.
   (a) When tickets sell out, which condition(s) for economic efficiency might not be satisfied?
   (b) Do scalpers improve economic efficiency?
   (c) If the ticket agencies auctioned the tickets rather than selling them for fixed prices, what would be the impact on scalpers?
2. Household incomes and the cost of living are higher in urban than rural areas. A non-profit group of hospitals operates across urban and rural areas. The group sets the same prices and pays the same salaries for doctors and other professional staff at all hospitals.
   (a) Management has noticed that there are long waiting lists for treatment at its urban hospitals. Can you explain this problem?
   (b) The company has had great difficulty in recruiting professional staff for its urban hospitals. Can you explain this problem?
   (c) What advice would you give to management?
3. LaGuardia Airport is one of three major airports that serve New York City. The heavy demand for flights to and from the airport has caused systematic delays. The entry of new carriers and expansion of service by existing carriers would increase congestion. In 2000, the airport management decided to allocate a limited number of new takeoff and landing slots among the various airlines by lottery. Incumbent carriers were allowed to retain existing slots.
   (a) With a limited number of takeoff and landing slots allocated by lottery, which condition for economic efficiency might be violated?
   (b) Comment on the following measures in terms of economic efficiency: (i) giving the incumbent carriers ownership over their slots and allowing them to lease or sell their slots; (ii) auctioning the right to new slots.
4. Jupiter Mines produces silver from several mines. Until recently, corporate headquarters set production targets for each mine based on average production costs. Then management consultants recommended a new policy: each mine must aim to maximize profits given the prevailing price of silver.
   (a) Under Jupiter's old production policy, which condition(s) for economic efficiency might not be satisfied?

(b) Does the new production policy improve economic efficiency?

(c) Explain the role of price under the new policy.

5. China Petroleum & Chemical Corporation (Sinopec) is an integrated producer of oil and chemicals. Sinopec's refining division sells most of its production to the marketing and distribution division. The company's policy is to set inter-segment transfer prices according to the market price or cost plus an appropriate margin. In early 2014, Sinopec announced that it would partially privatize the marketing and distribution division.

(a) How does the transfer price of refined products affect the profits of the marketing and distribution division?

(b) China is a large country with refineries sourcing crude oil from diverse sources, including foreign countries. Would the market prices of refined products be the same in all places?

(c) Suppose that Sinopec allows the marketing and distribution division to outsource its supply of refined products. How would that affect the refining division's sales to the marketing and distribution division?

6. Some marketing consultants argue that cents-off coupons are more effective in reducing retail prices than cuts in wholesale prices. They believe that retailers would absorb cuts in wholesale prices instead of passing the price cuts to consumers. By contrast, they believe that consumers would benefit fully from coupons.

(a) Consider the retail market for a brand of shampoo. Using relevant demand and supply curves, illustrate the market equilibrium at a price of $4 per bottle and a quantity of 500 million bottles a year. (*Hint*: You are free to assume any data necessary to draw the curves.)

(b) Suppose that the manufacturer cuts the wholesale price by 25 cents. Draw a new retail supply curve, shifted down by 25 cents. Identify the new equilibrium quantity and price.

(c) Suppose, instead, that the manufacturer distributes 25-cent coupons and that all consumers use these coupons. Draw a new retail demand curve, shifted down by 25 cents. Identify the new equilibrium quantity and price.

(d) Compare the equilibria under (b) and (c). Do you agree with the marketing consultants?

7. Online retailers differ in charges for shipping. In November 2014, R.T. Edwards offered a Samsung 65-inch high definition LED TV for A$4,238 with free shipping, while Exeltek offered the same TV for A$4,095 with shipping charge of A$145 to Perth, Western Australia.

(a) Using relevant demand and supply curves, explain whether it matters for consumers if the retailer offers free shipping or charges for shipping. (*Hint*: You are free to assume any data necessary to draw the curves.)

(b) If consumers view R.T. Edwards and Exeltek as equivalent (in terms of quality of service), how should their prices for the same TV compare? Are the prices consistent with your answer in (a)?

(c) If consumers are biased in decision-making by anchoring, how would that affect your answer in (a)?

8. The Internet has drastically reduced the cost of intermediary services of travel agencies, real estate brokers, and investment advisors. Consider the market for air travel. Suppose that, with booking through travel agencies, the market equilibrium price is $500 per ticket, including a $25 cost of intermediation. The quantity bought is 2 million tickets a year. With Internet bookings, however, the intermediation cost falls to $2 per ticket.

   (a) Using suitable demand and supply curves, illustrate the original equilibrium with booking through travel agencies. Represent the intermediation cost by shifting the supply curve.

   (b) Illustrate the new equilibrium with online booking.

   (c) Under what conditions of demand and supply would consumers benefit the most from online bookings?

9. Mainland Chinese visitors are among the most free-spending shoppers at Hermes, Louis Vuitton, Prada, and other luxury stores in Hong Kong. The government of China levies value-added tax (VAT) at 17% on the retail sales of imported goods within China. Shenzhen, on the border with Hong Kong, is China's highest-income city.

   (a) Suppose that Chinese tourists can avoid VAT when bringing luxury items back to China. How would this affect the demand among Chinese for luxury goods: (i) in Hong Kong, and (ii) within China?

   (b) If the demand among Chinese for luxury goods within China is very elastic (owing to ready access to shops in Hong Kong), what would be the relation of prices in Shenzhen to those in Hong Kong?

   (c) To what extent would your analysis in (a) and (b) also apply to consumer goods such as shampoo and baby diapers?

You are the consultant!

Consider some input that your organization uses to produce the goods and services that it sells.

(a) Are all users of the input getting the same marginal benefit from the input?

(b) Compare the marginal benefit from use of the input with the marginal cost of producing the input.

(c) How could your organization increase the efficiency of the use of the input?

Notes

1   This discussion is based in part on "Congestion management rule for John F. Kennedy International Airport and Newark Liberty International Airport: Final regulatory evaluation," US Federal Aviation Administration, Office of Aviation Policy and Plans, Aircraft Regulatory Analysis Branch, October 10, 2008.

2   Adam Smith, *The Wealth of Nations*, 2nd edition, London: W. Strahan and T. Cadell, 1778, Vol. II, Book IV, p. 35 (first published in 1776).

Market Power

COMPANION @ WEBSITE

CHAPTER

Costs

LEARNING OBJECTIVES

- Understand opportunity costs and apply in business decisions.
- Apply the concept of opportunity cost to the cost of capital and transfer pricing.
- Appreciate that sunk costs should be ignored in business decisions.
- Understand economies of scale and apply in business decisions.
- Understand economies of scope and apply in business decisions.
- Understand the experience curve and apply in business decisions.
- Recognize and avoid behavioral biases in cost decisions.

1. Introduction

The Canadian aerospace manufacturer, Bombardier, is well-established in the production of regional jets. It long aspired to expand into large jets and announced the development of the CSeries in 2004. However, it did not actually commence development until 2008, upon securing a letter of interest for 60 planes from Deutsche Lufthansa. The new CSeries is scheduled to enter service in 2015. It will reduce fuel consumption by 20% through the use of advanced materials and a more fuel-efficient engine, the Pratt & Whitney PW1000G.[1]

COMAC of China and Irkut of Russia have begun development of large jets. Acutely conscious of the competitive threat, Airbus and Boeing are under pressure to respond. In December 2010, Airbus launched a new version of one of its large jets, the A320neo, with a "new engine option" offering better fuel economy.

In March 2011, Airbus announced that it would raise production of the A320 family from 34 to 36 units per month.

In June 2011, at the Paris Air Show, Boeing had still not decided its strategy – whether to replace the Boeing 737 with a completely new model, or, like Airbus, offer a new version. Earlier, Boeing announced an increase in 737 production from 31.5 units to 42 units per month.

Why was Bombardier so cautious about commencing development of the CSeries? For Airbus, what are the advantages of meeting the competition with the A320neo rather than a completely new plane? How would Airbus's increase in A320 production affect its unit costs?

To address these questions, we introduce a framework for understanding costs. Within a single period of production, costs are either sunk (have been committed and cannot be avoided) or avoidable (see Figure 7.1). Practically, the most readily available information on profit is the accounting measure. The concept of economic profit is related to but differs from accounting profit. Specifically, economic profit differs from accounting profit by excluding opportunity cost and including sunk cost:

$$\text{Economic profit} = \text{Accounting profit} - \text{Opportunity cost} + \text{Sunk cost}. \quad (7.1)$$

> **Economic profit:**
> Accounting profit less opportunity cost plus sunk cost.

Strategically, looking forward, businesses must take care before incurring sunk costs. Bombardier estimates the cost of developing the CSeries to be $2.5 billion, or a quarter of the company's market capitalization. The company is prudent to be cautious about sinking so large an amount.

Among the avoidable costs, some are not reported in accounting statements but are relevant to management decisions. These are *opportunity costs*, which must be forgone to continue with the current course of action.

The avoidable costs can be analyzed in two ways. One way is fixed and variable costs. Fixed costs do not vary with the scale of production, while variable costs do. Which costs are fixed and which are variable depends on the technology of

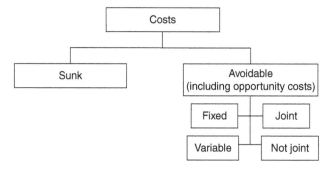

FIGURE 7.1 Costs in a single period of production.

Notes: The division of costs into sunk and avoidable depends on past commitments and the current planning horizon. The division of avoidable costs into fixed and variable and into joint and not joint depends on the production technology.

production. Fixed costs are an essential reason for economies of scale. If fixed costs are substantial in the manufacturing of Airbus jets, then Airbus can reduce its unit costs by increasing the rate of production.

Joint costs do not vary with the number of products, and are an essential reason for economies of scope. They explain, in part, why Airbus chose to launch a new version of an existing plane, the Airbus 320neo, instead of a completely new plane. By doing so, it could exploit economies of scope across the existing and new planes.

Over time, the cost of production may fall with cumulative production according to an experience curve. Indeed, the cost of airplane manufacturing falls substantially with cumulative production. Given the cost-reducing effect of experience, it would not be economic to produce a small number of planes. This also explains why Bombardier waited until securing substantial interest from Lufthansa before developing the CSeries.

For decisions in any context – for profit, non-profit, and government – managers need to understand costs from more than a pure accounting perspective. They can apply the framework and analyses of this chapter to make more effective decisions in investment, performance evaluation, outsourcing, and pricing.

2. Opportunity Cost

Analyses of costs usually begin with accounting statements. These, however, do not always provide the appropriate information for effective business decisions. It is often necessary to look beyond conventional accounting statements.

To illustrate, suppose that Luna Biotech has accumulated cash of $10 million. It is considering a $10 million research and development project to develop a new drug to treat a rare disease. The new drug is expected to generate a profit contribution of $20 million. (Profit contribution is revenues less variable cost, excluding R&D expenditures.) Luna Biotech has not yet commenced R&D.

Meanwhile, an independent scientist has already developed a similar drug to treat the same disease. The scientist has offered to sell her invention to Luna Biotech for $2 million. The scientist's drug would be just as good and also yield a profit contribution of $20 million. How should Luna choose between commencing R&D on its own drug and buying the scientist's invention?

Alternative Courses of Action

Table 7.1 presents a projected income statement for the R&D project. The profit contribution is $20 million for an R&D expense of $10 million. So, the projected

Table 7.1 Conventional income statement ($ million)

Profit contribution	20
R&D expense	10
Profit	10

Table 7.2 Income statement showing alternatives ($ million)

	Commence R&D	Cancel R&D and buy drug
Profit contribution	20	20
R&D expense	10	0
External purchases	0	2
Profit	10	18

Table 7.3 Income statement showing opportunity cost ($ million)

	Commence R&D
Profit contribution	20
R&D expense	10
Opportunity cost	18
Profit	-8

profit is $10 million for an investment of $10 million. The return on investment, 10/10 = 100%, looks very good.

However, the income statement overlooks a significant cost of continuing the R&D project. A proper evaluation of performance should consider the alternative uses of Luna's investment funds. Specifically, the scientist is willing to sell her drug, which would be just as profitable, to Luna Biotech for $2 million.

The income statement, as conventionally presented, does not present the revenues and costs from alternative courses of action. Table 7.2 presents an expanded income statement that explicitly shows the alternatives. This makes it very clear that Luna should cancel its own R&D and buy the scientist's drug.

Identifying Opportunity Cost

By commencing its own R&D, Luna forgoes the opportunity to buy the scientist's drug, which would yield a profit of $18 million. The **opportunity cost** of the current course of action is what must be forgone from the best alternative course of action. In Luna's case, there is only one alternative to its own R&D and the opportunity cost is $18 million.

> **Opportunity cost:** What must be forgone from the best alternative course of action.

We can apply the concept of opportunity cost to present the revenues and costs of continuing the R&D project in another way. Following equation (7.1), this method includes opportunity costs among the costs of the business. Table 7.3 presents a single income statement, showing both the R&D expense and the opportunity cost. The (economic) profit from commencing R&D is -$8 million, which is a loss. This approach leads to the same decision as in Table 7.2, which explicitly shows the two alternative courses of action.

So, there are two ways to uncover relevant costs: explicitly consider the alternative courses of action or use the concept of opportunity cost. When applied correctly, both approaches lead to the correct decision.

In Luna's case, there is one alternative to the existing course of action. Where there is more than one alternative, the explicit approach still works well. The opportunity cost approach, however, becomes more complicated: first identify the best of the alternatives, and then charge the profit contribution from that alternative as the opportunity cost of the current course of action.

Conventional methods of cost accounting focus on the costs of the course of action that management has adopted. They do not consider the revenues and costs of alternative courses of action; hence, they ignore costs that are relevant but do not involve cash outlays. One reason for these omissions is that alternative courses of action and opportunity costs change with the circumstances and hence are more difficult to measure and verify. Conventional methods of cost accounting focus on easily verifiable costs, and so overlook opportunity costs.

PROGRESS CHECK 7A

If the scientist demands $12 million for her drug, what is Luna's opportunity cost of commencing R&D and what is the right decision?

FREE LUNCH: DAVID HOCKNEY VERSUS WARREN BUFFET

The following story is apocryphal. The billionaire investor, Warren Buffet, and the famous artist, David Hockney, had lunch at the Smith & Wollensky restaurant. At the end of a fine meal, David Hockney reached for the bill: "Let me pay. I'll write a personal check, draw a few squiggles, and sign it. The manager won't ever cash it. She will display it as a work of art. And we'll have a free lunch."

Warren Buffet would not agree. "No, allow me to write a personal check. Remember, the name Warren Buffet is good as gold. The manager won't cash my check. She can use it just like money and our lunch will be free."

Who was right? The correct answer is that it was neither. By drawing a few squiggles, David Hockney was adding to the world's stock of his works. The increase in the supply would reduce the price that he could get for future works. David Hockney would not get a free lunch – he was bartering a picture for a lunch.

Warren Buffet was also wrong. Each check that he wrote would add to his stock of debts and, ultimately, reduced his creditworthiness. He could not issue an unlimited number of checks. So, by creating a check, Warren Buffet was exchanging a lunch for a reduction in his creditworthiness. In believing that they could get a free lunch, both David Hockney and Warren Buffet overlooked opportunity cost.

Opportunity Cost of Capital

Conventional accounting methods require the expensing of interest payments but do not require the expensing of expected dividends. Consequently, a business that is partly financed by debt will appear to be "less profitable" than an otherwise identical business that is completely financed by equity. Indeed, many loss-making businesses have returned to profit by persuading their creditors to convert their loans to shares.

However, from a managerial perspective, equity capital is not costless; it has an opportunity cost. The shareholders of a business would like management to earn a rate of return on equity that at least matches the return from other investments with the same risk profile. Businesses that evaluate performance in terms of accounting profit will tend to be biased in favor of capital-intensive activities.

The appropriate mix between debt and equity as sources of investment funds is a deep and complicated issue of corporate finance. It is beyond the scope of a managerial economics book. Our point here is that a complete measure of business performance should take account of the opportunity cost of equity capital.

One way to evaluate business performance without distortion by debt–equity capital structure is EBITDA, which is earnings before interest, taxes, depreciation, and amortization. As EBITDA does not deduct interest, it is not affected by the debt–equity capital structure. Hence, evaluation will be neutral with respect to capital intensity.

3. Transfer Pricing

As introduced in Chapter 6, a **transfer price** is the price for the sale of an item within an organization. Suppose that Luna Biotech comprises two divisions – manufacturing and marketing. The manufacturing division produces drugs by cell and tissue culture for the marketing division which sells the drugs to hospitals and clinics. How should it price the cultures?

Transfer price: The price for the sale of an item within an organization.

Figure 7.2 shows the manufacturing division's marginal cost of culturing a batch of drugs. It also shows the marketing division's marginal benefit from the culture, which reflects the additional profit generated by one more batch of drugs. Luna's overall profit would be maximized at a quantity of 16,000 batches per month, where the marketing division's marginal benefit equals the manufacturing division's marginal cost.

Suppose that Luna sets the transfer price at $2,000 per batch, and allows the marketing division to buy as many batches as it wants at that price. Comparing its marginal benefit with the transfer price, the marketing division will buy 16,000 batches per month, which is exactly the quantity that maximizes Luna's overall profit.

Generally, the organization will maximize its entire profit by setting the transfer price of an internally produced input equal to its marginal cost. Equivalently, the

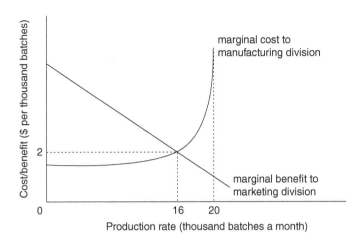

FIGURE 7.2 Transfer price.

Notes: Luna's manufacturing division has a maximum capacity of 20,000 batches a month. Luna maximizes its overall profit at a production rate of 16,000 batches a month, where the manufacturing division's marginal cost equals the marketing division's marginal benefit.

profit-maximizing transfer price is the marginal cost of the input. Recall that the marginal cost is the change in total cost due to the production of an additional unit. There are two important special cases, which we discuss below.

> **Profit-maximizing transfer price:** The marginal cost of the input.

Perfectly Competitive Market

One special case is where there is a perfectly competitive market for the input. We discussed this case in Chapter 6 when considering decentralized management. Rather than measure the marginal cost, it is simpler to set the transfer price equal to the market price. In a perfectly competitive market, a profit-maximizing business would produce the input at a rate where its marginal cost equals the market price. Hence, the transfer price (set at the market price) will also be the marginal cost.

Full Capacity

The other special case is where the (upstream) division that supplies the input is operating at full capacity. Then the marginal cost of the input is not well defined. For instance, referring to Figure 7.2, if Luna's manufacturing division is producing at a rate of 20,000 batches a month, the marginal cost curve is vertical and hence the marginal cost of a chip is not defined.

In this case, the transfer price should be set equal to the opportunity cost of the input, which is the marginal benefit that the input provides to the current user. To understand why, suppose that Luna reallocates one batch away from the marketing division to an external customer. Since the manufacturing division's total production remains the same, there will be no effect on its production costs. However, the reallocation will result in an opportunity cost – the reduction in profit for the marketing division.

To ensure that the alternative use of the batch raises overall profit, the transfer price should be set equal to the marketing division's marginal benefit from that batch. The alternative user will only buy the batch if the benefit exceeds the transfer price, and hence only if its benefit exceeds the marketing division's benefit. Accordingly, this rule will maximize the profit of the entire organization.

> **PROGRESS CHECK 7B**
>
> How should an organization set the transfer price for an internally produced input when: (i) the market for the input is competitive; and (ii) production of the input is at full capacity?

4. Sunk Costs

Since conventional accounting statements do not present alternative courses of action, they may fail to reveal costs which are important to effective business decisions. Another shortcoming of conventional accounting statements is that they present some costs which are not relevant to effective business decisions and should be ignored.

Sunk cost: Cost that has been committed and cannot be avoided.

As introduced in Chapter 4, a **sunk cost** is a cost that has been committed and so cannot be avoided. Since sunk costs cannot be avoided, they are not relevant to business decisions and managers should ignore them.

To appreciate the concept of sunk costs and why they should be ignored, let us slightly modify the example of Luna Biotech. Suppose that Luna had agreed to pay $10 million to an external contractor for the R&D to develop the new drug. The new drug is expected to generate a profit contribution of $20 million.

Meanwhile, the independent scientist has sold her drug to a competing manufacturer, which has filed a patent, and will soon commence sales. Faced with this competition, Luna has reduced the expected profit contribution from its own drug from $20 million to $8 million. Should Luna cancel the R&D project?

Alternative Courses of Action

Table 7.4 presents a projected income statement for the R&D project. The profit contribution is $8 million for an R&D expense of $10 million. So the projected profit is –$2 million, that is, a $2 million loss for an investment of $10 million. Apparently, Luna should cancel the R&D.

However, the income statement overlooks the fact that Luna would incur a substantial part of the R&D expense even if it canceled the project. A proper

Table 7.4 Conventional income statement ($ million)

Profit contribution	8
R&D expense	10
Profit	-2

Table 7.5 Income statement showing alternatives ($ million)

	Continue R&D	Cancel R&D
Profit contribution	8	0
R&D expense	10	6
Profit	-2	-6

Table 7.6 Income statement omitting sunk costs ($ million)

	Continue R&D
Profit contribution	8
R&D expense	4
Profit	4

evaluation of the decision to continue the R&D project should consider the profit from canceling the project.

Table 7.5 lays out the revenues and costs associated with the alternative courses of action. If Luna continued with the R&D, its profit contribution would be $8 million. Subtracting the R&D expense of $10 million, Luna's profit would be –$2 million, that is, a loss.

By contrast, if Luna canceled the R&D, its profit contribution would be zero. Suppose that, if Luna cancels the R&D, it must still pay the R&D contractor $6 million. Hence, if Luna decided to cancel the R&D, its profit would be –$6 million. Evidently, Luna should continue with the R&D. Continuation yields a loss which is smaller than the loss from cancelation.

Identifying Sunk Costs

By canceling the R&D, Luna does not save the entire R&D budget of $10 million. Part has already been spent or committed, and is now sunk, and so should be ignored in any business decision. Another way in which Luna can correctly decide whether or not to continue the launch applies equation (7.1) – this uses a single income statement that omits sunk costs and includes only avoidable costs.

Table 7.6 presents this information, showing only avoidable costs rather than cash outlays. The profit contribution is $8 million. The avoidable cost of the R&D project is just $4 million. If Luna continues with the R&D, it will earn an (economic) profit of $4 million. Accordingly, the correct decision is to continue with the R&D.

We have shown two ways of dealing with sunk costs: explicitly consider the alternative courses of action or remove all sunk costs from the income statement. When applied correctly, both approaches lead to the same business decision.

In Luna's case, there is one alternative to the existing course of action. Where there is more than one alternative, the explicit approach still works well. The sunk cost approach, however, becomes more complicated. Which costs are sunk depends on the alternative at hand. Accordingly, it is easier to consider the alternative courses of action explicitly.

Conventional methods of cost accounting focus on the cash outlays associated with the course of action that management has adopted. These methods report all costs that involve cash outlays, even sunk costs. To make effective business decisions, managers must look beyond conventional accounting statements and ignore sunk costs.

Commitments and Planning Horizon

The extent of sunk costs depends on two factors: past commitments and the planning horizon. Suppose that Luna Biotech's contract with the external R&D provider specifies six months' notice of termination. Then, from the current standpoint, the R&D expenditure is sunk for a six-month planning horizon but not beyond.

If Luna's contract were different, the sunk cost would also be different. Suppose that the contract specifies only three months' notice of termination. Then, from the current standpoint, the R&D expenditure is sunk for only the next three months. For planning beyond the third month, the expense is avoidable.

This example also illustrates how the extent to which a cost is sunk depends on the planning horizon. Generally, the longer the planning horizon, the more time there will be for past commitments to unwind and hence the greater will be management's freedom of action.

Chapter 4 distinguishes between short-run and long-run planning horizons. The short run is a time horizon in which at least one input cannot be adjusted. By contrast, the long run is a time horizon long enough that all inputs can be freely adjusted. Consequently, in a short-run planning horizon there will be some sunk costs, while in a long-run horizon there will be no sunk costs.

Strategic Implications

Generally, managers should ignore sunk costs and consider only avoidable costs. Sunk costs, once incurred, are not relevant for investment, pricing, or any other business decision. Managers who consider sunk costs may stumble into serious mistakes.

If a substantial portion of costs are sunk, then the avoidable costs are relatively low. For the participation decision, this implies that the break-even revenue will be relatively low. The business should continue in operation even with relatively low revenues – provided that the revenues cover the avoidable costs.

For the extent decision (how much to produce, at what scale to operate), substantial sunk costs may imply that marginal costs will be relatively low. To that extent, the business should price relatively low and aim to serve larger demand.

From a prospective viewpoint, managers should be very careful before committing to costs that will become sunk, since such commitments cannot be reversed. In Chapter 10, we discuss how businesses can exploit investments in sunk costs as a way to strategically influence the behavior of competitors.

PROGRESS CHECK 7C

Suppose that, if Luna canceled the R&D contract, the R&D expenditure would be $1 million. What is Luna's cost of continuing R&D and what is the right decision?

DAMPIER–BUNBURY PIPELINE: YOUR LOSS, MY PROFIT

The 1,530-kilometer Dampier–Bunbury pipeline transports natural gas from the vast North Western Shelf gas fields into the state of Western Australia. The pipeline is the state's largest. In 1998, the state sold the pipeline to Epic Energy, a joint venture of US companies El Paso and Dominion Resources, for A$2.4 billion. Epic financed the purchase with A$1.85 billion of loans from a consortium of 28 banks.

The investment, however, did not perform to expectation, and, in October 2003, Epic decided to sell the pipeline. Epic blamed the gas regulator for imposing unacceptably low tariffs. However, Australian Competition and Consumer Commissioner Edward Willett remarked that Epic had overpaid for the pipeline by A$1 billion.

In April 2004, with Epic's pipeline company failing to meet its debt obligations, the consortium of banks forced the company into receivership. In August, the receivers named a consortium led by Diversified Utility and Energy Trusts (DUET) as their preferred buyer at a price of A$1.86 billion. The consortium also included Western Australia's largest gas retailer, Alinta, and the pipeline's largest customer, aluminum manufacturer, Alcoa, each with a 20% share. DUET Chief Executive Peter Barry remarked that "with the appropriate acquisition structure" the pipeline would yield very attractive returns.

How could the pipeline be unprofitable for Epic Energy while being "attractive" to DUET? One possible reason is that Epic (and its bankers) would not ignore the sunk cost of Epic's investment. If, as Willett said, Epic had overpaid by A$1 billion, then the true market value of the pipeline was A$1.86 billion with A$1.85 billion of debt outstanding, and the net equity of the pipeline was just A$10 million.

Sources: "Receivers looming for Epic Energy," *Sydney Morning Herald*, April 12, 2004; "Joint venture to buy Australian pipeline," *International Herald Tribune*, September 1, 2004.

5. Economies of Scale

For effective business decisions, managers must identify all relevant costs and appreciate how those costs vary with business decisions – specifically, scale, scope, and experience. A fundamental issue for any organization is whether to operate on a small scale or large scale.

Large-scale production means mass marketing and relatively low pricing; by contrast, small-scale production is associated with niche marketing and relatively high pricing. So, how do costs depend on the scale or rate of production? (We shall treat the *scale* and *rate* of production as synonymous.)

To address this question, recall the distinction between fixed and variable costs introduced in Chapter 4. The *fixed cost* is the cost of inputs that do not change with the production rate. So the fixed cost supports the production of multiple units of output. The *variable cost* is the cost of inputs that change with the production rate. The distinction between fixed and variable costs applies in the short and long run.

Fixed and Variable Costs in the Long Run

To illustrate the distinction between long-run fixed and variable costs, consider the production of a newspaper, the *Daily Globe*. The production process begins when the printing department receives a photographic negative containing the text of the forthcoming edition. The negative is "burned" on to an aluminum plate, which is then mounted on electric-powered printing presses. The presses can be fed a continuous flow of newsprint and ink to produce the newspaper.

Table 7.7 reports the daily expenses for production rates up to 90,000 copies a day, in the four categories of labor, printing press, ink and paper, and electric power. Table 7.8 assigns each of the costs of newspaper production into the two categories of fixed and variable costs.

Table 7.7 Daily expenses for newspaper production

Daily production (thousands)	Labor ($)	Printing press ($)	Ink and paper ($)	Electric power ($)	Total ($)
0	5,000	1,000	0	200	6,200
10	5,000	1,500	1,200	300	8,000
20	5,000	2,000	2,400	400	9,800
30	5,000	2,500	3,600	500	11,600
40	5,000	3,000	4,800	600	13,400
50	5,000	3,500	6,000	700	15,200
60	5,000	4,000	7,200	800	17,000
70	5,000	4,500	8,400	900	18,800
80	5,000	5,000	9,600	1,000	20,600
90	5,000	5,500	10,800	1,100	22,400

Table 7.8 Analysis of fixed and variable costs

Daily production (thousands)	Fixed cost ($)	Variable cost ($)	Total cost ($)	Marginal cost ($)	Average fixed cost ($)	Average variable cost ($)	Average cost ($)
0	6,200	0	6,200				
10	6,200	1,800	8,000	0.18	0.62	0.18	0.80
20	6,200	3,600	9,800	0.18	0.31	0.18	0.49
30	6,200	5,400	11,600	0.18	0.21	0.18	0.39
40	6,200	7,200	13,400	0.18	0.16	0.18	0.34
50	6,200	9,000	15,200	0.18	0.12	0.18	0.30
60	6,200	10,800	17,000	0.18	0.10	0.18	0.28
70	6,200	12,600	18,800	0.18	0.09	0.18	0.27
80	6,200	14,400	20,600	0.18	0.08	0.18	0.26
90	6,200	16,200	22,400	0.18	0.07	0.18	0.25

Production involves a fixed cost of $6,200. Indeed, a substantial fixed cost is a distinctive feature of the newspaper industry. The industry has given the name *first copy cost* to the fixed cost. It is the cost of producing just one copy a day.

By contrast, as the print run increases from 0 to 90,000 copies a day, the variable cost rises from nothing to $16,200. By distinguishing between fixed and variable costs, the management of a business can understand which cost elements will be affected by changes in the scale of production.

Marginal and Average Costs

Applying the analysis of fixed and variable costs, we can see how costs depend on the scale of production. Chapter 4 introduced the concepts of marginal and average costs. The marginal cost is the change in total cost due to the production of an additional unit. The average (or unit) cost is the total cost divided by the production rate or scale.

Let us study the marginal and average costs of production of the *Daily Globe*. Table 7.8 shows that, as the print run increases from 0 to 90,000 copies a day, the total cost of production increases from $6,200 to $22,400.

The marginal cost of the first 10,000 copies is $8,000 − $6,200 = $1,800, or $1,800/10,000 = 18 cents per copy. The marginal cost is constant at 18 cents at all scales of production. Recall from Chapter 4 that the marginal cost equals the rate of change of the variable cost. For the *Daily Globe*, the average variable cost remains constant at 18 cents per copy. Hence, the marginal cost is also constant at 18 cents per copy.

Dividing total cost by the scale of production, we can obtain the average cost. The average cost drops from 80 cents at a scale of 10,000 copies a day to 25 cents at 90,000 copies a day. To understand why the average cost decreases with the scale of production, recall that the average cost is the average fixed cost plus the

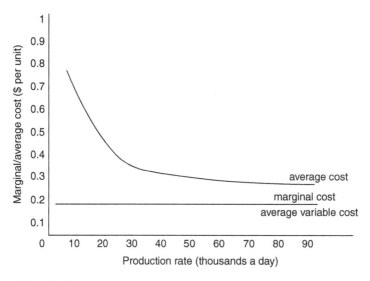

FIGURE 7.3 Economies of scale.

Notes: The marginal and average variable costs are identical and do not change with the scale of production. The average cost decreases with the scale of production.

average variable cost. The average fixed cost is the fixed cost divided by the production scale. With a larger scale of production, the fixed cost will be spread over more units of production and the average fixed cost will be lower.

The average variable cost is constant at 18 cents per copy. Therefore, the average cost declines as the scale of production increases. Figure 7.3 graphs the marginal, average variable, and average costs against the scale of production. The marginal and average variable cost curves are identical and flat. The average cost curve slopes downward.

A business for which the average cost decreases with the scale of production is

> **Economies of scale**
> (increasing returns to
> scale): Average cost
> decreases with the scale
> of production.

said to exhibit **economies of scale** or **increasing returns to scale**. With economies of scale, the marginal cost will be lower than the average cost. Since the marginal unit of production costs less than the average, any increase in production will reduce the average. Therefore, the average cost curve slopes downward.

Intuitive Factors

The basic reason for economies of scale is either fixed inputs, that is, inputs that can support any scale of production, or inputs that increase less than proportionately with the scale of production. Consider fixed inputs. At a larger scale, the cost of the fixed inputs will be spread over more units of production, so that the average fixed cost will be lower. If the average variable cost is constant or does not increase very much with the scale of production, then the average cost will fall with the scale.

Any business with a strong element of composition, design, or invention has substantial fixed inputs. For instance, the cost of developing a new pharmaceutical is fixed (with respect to the quantity produced). Regardless of the production rate, the development cost will remain the same. Similarly, the cost of preparing the computer code for a software package is fixed. It is the same whether the publishers produces 1 million copies or only one. Accordingly, there are strong economies of scale in these industries. Indeed, for pharmaceuticals, software, and other knowledge-intensive industries, the marginal production cost is tiny compared with the average cost.

The other basic reason for economies of scale is inputs that increase less than proportionately with the scale of production. This explains scale economies in transportation. To double the capacity of a tanker or pipeline requires less than double the material (to be precise, the proportion is $\sqrt{2}$).

PROGRESS CHECK 7D

Using the data in Table 7.8, draw the average fixed cost in Figure 7.3.

Diseconomies of Scale

A business where the average cost increases with the scale of production is said to exhibit **diseconomies of scale** or **decreasing returns to scale**. A business will have diseconomies of scale if the fixed cost is not substantial and the variable cost rises more than proportionately with the scale of production.

> **Diseconomies of scale (decreasing returns to scale):** Average cost increases with scale of production.

To illustrate diseconomies of scale, consider a hairdressing salon. The salon does not involve a significant fixed cost. The main variable cost is labor. To the extent that additional workers are less productive, the cost of labor rises more than proportionately with the scale of production.

The average cost is the average fixed cost plus the average variable cost. For the salon, the average cost initially decreases with the scale because of the decreasing average fixed cost. Since the variable cost rises more than proportionately with the scale of production, the average variable cost is increasing.

Hence, there is a scale at which the decreasing average fixed cost is outweighed by the increasing average variable cost. Then the average cost reaches a minimum and rises with further increases in the scale. The average cost curve is U-shaped.

Strategic Implications

The relation between average cost and the scale of production influences the structure of the industry. If there are economies of scale, a business operating on a relatively large scale will achieve a lower average cost than smaller-scale competitors. Large-scale production means mass marketing and relatively low pricing.

An industry where individual producers have economies of scale tends to be concentrated, with a few producers serving the entire market. There are strong economies of scale in providing broadband service. The essential input is the network. With the network in place, the provider can serve additional customers at relatively low marginal cost. Owing to the strong economies of scale, most communities are served by a small number of broadband providers. In Chapter 8, we analyze the extreme case of a monopoly, where there is just one producer.

> In an industry with economies of scale, large producers dominate and the industry will be concentrated.

By contrast, in an industry with diseconomies of scale, the management should aim at a relatively small scale. Small-scale production is associated with niche marketing and relatively high pricing. Industries where individual producers have diseconomies of scale tend to be fragmented. The extreme case is the model of perfect competition in Chapter 5, where there are many producers, none of whom can influence the market demand.

Sunk and Fixed Costs

In popular as well as professional parlance, the term "fixed cost" is often used in two different senses: a cost that cannot be avoided once incurred (properly called *sunk cost*); and the cost of inputs that do not change with the production rate (properly called *fixed cost*).

Referring to Figure 7.1, it is important to distinguish sunk from fixed costs because the two concepts have very different implications for business decisions. Managers should ignore sunk costs that have been incurred, as these cannot be avoided. By contrast, the presence of fixed costs tends to give rise to economies of scale, and so management should aim to operate on a large scale. (The confusion between the two concepts arises because economics tends to assume that, in the short run, all fixed costs are sunk.)

Some fixed costs become sunk once incurred. Consider, for instance, a manufacturer of sports shoes. The manufacturer must pay for the design of the shoes. The design can support the production of any number of shoes. So, the cost of *design* is a fixed cost. Moreover, once the manufacturer has committed to the design, the cost cannot be avoided. Hence, once incurred, the design cost is a sunk cost.

Sunk costs, however, are not fixed in the sense of supporting any scale of operations. Having designed the shoes, the manufacturer needs one set of molds (left and right) to begin production of shoes. The cost of making the molds is sunk, once incurred. If the demand for the shoes is sufficiently high, the manufacturer might have to invest in a second production line. Then it will need a second set of molds, which requires an additional investment. So, the cost of making molds is not a fixed cost. Rather, it depends on the scale of production.

Not all fixed costs become sunk. Wireless telecommunications providers need a government license to operate on the electromagnetic spectrum. Supposing that the license fee is a lump sum, the fee is a fixed cost of providing service. However, if the license is transferable, the fee need not be sunk. Only the part of the fee that cannot be recovered from resale is sunk.

ECONOMIES OF SCALE IN TANKER CONSTRUCTION

In 1833, Marcus Samuel opened a shop in London to sell seashells. While procuring shells in the Caspian Sea, Marcus Samuel's son spotted a new business opportunity – the export of kerosene from Russia to the Far East. This business grew into Shell Transport and Trading.

Historically, oil had been transported in wooden barrels on cargo ships. In 1892, Marcus Samuel Junior conceived the idea of building a ship in the shape of a tank. This became the world's first oil tanker.

An oil tanker is like a pipeline in the sense that its capacity increases with the cross-sectional area, and hence the square of the radius of the cross section, but the material and construction costs increase with the circumference, and hence the radius of the cross section.

Figure 7.4 shows the price of new tankers per deadweight ton for four standard tanker sizes. Clearly, larger tankers are cheaper, presumably because they are less costly to build.

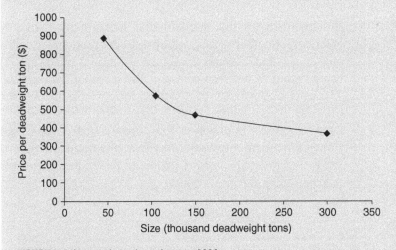

FIGURE 7.4 New tanker prices: January 2006.

Sources: Shell Oil Company, "Shell heritage," www.shellenergy.com, September 7, 2004; *Lloyd's Shipping Economist*, February 2004; Platou Report 2005, www.platou.com.

AIRBUS: INCREASING PRODUCTION

In March 2011, Airbus announced that it would raise production of the A320 family from 34 to 36 units per month. Subsequently, Boeing announced a progressive increase in production of the 737 from 31.5 units to 42 units per month.

How would these changes affect the costs of production? The impact of higher rates of production on average costs depends on the proportion of fixed and variable costs and the impact on average variable costs. Both Airbus and Boeing depend on external contractors for many essential components, including avionics, composites, and titanium parts.

Opinions differ on the ability of suppliers to increase the rate of production, and so the impact on the average variable costs of Airbus and Boeing. Robert P. Barker, President of Parker Aerospace, stressed: "It's very manageable for us to take on these added quantities in our factories . . . . We can go from 35 actuators a month to 42 pretty easily over a period of time."

By contrast, Donald Majcher, Vice President at the Ohio Aerospace Institute in Cleveland, Ohio questioned: "In recent years you've seen a consolidation in the supply base . . . . The question is, how much of an increase can it now support?"

Source: "Can suppliers keep up with aircraft orders?" *Aviation Week*, July 7, 2011.

6. Economies of Scope

> **Economies of scope:** The total cost of production is lower with joint than it is with separate production.

> **Diseconomies of scope:** The total cost of production is higher with joint than it is with separate production.

Besides scale, another fundamental strategic issue for any business is whether to offer many different products or focus on a single item. The answer to this question depends in part on the relation between cost and the scope of production. There are **economies of scope** across two products if the total cost of production is lower when two products are produced together than when they are produced separately. Conversely, there are **diseconomies of scope** across two products if the total cost of production is higher when two products are produced together.

Joint Cost

Consider how costs depend on the scope of production through the following example. Suppose that the management of the *Daily Globe* is considering whether to launch an afternoon paper, the *Afternoon Globe*. Table 7.9 shows three categories of expenses required to produce the *Daily Globe* and the *Afternoon Globe*, assuming a print run of 50,000 copies a day for each paper.

Table 7.9 Expenses for two products

Organization	Daily production ('000)	Labor ($)	Printing press ($)	Ink, paper, electric power ($)	Total cost ($)
Separate production					
Daily Globe	50	5,000	3,500	6,700	15,200
Afternoon Globe	50	5,000	3,500	6,700	15,200
Combined production	100	10,000	3,500	13,400	26,900

If the two newspapers are printed in separate facilities, then the total production cost is $15,200 a day for each paper, or $30,400 for the two papers. If, however, both newspapers are printed in the same facility, then the total cost of producing the two newspapers is $26,900. The cost of producing both newspapers in the same facility is 11.5% lower than if they were produced separately.

What explains the difference in cost? The key is that the same printing press can be used in the night to print the morning paper, and in the late morning to print the afternoon paper.

To produce the *Daily Globe* by itself, the publisher must spend $3,500 a day on the printing press. Likewise, to produce the *Afternoon Globe* by itself, the publisher must spend $3,500 a day on the printing press. To produce both newspapers from the same facility, however, the publisher spends $3,500 only once.

The expense of the printing press is a *joint cost* of the morning and afternoon newspapers. The **joint cost** is the cost of inputs that does not change with the scope of production. The joint cost supports the production of multiple products. Economies of scope arise wherever there are significant joint costs.

> **Joint cost:** The cost of inputs that does not change with the scope of production.

Strategic Implications

Where two products are linked by economies of scope, it will be relatively cheaper to produce the products together. Then a supplier of both items can achieve a relatively lower cost than competitors that specialize in one or the other product. Subject to conditions of market demand and competition, the management should offer both products. Multi-product suppliers dominate industries with economies of scope.

Broadband service and cable TV provide an important example of scope economies. Broadband service can be provided through a wire network to potential subscribers. Similarly, cable TV requires a wire network connecting potential subscribers. In this case, the cost of building and maintaining the network is a significant joint cost. Consequently, there are very substantial economies of scope across the broadband and cable TV businesses. Combined providers of broadband and cable TV service can deliver the services at relatively lower cost than specialized services.

Economies of scope in advertising and promotion are essential for the strategy of *brand extension* in marketing. When Sony spends $1 million to advertise Sony, it promotes the sales of every Sony-branded product, including computers, TV sets, and game consoles. Accordingly, the expenditure on advertising a brand is a joint

> In an industry with economies of scope, businesses supply multiple products.

cost of marketing all the products marked with the brand. This joint cost gives rise to economies of scope in advertising and promotion. Through a brand extension, the owner of an established brand can introduce new products at relatively lower cost than a competitor with no established brand.

Diseconomies of Scope

There are diseconomies of scope across two products if the total cost of production is higher when the two items are produced together than when they are produced separately. Diseconomies of scope arise where joint costs are not significant and making one product increases the cost of making the other in the same facility.

Where diseconomies of scope prevail, it will be relatively cheaper to produce the various items separately. Hence, specialized producers can achieve relatively lower costs than competitors that combine production. In such circumstances, the management should aim for a narrow scope and focus on one product.

PROGRESS CHECK 7E

Referring to Table 7.9, suppose that, with combined production, the expenses on the printing press were $7,000 a day. Are there economies or diseconomies of scope?

BANKING AND INSURANCE: DISECONOMIES OF SCOPE?

During the 1990s and into the early 2000s, banks and insurers worldwide rushed to merge. In 1998, Citibank combined with the insurer, Travelers Group, in one of the world's largest mergers to form Citigroup. In 2001, the German insurer, Allianz, acquired Dresdner Bank.

The French *bancassurance* model promised higher profits through boosting demand and economies of scope in service provision. The underlying theory was that the same institution could provide clients with a wide range of services and products, including loans, deposits, investments, and insurance.

However, in reality, the economies of scope were difficult to realize. Consumers make deposits and use many other banking services on a routine basis. By contrast, investments and insurance are relatively big-ticket items which consumers buy infrequently. So marketing and supporting investments and insurance requires different skills than those needed for banking services.

In 2002, just four years after the merger, Citigroup spun off Travelers Property and Casualty insurance to its shareholders. In 2008, Allianz sold Dresdner to Commerzbank for €5.5 billion.

7. Experience Curve

We have discussed how the cost of production varies with the scale and scope of production within any time period. The cost of production may also vary with experience – as measured by accumulated production – over time.

Experience matters especially in industries characterized by relatively short production runs. In aerospace manufacturing, as engineers and workers gain experience in production, they devise new ways to reduce cost, including developing better tools and faster processes. Even in semiconductor manufacturing, a large-scale process, experience matters as the rate of defects falls with accumulated production. In surgery, with accumulated experience, the medical professionals become more proficient individually and as teams.

Accordingly, the unit cost of production falls with accumulated experience, which motivates the concept of the *experience curve*, which is also called the *learning curve*. Typically, experience is measured by cumulative production, hence the **experience curve** shows how the unit (average) cost of production falls with cumulative production over time.

> **Experience curve:**
> The unit (average) cost of production falls with cumulative production over time.

Figure 7.5 illustrates an experience curve, where the unit (average) cost of production is indexed to 100 for the first unit produced. The unit cost falls most sharply with the initial units of cumulative production. Assuming a 20% cost reduction for every doubling of cumulative production (that is, a learning percentage of 80%), by the fourth unit of cumulative production the unit cost drops to 64, by the 32nd unit to 32.77, etc.

The learning percentage determines the rate at which the unit cost falls with cumulative production. The lower the learning percentage, the higher the rate

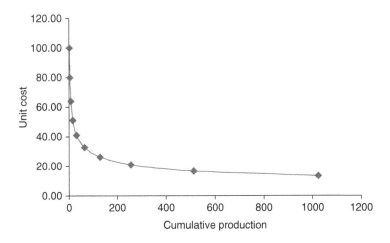

FIGURE 7.5 Experience curve.

Notes: The experience curve shows how the unit cost of production falls with cumulative production over time. An 80% learning percentage is shown, and the unit cost of production is indexed to 100 for the first unit produced.

of cost reduction from doubling cumulative output. The learning percentage depends on the particular technology and process of manufacturing, and so varies with product and industry.

The experience curve is distinct from economies of scale. The experience curve relates cumulative production over *preceding periods* to production costs in one period. By contrast, economies of scale relate the scale of production within one period to production costs in the *same period*.

Strategic Implications

In any industry where production costs are subject to a substantial experience curve relative to cumulative sales, it is crucial to forecast cumulative production accurately. Accurate forecasting of cumulative production is crucial for both planning investments and setting prices. The challenge is especially great to the extent that sales, and hence cumulative production, depend on pricing and competitors' strategies.

For instance, referring to Figure 7.5, if the manufacturer plans for cumulative production of 500 units, its unit (average) cost would be about 17. Hence, it can break even with a price of 17 or more. By contrast, if the manufacturer plans for cumulative production of 100, the unit cost would be about 29, which is 70% higher than with cumulative production of 500 units.

The experience curve also motivates a strategy of cutting price to increase sales and so gain more cumulative production. The business that gets ahead in cumulative production can then outcompete competitors on costs. So, the experience curve can justify a strategy of competing for market share.

PROGRESS CHECK 7F

On Figure 7.5, draw a new experience curve with a smaller reduction (lower than 20%) in unit cost for every doubling of cumulative production.

BOMBARDIER: WAITING FOR LUFTHANSA

The cost of aircraft manufacturing is strongly affected by accumulated experience. Airbus, Boeing, and other airplane manufacturers must set prices for aircraft based on projections of forecast cumulative sales. If the sales fall short of target, unit costs will be higher than planned, and the manufacturer may incur a substantial loss on the plane.

Bombardier is well established in the production of regional jets. Long aspiring to expand into large jets, it announced the CSeries in 2004. Bombardier estimated the cost of development to be $2.5 billion, with part of the cost being born by the governments of Canada and the United Kingdom, and suppliers.

Much of the development cost would be sunk, once incurred. In January 2006, with no significant orders, Bombardier scaled back plans and reallocated resources to produce the CRJ1000 regional jet.

Then, in July 2008, Bombardier secured a letter of interest for 60 CSeries planes, including 30 options, from Deutsche Lufthansa. Bombardier then committed to development, with commercial service to begin in 2013. Given the experience curve and that the costs of development would be substantially sunk once incurred, Bombardier was prudent in delaying commitment until securing a big order.

Source: Richard Tortoriello, "Aerospace & defense," *Standard & Poor's Industry Surveys*, February 10, 2011; "Bombardier jet strains to take off," *Wall Street Journal Online*, June 16, 2011; "Bombardier CSeries," Wikipedia (accessed July 25, 2011).

8. Bounded Rationality

Being human, managers, like consumers, are subject to bounded rationality in decision-making. In decisions with respect to costs, managers are particularly prone to status quo bias, the sunk-cost fallacy, and what I call the "fixed-cost fallacy." The techniques of this chapter are even more pertinent to the extent that managers fall prey to these biases in their costing decisions.

- *Status quo bias*. Human beings tend to be biased toward the status quo, perhaps because of inertia. To the extent that the status quo involves opportunity costs, the status quo bias reinforces any systematic failure to account for opportunity costs. The result is an even stronger bias toward continuing with the status quo, rather than taking an alternative course of action, which might actually be more profitable.
- *Sunk-cost fallacy*. One human response to sunk costs is to rationalize the sunk costs by increasing usage or consumption. An (in)famous example is the Anglo-French supersonic airliner, Concorde. Having invested heavily, Britain and France continued to pour additional resources into the project long after it was clear that Concorde was not commercially viable. Their actions exemplified the sunk-cost fallacy. This human tendency to rationalize costs that are already sunk by additional expenditures results in *over*investment.
- *Fixed-cost fallacy*. Related to the sunk-cost fallacy, but resulting in the opposite outcome, is what might be called the "fixed-cost fallacy." This is the tendency, which is common, for managers to treat fixed costs as variable. The mistake is to set a target production rate and allocate the fixed cost to each unit of production. Essentially, this allocation increases the perceived variable cost and so results in *under*production relative to the profit-maximizing level.

KEY TAKEAWAYS

- For effective decision-making, consider alternative courses of action, take account of opportunity costs and ignore sunk costs.

- The opportunity cost is what must be forgone from the best alternative course of action.
- Businesses financed by equity should take account of the opportunity cost of equity capital.
- To maximize profit, set the transfer price equal to the marginal cost of the input.
- Commit to sunk costs with caution as they cannot be reversed.
- Economies of scale arise from fixed costs, which support the production of multiple units of output.
- With economies of scale, businesses should produce on a large scale and the industry will tend to be concentrated.
- Economies of scope arise from joint costs, which support production of multiple products.
- With economies of scope, businesses should produce multiple products.
- The experience curve shows that unit (average) cost of production falls with cumulative production over time at a rate according to the learning percentage.
- With the experience curve, it is important to forecast cumulative production and the business can gain from increasing market share.
- Managers should take care to avoid behavioral biases in decisions with respect to costs.

REVIEW QUESTIONS

1. A salesman buys lunch for a potential client. Why is this lunch *not* free for the client?
2. A social enterprise provides free primary school education in West Africa. It charges fees to just cover costs. The enterprise is completely financed by European charities. Compare the school's value added (according to the definition in Chapter 1) and EBITDA.
3. There is a perfectly competitive market for lumber. How much should Saturn's residential development group pay the building materials division for lumber?
4. Luna Biotech's manufacturing division uses a unique patent-protected process to culture drugs. Presently, the division is operating at full capacity. How should it price its services to Luna's marketing division?
5. Mercury Transport is wholly equity-financed, while Jupiter Trucking has borrowed from banks to finance its business. The two businesses are otherwise identical. Jupiter is losing money, while Mercury is profitable. Compare the two businesses in terms of EBITDA.
6. "Our costs are very high because of the huge pensions of our retirees." Are the pensions of retired employees relevant for forward-looking business decisions?
7. In which situation are sunk costs more significant: (a) Tre Stagioni, which has a permanent staff of two chefs and five waiters; or (b) Campus Deli, which relies mainly on part-time workers, hired on a monthly basis?
8. The most substantial cost in family medicine practice is human resources. To treat twice as many patients, a clinic will probably need twice as many doctors, nurses, and other professional staff. Does this business have economies of scale?
9. Explain the difference between fixed cost and sunk cost.
10. What are the strategic implications of economies of scale?
11. Explain the difference between economies of scale and economies of scope.

12. What are the strategic implications of economies of scope?
13. Draw an experience curve with a learning percentage of 100%.
14. What are the strategic implications of the experience curve?
15. Explain the fixed-cost fallacy in the context of producing a newspaper.

DISCUSSION QUESTIONS

1. The Great Recession of 2007–2009 severely depressed world trade, the demand for tanker services, and the daily rental rate for tankers. Herbjorn Hansson, CEO of Nordic American Tanker Shipping, remarked: "Those who have a lot of debt are suffering . . . . If you're collecting $10,000 a day and you have a cash break-even of $25,000 a day, that's a $15,000 a day loss." By contrast, Hansson felt that his company was well placed to survive the downturn as it carried no debt. Its ships could make a profit with rates of $10,000 a day. (Source: "Oil tanker owners see rates fall," *Financial Times*, May 5, 2009.)
    (a) Suppose that the operating costs of a tanker are $8,000 a day, and, for a debt-financed tanker, the interest cost is $17,000 a day. Given revenues of $10,000 a day, construct a conventional income statement.
    (b) Suppose that the operating cost of a laid-up tanker is $1,500 a day. Construct an income statement showing two alternative courses of action – continuing operations and laying up the vessel. Should the tanker owner lay up the ship?
    (c) In discussing the situation of tanker owners financed by debt, what mistake did Hansson make?
    (d) By 2010, the world demand for oil and tanker rates had recovered. From a long-run perspective, tankers that are equity-financed yield higher profit than debt-financed tankers. (i) Why do equity-financed tankers yield higher profit? (ii) Explain a better way to compare the performance of equity- and debt-financed tankers.
2. Consider a distributor of luxury American and European cars in China. In January 2011, it ordered shipments of high-end BMWs from Germany at €50,000 each and Cadillac SUVs from the United States at $40,000 each. By July 2011, the Chinese yuan had depreciated by 3% from 8.93 yuan against the euro and appreciated by 2% from 6.58 yuan against the US dollar.
    (a) For purposes of pricing, what is the relevant cost of the BMWs?
    (b) For purposes of pricing, what is the relevant cost of the Cadillacs?
    (c) Use the examples in (a) and (b) to explain the concepts of opportunity cost and sunk cost.
3. Following a collapse of sales in the wake of the subprime financial crisis, the US automobile manufacturer Chrysler LLC filed for bankruptcy in April 2009. It then sold its brands and various other assets to Fiat SpA. Table 7.10 lists the estimated recovery value of Chrysler's property, plant, and equipment in the event of liquidation.
    (a) Which of the following best describes the difference between book value and estimated recovery value: (i) opportunity cost; (ii) sunk cost; or (iii) joint cost? Explain your answer.

Table 7.10 Chrysler LLC liquidation ($ million)

Assets	Book value	Recovery value	
		Low estimate	High estimate
Assembly plants	2,205	110	220
Stamping plants	1,129	113	226
Powertrain plants	3,513	352	702
Tooling	1,337	–	67
Furniture, fixtures, etc.	487	5	24

Source: Chrysler LLC, Preliminary Hypothetical Liquidation Analysis – Orderly Liquidation, January 31, 2009.

(b) Use the low and high estimates of recovery value to calculate the average recovery value.

(c) Define *specificity* as the ratio of book value less average estimated recovery value to book value, in percentage terms. Calculate the specificity of each category of assets.

(d) Explain the relation between sunk costs and specificity.

(e) Stamping equipment is heavy machinery used to produce metal parts such as car bodies. Tooling is equipment designed to produce particular models of cars. Explain why Chrysler's tooling has a higher specificity than the stamping plants.

4. Elevators generally break down at random times and for different reasons. Elevator maintenance contractors must have trained service personnel to provide routine and emergency service. Shan On Elevator, Hong Kong, has 200 service personnel to maintain 1,000 elevators.

(a) Suppose that Shan On has received a contract to maintain an additional 1,000 elevators. Do you expect that Shan On will need to double service personnel? Why or why not?

(b) Does the example in (a) illustrate economies of scale or scope?

(c) Escalators and elevators use quite different technology and parts. But many clients operate both escalators and elevators. Are there any economies of scope for a contractor to maintain both escalators and elevators?

5. Generators of electric power produce electricity in large-scale plants with capacities of hundreds of megawatts. However, when electricity is transmitted over cables, resistance causes loss of energy. The loss of energy increases with the distance of transmission.

(a) Draw a graph to illustrate the average cost of generating electricity at different scales of production (megawatt hours per month).

(b) Draw a graph to illustrate the average cost of transmitting electricity for different distances.

(c) If a producer of electricity increases the scale of generation to reduce average cost of generation, what will be the effect on the average cost of transmission?

(*Hint*: You are free to assume any data necessary to draw the curves.)

6. Airbus and Boeing dominate the large commercial jet aircraft industry. Each company manufactures jet aircraft for commercial use by passenger and cargo airlines as well as for military use by national air forces. In February 2011, Boeing won a US Air Force tender for 179 aerial refueling tankers at an estimated price of $35 billion. The Boeing tanker is based on Boeing's 767 wide-body commercial aircraft.

    (a) Which one of the following concepts best explains Boeing's adaptation of the Boeing 767 to supply an aerial tanker: (i) economies of scale; (ii) economies of scope; (iii) experience curve? Explain your answer.

    (b) Following the initial tender for 179 tankers, the US Air Force is expected to buy additional tankers. Apply relevant cost concepts to explain Boeing's advantage in competing for follow-on orders.

    (c) "The more an aircraft manufacturer spends on R&D, the higher the price that it must charge to recover its investment." Comment.

7. Punch Taverns owns over 3,500 pubs (bars) in Britain. The group borrowed heavily to grow, but was hit by a ban on smoking in bars, higher taxes on beer, and the Great Recession. In October 2014, the group negotiated with creditors to exchange £0.6 billion of debt for equity. The restructuring reduced the group's debt by a quarter to £1.8 billion and left the original shareholders with just 15% of the shares. Table 7.11 reports the group's income statement for 2014. (Sources: "Punch Taverns wins final restructuring approval," *Financial Times*, October 7, 2014; Punch Taverns PLC, Preliminary Results, August 23, 2014.)

    (a) Explain which concept of cost can justify Punch Tavern's expansion strategy.

    (b) Which items in the income statement would the restructuring affect?

    (c) How would the restructuring affect Punch Tavern's EBITDA?

    (d) If the income statement took account of the opportunity cost of equity capital, would the restructuring improve the group's financial performance?

8. In August 2004, Infineon announced a deal with Taiwan's Winbond Electronics to build a new dynamic random-access memory (DRAM) factory. Infineon executive Ralph Heinrich hoped to secure a quarter of the global DRAM market: "the fight to survive in the DRAM industry depends largely on size – since the more chips a company churns out, the lower the cost per chip." DRAMs are cut from circular wafers of semiconductors. Wafers of 300 millimeter (mm) diameter potentially yield more than twice as many DRAMs as 200 mm wafers. A 300 mm wafer fabrication facility costs more to build and set up than a

Table 7.11 Punch Taverns (£ million)

	2014
Revenue	448
Operating costs and joint venture profit	−270
EBITDA	178
Depreciation, amortization, impairment etc.	−55
Operating profit	123
Finance income and costs	−363
Profit before tax	−240

200 mm facility. (Source: "Infineon's deal with Winbond reaffirms outsourcing strategy," *Asian Wall Street Journal*, August 10, 2004.)

(a) Assume that the variable costs of manufacturing 200 mm and 300 mm wafers are the same. Explain why the economies of scale in manufacturing DRAMs from 300 mm wafers are larger than with 200 mm wafers.

(b) Infineon produces DRAMs from multiple factories, some of which are joint ventures with Taiwanese manufacturers. Does the cost per DRAM depend on the total quantity produced by the entire company or each individual factory?

(c) When a wafer fabrication facility is first commissioned, the percentage of output that meets product standards (the "yield") tends to be low. Engineers then fine-tune the manufacturing process to increase the yield. What principle of cost does this illustrate?

9. In April 2004, Boeing launched the new 787 Dreamliner with 50 firm orders from All Nippon Airways of Japan. Boeing aimed to secure 200 firm orders by December. However, by December 2004, Boeing had only 52 orders. Then Airbus introduced the A350, a derivative of the existing A330, enhanced with a new wing, more fuel-efficient engines, and other new technologies. Airbus's Chief Commercial Officer, John Leahy, predicted that the A350 would draw Boeing customers and so "put a hole in Boeing's Christmas stocking." (Source: "350: Airbus's counter-attack," *Flight International*, January 25, 2005.)

(a) Draw a timeline to mark when a manufacturer incurs the costs of development and production.

(b) How would the costs of developing the 787 Dreamliner vary with the total quantity manufactured?

(c) Referring to Figure 7.5, compare Boeing's average cost with cumulative production of 50 and of 200 units. (Note that, in Figure 7.5, the average cost is not absolute but rather indexed to 100 with production of the first unit.)

(d) Suppose that the price of a Boeing 787 is $120 million and that Boeing would just break even on the costs of development ($10 billion) and manufacturing with cumulative production of 200 units. How much would Boeing lose with cumulative production of 50 units?

You are the consultant!

Consider your organization's various lines of business. For each line of business, consider the revenues and costs from alternative uses of the resources – people, property, and funds. Is every line of business maximizing profit?

Note

1   This discussion is based, in part, on Richard Tortoriello, "Aerospace & defense," *Standard & Poor's Industry Surveys*, February 10, 2011; "Boeing likely to boost 737, 777 production rates," *ATWOnline*, March 18, 2010; "Bombardier jet strains to take off," *Wall Street Journal Online*, June 16, 2011; "Airbus and Boeing call end to 'duopoly,'" *Financial Times*, June 21, 2011; "Airbus-Boeing duopoly holds narrow-body startups at bay at Paris Air Show," *Bloomberg*, June 23, 2011.

Monopoly

1. Introduction

Atorvastatin, marketed by Pfizer under the brand name Lipitor, inhibits the liver enzyme, HMG-CoA reductase, and so reduces the level of low-density lipoprotein cholesterol in the human body. In 2010, Lipitor was Pfizer's best-selling drug, with sales revenue of $10.7 billion, or 15.7% of the company's total revenue.[1]

Lipitor faced competition from other statins – particularly simvastatin. In June 2006, Merck's US patent on simvastatin expired and Merck cut the price of its branded simvastatin, Zocor. Moreover, Pfizer's US patent on atorvastatin was initially due to expire in June 2011.

In 2003, the Indian generic drug manufacturer, Ranbaxy Laboratories, filed an Abbreviated New Drug Application (ANDA) with the US Food and Drug Administration (FDA) for a generic version of atorvastatin. The Hatch-Waxman Act provides six months of exclusivity to the first generic manufacturer approved by the FDA. The six-month period of generic exclusivity begins immediately after the expiry of the patent of the original drug. Typically, the exclusive generic manufacturer will price its drug at 70–80% of the price of the patented drug. Once the generic exclusivity expires and open competition ensues, the price will fall even further.

Following its ANDA, Ranbaxy sued Pfizer to establish the expiry of Pfizer's US patents. In June 2008, the two companies settled: Pfizer dropped its opposition to Ranbaxy's generic atorvastatin and Ranbaxy agreed to delay selling the generic in the United States until November 2011, giving Pfizer an additional five months of exclusivity. Pfizer also agreed to Ranbaxy selling the generic atorvastatin in Australia, Canada, and specific European countries.

Ranbaxy expected to earn $600 million in profit from atorvastatin during the six months of generic exclusivity. This profit was significant for a company with $1.9 billion in revenue and $459 million in earnings. Pfizer itself prepared to manufacture a generic version of atorvastatin for distribution by Watson Pharmaceuticals.

Blockbuster drugs like atorvastatin require millions of dollars of investment in research and development. For every blockbuster drug, many molecules fail in the market and many more do not make it beyond the laboratory. Yet R&D is key for branded pharmaceutical manufacturers to differentiate themselves from generic manufacturers. How much should Pfizer spend on R&D?

Lipitor already competed with simvastatin and other statins. Generic competition was imminent in the market for atorvastatin in the United States and Europe. Pfizer had to decide how to manage the competition. How much should it spend on advertising? At what scale should Pfizer produce the branded drug, Lipitor, and the generic version? How would generic production of atorvastatin affect the market for the ingredients in the production of the drug?

To address these questions, we must understand the behavior of buyers or sellers that have the power to influence market conditions. A buyer or seller that can influence market conditions is said to have **market power**. A buyer with market power can influence market supply – in particular, the price and quantity supplied. A seller with market power can influence market demand – in particular, the price and quantity demanded.

> **Market power:** The ability of a buyer or seller to influence market conditions.

Economic profit is the difference between revenue and cost. Businesses can use their market power to increase revenue and reduce cost, and so increase profit. Here, we ask how to build market power and how to use it. For simplicity, we focus on markets in which there is either just one seller or one buyer. If there is only one seller in a market, that seller is called a **monopoly**. If there is only one buyer in a market, that buyer is called a **monopsony**.

> **Monopoly:** One seller in a market.

> **Monopsony:** One buyer in a market.

This chapter begins with the sources of market power. Then we analyze how a profit-maximizing monopoly determines its scale of production and price. This then shows how the producer should adjust production and price in response to changes in demand and costs. Applying this analysis, we can address the issues of how Pfizer should adjust production of Lipitor and at what scale to produce the generic atorvastatin.

Next, we consider how much a monopoly should spend on advertising and R&D, and explain how competing sellers can benefit by restricting competition among themselves. These analyses explain how much branded pharmaceutical manufacturers like Pfizer should spend on advertising and R&D.

Finally, we consider monopsony and analyze how a monopsony that maximizes net benefit would set the scale and price of purchases. This explains how the expiry of the patents on atorvastatin would affect the market for the ingredients in the production of the drug.

2. Sources of Market Power

Market power has two ingredients – one is barriers to competition, and the other is the elasticity of demand or supply. For a monopoly or monopsony to exist, competitors must be deterred or prevented from entering the market to compete for the business. So, one source of market power is the barriers that keep competitors out.

> **Sources of market power:**
>
> - product differentiation;
> - intellectual property;
> - economies of scale, scope, and experience;
> - regulation.

However, even a monopoly cannot increase profit unless it can influence demand conditions – in particular, by raising price. Likewise, a monopsony cannot increase profit unless it can influence supply conditions. So, the other ingredient to market power is the elasticity of demand or supply.

Here, we focus on the seller's market power, while noting that the ingredients for the buyer's market power are quite symmetric. Sellers can reduce the price elasticity of demand and create barriers to competition in four ways.

Product Differentiation

Chapter 3 presented the intuitive conditions for demand to be inelastic with respect to price. Here, we emphasize one factor – *product differentiation*. To the extent that the differentiation appeals to buyers, it would increase the demand and reduce the price elasticity of demand, and so contribute to market power.

Broadly, sellers can differentiate their products in four ways:

- *Design* provides the potential buyer's first impression of a product. Hence, an obvious way to differentiate products is by distinctive design – the appearance, form, and feel. Appealing design can transform utilitarian products into distinctive offerings that buyers value and prefer.

- *Function* is, besides design, the other aspect of the day-to-day benefit that the product provides to the user.
- *Distribution* channels make products available to buyers at a time and place of their convenience. So another way to differentiate products is through distribution channels. Manufacturers of luxury products use exclusive distribution to build brand image and demand. By contrast, producers of mass consumer goods use intensive distribution to provide wide and timely availability.
- *Advertising and promotion* introduce buyers to products and communicate the brand image. Hence, yet another way to differentiate products is through advertising and promotion that influence and sustain buyers' preferences.

Intellectual Property

Product differentiation builds, in part, on innovation. To encourage particular forms of innovation, society may award the innovator a period of exclusive use through *intellectual property*. Innovators may be able to exclude competitors and so contribute to market power by establishing intellectual property over their innovations.

- A *patent* gives the owner an exclusive right to an invention for a specified period of time. Pfizer's patent on atorvastatin provided the manufacturer with a monopoly until 2011.
- *Copyright* provides exclusivity over published expressions for a specified period of time. Microsoft's copyright over the Windows operating system and Office application suite provides the software publisher with a monopoly over the software.
- A *trademark* provides exclusivity over words or symbols associated with a good or service. Trademarks are the basis for branding and advertising and promotion. Pfizer's Lipitor trademark complements its patent, and Microsoft's Windows trademark complements its copyright.
- *Trade secrecy* provides exclusivity over information that is not generally known and that provides commercial advantage. The scope of secrecy extends to business information such as customer lists and technical information that possibly cannot be patented, such as algorithms. Google famously protects its technologies through secrecy.

Economies of Scale, Scope, and Experience

A third source of market power is *economies of scale, scope, and experience*. In an industry characterized by economies of scale, scope, or experience, an incumbent producer will have a cost advantage over potential competitors. By establishing a sufficient cost advantage, the incumbent producer may be able to deter entry by competitors and so gain market power.

The combined provision of broadband and cable television illustrates economies of scope. Both services depend on a network of cables from the service provider to subscribers. Owing to economies of scope, a combined provider of broadband and cable television can achieve lower costs than specialized providers.

Further, the cable network also exhibits economies of scale – it involves large fixed costs and relatively low variable costs. Consequently, the broadband and cable television industries tend to be dominated by a few providers, each of which provides both services.

Regulation

Finally, for various reasons, including economic or social policy, the government may decide to limit competition, and in the extreme, allow only a single producer. A producer with the government license is shielded from competition by law, and so gains market power.

An important economic reason for such *regulation* is the presence of large fixed costs in production. So, for example, most governments limit competition in the distribution of electricity, natural gas, and water. The policy helps to avoid duplication of the fixed costs of the distribution network.

Governments may limit competition in particular markets for social reasons. Examples include sports and mass media, retailing of alcohol and tobacco, and gambling.

PROGRESS CHECK 8A

What are the two ingredients of market power?

APPLE: PRODUCT DIFFERENTIATION AND INNOVATION

Most manufacturers of personal computers produce utilitarian machines and market their products on function and price. Apple famously took a different approach. From the first Apple computer to the latest Mac, Apple founder Steve Jobs emphasized design as much as function. Apple has consistently priced the Mac above other brands of personal computers and earned higher margins.

Apple has also pioneered differentiation through exclusive distribution to connect directly with consumers. In 2001, Apple opened its first dedicated retail stores in Tyson's Corner, Virginia, and Glendale, California. To staff the stores, Apple carefully selects passionate people who are keen to collaborate and ready to learn.

And, of course, Apple reinforces its brand through advertising and creates new products through R&D. In 2013, Apple spent $1.1 billion on advertising and $4.5 billion on R&D – amounting to 0.6% and 2.6% respectively of its $170.9 billion sales revenue.

Source: Apple Inc., Annual Report 2013.

COKE: 17 YEARS WAS TOO SHORT

In 1886, pharmacist John Pemberton sold the first glass of Coca-Cola for 5 cents at Jacobs' Pharmacy in downtown Atlanta. The Coca-Cola Company famously did not patent its invention. Applying for a patent would require disclosure of the formula for the beverage. And, upon the expiry of the patent (after 17 years), competitors would be free to produce the "real thing." So, Coca-Cola has relied on secrecy to protect the formula.

There are many competing colas in the retail market. Besides its secret formula, Coca-Cola advertises heavily to reinforce its brand and differentiate its products. In 2010, Cola-Cola spent $2.9 billion or 8.3% of its $35.1 billion sales revenue on advertising. The advertising supports a price premium over competing beverages.

Source: Coca-Cola Company, Annual Report 2010.

3. Profit Maximum

Having gained market power, how should a seller use it? Here, we consider the scale of production and price. Suppose that Venus Pharmaceutical has a monopoly over a drug, Gamma-1, that cures bone-marrow cancer. Venus faces the two basic business decisions. One is participation – should it produce the drug? The other is extent – how much should it produce and sell (and how should it price the drug)?

Supposing that Venus decides to produce the drug, we first analyze the profit-maximizing sales and price. Then we consider whether Venus should produce the drug at all.

The essence of market power is that the seller faces a demand curve that slopes downward. Venus Pharmaceutical, being a monopoly, faces the market demand curve. Unlike a perfectly competitive seller, a monopoly has to consider how its sales will affect the market price.

Given the market demand curve, a monopoly can either decide how much to sell and let the market determine the price at which it is willing to buy that quantity, or set the price and let the market determine how much it will buy. If the monopoly tries to set both sales and price, the sales and price may be inconsistent in the sense that, at that price, the market wants to buy more or less than the quantity the monopoly is selling. In terms of a graph, inconsistency means that the monopoly is choosing a combination of sales and price off the demand curve. Accordingly, a monopoly can set either sales or price, but not both.

Let us focus on the decision on sales. For simplicity, we ignore inventories and hence production equals sales. So, scale of production and sales are equivalent. To analyze the profit-maximizing sales, we need to know how Venus's sales affect its revenues and costs.

Revenue

First, consider the relationship among price, sales, and revenue. Table 8.1 shows the demand for Gamma-1. Specifically, the second column shows, for every price, the quantity that Venus expects to sell. The quantity demanded increases by 200,000 units for every $10 reduction in price. Using this information, we can then calculate Venus's *total revenue* for every price, which is price multiplied by sales.[2] From the total revenue, we can then calculate *marginal revenue*, which is the change in total revenue arising from selling an additional unit.

To sell additional units, Venus Pharmaceutical must reduce its price. So, when increasing sales by one unit, Venus will gain revenue from selling the additional (or marginal) unit, but it will lose revenue on the *inframarginal units*. The **inframarginal units** are those units sold other than the marginal unit. Venus would have sold the inframarginal units without reducing the price.

> **Inframarginal units:**
> Units sold other than the marginal unit.

For example, referring to Table 8.1, to increase sales from 200,000 to 400,000 units, Venus must reduce the price from $190 to $180. Hence, Venus will gain revenue of $180 × 200,000 = $36 million on the additional units, but lose $(190 − 180) × 200,000 = $2 million on the inframarginal 200,000 units that it could have sold at $190. Thus, Venus's revenue for the additional 200,000 units is $36 million − $2 million = $34 million, which means that marginal revenue is $170 per unit.

In general, the marginal revenue from selling an additional unit will be less than the price of that unit. The reason for this is that the marginal revenue is the price of the marginal unit minus the loss of revenue on the inframarginal units.

The difference between the price and the marginal revenue depends on the price elasticity of demand. If demand is very elastic, then the seller need not reduce the price very much to increase sales; hence, the marginal revenue will be close to the

Table 8.1 Monopoly revenue, cost, and profit

Price ($)	Sales (million)	Total revenue ($ million)	Marginal revenue ($)	Total cost ($ million)	Marginal cost ($)	Profit ($ million)
200	0.0	0.00		50.00		−50.00
190	0.2	38.00	190	64.20	71	−26.20
180	0.4	72.00	170	78.40	71	−6.40
170	0.6	102.00	150	92.60	71	9.40
160	0.8	128.00	130	106.80	71	21.20
150	1.0	150.00	110	121.00	71	29.00
140	1.2	168.00	90	135.20	71	32.80
136	1.28	174.08	76	140.88	71	33.20
135	1.30	175.50	71	142.30	71	33.20
134	1.32	176.88	69	143.72	71	33.16
130	1.4	182.00	64	149.40	71	32.60
120	1.6	192.00	50	163.60	71	28.40
110	1.8	198.00	30	177.80	71	20.20
100	2.0	200.00	10	192.00	71	8.00
90	2.2	198.00	−10	206.20	71	−8.20

price. If, however, demand is very inelastic, then the seller must reduce the price substantially to increase sales; so the marginal revenue will be much lower than the price.

The marginal revenue can be negative, if the loss of revenue on the inframarginal units exceeds the gain on the marginal unit. Table 8.1 shows that, if Venus cut the price from $100 to $90, sales would increase from 2.0 to 2.2 million units. The change in revenue, however, is –$2 million for the additional 200,000 units, which means that marginal revenue is –$10 per unit.

PROGRESS CHECK 8B

If demand is extremely elastic, what will be the difference between the price and the marginal revenue?

Costs

We have considered the relation among price, sales, and revenue. The other side to profit is cost. Table 8.1 also shows data for Venus Pharmaceutical's production costs. It reports only avoidable costs. From the total cost at a zero production scale, we can infer that production requires a fixed cost of $50 million.

Total cost increases with the scale of production. Table 8.1 shows Venus's *marginal cost*, which is the change in total cost due to the production of an additional unit. The change in total cost arises from change in the variable cost. For simplicity, the marginal cost is $71 per unit at all scales of production.

Profit-Maximizing Scale

With information on both revenue and cost, we can calculate Venus's profit at every possible price and quantity. Profit is total revenue less total (fixed and variable) cost. The last column of Table 8.1 reports profit at each quantity of sales. Looking down the column, we see that Venus's maximum profit is $33.2 million. It achieves this profit with a price of $135 and sales of 1.3 million units.[3]

Profit-maximizing scale of production: The scale at which the marginal revenue balances the marginal cost.

Another way to identify the **profit-maximizing scale of production** is the scale at which the marginal revenue balances the marginal cost. At the price of $135, Venus's sales are 1.3 million units. The marginal revenue is $71 per unit (note that, to calculate the marginal revenue more precisely, we drilled down to a smaller increment between prices around the profit-maximizing level). The marginal cost is also $71 per unit. So, at the profit-maximizing scale, the marginal revenue equals the marginal cost.

This suggests a general rule: to maximize profit, a monopoly should produce at a scale where its marginal revenue balances its marginal cost. This rule applies to any seller and not only a monopoly.

Let us illustrate the profit-maximizing price and operation scale with a diagram. Figure 8.1 shows Venus Pharmaceutical's demand, marginal revenue, and marginal cost curves. The demand curve shows, for every price, the quantity that

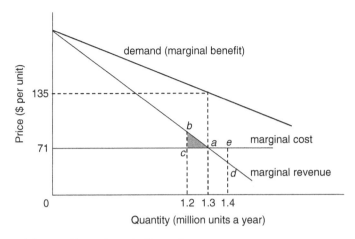

FIGURE 8.1 Monopoly production scale.

Notes: The marginal revenue and marginal cost curves cross at the quantity of 1.3 million units. From the demand (marginal benefit) curve, the profit-maximizing price is $135. At 1.2 million units, the marginal revenue exceeds the marginal cost.

the market will buy. Equivalently, it shows, for every quantity of purchases (on the horizontal axis), the maximum price (on the vertical axis) that the market will pay for that quantity.

The marginal revenue curve shows, for every quantity (on the horizontal axis), the marginal revenue (on the vertical axis). As we have explained, for every quantity, the marginal revenue is less than the price. Accordingly, at all quantities, the marginal revenue curve lies below the demand curve.

The marginal revenue and marginal cost curves cross at the quantity of 1.3 million units. From the demand curve, we see that the price at that quantity is $135. This is the profit-maximizing price.

Let us understand why a seller maximizes profit at a production scale where marginal revenue balances marginal cost. Suppose that Venus produces at a scale, such as 1.2 million units, where the marginal revenue exceeds the marginal cost. Then, if Venus increases production by 100,000 units, its revenue will increase by more than its cost; indeed, it will increase its profit by the area shaded *bca*.

By contrast, suppose that Venus produces at a scale such as 1.4 million units, where the marginal revenue is less than the marginal cost. Then, if Venus cuts production by 100,000 units, its revenue will fall by less than its cost; hence it will increase its profit by the area *ade*. Generally, a seller will maximize profit by producing at a scale where its marginal revenue balances its marginal cost.

Break-Even Analysis

What about the participation decision: should Venus produce Gamma-1 at all? We have already analyzed the profit-maximizing scale of production or sales, assuming that Venus does produce the drug. So Venus should produce the

Profit maximum:

- Produce if total revenue covers total cost.
- Produce at scale where marginal revenue equals marginal cost.

drug if the total revenue covers the total cost, with both revenue and cost calculated at the profit-maximizing scale.

Profit contribution: Total
revenue less variable cost.

Incremental margin:
Price less marginal cost.

**Incremental marginal
percentage:** The ratio
of incremental margin to
price.

Profit Measures

Later in this chapter, we discuss how much a seller with market power should spend on advertising and R&D. That discussion applies two measures of profit. One is the **profit contribution**, which is total revenue less variable cost. The other is the **incremental margin**, which is the price less the marginal cost. Further, the **incremental marginal percentage** is the ratio of the incremental margin (price less marginal cost) to the price.

PROGRESS CHECK 8C

Suppose that, at the current scale of production, Venus's marginal revenue is less than its marginal cost. How should management adjust its production?

BIG PHARMA VERSUS GENERICS

Branded pharmaceutical manufacturers such as Pfizer invest billions of dollars in R&D to discover and develop new drugs. Of every 10,000 compounds investigated, only five are tested in clinical trials, and, of those, only one receives approval for use among patients.

R&D expenditures are fixed costs in the sense that they do not vary with scale of production. To cover the R&D expenditures, Pfizer needs a large profit contribution. This comes from either a high incremental margin on each unit of sales or large scale of production or both.

Generic manufacturers such as Ranbaxy follow a different strategy. They jump in after the patents of branded manufacturers expire and focus R&D on developing generic equivalents. With lower R&D expenditures, they incur relatively lower fixed costs, and so can be profitable with smaller incremental margin and production.

In 2010, Pfizer earned revenues of $67.8 billion, with a gross margin of 76%, and spent $9.4 billion or 13.9% of revenues on R&D. By contrast, Ranbaxy earned revenues of 66.7 billion Indian rupees ($1.5 billion), with a gross margin of less than 67%, and spent 5.0 billion rupees or 9.5% of revenues on R&D.

Sources: Pfizer, Inc, Annual Report 2010; Ranbaxy Laboratories Ltd, Annual Report 2010; Pharmaceutical Research and Manufacturers of America, "Drug discovery and development," www.phrma.org.

4. Demand and Cost Changes

How should a seller with market power respond to changes in demand and cost? Generally, when there is a change in either demand or cost, the profit-maximizing adjustment to sales depends on both the marginal revenue and marginal cost curves. The seller should adjust the sales until its marginal revenue equals its marginal cost.

Demand Change

Suppose, for instance, that Venus Pharmaceutical increases advertising, and so boosts demand for Gamma-1. How should Venus adjust its sales? To address this question, Figure 8.2 shows the new demand curve. From the new demand curve, we can calculate the new marginal revenue curve.

The new marginal revenue curve lies further to the right. Since the upward-sloping marginal cost curve does not change, the new marginal revenue curve crosses the marginal cost curve at a larger scale. Specifically, the two curves cross at a scale of 1.4 million units, and the new profit-maximizing price is higher, at $140.

Only the demand has changed. However, to identify the new profit-maximizing scale and price, we need both the new marginal revenue and the original marginal cost.

Marginal Cost Change

We can use a similar approach to understand how a seller with market power should respond to a change in the marginal cost. Suppose, for instance, that,

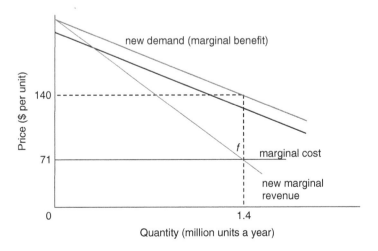

FIGURE 8.2 Demand increase.

Notes: The new marginal revenue curve and original marginal cost curve cross at the quantity of 1.4 million units a year. The new profit-maximizing price is $140.

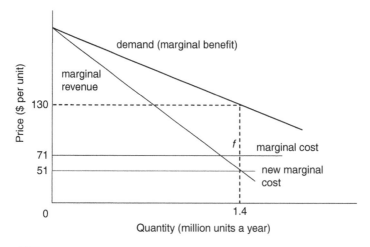

FIGURE 8.3 Reduction in marginal cost.

Notes: The marginal revenue curve and new marginal cost curve cross at the quantity of 1.4 million units a year. The new profit-maximizing price is $130.

relative to the data reported in Table 8.1, the marginal cost is $20 lower at all scales of production. Should Venus reduce the price of the drug by $20 as well?

To address this question, consider Figure 8.3, which shows Venus's marginal revenue and the new marginal cost. The marginal revenue and the new marginal cost cross at a larger scale of 1.4 million units. The new profit-maximizing price is lower, at $130.

Relative to the original maximum (Figure 8.1), Venus now maximizes profits by cutting its price by $10, which is less than the fall in the marginal cost. Further, although the change was only in the marginal cost, Venus must consider the marginal revenue as well as the new marginal cost to obtain the new profit-maximizing sales and price.

Fixed-Cost Change

We should stress that the seller's profit-maximizing sales and price do not depend in any way on the fixed cost (so long as it is not too large). Recall that a seller with market power maximizes profit by producing at the scale where its marginal revenue equals its marginal cost. Changes in the fixed cost will not affect the marginal cost curve; hence, they will not affect the profit-maximizing sales level.

If, however, the fixed cost is so large that the total cost exceeds total revenue, then the business should shut down. In Venus's case, referring to Table 8.1, if the fixed cost exceeds $84 million, the company should close.

The principle that the profit-maximizing sales and price do not depend on the level of fixed costs is crucial in knowledge-intensive industries such as media and publishing, pharmaceuticals, and software. In these industries, production is characterized by relatively high fixed costs and low variable costs.

PROGRESS CHECK 8D

In Figure 8.3, show how Venus should adjust sales if marginal cost increases by $20 at all scales of production.

5. Advertising

Any seller with market power can influence the demand for its products through advertising. Advertising can shift out the demand curve as well as cause it to be less price elastic. In the analysis of advertising, for simplicity, we take price as given. However, in practice, it is important to bear in mind that the seller should simultaneously maximize on price, advertising, and other influences on demand.

Profit-Maximizing Advertising

By shifting out the demand curve and causing it to be less price elastic, advertising can raise sales. The increase in sales will affect total revenue and variable cost. Accordingly, the benefit of advertising is to increase the profit contribution. To maximize profit, Venus should advertise up to the level that the marginal benefit of advertising equals the marginal cost.

Using the concepts of the incremental margin percentage and the *advertising elasticity of demand*, we can derive a simple rule for the profit-maximizing level of advertising. Recall from Chapter 3 that the advertising elasticity of demand is the percentage by which the demand will change if the seller's advertising expenditure rises by 1%, other things equal.

Advertising–Sales Ratio

When the marginal benefit equals the marginal cost of advertising, the **advertising–sales ratio** (the ratio of the advertising expenditure to sales revenue) equals the incremental margin percentage multiplied by the advertising elasticity of demand. This provides a simple rule for the profit-maximizing level of advertising expenditure.

> **Profit-maximizing advertising–sales ratio:** Incremental margin percentage multiplied by advertising elasticity of demand.

Strictly, the rule stipulates the ratio of advertising expenditure to sales *revenue*. So the ratio should be called the advertising–revenue ratio. However, in practice, it is usually called the advertising–sales ratio.

We can apply the advertising–sales ratio rule to determine the profit-maximizing level of advertising expenditure for Venus's new drug Gamma-1. Recall that, with the demand and costs in Table 8.1, the profit-maximizing price is $135 per unit and the marginal cost is $71. This means that the incremental margin percentage is $(135 − 71)/$135 = 0.474. Suppose that, at the price of $135, the advertising elasticity of the demand is 0.26. Then the profit-maximizing advertising–sales ratio is $0.474 \times 0.26 = 0.123$, or 12.3%.

At the $135 price, Gamma-1 revenue is 135×1.3 million $= \$175.5$ million. Hence, the profit-maximizing advertising expenditure is $0.123 \times \$175.5$ million $= \$21.6$ million.

The rule for advertising expenditures implies that, if the incremental margin percentage is higher, then the seller should spend relatively more on advertising. The reason is that each dollar of advertising produces relatively more benefit. Accordingly, when the incremental margin percentage is higher, the seller should increase advertising. This means that, whenever a seller raises its price or reduces its marginal cost, it should also increase advertising expenditure. By contrast, if a seller reduces its price or raises its marginal cost, it should reduce advertising expenditure.

Further, the rule for advertising expenditures implies that, if either the advertising elasticity of demand or the sales revenue is higher, then the seller should spend relatively more on advertising. Essentially, a higher advertising elasticity of demand or sales revenue means that the influence of advertising on buyer demand is relatively greater. In these circumstances, it makes sense to advertise more.

PROGRESS CHECK 8E

Suppose that the profit-maximizing scale of production for Gamma-1 is 1.3 million units. At that scale, the price is $135 per unit, the marginal cost is $71, and the advertising elasticity of demand is 0.14. How much should Venus spend on advertising?

PFIZER: MANAGING COMPETITION

Atorvastatin, marketed by Pfizer under the brand name Lipitor, reduces the level of low-density lipoprotein cholesterol in the human body. In 2010, Lipitor was Pfizer's best-selling drug, with sales revenue of $10.7 billion, or 15.7% of the company's total revenue.

However, in November 2011, Ranbaxy Laboratories introduced a generic version of atorvastatin. During a six-month period of generic exclusivity in the United States, Ranbaxy expected to set price at between 70% and 80% of the price of the patented Lipitor.

With Ranbaxy's generic taking part of the demand for Lipitor, it would have made sense for Pfizer to reduce its own production. Ranbaxy would draw price-sensitive patients who had a relatively weak preference for Lipitor. High sales of Lipitor could only be maintained if the remaining patients, with a strong preference for Lipitor, formed a relatively large group.

In response to the entry of generic simvastatin, Pfizer mounted an aggressive marketing campaign. Pfizer prepared to introduce its own generic to compete with other generics. The cost of maintaining the production line is fixed, so any additional profit contribution, whether from branded Lipitor or a generic, adds to profit.

Sources: "Pfizer deal with Ranbaxy means a delay for generic form of Lipitor," *New York Times*, June 19, 2008; "The War over Lipitor," CNN Money, May 6, 2011; "Atorvastatin," Wikipedia (accessed July 12, 2011).

6. Research and Development

A seller with market power can also influence demand through research and development. Especially in knowledge-intensive industries, R&D drives the pipeline of new products and refreshes existing products.

How much should a business invest in R&D? The principles are the same as for advertising. R&D shifts out the demand curve and causes it to be less price elastic. The benefit of R&D is to increase the profit contribution.

A simple rule for the profit-maximizing level of R&D expenditure applies the concept of the R&D elasticity. The **R&D elasticity** of demand is the percentage by which demand will change if the seller's R&D increases by 1%. The R&D elasticity of demand depends on two factors: one is the effectiveness of R&D in generating new products and enhancing existing products, and the other is the effect of new and enhanced products on demand.

> **R&D elasticity:** The percentage by which demand will change if the seller's R&D increases by 1%.

The rule for profit maximization is to spend on R&D up to the level where the **R&D–sales ratio** (the ratio of the R&D expenditure to sales revenue) equals the incremental margin percentage multiplied by the R&D elasticity of demand.

> **Profit-maximizing R&D–sales ratio:** Incremental margin percentage multiplied by R&D elasticity of demand.

By this rule, when the incremental margin percentage is higher (higher price or lower marginal cost), the seller should increase R&D expenditure relative to sales revenue. Conversely, when the incremental margin percentage is lower (lower price or higher marginal cost), the seller should reduce R&D expenditure relative to sales revenue.

Further, if either the R&D elasticity of demand or the sales revenue is higher, then the seller should increase R&D, and if either the R&D elasticity of demand or the sales revenue is lower, then the seller should reduce R&D.

PROGRESS CHECK 8F

If price is higher while marginal cost is lower, how should R&D expenditure be adjusted?

SPENDING ON ADVERTISING AND R&D

Table 8.2 presents the amounts that various manufacturers of foods, personal consumer products, information technology (IT), and telecom equipment spend on advertising and R&D. Manufacturers of foods and personal consumer products spend relatively more on advertising, while producers of IT and telecom equipment spend relatively more on R&D.

Table 8.2 Advertising and R&D, 2013

Industry/ company	Currency	Sales revenue	Advertising	Advertising– sales ratio	R&D	R&D– sales ratio
Foods and personal consumer products						
China Mengniu	RMB million	43,357	2,710	6.3%	57	0.1%
Proctor and Gamble	US$ million	83,062	9,236	11.1%	2,023	2.4%
Unilever	€ million	49,797	6,832	13.7%	1,040	2.1%
IT and telecom equipment						
Apple	US$ million	170,910	1,100	0.6%	4,475	2.6%
Microsoft	US$ million	77,849	2,600	3.3%	10,411	13.4%
Nokia	€ million	12,709	n.a.		2,619	20.6%
ZTE	RMB million	75,234	568	0.8%	7,384	9.8%

7. Market Structure

Monopoly, the case of a single seller, is one extreme of a range of market structures. At the other extreme lies perfect competition, where there are numerous sellers, each of whom is too small to affect market conditions. By comparing monopoly with perfect competition, we can understand how production and price depend on the competitive structure of the market.

Effects of Competition

Consider the market for trucking service between two cities. Assume that, in the long run, the provision of the service involves no fixed cost and the marginal cost is constant at 30 cents per pound of freight. Let us compare production and price when the trucking industry is perfectly competitive and when there is a monopoly.

First, suppose that the industry is perfectly competitive. Since provision requires only a constant marginal cost of 30 cents per pound, all truckers will be willing to supply unlimited service at 30 cents per pound. Hence, the market supply will be perfectly elastic at 30 cents per pound. Given the market demand, the supply will

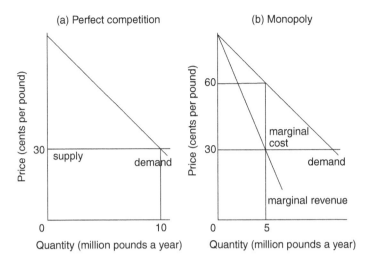

FIGURE 8.4 Market structure.

Notes:
(a) Under perfect competition, competition drives the market price down toward the long-run average cost of 30 cents. Production is 10 million pounds a year.
(b) Under a monopoly, the monopoly restricts production below the competitive level and sets a higher price of 60 cents to obtain larger profit.

balance demand at a price of 30 cents. Figure 8.4(a) illustrates the market equilibrium. The sales and production will be the quantity demanded at a price of 30 cents, say, 10 million pounds a year. In equilibrium, each trucker earns zero profit.

Next, suppose that the trucking industry is a monopoly. The monopoly will produce at a scale that balances marginal revenue and the marginal cost of 30 cents. Since the marginal revenue curve lies below the demand curve, marginal revenue equals marginal cost at a quantity of less than 10 million pounds a year. Accordingly, the monopoly will set the price above 30 cents. Suppose that the monopoly price is 60 cents and sales are 5 million pounds a year. Figure 8.4(b) depicts the monopoly price and sales. The monopoly will enjoy profits of $(0.60 - 0.30) \times 5 = $1.5 million a year.

The trucking example illustrates several general principles. First, a monopoly restricts production below the competitive level and, in so doing, can extract a relatively higher margin and thus larger profit. By contrast, competition drives the market price down toward the long-run average cost and results in more production. Further, the profit of a monopoly exceeds what would be the combined profit of all the sellers if the same market were perfectly competitive.

Potential Competition

We have just seen that competition will push down the market price toward the long-run average cost. It is worth emphasizing that, under specific conditions, even *potential* competition suffices to keep the market price close to the long-run average cost.

Consider a market in which sellers can enter and exit at no cost. Such a market is called **perfectly contestable**. A monopoly in a perfectly contestable market cannot raise its price substantially above its long-run average cost.

> **Perfectly contestable market:** Sellers can enter and exit at no cost.

To understand why, suppose that Jupiter Trucking has a monopoly on freight transport between the two cities. However, other truckers can easily switch their trucks among routes. So, if Jupiter raises its price above the long-run average cost, other truckers can profit by entering the route between the two cities. They would quickly enter to compete for a share of the market. The resulting increase in supply would drive the market price down toward the long-run average cost.

So, in a perfectly contestable market, even a monopoly cannot raise its price substantially above the long-run average cost. The degree to which a market is contestable depends on the extent of barriers to entry and exit. Earlier in this chapter, we reviewed barriers to entry. To the extent that there are barriers to entry, it will be more difficult for competing sellers to enter and, hence, it will be easier for a monopoly to raise its price above the long-run average cost.

The degree to which a market is contestable also depends on the extent of barriers to exit. Recall that, if Jupiter Trucking raises its price above long-run average cost, it might attract other truckers to enter. These other truckers are lured by the attraction of temporary profits, made possible by Jupiter's relatively high price. Once Jupiter lowers its price back toward long-run average cost, these other truckers will leave. But their brief presence in the market will have been profitable.

Now suppose that these other truckers must incur liquidation costs to exit the market. When deciding whether to enter the market, these other truckers must consider these exit costs. The higher are such exit costs, the less likely these other truckers are to enter when Jupiter raises its price. This illustrates how barriers to exit affect the degree to which a market is contestable.

Measuring Market Power

Having understood the potential effect of market power on production and price, it is worth considering how to measure market power. In a perfectly competitive market, every seller produces at a scale where its marginal cost equals the market price; hence, its incremental margin percentage is zero. By contrast, a seller with market power restricts sales to raise its price above its marginal cost. The more inelastic is the market demand, the more the seller can raise its price above its marginal cost.

We measure market power by the incremental margin percentage. This measure can be used to compare market power across different markets. Some drugs cost hundreds of dollars per dose, while others cost less than a dollar. It would not make sense to directly compare their prices or incremental margins. Even if the market for the expensive drugs were almost perfectly competitive, the price would be a few dollars above the marginal cost. This difference would exceed the incremental margin for the cheap drugs. Hence, to compare market power, it makes more sense to use the incremental margin percentage.

The incremental margin percentage also captures the impact of potential competition. If, owing to the presence of potential competitors, a monopoly sets a price close to its marginal cost, then the incremental margin percentage will also be relatively low.

VALUE OF A GAMBLING DUOPOLY

The state of Victoria, Australia, legalized slot machines in 1992. The state government issued master licenses to Tattersall's and Tabcorp for each to operate 13,750 slot machines at clubs and hotels across the state. The state also licensed Crown Casino for 2,500 machines in its casino. The master licenses expired in 2012.

By 2010, Tattersall's and Tabcorp operated 26,682 slot machines at 514 clubs and hotels. Revenues from slot machines, more properly called "player loss," were $2.6 billion, or more than half of all gambling revenues in Victoria.

In April 2008, the government announced that it would not renew the master licenses. Instead, it would open applications to individual clubs and hotels for licenses valid for 10 years from 2012. The market value of Tattersall's and Tabcorp fell by A$2.8 billion in one day.

The government issued the new licenses in two rounds. In the first round, 236 clubs with existing slot machines bought licenses for 8,712 machines. The license fee was a percentage of the historical revenue and averaged A$42,014. In the second round, licenses for 4,838 machines in clubs and 13,750 in hotels were auctioned for an average of A$14,134 and A$39,686, respectively. The government received a total of A$980 million for the new licenses.

Source: Victorian Auditor-General, *Allocation of Electronic Gaming Machine Entitlements*, Melbourne: Victorian Government Printer, June 2011.

8. Monopsony

A seller with market power will restrain sales to raise its price and so increase profit. What about a buyer with market power? How would its business decisions differ from those of a perfectly competitive buyer? For simplicity, we discuss a situation with a single buyer, that is, a *monopsony*. Since there are close parallels between monopoly and monopsony, we will focus on the important differences.

Benefit and Expenditure

Suppose that a key input into the production of Gamma-1 is an Indonesian herb. Venus is the only buyer of this herb; hence, it is a monopsony. By contrast, many growers produce the herb. Each grower is too small to affect market conditions, so the supply of the herb is perfectly competitive.

Since the herb is a key input into Venus's manufacturing process, it provides a benefit that can be measured as the revenue generated less the costs of other associated inputs. The herb, however, must be bought from Indonesian growers. Venus's expenditure is the market price of the herb multiplied by the quantity purchased. Accordingly, Venus's net benefit from the herb is its benefit less expenditure. We suppose that Venus's objective is to maximize its net benefit.

At what quantity of purchases will Venus maximize its net benefit? Referring to Figure 8.5, Venus's benefit depends on the quantity of its purchases: we suppose that the marginal benefit of a small quantity is very high and that the marginal benefit falls with the scale of purchases.

Also referring to Figure 8.5, the supply curve shows, for every quantity, the price at which competitive sellers will provide the herb. Equivalently, the supply curve represents the monopsony's average expenditure for every possible quantity of purchases. Since the price must be higher to induce a greater quantity of supply, the average expenditure curve slopes upward.

> **Marginal expenditure:**
> The change in expenditure resulting from an increase in purchases by one unit.

The **marginal expenditure** is the change in expenditure resulting from an increase in purchases by one unit. For the average expenditure curve to slope upward, the marginal expenditure curve must lie above the average expenditure curve and slope upward more steeply.

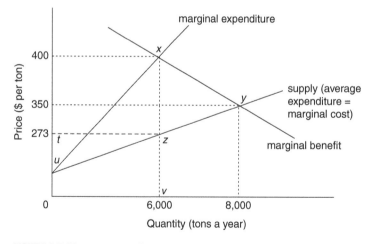

FIGURE 8.5 Monopsony purchasing.

Notes: The marginal benefit and marginal expenditure curves cross at a quantity of 6,000 tons. Reading from the supply curve, the price at that quantity is $273 per ton. The supply curve also shows the marginal cost. At 6,000 tons, the marginal benefit exceeds the marginal cost.

Maximizing Net Benefit

We can now state the following rule: a buyer with market power will maximize its **net benefit** by purchasing the quantity at which its marginal benefit equals its marginal expenditure.

To explain this rule, consider a scale of purchases where Venus's marginal benefit exceeds its marginal expenditure. Then, if Venus steps up purchases, its benefit will increase by more than its expenditure; hence it will obtain a larger net benefit. By contrast, if marginal bene-

> **Net benefit maximum:**
> Purchase at a scale such that marginal benefit equals marginal expenditure.

fit is less than marginal expenditure, Venus should reduce purchases: its benefit will drop by less than its expenditure. Venus will exactly maximize net benefit when it purchases the quantity where its marginal benefit balances its marginal expenditure.

Referring to Figure 8.5, the quantity that maximizes net benefit is 6,000 tons. At that quantity, the price is $273 per ton. Notice that the price of $273 per ton is less than the buyer's marginal benefit. By contrast, if the demand side were competitive and the marginal benefit curve represented the market demand, the equilibrium price would be $350 per ton and the quantity would be 8,000 tons. This illustrates a general point: a monopsony restricts purchases to get a lower price and increase its net benefit above the competitive level.

PROGRESS CHECK 8G

In Figure 8.5, shade the area that represents Venus's total expenditure on the herb.

GAVI: CHARITABLE MONOPSONY

Established with a US$750 million pledge from the Bill & Melinda Gates Foundation, the Global Alliance for Vaccines and Immunizations (Gavi) aims to increase vaccination of children in the world's poorest countries. By 2014, Gavi had extended vaccination to 440 million children, saving 6 million lives.

Gavi cleverly applies economic principles to carry out its mission. It consolidates purchases of vaccines and uses its buying power to get lower prices. In addition, it arranges large advance purchases to encourage manufacturers to keep open production lines for proven vaccines and to stimulate R&D to develop new vaccines.

Source: www.gavi.org (accessed December 1, 2014).

- Gain market power by limiting competition and making demand less price elastic.
- To maximize profit, produce if total revenue covers total cost, and produce at the scale where marginal revenue equals marginal cost.
- When demand or costs change, adjust production to the scale where marginal revenue equals marginal cost.
- To maximize profit, spend on advertising to the level where the advertising–sales ratio equals the incremental margin percentage multiplied by the advertising elasticity of demand.
- To maximize profit, spend on R&D to the level where the R&D–sales ratio equals the incremental margin percentage multiplied by the R&D elasticity of demand.
- Sellers with market power restrict sales to raise margins and profit.
- Measure market power by the incremental margin percentage.
- To maximize profit, purchase at the scale where marginal benefit equals marginal expenditure.

REVIEW QUESTIONS

1. By way of an example, explain how product differentiation contributes to market power.
2. What are the major forms of intellectual property?
3. Explain how economies of scale can contribute to market power.
4. For a seller with market power, why is marginal revenue less than or equal to price?
5. True or false? A seller with market power can either set the price and let the market decide how much to buy, or set the quantity to sell and let the market decide the price, but not set both price and quantity.
6. A software publisher has priced a new database program such that its marginal revenue is more than its marginal cost. Advise the company how to raise its profit.
7. Why should a seller take account of both the marginal revenue and the marginal cost when considering how to adjust price following a change in costs?
8. Why should a seller take account of both the marginal revenue and the marginal cost when considering how to adjust price following a change in demand?
9. The profit-maximizing price for a new electronic device is $100. At that price, the advertising elasticity of demand is 0.1 and sales are 500,000 units a year. The marginal cost of production is $40 per unit. How much should the publisher spend on advertising?
10. For a medical device, the advertising to sales ratio exceeds the incremental margin percentage multiplied by the advertising elasticity of demand. How can the manufacturer increase profit?
11. What factors affect the R&D elasticity of demand?
12. Explain the profit-maximizing rule for R&D expenditure relative to sales revenue.

13. For a monopoly, the incremental margin percentage would be infinite. True or false?
14. A buyer with market power restrains its purchases to reduce the market price. True or false?
15. Compare purchases and price with a monopsony and perfectly competitive buyers.

DISCUSSION QUESTIONS

1. Eli Lilly owns the patent to Xigris, which is the only approved drug for the treatment of sepsis. Sepsis is a severe illness caused by a bacterial infection which may lead to the failure of multiple organs. Bayer manufactures aspirin, which is not covered by patent, and is one of several drugs that relieve the symptoms of the common cold.
    (a) Which company has relatively more market power: Eli Lilly over treatments for sepsis, or Bayer over drugs for relieving the common cold? Explain your answer.
    (b) How is the difference between price and marginal revenue related to the price elasticity of demand?
    (c) Compare the incremental margin percentage at profit maximum for Lilly's Xigris and Bayer's aspirin.
2. Table 8.1 describes the demand and costs for Venus Pharmaceutical's Gamma-1 drug. Suppose that the costs are a fixed cost of $60 million and a constant marginal cost of $50 per unit. The demand remains the same.
    (a) Prepare a new table of revenues and costs according to the new data.
    (b) What are the profit-maximizing scale of production and price?
    (c) At that production scale, what are the marginal revenue, marginal cost, and incremental margin percentage?
3. Apple outsources manufacturing of iPhones and iPads to Foxconn, with 800,000 workers at factories in Shenzhen, Chengdu, and elsewhere in China. Faced with increased competition for labor, Foxconn has raised wages and increased benefits for its workers. In April 2012, Samsung sued Apple for violating various Samsung patents to produce mobile phones. (Sources: "Foxconn to raise salaries 20% after suicides," *Financial Times*, May 28, 2010; "Samsung sues Apple on patent-infringement claims as legal dispute deepens," *Bloomberg*, April 22, 2011.)
    (a) Using a suitable diagram, explain how Apple should set the production and price of the iPhone to maximize profit. (*Hint*: You are free to assume any data necessary to draw the diagram.)
    (b) Using your diagram in (a), explain how Apple should adjust its production and price if Foxconn raises its prices for contract manufacturing.
    (c) Suppose that Apple must pay Samsung a royalty on each mobile device that it produces. How should Apple adjust its production and price in response to the royalty?
    (d) How would you change your answer to (b) if Apple must pay Samsung a lump sum in damages rather than a royalty per unit produced?

Table 8.3 Google profit and loss, 2010–2013

$ millions	2013	2012	2011	2010
Revenue	59,825	50,175	37,905	29,321
Cost of goods sold	25,858	20,634	13,188	10,417
Gross profit	33,967	29,541	24,717	18,904
R&D	7,952	6,793	5,162	3,762
Selling, general, and administrative expenses	12,049	9,988	7,813	4,761
Operating income	13,966	12,760	11,742	10,381

4. Atos Origin, Coca-Cola, Eastman Kodak, General Electric, John Hancock Financial Services, Lenovo Group, McDonald's, Panasonic, Samsung, and Visa paid a total of $866 million to the International Olympic Committee to be global sponsors for the years 2004–2008. The sponsorship period included the 2006 Winter Olympics in Turin and the 2008 Summer Olympics in Beijing. By contrast, total sponsorship for the years 2000–2004, including the Salt Lake City winter games and the Athens summer games, amounted to $666 million. (Source: "For Olympic sponsors, it's on to Beijing," *International Herald Tribune*, August 31, 2004.)

   (a) Compare the benefit from Olympics sponsorship for global brands such as Kodak and Samsung relative to regional and local brands.

   (b) Considering the relative sizes of the Greek and Chinese consumer markets, explain why sponsors paid more for the 2004–2008 Olympics than the 2000–2004 Olympics.

   (c) Atos Origin's customers are primarily other businesses, while Lenovo's market is mainly within China. Compare the benefit from Olympic sponsorship for these two companies with the benefit for other sponsors.

5. At Google's 2013 third quarter earnings call, analyst Carlos Kirjner remarked, "the perception by people outside the company is that Google spends a material amount in long-term R&D that will not generate revenue in the next two years or so." CEO Larry Page countered that, with respect to large innovations, "I think you overestimate short-term and underestimate long-term." He then pointed to how Google had transformed the concept of self-driving cars from being far-fetched to inevitable.

   (a) Explain the formula for the profit-maximizing level of R&D relative to sales revenue in terms of the R&D elasticity of demand and incremental margin percentage.

   (b) Interpret the discussion between analyst Carlos Kirjner and CEO Larry Page in terms of the R&D elasticity of demand.

   (c) Referring to Table 8.3, calculate the ratio of R&D to sales in the years 2010–2013.

   (d) Approximate the incremental margin percentage by the ratio of gross profit to revenue. Suppose that the R&D elasticity of demand in the years 2010–2013 is 0.2. Calculate the R&D expenditure that would have maximized Google's profit in each of the years 2010–2013.

(e) Compare your calculations in (d) with Google's actual R&D expenditure.

6. In 1992, the state of Victoria, Australia, issued 10-year master licenses to Tattersall's and Tabcorp for each to operate 13,750 slot machines at clubs and hotels. Eventually, they set up 26,682 machines at 514 locations. In 2008, the government decided to replace the master licenses with individual transferable 10-year licenses. The market value of Tattersall's and Tabcorp fell by A$2.8 billion in one day. Subsequently, the government issued 27,290 new licenses for fees totaling A$980 million. (Source: Victorian Auditor-General, *Allocation of Electronic Gaming Machine Entitlements*, Melbourne: Victorian Government Printer, June 2011.)

   (a) Consider a club that has acquired one of the new 10-year licenses. Using a suitable diagram, explain how the club should set the price of gambling to maximize profit. (*Hint*: You are free to assume any data necessary to draw the diagram.)

   (b) How should the club take account of the once-only license fee in its decisions: (i) whether to continue in business; and (ii) its scale of operations? How does it matter that the license is transferable?

   (c) Comparing the master and individual licensing systems, what effect do you expect on the quantity and price of gambling?

7. The National Collegiate Athletic Association (NCAA) regulates competitive sports at member colleges and universities. The NCAA restricts the pay of student athletes (generally limited to the full cost of their education) and requires student athletes to attend full-time programs of study.

   (a) What market power does the NCAA have, and what are its source(s)?

   (b) In April 2014, football players at Northwestern University voted in a secret ballot on whether to form a union. Explain why the NCAA vigorously opposed the vote.

   (c) If the US government were to forbid the NCAA from restricting pay to student athletes, how would that affect: (i) the earnings of student athletes; and (ii) professional sports leagues?

8. Cricket is India's top spectator sport. Under Indian law, private broadcasters must share any coverage of Indian cricket matches with the national television and radio broadcasters, Doordarshan and All India Radio. However, the law does not require national broadcasters to share their cricket telecasts with private channels. (Source: "DD may get a blank cheque," *Times of India*, August 13, 2004.)

   (a) How would the Indian law affect the ability of a private television channel to differentiate itself from Doordarshan?

   (b) How would the law affect the amount that a private television channel would bid for rights to broadcast Indian cricket matches?

   (c) How would the law affect Doordarshan's degree of market power relative to: (i) television viewers; and (ii) the organizers of Indian cricket matches?

(d) Some predicted that, owing to the law, only national broadcasters would bid for rights to broadcast Indian cricket matches, and private broadcasters would not bid. Do you agree?

9. Some automobile parts, such as batteries and tires, wear out with use and must be replaced frequently. Suppliers of these parts sell their products both as original equipment to auto manufacturers and as replacement parts to car owners. By contrast, supplies of air bags and ignition systems sell mainly to auto manufacturers.

   (a) Assess the power of automobile manufacturers over suppliers of (i) batteries and tires as compared to (ii) air bags and ignition systems.
   (b) For products like batteries and tires, do you expect prices to be higher in the original equipment market or the replacement market?
   (c) Suppose that the supply of batteries is perfectly competitive. Using an appropriate diagram, explain how an automobile manufacturer would determine the quantity of batteries to buy.

You are the consultant!

Consider some good or service that your organization produces. If your organization produced and sold 5% more, what would be the effect on revenue and cost? If your organization produced and sold 5% less, what would be the effect on revenue and cost? Is your organization maximizing profit?

Notes

1   The following discussion is based, in part, on: "Pfizer deal with Ranbaxy means a delay for generic form of Lipitor," *New York Times*, June 19, 2008; "The War over Lipitor," CNN Money, May 6, 2011; "Atorvastatin," Wikipedia (accessed July 12, 2011).

2   Chapter 9 introduces the concept of price discrimination. With price discrimination, different units are sold at different prices, so total revenue is not simply price multiplied by sales.

3   According to Table 8.1, Venus can earn the same profit of $33.2 million with a price of $136 and sales of 1.28 million. This ambiguity is due to our considering increments of sales of 200,000 units. The rule presented in this section – choosing the scale of production where marginal revenue equals marginal cost – is more precise, and essentially considers sales in infinitesimal increments.

CHAPTER 9

Pricing

LEARNING OBJECTIVES

- Apply uniform pricing.
- Appreciate how price discrimination can increase profit beyond uniform pricing.
- Understand complete price discrimination.
- Apply direct segment discrimination.
- Apply indirect segment discrimination.
- Appreciate the choice between alternative pricing policies.

1. Introduction

Founded in Australia in 1920 as Queensland and Northern Territory Air Services, the Qantas Group is a leading international carrier. The Qantas Group operates the Qantas and Jetstar airlines. In the year 2012–2013, the group earned A$13.7 billion in revenue and its seat factor (capacity utilization) was 79.3%. Its fleet comprised 312 aircraft, with an average age of 7.9 years.[1]

On January 6, 2015, passengers traveling in economy class on Qantas flight QF401 from departing Sydney at 6 am to Melbourne who compared tickets might have been surprised at the differences among their fares. The fully flexible fare was A$600, the Flexi Saver fare was A$365, while the Red e-Deal fare was A$245. If they had traveled half an hour later, at 6:30 am, they could have got the Red e-Deal for just A$155.

Each fare is subject to different conditions. The fully flexible fare is fully refundable. The Flexi Saver is not refundable but allows changes up to the time of the flight, subject to fees. The Red e-Deal is not refundable but allows changes up to the day before the flight, subject to fees.

Until April 2014, Qantas offered a 20% discount on flexible fares to seniors aged 60 and over, and to children traveling with adults. However, the airline did not allow any discount on Red e-Deal fares.

Pricing is crucial for Qantas, as for any airline. Travelers vary widely in the amount that they are willing to pay for the same flight. Moreover, airline operations involve substantial fixed costs and relatively low variable costs. Consequently, airlines have invested substantial amounts in reservations and yield management systems to adjust fares and allocate seats.

Since variable costs are low, why doesn't Qantas fill all its seats and earn more profit? Why did it offer senior discounts? Why is the Red e-Deal cheaper for the 6:30 am flight? Why does Qantas set different conditions for changes in the Flexi Saver and Red e-Deal fares?

This chapter ties threads from previous chapters on demand, elasticity, costs, and monopoly to analyze how a seller with market power should set prices to maximize profit. We first apply the price elasticity of demand and marginal cost. Our rule will explain why Qantas doesn't fill all its seats. Essentially, the reason is that, to fill all the empty seats, it must cut fares to a point that would reduce overall profit.

Next, we show how to increase profit by setting different prices that realize different margins from various market segments. This depends on the extent of the seller's information about the individual buyer's demand. We consider situations where the seller has complete information as well as those where the seller has limited information.

Where the seller has sufficient information to directly identify consumer segments, it can apply direct segment discrimination. This explains why Qantas offered discounts for seniors. By doing so, it might raise profit.

However, even if the seller lacks sufficient information or the ability to discriminate directly, it might be able to apply indirect segment discrimination. This explains why Qantas sets different prices for different flights, and imposes different conditions for change in the Flexi Saver and Red e-Deal fares. By doing so, it can earn more profit from travelers who prefer particular times, and from travelers who might change their plans.

Any seller with market power can use the techniques of pricing presented in this chapter to better achieve its objectives and, in particular, increase profit. Non-profits can use pricing techniques to increase production and serve more customers.

2. Uniform Pricing

Whenever managers are asked why they do not set a higher price, the most frequent response is: "Because I would lose sales." This does not, however, answer the question. Unless the demand is completely inelastic, a higher price will always result in lower sales. The real issue is how the increase in price will affect the profit of the business. As we will show, the answer depends on the price elasticity of demand and the marginal cost.

Here, we begin with the simplest pricing policy – **uniform pricing**, where the seller charges the same price for every unit of the product.

> **Uniform pricing:** The same price for every unit of the product.

Price Elasticity

Suppose that Mercury Airlines offers air service and the cost of service comprises a constant marginal cost of $80 per passenger. How should Mercury price the service? For simplicity, we suppose that the profit contribution is large enough to exceed the fixed cost, so Mercury should continue in operation.

Recall from Chapter 3 that demand is *elastic* if a 1% price increase causes the quantity demanded to drop by more than 1%, and *inelastic* if a 1% price increase causes the quantity demanded to fall by less than 1%. Generally, if the demand is inelastic, an increase in price will lead to a higher profit. Accordingly, a seller that faces an inelastic demand should raise the price.

Profit-Maximizing Price

Indeed, the seller should raise price until the demand is elastic. In the price elastic range, what price maximizes the seller's profit? Chapter 8 identified the profit-maximizing sales and price by the rule that marginal revenue equals marginal cost. Figure 9.1 shows the profit-maximizing sales and price for Mercury Airlines.

> **Profit-maximizing price:** The incremental margin percentage equals the reciprocal of the absolute value of the price elasticity of demand.

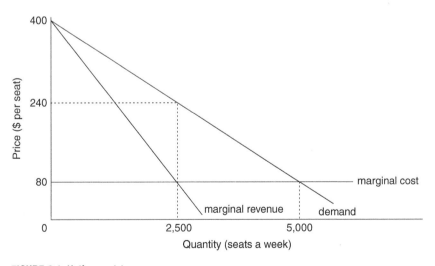

FIGURE 9.1 Uniform pricing.

Note: At the profit maximizing quantity of sales, the marginal revenue equals the marginal cost. Equivalently, the incremental marginal percentage equals the reciprocal of the absolute value of the price elasticity of demand.

Managers usually do not readily have information about marginal revenue. Typically, however, they have better information about the price elasticity of demand. So, it is more convenient to have a pricing rule based on elasticity.

A rule equivalent to marginal revenue being equal to marginal cost is that the incremental margin percentage equals the reciprocal of the absolute value of the price elasticity of demand. So a seller maximizes profit by setting a **price** where

$$\text{incremental margin percentage} = -\frac{1}{\text{price elasticity of demand}}. \tag{9.1}$$

The price elasticity of demand is negative; hence, the minus sign on the right-hand side of the pricing rule ensures that the entire right-hand side is positive.

Let us apply the rule to Mercury's pricing. Suppose that the price elasticity of demand is −1.5. Then, for Mercury to maximize its profit, the incremental margin percentage must be $1/1.5 = 2/3$. Representing the price by p, and recalling that the marginal cost is $80, the rule implies that

$$\frac{p-80}{p} = \frac{2}{3}. \tag{9.2}$$

By solving this equation, we find that $p = 240$. Hence, the price that maximizes Mercury's profit is $240 (as Figure 9.1 shows, we get the same price if we look for the sales where the marginal revenue equals the marginal cost). At the price of $240, the quantity demanded is 2,500 seats per week. Hence, Mercury's total revenue is $240 \times 2,500 = \$600,000$ a week. Mercury's total cost is $80 \times 2,500 = \$200,000$. Thus, its profit contribution is $400,000 a week.

The price elasticity may vary along a demand curve. Further, the marginal cost may change with the scale of production. Accordingly, determining the profit-maximizing price involves a series of trials with different prices until a price is found such that the incremental margin percentage equals the reciprocal of the absolute value of the price elasticity.

Demand and Cost Changes

The pricing rule shows how a seller should adjust its price when there are changes in the price elasticity of demand or marginal cost. Consider changes in the price elasticity. If the demand is more elastic, then the price elasticity will be a larger negative number. So, by the rule, the seller should aim for a lower incremental margin percentage.

For instance, suppose that, in Mercury's case, the price elasticity is −2 rather than −1.5. Then the profit-maximizing incremental margin percentage will be $1/2 = 50\%$. Letting the price be p, we have $(p - 80)/p = 0.50$, which implies that the profit-maximizing price is $160.

By contrast, if the demand were less elastic, say, with an elasticity of -1.33, then the profit-maximizing incremental margin percentage would be $1/1.33 = 75\%$. Again, representing the price by p, we would then have $(p - 80)/p = 0.75$, which implies that the profit-maximizing price would be \$320.

Next, let us consider changes in the seller's marginal cost. In our original example, the price elasticity was -1.5, while the marginal cost was \$80. Suppose that the marginal cost is lower at \$60. How should Mercury adjust its price? Using the pricing rule, the profit-maximizing price must satisfy $(p - 60)/p = 1/1.5$, which implies that $p = 180$. Notice that, although the marginal cost is \$20 lower, the profit-maximizing price is \$60 lower.

Similarly, we can show that, if the marginal cost is higher, Mercury should not raise its price by the same amount. The reason is that Mercury must consider the effect of the price change on the quantity demanded.

These examples demonstrate that the way a seller should adjust its price to changes in either the price elasticity or the marginal cost depends on both the price elasticity and the marginal cost. In particular, this means that a seller should not necessarily adjust the price by the same amount as a change in marginal cost.

PROGRESS CHECK 9A

In the case of Mercury Airlines, suppose that the price elasticity of demand is -2, while the marginal cost is \$70 per seat. Calculate the price that maximizes profit.

Common Misconceptions

A common mistake in pricing is to set the price by marking up average cost. Cost-plus pricing is problematic. In businesses with economies of scale, the average cost depends on the scale of production. So, to apply cost-plus pricing, the seller must make an assumption about the scale. But the sales and production scale depend on the price, hence cost-plus pricing leads to circular reasoning.

Moreover, cost-plus pricing gives no guidance as to the appropriate mark-up on average cost. Should a seller apply the same or different mark-ups to different products? Suppose that a seller wants to set the mark-up to maximize profits. Then the seller must go back to considering the price elasticity of demand and the marginal cost.

Another common mistake is to believe that the profit-maximizing price depends only on the price elasticity. To illustrate the correct approach, consider the mini-bars provided by many hotels. The mini-bar has considerable market power, especially in the early hours of the morning, when it would be inconvenient if not hazardous to venture out of the hotel for a beverage.

Suppose that the price elasticities of demand for Heineken beer and Coca-Cola in the mini-bar are the same. Should the hotel set the same price for both items? Absolutely not. The hotel should set the same incremental margin percentage on the two items. Since the marginal cost of Heineken beer is higher than that of Coca-Cola, the hotel should set a higher price for the Heineken.

A common mistake in the pricing of services is to aim to fully utilize the available capacity. Capacity utilization is a useful metric of cost efficiency. However, to achieve 100% utilization means increasing sales. In turn, with uniform pricing, that means cutting the price and losing revenue on inframarginal buyers. So, increasing capacity utilization may lead to lower profit!

PRICE ELASTICITY: WHO IS THE CUSTOMER?

Whenever a damaged car arrives at a repair shop, one of the first questions that the car owner must answer is: "Do you have insurance for the damage?" Why does the repair shop care whether the owner has insurance coverage?

Automobile repair is a case where there are two persons on the demand side: the car owner who makes the buying decision and the insurer who pays the bill. The owner of a damaged car will be relatively less sensitive to the price of repairs. Indeed, the owner may ask the repair shop to fix some other outstanding damage at the insurer's expense.

Generally, demand is less sensitive to price whenever there is a split between the party that makes the buying decision and the party that pays the bill. Auto repair shops understand and exploit this split. However, the car owner will be concerned about the price of repairs to the extent that his or her future insurance premium or policy renewal depends on past claims.

3. Complete Price Discrimination

The previous section introduced a rule for uniform pricing: set the price so that the incremental margin percentage equals the reciprocal of the absolute value of the price elasticity of demand. In Figure 9.2, we illustrate the profit-maximizing uniform price for Mercury Airlines. On closer examination, however, we can show that uniform pricing does not yield the maximum possible profit. This suggests that we should look for better pricing policies.

Shortcomings of Uniform Pricing

Recall that the demand curve for a product also reflects the marginal benefits of the various buyers. At the price of $240 per seat, the benefit of a flight for the marginal buyer is just equal to the price. For all the other (inframarginal) buyers, who account

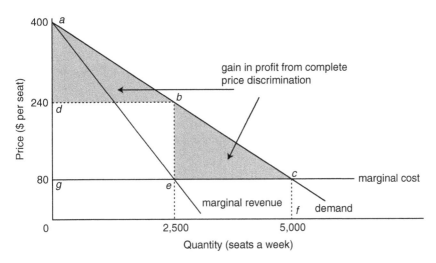

FIGURE 9.2 Complete price discrimination.

Notes: With complete price discrimination, the seller prices each unit at the buyer's benefit and sells a quantity such that the marginal benefit equals the marginal cost. The increase in profit over uniform pricing is the shaded area *abd* plus the shaded area *bec*.

for 2,499 seats, the benefit exceeds the price. Each of these inframarginal buyers enjoys some buyer surplus. The market buyer surplus is the area *abc* in Figure 9.2.

With uniform pricing, the inframarginal buyers do not pay as much as they would be willing to pay. This suggests that, by taking some of the buyer surplus, Mercury could increase its profit.

Another shortcoming of uniform pricing is that it sells an economically inefficient quantity. (Recall from Chapter 6 on economic efficiency that the allocation of an item is economically efficient if the marginal benefit equals the marginal cost.)

The marginal buyer derives a benefit of $240, while the marginal cost is only $80. This economic inefficiency identifies an opportunity for profit. By providing the service to everyone whose marginal benefit exceeds the marginal cost, Mercury can increase profit.

> **Shortcomings of uniform pricing:**
>
> - It does not extract the entire buyer surplus.
> - It does not provide the economically efficient quantity.

PROGRESS CHECK 9B

What are the two shortcomings of uniform pricing?

Price Discrimination

Ideally, Mercury should sell each seat at the respective buyer's benefit. Referring to Figure 9.2, this would be like selling down the market demand curve. Then Mercury would earn a higher incremental margin from buyers with higher benefit and a smaller margin from buyers with lower benefit.

Any pricing policy under which a seller sets prices to earn different incremental margins on various units of the same or a similar product is called **price discrimination**. (This term simply means setting different prices, and is not intended to have any negative connotation. An equivalent term would be "price differentiation.")

> **Price discrimination:** Pricing so as to earn different incremental margins on various units of the same or a similar product.

Complete price discrimination is the pricing policy which prices each unit at the buyer's benefit and sells a quantity such that the marginal benefit equals the marginal cost. This policy is called "complete" because it charges every buyer the maximum that they are willing to pay for each unit. Hence, the policy leaves each buyer with no surplus.

> **Complete price discrimination:** Pricing each unit at the buyer's benefit and selling a quantity such that marginal benefit equals marginal cost.

To illustrate complete price discrimination, consider Mercury Airlines' pricing of air service. Referring to Figure 9.2, the demand curve is a straight line with a slope of $-320/5{,}000 = -0.064$. This means that the first traveler is willing to pay $400 - 0.064 = \$399.936$ for a seat, the second traveler $400 - 2 \times 0.64 = \$399.872$, and so on. Hence, under complete price discrimination, Mercury should charge the first traveler $399.936, the second traveler $399.872, and so on.

Mercury should *not* stop selling at the 2,500th seat. The reason is that the 2,501st traveler derives a benefit of $240 - 0.064 = \$239.936$, which exceeds Mercury's marginal cost of $80. This means that Mercury can raise its profit by selling a seat to that traveler.

Indeed, Mercury should sell up to the quantity where the marginal benefit just equals the marginal cost. Referring to Figure 9.2, this balance occurs at a quantity of 5,000 seats a week. The 5,000th traveler is willing to pay exactly $80 for a seat, which is Mercury's marginal cost. If Mercury tried to sell beyond 5,000 seats, it would make a loss on additional units. Under complete price discrimination, the buyer of the 5,000th seat is the marginal buyer.

With complete price discrimination, Mercury's total revenue is the area $0fca$ under the demand curve from the quantity of 0 up to 5,000 seats a week. This area is $(400 + 80)/2 \times 5{,}000 = \$1.2$ million a week. As for costs, Mercury's total cost is area $0fcg$, which is $80 \times 5{,}000 = \$0.4$ million a week. Hence, with complete price discrimination, Mercury's profit contribution is $800,000 a week.

By contrast, in the preceding section, we showed that Mercury's maximum profit contribution with uniform pricing would be $400,000 a week. So, Mercury earns a higher profit with complete price discrimination than with uniform pricing.

Under a policy of complete price discrimination, the seller should sell each unit for the benefit that it provides its buyer and sell the quantity where the buyer's marginal benefit just equals the marginal cost. Complete price discrimination resolves the two shortcomings of uniform pricing:

- By pricing each unit at the buyer's benefit, the policy extracts all the buyer surplus.
- It provides the economically efficient quantity; hence, it exploits all opportunity for additional profit through increasing sales.

In the example of Mercury Airlines, the policy of complete price discrimination enables Mercury to extract higher prices for the 2,499 seats that would be inframarginal under uniform pricing. This increase in profit contribution is represented by the area *adb* in Figure 9.2. Second, with complete price discrimination, Mercury would sell 2,500 more seats. These additional seats raise the profit by the area *bec* in Figure 9.2. The total increase in profit contribution is the sum of the areas *adb* and *bec*.

Economic Efficiency

We have given a motivation for complete price discrimination as a way to increase profit. It is interesting to note that it also achieves economic efficiency. In this sense, maximizing profit is aligned with the social goal of economic efficiency, that is, allocating resources so that no person can be better off without making another person worse off.

To the extent that price discrimination achieves economic efficiency, it is useful for non-profit and government organizations such as hospitals, museums, and universities. By applying price discrimination, they may be able to expand their service to more people. For instance, by charging more to customers who are willing to pay more, a non-profit can use the additional revenue to provide service to poorer customers.

Information and Resale

Under complete price discrimination, the seller charges each buyer a different price for each unit of the product. To implement complete price discrimination:

* The seller must know each potential buyer's individual demand curve. It is not enough to know the price elasticities of the individual demand curves. Rather, the seller must know the entire individual demand curve of each potential buyer.
* The seller must be able to prevent customers from buying at a low price and reselling to others at a higher price.

Typically, it is more difficult to resell services, especially personal services, than goods. For instance, it is more difficult to resell medical treatment than pharmaceuticals, and it is more difficult to resell tax planning advice than tax preparation software. Accordingly, price discrimination is relatively more widespread in services than goods and is especially common in personal services.

PROGRESS CHECK 9C

In Figure 9.2, the profit contribution from complete price discrimination exceeds the profit contribution from uniform pricing by areas *adb* and *bec*. Calculate the dollar values of these areas.

DOES THE DOCTOR REALLY NEED TO KNOW YOUR OCCUPATION?

Price discrimination is common in medical services. Doctors treat patients on an individual basis. A doctor's first step in treatment is always to record the patient's history. This routinely includes questions about the patient's occupation, employer, home address, and insurance coverage. This information is very useful in gauging a patient's ability and willingness to pay as well as the patient's health.

To the extent that a patient is paying her or his own bill, the doctor can use this information to charge different prices to various patients for the same treatment. The result is close to complete price discrimination. Indeed, the healthcare scholars Victor Fuchs and Alan M. Garber remarked approvingly: "Medicine has a long and generally honorable history of price discrimination. Doctors have provided free or heavily discounted care to the needy, and drug companies have charged lower prices to those less able to pay full price."

Source: Victor Fuchs and Alan M. Garber, "Medical innovation: promises & pitfalls," *Brookings Review*, Vol. 21, No. 1 (Winter 2003), pp. 44–48.

SELLING DOWN THE DEMAND CURVE: SALESFORCE.COM

With broadband Internet service pervasive and reliable, software publishers are mimicking automobile manufacturers and movie studios. Auto manufacturers offer leases to drivers who do not wish to buy. Similarly, movie studios sell videos to rental stores that cater to low-benefit viewers. Not every potential customer derives enough benefit to justify outright purchase.

The same principle applies to software. Systems for customer relationship management (CRM) can be very expensive. Prices are out of reach for many businesses. Yet the marginal cost of software is low. Enter the application service provider (ASP) to offer software "on tap" through the Internet. The ASP charges by usage and so reaches down the demand curve to low-benefit users.

Marc Benioff founded Salesforce.com in 1999 to provide CRM through the Internet to clients of all sizes. By 2011, Salesforce.com served 97,700 customers worldwide, earning revenues of $1.78 billion and gross profit of $1.33 billion. The company's market value was $21.3 billion.

Sources: Salesforce.com; Yahoo! Finance

4. Direct Segment Discrimination

To implement complete price discrimination, a seller must know the entire individual demand curve of each potential buyer. What if the seller does not have so much information? A seller without sufficient information to price on an individual basis may still be able to discriminate among *segments* of buyers. A **segment** is a significant cohesive group of buyers within a larger market.

> **Segment:** A significant cohesive group of buyers within a larger market.

Homogeneous Segments

Suppose that Mercury Airlines transports adults and seniors at the same marginal cost of $80. Then Mercury can divide the market into two segments according to age. We give the name **direct segment discrimination** to the policy of setting different incremental margins for each identifiable segment.

> **Direct segment discrimination:** Pricing to earn different incremental margins from each identifiable segment.

In Mercury's case, there are two identifiable segments: adults and seniors. Suppose that adults are willing to pay exactly $360 for travel, while seniors are willing to pay just $90. The willingness to pay of both segments exceeds Mercury's marginal cost, which is $80. Accordingly, Mercury Airlines should set the regular adult fare at $360 and the senior fare at $90. Mercury would earn incremental margins of 360 − 80 = $280 from each adult passenger, and 90 − 80 = $10 from each senior.

In this simple scenario, Mercury is able to achieve complete price discrimination through direct segment discrimination. However, as discussed next, if the buyers within each segment are heterogeneous and Mercury lacks sufficient information to identify sub-segments, then direct segment discrimination will not achieve complete price discrimination.

Heterogeneous Segments

What if adults differ in their willingness to pay, or seniors differ in their willingness to pay? Then the profit-maximizing pricing policy depends on whether Mercury can identify sub-segments within the broader segments of adults and seniors and prevent resale within the sub-segments.

If Mercury does not have sufficient information to identify such sub-segments or cannot prevent resale within segments, it has two choices for pricing within the adult and senior segments. One is to apply uniform pricing *within* each segment. The other is to apply *indirect* segment discrimination within each segment. Here, we focus on within-segment uniform pricing, leaving indirect segment discrimination to Section 6.

Within each segment, applying the rule for uniform pricing, the price should be such that the incremental margin percentage equals the reciprocal of the absolute value of the price elasticity of demand.

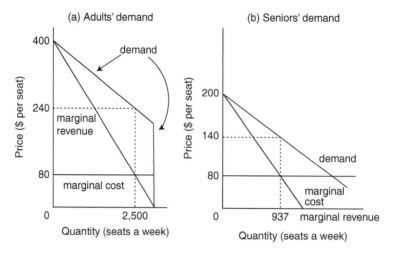

FIGURE 9.3 Direct segment discrimination.

Note: The demand for adult seats is relatively less elastic, so the seller should set a relatively higher incremental margin percentage on adult seats.

Let the adults' and seniors' demands be as shown in Figure 9.3. Consider first the demand from adults. Suppose that the profit-maximizing price is a. Through a process of trial and error, we find that, at the price a, the price elasticity of demand is -1.5. Accordingly, Mercury should set the price a so that the incremental margin percentage is $1/1.5 = 67\%$. This means $(a - 80)/a = 0.67$; hence, the price of an adult fare is $a = \$240$. Suppose that, at this price, the quantity demanded is 2,500 seats.

Next, consider the demand from seniors. Seniors derive lower marginal benefits; hence, their demand curve is lower than that of adults. Suppose that the profit-maximizing price is s. Through trial and error, we find that, at the price s, the price elasticity of demand is $-7/3$. Hence, Mercury should set the senior fare so that the incremental margin percentage is $3/7$. Then $(s - 80)/s = 3/7$, which implies that the senior fare is $s = \$140$. Suppose that, at this price, the quantity demanded is 937 seats.

In this example, the adult demand is less elastic. Therefore, Mercury should set a relatively higher incremental margin percentage on regular adult fares. Mercury's profit contribution from the adult segment is $(240 - 80) \times 2,500 = \$400,000$. Further, its profit contribution from the senior segment is $(140 - 80) \times 937 = \$56,220$. So, its total profit contribution with direct segment discrimination is $\$456,220$ a week. By contrast, its profit contribution with complete price discrimination is $\$800,000$ a week, while its profit contribution with uniform pricing is $\$400,000$ a week.

Generally, in a policy of direct segment discrimination coupled with uniform pricing within segments, the seller should set prices in the following way. Get a relatively lower incremental margin percentage from the segment with the more elastic demand and a relatively higher incremental margin percentage from the segment with the less elastic demand.

Implementation

To implement direct segment discrimination, the seller must identify and be able to use some identifiable and fixed buyer characteristic that segments the market. The characteristic must be fixed; otherwise, a buyer might switch segments to take advantage of a lower price.

The demand for movies and theme parks varies with such buyer characteristics as income, occupational status, and age. Movie theaters and theme parks cannot observe a customer's income, but they can check a customer's age and whether a customer is a student.

Age is a characteristic that fits the conditions for direct segment discrimination. It is easy to identify and impossible to change. A middle-aged adult cannot buy a senior citizen's ticket. Accordingly, movie theaters and theme parks set prices so as to extract lower margins from senior citizens and children. Assuming that the marginal cost of serving all patrons is the same, the result is lower prices for senior citizens and children and higher prices for middle-aged adults.

The other condition for direct segment discrimination is that the seller must be able to prevent consumers getting lower prices from reselling to those targeted with higher prices. Movie theaters mark their tickets as "not transferable." To the extent that theaters can prevent buyers from reselling tickets, they can discriminate effectively.

PROGRESS CHECK 9D

Referring to Figure 9.3, suppose that the marginal cost is $100. Use the graph to illustrate the new prices for adult and senior fares.

HEINZ KETCHUP: "NOT FOR RETAIL SALE"

The market for ketchup comprises a retail consumer segment and an institutional segment. Institutional customers include restaurants, catering services, airlines, schools, and even prisons. Institutions order larger quantities and often employ professional purchasing staff who aim to secure better deals. Typically, the institutional demand is more price elastic than the retail demand.

Ketchup manufacturers supply retail consumers through supermarkets and grocery stores. To the extent that manufacturers can prevent institutional customers from reselling ketchup to retail stores, they can implement direct segment discrimination. This means setting prices for a lower incremental margin from institutional customers. It is no coincidence that bottles of Heinz ketchup served in restaurants are marked "not for retail sale."

The National University Hospital is a tertiary referral healthcare and teaching facility that is affiliated with the National University of Singapore. Like other public-sector hospitals, the National University Hospital charges different prices to Singaporeans and foreigners.

Subsidized rates, which range from S$27 to S$31 for the first consultation and from S$25 to S$28 for follow-up consultations, are available only to Singapore citizens and permanent residents. The rates vary by the seniority of the attending doctor. Foreigners must pay the unsubsidized, private rates, which range from S$66.90 to S$85.95 for the first consultation and from S$43.10 to S$62.14 for follow-up consultations.

5. Location

To the extent that a product is costly to transport and the seller can identify a buyer's location, the seller can discriminate on the basis of the buyer's location. Generally, there are two ways of pricing to buyers in different locations.

> **FOB price:** Does not include the cost of delivery to the buyer.

> **CF price:** Includes the cost of delivery to the buyer.

One way is to set a common price to all buyers that does not include delivery. Such a price is called ex-works or **free on board (FOB)**. Each buyer pays the FOB price plus the cost of delivery to its respective location. With FOB pricing, the differences among the prices at various locations are exactly the differences in the costs of delivery to those locations.

The alternative way of pricing to different locations is to set prices that include delivery. The price is called **cost including freight (CF)**. With CF pricing, the differences among the prices at various locations need not correspond to the differences in the cost of delivery to the respective locations.

FOB and CF Pricing

To explain FOB and CF pricing (with uniform pricing in each market), suppose that Jupiter Bikes sets a price of $350 for a racing bike in its domestic market and the cost of freight to Japan is $30. Then the FOB price would be $350 + $30 = $380. With an exchange rate of 100 to the dollar, the FOB price in Japanese currency would be 38,000.

FOB pricing, however, ignores the differences between the price elasticities of demand in the various markets. Suppose that Jupiter can implement direct segment discrimination across the two markets. Then Jupiter should apply the analysis presented in the previous section to set a CF price. The incremental margin percentage in Japan should equal the reciprocal of the absolute value of the price elasticity of demand.

If Japanese demand is more elastic than domestic demand, then Jupiter should set prices so that its incremental margin percentage is lower in Japan than in the home market. A lower margin, however, does not necessarily mean a lower price, because Jupiter's marginal cost of supplying the Japanese market is higher owing to the cost of freight.

By contrast, if the Japanese demand is less elastic than domestic demand, then Jupiter should set prices so that its incremental margin percentage is higher in Japan than in the domestic market. Taking into account the higher marginal cost of supplying the Japanese market, this definitely means that Jupiter's price in Japan should exceed that in the domestic market.

With CF pricing, the difference in the prices between the two markets will simply be the result of the different incremental margin percentages and the different marginal costs of supplying the two markets. In particular, the price difference need not necessarily be the cost of freight from the domestic to the foreign market.

Earlier we showed that, generally, direct segment discrimination provides more profit than uniform pricing. Similarly, CF pricing yields more profit than FOB pricing – because it takes account of differences in the price elasticity of demand.

Parallel Imports

For discrimination by buyer's location, the various buyers must not be able to adjust location to take advantage of price differences. For most goods, the seller can control only the location at which it sells the product and cannot directly monitor the buyer's location.

If the difference between the prices of a product in two markets exceeds the transportation cost, retailers, and even consumers, might buy the item in one market and ship it to another. Such *parallel imports* are a particular challenge for lightweight high-price items such as pharmaceuticals and cosmetics.

Manufacturers deal with parallel imports in several ways. One is to customize the product to fit the market. English consumers are less likely to buy medicines labeled in Swahili. Another way is to limit sales to the sources of parallel imports. Manufacturers estimate the potential demand in low-price markets and limit sales to such markets accordingly. With durable goods, manufacturers may restrict warranty service to the country of purchase. This would discourage consumers from buying the good away from home.

PROGRESS CHECK 9E

Suppose that the price elasticity of demand for Jupiter bikes in Japan is −2.5 and the marginal cost including freight is ¥30,000. Calculate Jupiter's CF price in Japan. If Jupiter's domestic price is $350, and the exchange rate is ¥100 to $1, what is the difference between the Japanese and domestic prices?

6. Indirect Segment Discrimination

For a policy of direct segment discrimination, the seller must be able to identify some fixed buyer characteristic that divides the market into segments with different demand curves. A seller may know that specific segments have different demand curves but cannot find a fixed characteristic with which to discriminate directly. Under these circumstances, the seller may still be able to discriminate on price, but *indirectly*.

Suppose that the demand for Mercury Airlines' service comprises two segments – business and leisure travelers. Each segment is homogeneous. As Table 9.1 shows, the benefit of travel to business travelers is $501, and the benefit to leisure travelers is $201.

Ideally, Mercury would apply direct segment discrimination – charging the business travelers $500 and the leisure travelers $200. But how can it distinguish business from leisure travelers? The airline's check-in staff might ask every traveler to declare their purpose of travel. Then every passenger would claim to be going on vacation. Alternatively, Mercury's staff might check whether passengers are wearing business attire or casual clothes. But what if business travelers dress casually?

Structured Choice

Let us now consider another method of price discrimination, which uses an *indirect* means to discriminate. Consider the travelers' plans in more detail. Vacationers can fix their plans well in advance. By contrast, business travelers may need to change

Table 9.1 Indirect segment discrimination in air services

	Benefit ($)		Price ($)	Marginal cost ($)	Profit contribution per traveler ($)
	Business travelers	Leisure travelers			
Unrestricted fare	501	201	500	80	420
Restricted fare	101	181	180	80	100

their plans to fit work requirements. So, business and leisure travelers are differentially sensitive to fees for changes in flight bookings.

Mercury could offer two fares: a more expensive, unrestricted fare with no fees for changes; and a cheaper, restricted fare with a fee and limitations on changes. As Table 9.1 shows, the benefit of the restricted fare to business travelers is $101, and the benefit to leisure travelers is $181. Both business and leisure travelers get more benefit from unrestricted than restricted fares. However, business travelers get relatively more benefit from unrestricted fares and relatively less benefit from restricted fares.

Suppose, for instance, that Mercury prices the unrestricted fare at $500, and the restricted fare at $180. How would the business travelers choose? They would not buy the restricted fare, as the price exceeds their benefit. They would buy the unrestricted fare, and get a buyer surplus of $501 – $500 = $1. As for the leisure travelers, they would not buy the unrestricted fare, as the price exceeds their benefit. They would buy the restricted fare, and get a buyer surplus of $181 – $180 = $1. Table 9.1 shows the airline's profit contribution from each traveler.

The two segments – business and leisure travelers – have different demand curves. The airline, however, has no way to directly identify the segments. So instead it structures a choice between unrestricted and restricted fares to exploit the differential sensitivity of business and leisure travelers to fees for changes. We give the name **indirect segment discrimination** to the policy of structuring a choice for buyers so as to earn different incremental margins from each segment.

> **Indirect segment discrimination:** Structuring choice for buyers to earn different incremental margins from each segment.

Indirect segment discrimination uses product attributes to discriminate indirectly among the various buyer segments. Essentially, the product attributes are a proxy for the buyer attributes. To determine the profit-maximizing prices, the seller must consider how buyers with different attributes substitute among the various choices. Accordingly, the seller must not price any product in isolation. Rather, it must set the prices of all products together.

Implementation

To implement indirect segment discrimination, the seller must control some variable to which buyers in the various segments are differentially sensitive. The seller can then use this variable to structure a set of choices that will discriminate among the segments.

Since indirect segment discrimination allows each buyer a choice of products, the seller obviously cannot direct buyers to particular products. The other condition for indirect segment discrimination is that buyers must not be able to circumvent the discriminating variable.

Suppose, for instance, that Mercury were to allow travelers holding restricted fares to change their flights without any fee. Then business travelers would switch from unrestricted to restricted fares. Such switching would undermine the segment discrimination. In practice, airlines strictly enforce the conditions of restricted fares.

PROGRESS CHECK 9F

Referring to Table 9.1, suppose that the business traveler's benefit from the restricted fare is $401, and the leisure traveler's benefit from the restricted fare is $101. Calculate the business traveler's buyer surplus from the unrestricted and restricted fares, and the leisure traveler's buyer surplus from the unrestricted and restricted fares. Can Mercury Airlines implement indirect segment discrimination?

QANTAS: RED E-DEAL, FLEXI SAVER, OR FULLY FLEXIBLE?

Price discrimination is widespread in airline travel. Airlines are careful to match passengers to tickets (indeed, with increases in airport security, the government lends a helping hand). So, passengers cannot resell tickets to one another.

Fares vary by day of the week and time of day, and by the changes allowed and the fees for changes. On flight QF401 from Sydney to Melbourne, scheduled for January 6, 2015, Qantas offered three fares – a fully flexible fare of A$600, a Flexi Saver fare of A$365, and a Red e-Deal fare of A$245.

The more expensive the fare, the more flexibility it allows. The fully flexible fare is fully refundable. The Flexi Saver is not refundable but allows changes up to the time of the flight, subject to fees. The Red e-Deal is not refundable but allows changes up to the day before the flight, subject to fees. Obviously, the more flexible fares target business travelers, and the more restricted fares are aimed at leisure travelers.

Source: Qantas Airlines.

7. Selecting the Pricing Policy

Generally, the pricing policy that yields the most profit is complete price discrimination. This, however, also requires the most information. The next most profitable pricing policy is direct market segmentation. With direct segment discrimination, the seller discriminates directly on some fixed attributes of the buyer. The seller must be able to identify each buyer segment and prevent one segment from buying the product targeted at another segment.

The next most profitable pricing policy is indirect segment discrimination, which works indirectly through product attributes rather than directly through buyer attributes. Indirect segment discrimination is less profitable than direct segment discrimination for two reasons.

*   *Buyer benefit.* To induce buyers with different attributes to choose different products, the seller may resort to designing low-end products in a less appealing way. So, the products provide less benefit to buyers. For instance, with indirect discrimination, airlines deliberately impose unattractive conditions on restricted fares. The main purpose is to make them unappealing to business travelers.
*   *Cost.* Indirect discrimination may involve relatively higher costs. For instance, consumer products manufacturers use cents-off coupons to indirectly discriminate among consumers with different price elasticity. Coupons impose costs on manufacturers, retailers, and consumers.

The least profitable pricing policy is uniform pricing. This involves no discrimination at all. However, it is also the simplest, requiring the least information. Table 9.2 ranks the various pricing policies in order of profitability and information requirement.

Technology

The rapid development of information technology, especially the Internet, has had profound but conflicting effects on price discrimination. Information technology both facilitates and impedes price discrimination.

Table 9.2 Pricing policies: profitability and information

Profitability	Policy	Information and administration
lowest	Uniform pricing	lowest
	Indirect segment discrimination	
⬇	Direct segment discrimination	⬇
highest	Complete price discrimination	highest

The explosion in consumer usage of the Internet has enabled marketers to collect large volumes of detailed information about consumer preferences. In addition, falling costs of computing power and storage have lowered the cost of storing, analyzing, and applying the consumer information. So sellers can better design and target offers to particular segments.

For instance, airlines and supermarkets apply information technology to manage loyalty programs, tracking consumer purchases and targeting members with special offers. Online auctions enable sellers to fine-tune prices according to each individual buyer's willingness to pay. With computerized production and online delivery, producers can create multiple versions of a product and target different customer segments.

On the other hand, the falling costs of computing power and storage have also promoted the growth of consumer-oriented search services. Continuously prowling the Internet, these services help consumers to compare products and prices, thus identifying the best offer and circumventing price discrimination.

Cannibalization

We mentioned earlier that sellers may deliberately design low-end products in an unappealing way. They fear *cannibalization*, that is, high-benefit segments buying the item aimed at low-benefit segments. Cannibalization reduces the profitability of indirect segment discrimination.

> **Cannibalization:**
> Buyers switch from high incremental margin products to low incremental margin products.

Cannibalization occurs when buyers switch from high incremental margin products to low incremental margin products. Some examples of cannibalization are business travelers flying on restricted fares, high-income consumers redeeming coupons, and wealthy families buying basic sedans rather than high-end luxury cars.

The fundamental reason for cannibalization is that the seller cannot discriminate directly, and hence must rely on a structured choice of products to discriminate indirectly. To the extent that the discriminating variable does not perfectly separate the buyer segments, cannibalization will occur.

There are several ways to mitigate cannibalization. One is to use product design. Upgrading the high-margin item would make it relatively more attractive, and hence, less likely to be cannibalized. Degrading the low-margin item would make it less attractive, and thus less likely to cannibalize the demand for the high-margin item.

Further, the products can be designed with multiple discriminating variables. For instance, airlines specify multiple conditions for restricted fares, including minimum and maximum stay, limits on stopovers at intermediate destinations, and penalties for cancelation or changes in itinerary. Each of these conditions helps to reduce the degree to which the restricted fare would cannibalize the demand for the unrestricted fare.

Finally, cannibalization can be mitigated by controlling availability. Limiting the availability of the low-margin item would make it less attractive. Airlines, for instance, limit the number of seats allocated to lower fares.

PROGRESS CHECK 9G

Explain why indirect segment discrimination yields less profit than direct segment discrimination.

THE HERMITAGE: MUSEUM PRICING

Founded by Empress Catherine II (the Great), the Hermitage in St Petersburg, Russia, is one of the world's great art museums. Following the October Revolution, the Soviet government opened the Hermitage to the public. Subsequently, the Soviet government substantially expanded the museum by incorporating the Winter Palace of the former imperial family and adding works seized from private art collectors.

The Hermitage's pricing policy combines direct and indirect segment discrimination. General admission is free for all students and children and Russian pensioners. The price is 350 roubles for Russian adults, and 400 roubles (equivalent to $6) for foreign adults.

Through its website, the Hermitage encourages visitors to buy tickets through the Internet at a price of $17.95 and so "avoid a long line at the ticketing office." The Hermitage also offers free admission to all visitors on the first Thursday of each month.

Source: Hermitage Museum, www.hermitagemuseum.org (accessed July 20, 2011).

KEY TAKEAWAYS

- To maximize profit with uniform pricing, set the price so that the incremental margin percentage equals the reciprocal of the absolute value of price elasticity of demand.
- Price discrimination can increase profit by taking buyer surplus and providing a quantity closer to economically efficient.
- Complete price discrimination charges a different price for each unit of the product.
- Direct segment discrimination sets prices to earn different incremental margins from each segment.
- Indirect segment discrimination structures a choice for buyers to earn different incremental margins from each segment.
- Location is one profitable basis for segment discrimination.

- The ranking of pricing policies from most to least profitable is complete price discrimination, direct segment discrimination, indirect segment discrimination, and uniform pricing.

REVIEW QUESTIONS

1. Many supermarkets sell both branded and own-label merchandise. A supermarket estimates that the demand for its own-label cola is less elastic than the demand for Coca-Cola. Should it set a higher price for own-label cola?
2. Sol Electric manufactures low-energy light bulbs. The marginal production cost is $2 per unit, while the price elasticity of demand is –1.25. With uniform pricing, what is the profit-maximizing price?
3. Using a new manufacturing process, Saturn Tire has reduced the marginal cost of a tire from $50 to $40. Should it reduce the selling price of a tire by $10?
4. Book publishers typically set prices by the number of pages multiplied by a standard price per page. Comment on this pricing policy.
5. How does complete price discrimination increase profit as compared with uniform pricing?
6. What conditions are necessary to implement complete price discrimination?
7. Give an example of direct segment discrimination. Discuss whether the example meets the conditions for such discrimination.
8. Explain the difference between FOB and CF prices.
9. On which of the following products would it be easier to discriminate by the buyer's location: newspapers or scientific journals? Explain your answer.
10. Give an example of indirect segment discrimination. Discuss whether the example meets the conditions for such discrimination.
11. Typically, car rental agencies charge much higher prices for gasoline than nearby gas stations. Explain how this indirectly segments between drivers who are paying for the rental themselves and those who are renting at the expense of others.
12. How can consumer goods manufacturers use coupons to discriminate on price?
13. Rank the various pricing policies in terms of profit.
14. How does information technology affect a seller's ability to discriminate on price?
15. What is cannibalization and how can it be managed?

DISCUSSION QUESTIONS

1. In November 2014, Morgan Stanley, Citigroup, Deutsche Bank, and JP Morgan led the syndication of a three-year $300 million loan to Alibaba. The interest rate on the loan was set at the London Interbank Offer Rate (Libor) plus a spread of 52 basis points (0.52%). Banks source funds from demand, savings, and time deposits, as well as the interbank market. However, Libor is relatively higher than interest rates on deposits. (Source: "Alibaba smashes Asian bond records," *IFR Asia*, November 22, 2014.)

Table 9.3 DEWA: electricity rates

Residential/commercial customers		Industrial customers	
Monthly usage (kWh)	Fils per kWh	Monthly usage (kWh)	Fils per kWh
0–2,000	23	0–10,000	23
2,001–4,000	28	10,001 and above	38
4,001–6,000	32		
6,001 and above	38		

Source: Dubai Electricity and Water Authority.

(a) Does Libor reflect a typical bank's average or marginal cost of funds?

(b) For purposes of pricing, which is relevant – average or marginal cost?

(c) Explain the banks' pricing policy in terms of the incremental margin percentage and the price elasticity of demand.

2. Doctors routinely ask patients for personal information such as occupation, employer, home address, and insurance coverage.

(a) How do the following factors affect the scope for price discrimination in medical services? (i) Doctors treat patients on an individual basis and it is physically impossible to transfer medical treatment from one person to another. (ii) Characteristics such as occupation and home address are quite fixed.

(b) Explain how, if doctors use price discrimination, they can treat more patients than if they use uniform pricing.

3. Dubai Electricity and Water Authority (DEWA) supplies electricity and water. In 2009, DEWA produced 30,056 GWh of electricity, of which 29.25% was used by residential customers, 44.53% by commercial customers, and 8.45% by industrial customers. Table 9.3 presents rates for electricity as of January 2011.

(a) When applying direct segment discrimination coupled with uniform pricing within segments, how should a seller set prices?

(b) Assuming that DEWA sets prices to maximize profits, do the rates suggest that industrial demand is more or less elastic than residential and commercial demand?

(c) A necessary condition for price discrimination is no resale of the good. In this regard, what is the challenge to DEWA?

(d) DEWA can inspect customer premises for technical reasons. Does this help to address the challenge in (c)? Explain your answer.

4. Up to 2 million US consumers buy pharmaceuticals from online Canadian pharmacies, where prices are substantially lower than in the United States. Monthly sales reached a peak of $43.5 million in early 2004. Then US pharmaceutical manufacturers restricted supplies to Canadian wholesalers that sold to online pharmacies. In response, Universal Drugstore and other Canadian pharmacies sourced drugs from wholesalers in Australia, New Zealand and Britain. (Source: "Kinks in Canada drug pipeline," *New York Times*, April 7, 2006.)

(a) By considering price elasticities of demand, and production and shipping costs, explain why US pharmaceutical manufacturers set higher prices in the United States than in Australia and New Zealand.

(b) How do parallel imports affect US pharmaceutical manufacturers?

(c) Compare the problem of parallel imports for drugs administered by medical professionals relative to other drugs.

5. Every year, Heinz sells 650 million bottles and over 13 billion packets of ketchup worldwide (Source: H.J. Heinz Company). The demand side of the ketchup market comprises a retail segment and an institutional segment. Institutions order larger quantities and may employ professional purchasing staff. Retail consumers are supplied through supermarkets and grocery stores.

(a) Explain why institutional demand for ketchup is likely to be more price elastic than retail demand. How would Heinz like to apply direct segment discrimination?

(b) If Heinz supplies both institutional customers and retail distribution channels through wholesalers, explain how the wholesalers might undermine direct segment discrimination.

(c) Compare the problem in (b) for ketchup in bottles as compared with packets.

(d) Why does Heinz mark ketchup sold to restaurants "not for retail sale"?

6. In 2010, Google earned revenues of $29.3 billion, of which 96% derived from advertising. Google's AdWords is a service that places advertisements in Google search pages and websites. In a continuous auction, Google scores each advertisement by the advertiser's maximum bid per click multiplied by the click-through rate. Google displays the advertisements in decreasing order of score. Advertisers pay for each click according to the score of the next highest advertisement divided by their own click-through rate. (Source: Austin Rachlin, "Introduction to the ad auction," adwords.blogspot.com.)

(a) Explain Google's AdWords auction in terms of complete price discrimination. Discuss whether Google meets the conditions for such discrimination.

(b) Explain Google's AdWords auction in terms of indirect segment discrimination. What induces advertisers who value the advertising space more to bid higher?

(c) Considering the consumer demand for Google search and Google websites, explain why Google takes account of both the advertiser's bid and click-through rate in allocating advertising space.

7. The Chinese Visa Application Center in London charges applicants for visas an application service fee and a visa fee. The application service fee is £35.25 for processing within four working days and £47 for processing within three working days. The single-entry visa fee is £30, £65, and £20 for citizens of the United Kingdom, United States, and other countries respectively. The corresponding double-entry visa fees are £45, £65, and £30. (Source: Chinese Visa Application Center, London, January 5, 2010.)

(a) Explain the Visa Center's pricing policies in terms of direct segment discrimination. Discuss whether issuance of visas meets the conditions for such discrimination.

    (b) Explain the Visa Center's pricing policies in terms of indirect segment discrimination between tourists and business travelers. Discuss whether issuance of visas meets the conditions for such discrimination.

    (c) Should the Chinese government set the same visa fees in all foreign countries?

8. Qantas sells tickets through conventional travel agents, online intermediaries, its own telephone call center, and its own website. Typically, an airline's cost per transaction is lowest for bookings through its own website and highest for bookings through conventional travel agents. Qantas's cheapest fare, the Red e-Deal, is only available for online booking.

    (a) How does technology affect an airline's ability to discriminate on price?

    (b) Considering Qantas's cost of bookings and travelers' elasticity of demand, explain why the airline offers the Red e-Deal only through online booking.

    (c) For flight QF401 departing Sydney on January 6, 2015 at 6 am for Melbourne, the Red e-Deal fare was A$245. For the next flight, departing at 6:30 am, the Red e-Deal fare was A$155. Explain the difference in pricing.

    (d) Explain why Qantas limits the number of seats sold by the Red e-Deal.

9. Founded by Empress Catherine II (the Great), the Hermitage in St Petersburg, Russia, is one of the world's great art museums. General admission is free for all students and children, and Russian pensioners. The price is 350 roubles for Russian adults, and 400 roubles (equivalent to $6) for foreign adults. Through its website, the Hermitage encourages visitors to buy tickets through the Internet at a price of $17.95 and so "avoid a long line at the ticketing office." The Hermitage also offers free admission to all visitors on the first Thursday of each month.

    (a) Explain how the Hermitage uses direct segment discrimination. Discuss whether Hermitage pricing meets the conditions for such discrimination.

    (b) Explain how the Hermitage uses indirect segment discrimination. Discuss whether Hermitage pricing meets the conditions for such discrimination.

    (c) Comment on the free admission on the first Thursday of each month with regard to: (i) maximizing the number of visitors served for a given budget; and (ii) cannibalization.

You are the consultant!

Consider your organization's various lines of business. For each line of business, consider the revenues and costs from alternative uses of the resources – people, property, and funds. Is every line of business maximizing profit?

Note

1   The following discussion is based, in part, on Qantas Annual Report 2013 and "Qantas slugs families, elderly on fares by cancelling discounts," *The Australian*, April 30, 2014.

10 CHAPTER

Strategic Thinking

LEARNING OBJECTIVES

- Appreciate strategic situations.
- Apply games in strategic form to situations with simultaneous moves.
- Appreciate the use of randomization in competitive situations.
- Distinguish zero-sum and non-zero-sum games.
- Apply games in extensive form to situations with sequential moves.
- Plan strategic moves and conditional strategic moves, both threats and promises.
- Appreciate strategy in repeated situations.

1. Introduction

The market for narrow-body medium-range commercial aircraft has been very profitable for Airbus and Boeing. However, manufacturers from Brazil, Canada, China, and Russia are poised to challenge Airbus's A320 family and Boeing's 737. Indeed, at the Paris Air Show in June 2011, Jim Albaugh, CEO of Boeing Commercial Airplanes, conceded: "The days of the duopoly with Airbus are over."[1]

In 1969, Empresa Brasileira de Aeronáutica (Embraer) was founded to manufacture military and agricultural aircraft. In 2000, it was privatized and listed on the São Paulo and New York stock exchanges. Embraer is now a well-reputed manufacturer of regional jets (aircraft with up to 120 seats). While Bombardier, COMAC, and Irkut have committed to build large planes, Embraer hesitated. At the Paris Air Show in June 2011, Frederico Curado, CEO, remarked: "Going up against Boeing and Airbus in head-to-head competition is really tough, not only because of their size, but because of their existing product line and industrial capacity .... They can have a very quick response and literally flood the market."

The government of China established the Commercial Aircraft Corporation of China (COMAC) to spearhead a national plan to produce commercial jets. COMAC is owned by the state-owned Assets Supervision and Administration Commission and various state-owned enterprises. In 2006, COMAC launched the C919. In November 2010, COMAC announced 100 orders, mainly from Chinese airlines. The C919 is scheduled to fly in 2015 and begin commercial deliveries in 2018.

As national champion in aviation manufacturing, COMAC is the successor to the Aviation Industry Corporation of China. COMAC is indirectly owned and controlled by the government of China. By contrast, Embraer is a publicly listed company.

How does the difference in ownership between COMAC and Embraer affect the decisions of the two manufacturers? Why do airplane manufacturers heavily publicize new orders, especially of new models under development? Given the established positions of Airbus and Boeing, and the commitment to enter by Bombardier, COMAC, and Irkut, should Embraer have proceeded?

The situation among Airbus, Boeing, Bombardier, and COMAC is *strategic*. A **strategic situation** is one where the parties consider interactions with one another in making decisions. Airbus and Boeing watch each other closely, and both pay great attention to the plans of COMAC and Embraer, and vice versa. A **strategy** is a plan for action in a strategic situation.

> **Strategic situation:** Where the parties consider interactions with one another in making decisions.

This chapter considers how to organize thinking about strategic decisions, choose among alternative strategies, and make more effective strategic decisions. The chapter is based on a set of principles to guide strategic thinking called *game theory*.

> **Strategy:** A plan for action in a strategic situation.

The first set of principles is the model of games in *strategic* form, which applies to situations where parties choose strategies at the same time. COMAC and Embraer can each apply a game in strategic form in its decision whether to produce a narrow-body jet. The same model applies to competition in markets with few sellers. It explains why competing sellers tend to cut price, although collectively they could raise profit by avoiding price competition.

The second set of principles is the model of games in *extensive* form, which applies to situations where parties act in sequence. Applying a game in strategic form, Embraer can appreciate that, through government support and the commitment of orders for 100 planes, COMAC has established a first-mover advantage. Managers can apply the same model to plan strategic moves and conditional strategic moves, both threats and promises.

The ideas and principles of game theory provide an effective guide to strategic decision-making in many situations. Corporate financiers apply game theory in leveraged buyouts and takeovers. Unions apply game theory in bargaining with employers. And, of course, game theory is useful to any business with market power in deciding competitive strategy.

PROGRESS CHECK 10A

The nail manufacturing industry is almost perfectly competitive. Your company is deciding whether to manufacture nails. Explain why this decision is *not* *strategic.*

---

2. Nash Equilibrium

To introduce a framework for situations where parties choose strategies at the same time, consider the following example. Jupiter Gasoline and Saturn Fuel operate adjacent gasoline stations. Each station independently decides its price. Should Jupiter maintain or cut price? What about Saturn?

The situation between Jupiter and Saturn is clearly strategic. Consumers are price sensitive and would switch to the station offering a lower price. Jupiter's sales and profit depend on Saturn's price, and likewise, Saturn's sales and profit depend on Jupiter's price. How should Jupiter act?

Let us try to clarify Jupiter's position in the following way. Jupiter has a choice of two strategies – maintain price or cut price. Likewise, Saturn has a choice of the same two strategies. Accordingly, there are four possible outcomes: Jupiter and Saturn both maintain price; Jupiter maintains price while Saturn cuts price; Jupiter cuts price while Saturn maintains price; and both stations cut price.

We can gather this information in Table 10.1 as follows. Record Jupiter's alternative strategies along the rows, and Saturn's strategies along the columns. The columns and rows delineate four cells, each representing one of the four possible outcomes. In each cell, the first entry is Jupiter's daily profit and the second entry is Saturn's daily profit. For instance, in the cell where both Jupiter and Saturn maintain price, write "J: 1,000" to show that Jupiter's profit would be $1,000, and "S: 1,000" to show that Saturn's profit would be $1,000. Similarly, in the cell where Jupiter cuts price and Saturn maintains price, write "J: 1,300" to show that Jupiter's profit would be $1,300, and "S: 700" to show that Saturn's profit would be $700. Table 10.1 is called a **game in strategic form**. It helps to organize thinking about strategic decisions that parties must take simultaneously.

Game in strategic form: Depicts one party's strategies in rows, other party's strategies in columns, and consequences in corresponding cells.

Let us use the game in strategic form to consider how Jupiter should act. First, look at the situation from Saturn's position. If Jupiter maintains price, then Saturn will earn $1,000 if it maintains price or $1,300 if it cuts price, so Saturn prefers to cut price. Now, if Jupiter cuts price, then Saturn will earn $700 if it maintains price or $800 if it cuts price, so, Saturn prefers to cut price.

Table 10.1 Gasoline stations: price war

| | | Saturn | |
		Maintain price	Cut price
Jupiter	Maintain price	J: 1,000 S: 1,000	J: 700 S: 1,300
	Cut price	J: 1,300 S: 700	J: 800 S: 800

Hence, regardless of Jupiter's move, Saturn should cut price. For Saturn, the strategy of maintaining price is *dominated* by the strategy of cutting price. A strategy is **dominated** if it generates worse consequences than some other strategy, regardless of the other party's choices. It makes no sense to adopt a dominated strategy.

For Saturn, maintaining price is a dominated strategy. Accordingly, Jupiter can guess that Saturn will cut price. Similarly, by studying the situation from Jupiter's position, it is easy to see that, for Jupiter also, maintaining price is a dominated strategy. Hence, Jupiter also should cut price.

> **Dominated strategy:** Generates worse consequences than some other strategy, in all circumstances.

This situation is called the *cartel's dilemma*. As Chapter 11 explains, a cartel is an agreement to restrain competition. Both stations know that, if they maintain price, then they can increase their profit. The snag, however, is that when each station acts independently, it will cut price. The final outcome is that both stations lose profit.

Definition

The pair of strategies – for Jupiter, to cut price, and for Saturn, to cut price – is the obvious way for the two stations to act. Moreover, this pair of strategies is a stable situation in the following sense. Even if Saturn knows that Jupiter will cut price, Saturn's best action is to cut price, so it will not change its strategy. Likewise, even if Jupiter knew that Saturn would cut price, Jupiter would still cut price.

In a game in strategic form, a **Nash equilibrium** is a set of strategies such that, given that the other parties choose their Nash equilibrium strategies, each party prefers its own Nash equilibrium strategy. In the cartel's dilemma, the pair of strategies in which both Jupiter and Saturn cut price is a Nash equilibrium.

> **Nash equilibrium:** Given that the other parties choose their Nash equilibrium strategies, each party prefers its own Nash equilibrium strategy.

What justifies a Nash equilibrium as a reasonable way for the relevant parties to act? In many typical strategic situations such as the cartel's dilemma, the Nash equilibrium strategies seem the most reasonable and obvious way to behave. By extension, this provides grounds for believing that in other, less intuitive settings, the relevant parties should also act according to Nash equilibrium strategies.

Solving Equilibrium – Formal Method

How should parties solve a game in strategic form for the Nash equilibrium? The formal solution for a Nash equilibrium is, first, to rule out dominated strategies and, next, to check all the remaining strategies, one at a time.

The cartel's dilemma is easy to solve. First, rule out the dominated strategies: for Jupiter, maintaining price is dominated, and for Saturn, maintaining price is dominated. Then each station has only one strategy left – to cut price – so that must be the equilibrium.

To illustrate the solution for Nash equilibrium in another setting, consider the Battle of the Bismarck Sea in World War II.[2] In late February 1943, the Japanese commander Rear-Admiral Kimura assembled a convoy of 16 transport ships and destroyers at the port of Rabaul. Kimura's mission was to bring the convoy to Lae, on the mainland of New Guinea. US Lieutenant-General Kenney, commander of Allied Air Forces in the area, sought to intercept and destroy the Japanese convoy.

Kimura had to choose between sailing along a northern route through the Bismarck Sea and a southern route. Meteorologists forecast that there would be rain on the northern route, which would reduce visibility. The weather on the southern route, however, would be fine.

Kenney had to decide the direction in which to concentrate his reconnaissance aircraft. Once his aircraft spotted the Japanese convoy, Kenney would dispatch his bombers. The dilemma for Kenney was that his best decision depended on what he believed Kimura would do.

Table 10.2 represents the Battle of the Bismarck Sea in strategic form. In each cell, the first entry represents the number of days of bombing that Kenney could inflict on the Japanese, while the second entry represents the number of days of bombing that Kimura would suffer (as a negative number).

Recall that the solution for a Nash equilibrium is, first, to rule out dominated strategies and, next, to check all the remaining strategies, one at a time. First, look at the situation from Kimura's position. If Kenney goes north, then Kimura will

Table 10.2 Battle of the Bismarck Sea

		Japan (Kimura)	
		North	South
US (Kenney)	North	US: 2 ↑ Japan: −2 ↔ US: 1	US: 2 ↕ Japan: −2 US: 3
	South	Japan: −1 ←	Japan: −3

suffer 2 days of bombing whether he goes north or south, so Kimura is indifferent between the strategies. If Kenney goes south, then Kimura will suffer 1 day of bombing if he goes north or 3 days of bombing if he goes south, so Kimura prefers to go north. Hence, regardless of Kenney's strategy, Kimura should go north; the south strategy is dominated by the north strategy.

Next, look at the situation from Kenney's position. Knowing that Kimura would go north, his choice is between north, which yields 2 days of bombing, and south, which yields only 1 day of bombing, so Kenney should go north.

Indeed, on February 28, Admiral Kimura set sail on the northern route. On March 2, General Kenney's planes discovered the Japanese convoy and destroyed it over two days of bombing.

Solving Equilibrium – Informal Method

A simple, informal method of finding a Nash equilibrium is to draw arrows between the cells as follows. Suppose that Kenney chooses north, then for Kimura draw a double-headed arrow between −2 in the top left-hand cell and −2 in the top right-hand cell (this double-headed arrow represents Kimura being indifferent between strategies). Next, suppose that Kenny chooses south, then for Kimura draw an arrow from −3 in the bottom right-hand cell pointing toward −1 in the bottom left-hand cell (this arrow represents Kimura preferring north).

Now, suppose that Kimura chooses north, then for Kenney draw an arrow from 1 in the bottom left-hand cell to 2 in the top left-hand cell (this arrow represents Kenney preferring north). Finally, suppose that Kimura chooses south, then for Kenney draw an arrow from 2 in the top right-hand cell pointing toward 3 in the bottom right-hand cell (this arrow represents Kenny preferring south).

Using this "arrow" technique, we can easily see if a strategy is dominated. A strategy is dominated if the row or column corresponding to the strategy has all the arrows pointing out. From Table 10.2, for Kimura, south is dominated. The arrow technique also easily identifies an equilibrium. If there is a cell with all arrows leading in, then the strategies marking that cell are a Nash equilibrium.

By the arrow technique, the Nash equilibrium is for Kenney to fly north and Kimura to sail north.

Non-equilibrium Strategies

We have explained how to analyze a strategic situation using the concept of a Nash equilibrium. Given that the other players choose their Nash equilibrium strategies, each party's best choice is its own Nash equilibrium strategy. But what if some party does not follow its Nash equilibrium strategy? Then the other parties may find it better to deviate from their respective Nash equilibrium strategies.

For example, from Table 10.2, Kenney's Nash equilibrium strategy is north, while Kimura's Nash equilibrium strategy is north. Suppose, however, that Kimura decides, for some reason, to go south and that Kenney has this information. Then Kenney can score three days of bombing and win a bigger victory by flying *south*.

Accordingly, in the Battle of the Bismarck Sea, if Kimura does not follow his Nash equilibrium strategy, then it is better for Kenney to choose a strategy that is not a Nash equilibrium strategy.

However, if the alternative to the Nash equilibrium strategy is a dominated strategy, then the Nash equilibrium strategy is better, even if the other party does not follow its Nash equilibrium strategy. For instance, suppose that Kenney decides to fly south. Then Kimura should still go north. The alternative strategy, south, is dominated.

PROGRESS CHECK 10B

In Table 10.1, use the arrow technique to identify the Nash equilibrium strategies.

EMBRAER: TO ENTER OR NOT TO ENTER

Boeing forecasts demand for 23,370 new narrow-body jets in the next 20 years. Given the finite demand, Airbus CEO, Tom Enders, cautioned that there might not be room for Airbus, Boeing, and four new manufacturers.

Focusing on COMAC and Embraer, suppose that COMAC would have an advantage in selling to Chinese airlines, while both manufacturers would compete on an equal basis for sales to other carriers. If both enter the market, COMAC would lose $1 billion, while Embraer would lose $2 billion. If only Embraer enters, it would earn $1 billion, while if only COMAC enters, it would earn $2 billion.

Table 10.3 presents the game in strategic form. Drawing the arrows shows two equilibria. In one equilibrium, COMAC enters and Embraer does not enter. In the other equilibrium, Embraer enters and COMAC does not enter. So, the game in strategic form is ambiguous about the actual outcome.

Table 10.3 Narrow-body jets: new entry

		Embraer	
		Enter	Do not enter
COMAC	Enter	C: –1 / C: 0 / E: –2	C: 2 / C: 0 / E: 0
	Do not enter		E: 1 / E: 0

Source: Richard Tortoriello, "Aerospace & defense," *Standard & Poor's Industry Surveys*, February 10, 2011.

3. Randomized Strategies

When the various parties act strategically, it seems reasonable for them to choose Nash equilibrium strategies. In some situations, however, there is no Nash equilibrium of the type that we have been considering. To illustrate, suppose that Table 10.4 represents the competitive situation between the two gasoline stations. The change from the original scenario is that Jupiter has a segment of loyal customers, so, if Saturn cuts price, Jupiter earns more by maintaining price.

By applying the arrow technique to Table 10.4, we can see that there is no Nash equilibrium in *pure strategies*: no cell has all the arrows leading inward. A **pure strategy** is one that does not involve randomization. In Table 10.4, Jupiter has two pure strategies, price high and price low, and Saturn also has two pure strategies, price high and price low.

> **Pure strategy:** Does not involve randomization.

Although there is no Nash equilibrium in pure strategies, there is another way for Jupiter and Saturn to act. Essentially, Jupiter does not want Saturn to know or predict its price. One way in which Jupiter can keep Saturn in the dark is to *randomize* the choice between maintaining and cutting price. If Jupiter randomizes its price, the station itself will not know its price. Then, of course, Saturn will not know either. Similarly, Saturn does not want Jupiter to know or predict its price. If Saturn randomizes its price, Jupiter cannot guess or learn it.

With a **randomized strategy**, the party specifies a probability for each of the alternative pure strategies. It then adopts each pure strategy randomly according to the probabilities. The probabilities must add up to 1.

> **Randomized strategy:** Choose each pure strategy according to a specified probability.

Nash Equilibrium in Randomized Strategies

Suppose that Jupiter adopts the following randomized strategy: maintain price with probability 1/2 and cut price with probability 1/2. To implement this strategy, Jupiter's manager marks a coin "maintain price" on one side and "cut price" on the other side, then gives the coin to the pump attendant. Jupiter then orders the pump attendant to toss the coin and fix the price according to which side of the coin faces up.

Table 10.4 Gasoline stations: price war (modified)

		Saturn	
		Maintain price	*Cut price*
Jupiter	Maintain price	J: 900 ↓ J: 1,300	J: 1,000 ↑ S: 900 ← — S: 800 J: 600
	Cut price	S: 500 — → S: 600	

Given that Jupiter has chosen this randomized strategy, how should Saturn act? Referring to Table 10.4, let us calculate the expected consequence for Saturn from maintaining price. Saturn's profit would be $900 if Jupiter maintains price, and $500 if Jupiter cuts price. Hence, Saturn's expected profit from maintaining price is ($900 × 1/2) + ($500 × 1/2) = $700. Similarly, we can calculate that, if Saturn cuts price, its expected profit would be ($800 × 1/2) + ($600 × 1/2) = $700.

What should Saturn do? Since Saturn gets the same expected profit from its two pure strategies, it is indifferent between the two. Accordingly, it would be willing to randomize between them. Specifically, suppose that Saturn prices high with probability 1/2.

How will Jupiter act? If Jupiter maintains price, its expected profit would be ($900 × 1/2) + ($1,000 × 1/2) = $950. Similarly, if Jupiter cuts price, its expected profit would be ($1,300 × 1/2) + ($600 × 1/2) = $950. Therefore, given Saturn's strategy, Jupiter is indifferent between maintaining and cutting price.

A Nash equilibrium in randomized strategies is like a Nash equilibrium in pure strategies: given that the other players choose their Nash equilibrium strategies, each party's best choice is its own Nash equilibrium strategy. The following randomized strategies constitute a Nash equilibrium in the (modified) situation between the gasoline stations: Jupiter prices high with probability 1/2 and Saturn prices high with probability 1/2. The appendix at the end of this chapter shows how to calculate the probabilities and thus solve the Nash equilibrium in randomized strategies.

Advantages of Randomization

Suppose that Jupiter has adopted the Nash equilibrium strategy of pricing high with probability 1/2. Suppose further that Saturn has learned of Jupiter's strategy through a spy. How can Saturn exploit this information? The answer is that it cannot – as we have calculated earlier, whether Saturn prices high or low, its expected profit will be $700. Generally, whenever a party adopts a Nash equilibrium strategy, the other parties cannot benefit from learning the strategy.

Randomization is useful in competitive contexts. The advantage of randomization comes from its being *unpredictable*. To implement the randomized strategy, Jupiter must leave the direction of its pricing to the coin toss. Jupiter must not make any conscious decision on pricing. If it chooses its price in a conscious way, Saturn may be able to guess or learn Jupiter's decision and act accordingly.

PROGRESS CHECK 10C

Referring to Table 10.4, suppose that Jupiter maintains price with probability 2/5. Calculate the expected consequences for Saturn if it: (a) maintains price; and (b) cuts price.

SUPERMARKET PRICING: HIGH OR LOW?

Supermarkets are torn between pricing high to extract buyer surplus from loyal consumers and pricing low to grab price-sensitive consumers. The dilemma is compounded in the presence of competition. Cutting price may not raise profit if a competing supermarket cuts price even lower.

The solution is to randomize the price discounts. Indeed, the dazzling array of "specials" in a supermarket advertisement does appear like randomized discounts. By discounting randomly, a supermarket can attract price-sensitive consumers while preventing competitors from undercutting on price.

4. Competition or Coordination

In the Battle of the Bismarck Sea, described in Table 10.2, if we add the outcomes for the United States and Japan in each cell, the sum is zero in every cell. By contrast, in the price war between the gasoline stations, described in Table 10.1, if we add the outcomes for Jupiter and Saturn in each cell, the sum varies from 1,600 to 2,000.

Strategic situations can be classified by the outcomes as either zero-sum games or positive-sum games. A **zero-sum game** is one where one party can become better off only if another is made worse off. If the outcomes for the parties add up to the same number (whether negative, zero, or positive) in every cell of the game in strategic form, then one party can become better off only if another is made worse off. Accordingly, such a strategic situation is a zero-sum game. A **positive-sum game** is one where one party can become better off without another being made worse off.

> **Zero-sum game:** One party can be better off only if another is worse off.

> **Positive-sum game:** One party can be better off without another being worse off.

A zero-sum game characterizes the extreme of *competition*: there is no way for all parties to become better off. By contrast, a positive-sum game involves at least some element of *coordination*. For instance, in the gasoline station price war, described in Table 10.1, both Jupiter and Saturn could agree that both maintaining price is better than both cutting price. However, the challenge for them is to enforce the agreement. Each station, acting independently, would cut the price.

Some situations involve elements of both competition and coordination. Consider two TV stations, Channel Z and TV Delta, choosing between two time slots for the evening news, 7:30 pm and 8:00 pm. Market research shows that the demand for news peaks at 8:00 pm and is lower at 7:30 pm.

Table 10.5 depicts the game strategic form. Each station has two pure strategies: broadcast at 7:30 pm or at 8:00 pm. Each cell presents the monthly profits of TV Delta and Channel Z in millions of dollars. The situation is a positive-sum game.

Table 10.5 Scheduling evening news

		Channel Z	
		7:30 pm	8:00 pm
TV Delta	7:30 pm	D: 1	D: 3
		↓	↑
		Z: 1 ———→ Z: 4	
		D: 4	D: 2.5
	8:00 pm		
		Z: 3 ←——— Z: 2.5	

The total profit of the two TV stations is not a constant. It is largest when the stations broadcast in different time slots.

While scheduling the evening news involves coordination, it also has an element of competition. Both stations will be better off if they schedule their news at different times. But one station will benefit relatively more – the station that gets the 8:00 pm slot. Accordingly, there are elements of competition (for the 8:00 pm slot) as well as coordination (choosing different slots).

Applying the arrows technique, we can identify two Nash equilibria in pure strategies: Channel Z broadcasts at 8:00 pm and TV Delta at 7:30 pm, or Delta broadcasts at 8:00 pm and Channel Z at 7:30 pm. There is also an equilibrium in randomized strategies, where each station chooses 7:30 pm with probability 1/7 and 8:00 pm with probability 6/7.

PROGRESS CHECK 10D

Check whether the following are zero-sum games: (a) entry into the market for narrow-body jets (Table 10.3); (b) modified gasoline price war (Table 10.4).

---

5. Sequencing

So far, we have focused on situations where the various parties move simultaneously. What if the parties move one at a time? To organize thinking about a strategic situation in which the parties act in sequence, we use the *game in extensive form*. A **game in extensive form** explicitly depicts the sequence of moves and the corresponding outcomes. It consists of nodes and branches: a node represents a point at which a party must choose a move, while the branches leading from a node represent the possible choices at the node.

Game in extensive form: Depicts the sequence of moves and corresponding outcomes.

Let us apply the game in extensive form to the scheduling of the evening news where Channel Z can schedule its news before Delta. In Figure 10.1, at the first node, *A*, Channel Z must choose between 7:30 pm (the upper branch) and 8:00 pm (the lower branch). TV Delta has the next move.

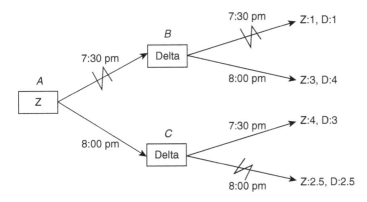

FIGURE 10.1 Scheduling the evening news: extensive form.

Note: At node *B*, Delta will choose 8:00 pm. At node *C*, Delta will choose 7:30 pm. By backward induction, at node *A*, Z will choose 8:00 pm.

Delta's node depends on Z's choice. If Z has chosen 7:30 pm, then Delta will be at node *B* and must decide between the two branches of 7:30 pm and 8:00 pm. If Z has chosen 8:00 pm, then Delta will be at node *C* and must decide between the two branches of 7:30 pm and 8:00 pm.

The consequences for TV Delta of choosing 7:30 pm or 8:00 pm depend on Z's choice. At the end of each branch, we mark the profits to Z and Delta, respectively. If Z chooses 7:30 pm and Delta also chooses 7:30 pm, they both earn $1 million. If Z chooses 7:30 pm while Delta chooses 8:00 pm, then Z makes $3 million and Delta earns $4 million. If Z chooses 8:00 pm while Delta chooses 7:30 pm, then Z makes $4 million and Delta earns $3 million. Finally, if both stations choose the peak time of 8:00 pm, they both earn $2.5 million.

Backward Induction

How should the two stations act? We solve the game in exten-sive form by **backward induction**, which means looking forward to the final nodes and reasoning backward toward the initial node. We can use this procedure to identify the best strategies for the two stations. There are two final nodes: *B* and *C*. At node *B*, TV Delta can choose 7:30 pm, which yields $1 million, or 8:00 pm, which yields $4 million. Clearly, at node *B*, Delta would choose 8:00 pm. Accordingly, we cancel the 7:30 pm branch. Now consider node *C*. Here, Delta must choose between 7:30 pm, which yields $3 million, and 8:00 pm, which yields $2.5 million. It will choose 7:30 pm, so we cancel the 8:00 pm branch.

> **Backward induction:**
> Look forward to final nodes and reason backward toward the initial node.

Having determined how TV Delta will act at each of its two possible nodes, *B* and *C*, we work back to consider the initial node, *A*. At node *A*, if Z chooses 7:30 pm, it can foresee that Delta will choose 8:00 pm, so Z will earn $3 mil-lion. On the other hand, if Z chooses 8:00 pm, it can foresee that Delta will choose 7:30 pm, so Z will earn $4 million. Therefore, Z should choose 8:00 pm.

Accordingly, in the scheduling of the evening news, when Z can move first, it will choose the 8:00 pm slot, while Delta will take the 7:30 pm slot.

Equilibrium Strategy

Equilibrium strategy:
The sequence of best actions, with each action decided at the corresponding node.

In a game in extensive form, a party's **equilibrium strategy** consists of a sequence of its best actions, where each action is decided at the corresponding node. In the evening news, when Channel Z can move first, Z's equilibrium strategy is to choose the 8:00 pm slot, while TV Delta's equilibrium strategy is to take the 7:30 pm slot.

We have assumed that Channel Z moves before TV Delta. If Delta can move first, then the game in extensive form will be like Figure 10.1, except that Delta would schedule its broadcast time at node A, and Z would schedule its broadcast time at node B or C. Then Delta's equilibrium strategy would be to take the 8:00 pm slot, and Z's equilibrium strategy would be to settle for 7:30 pm.

To decide on a strategy in a situation where the parties move in sequence, the basic principle is to look forward and anticipate the other party's responses. So when TV Delta can set its schedule before its competitor, Delta must look forward and anticipate how Z will respond to each of Delta's choices. In this way, Delta anticipates that, if it chooses 7:30 pm, then Z would choose 8:00 pm, while if it chooses 8:00 pm, then Z would choose 7:30 pm. By this procedure of backward induction, Delta and Z can determine their equilibrium strategies.

Practically, what is the difference between the equilibrium strategy in a game in extensive form and the Nash equilibrium strategy in a game in strategic form? In the evening news, when the two stations move simultaneously, there are two Nash equilibria in pure strategies (plus a Nash equilibrium in randomized strategies). But when the stations move in sequence, there is only one equilibrium. In the evening news, the equilibrium in the extensive form is also a Nash equilibrium in the corresponding strategic form. In other situations, however, the equilibrium in the extensive form may not be a Nash equilibrium in the corresponding strategic form.

Accordingly, when analyzing a strategic situation, it is important to consider carefully the structure of the moves: do the parties move simultaneously or sequentially? The equilibria with simultaneous moves and with sequential moves may be different.

First-Mover Advantage

First-mover advantage:
The party moving first gains an advantage.

In the evening news, the station that is first to commit its schedule will make the larger profit. The first mover has the advantage. There is **first-mover advantage** in any strategic situation where a party gains advantage by moving before others. To identify whether a strategic situation involves first-mover advantage, analyze the game in extensive form.

The first mover has an advantage in situations of coordination and competition. For instance, in the evening news, both stations can agree to broadcast at different times. But they cannot agree on who gets the 8:00 pm slot. The power of the first mover is to determine the equilibrium.

First-mover advantage is a concept that is much emphasized in corporate strategy. However, first-mover advantage is not a universal rule in strategic situations. Consider, for instance, the launch of a new product category, such as driverless cars. The pioneer must invest to develop infrastructure and educate consumers. Other manufacturers can piggyback on the pioneer's investment and introduce their products at lower cost.

Uncertain Consequences

In some situations, one party may not be certain about the consequences of the various actions of the other party. The situation should still be analyzed by backward induction, using all available information. Even if one party does not know the consequences of the various actions for the other party, it may be able to assess the probabilities with which the other party will choose between the alternative actions. It can apply backward induction using these probabilities.

For example, suppose that, in the battle for the evening news, Channel Z does not know TV Delta's profits, but Z can assess the probabilities of Delta's actions at each node. Figure 10.2 shows the specific probabilities.

Then Z can calculate as follows. At node B, Delta will choose 7:30 pm with probability 1/3 and 8:00 pm with probability 2/3, hence Z's expected profit would be $1/3 \times 1 + 2/3 \times 3 = \$2.33$ million. At node C, Delta will choose 7:30 pm with probability 1/2 and 8:00 pm with probability 1/2, hence Z's expected profit would be $1/2 \times 4 + 1/2 \times 2.5 = \$3.25$ million. Thus, at node A, looking forward, Z should choose 8:00 pm.

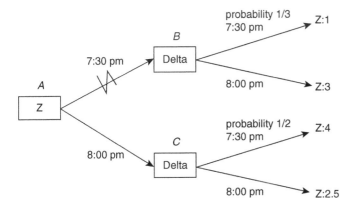

FIGURE 10.2 Scheduling the evening news: uncertain consequences.

Notes: At node B, Delta will choose 7:30 pm with probability 1/3 and 8:00 pm with probability 2/3. At node C, Delta will choose 7:30 pm with probability 1/2 and 8:00 pm with probability 1/2. By backward induction at node A, Z will choose 8:00 pm.

Strategic Thinking

PROGRESS CHECK 10E

In the gasoline station price war (Table 10.1), does the first mover have an advantage? Why or why not?

COMAC: FIRST-MOVER ADVANTAGE

Bombardier, COMAC, Embraer, and Irkut have entered or are poised to enter the market for narrow-body jets. Focusing on COMAC and Embraer, Table 10.3 represents the strategies and corresponding profits of the two manufacturers if they act simultaneously.

What if COMAC moves first? Figure 10.3 shows the situation. If COMAC enters, then, at node *B*, Embraer would not enter, and so COMAC would earn $2 billion. If COMAC does not enter, then, at node *C*, Embraer would enter, and so COMAC would earn zero. So, at node *A*, COMAC would choose to enter. Likewise, if Embraer moves first, it would choose to enter.

Clearly, this is a situation of first-mover advantage. COMAC has been marketing aggressively to sign up customers. If it can convince Embraer that it is committed to production, it might be able to persuade Embraer not to enter the market. Then COMAC would face one competitor fewer.

The government of China strongly supports COMAC. This government backing may further help to convince Embraer (as well as Bombardier and Irkut) that COMAC is committed to production, and persuade them to stay out. This would leave the field to just three manufacturers – Airbus, Boeing, and COMAC.

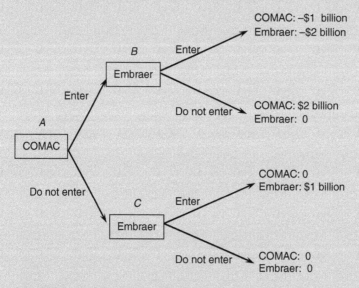

FIGURE 10.3 Narrow-body jets: new entry.

Note: At node *B*, Embraer would not enter, while at node *C*, Embraer would enter. Looking forward from node *A*, COMAC would enter.

6. Strategic Move

Scheduling the evening news is a strategic situation of first-mover advantage. Each station would like to move first and take the 8:00 pm slot, and have the other station accept the 7:30 pm slot.

Now, suppose that TV Delta outsources the recording studio and other news production facilities, and contracts to produce the news for broadcast at 8:00 pm. With the outsourcing, TV Delta is simply not able to broadcast news at 7:30 pm.

Figure 10.4 illustrates the game in extensive form (modified from Figure 10.1). We analyze by backward induction, beginning with the final nodes. At node *B*, Delta will choose the 8:00 pm slot, and similarly, at node *C*, Delta will also choose the 8:00 pm slot.

Hence, at node *A*, looking forward, Channel Z will reason that, whether it chooses to broadcast at 7:30 pm or 8:00 pm, TV Delta will choose 8:00 pm. So, Channel Z will earn more by broadcasting at 7:30 pm.

Thus, in equilibrium, Channel Z will broadcast at 7:30 pm, earning $3 million a month, while TV Delta will broadcast at 8:00 pm, earning $4 million a month. TV Delta's outsourcing illustrates a *strategic move*. By outsourcing the news production facilities, TV Delta reduces its profit from the 7:30 pm slot to zero, and thereby changes the equilibrium of the strategic situation.

A **strategic move** is an action to influence the beliefs or actions of other parties in a favorable way. In order to influence the other parties, the strategic move must be *credible*.

Suppose that, instead of outsourcing the news production facilities, TV Delta simply announces that it will only broadcast news at 8:00 pm. Is such an announcement credible? No, because the announcement does not change the strategic situation.

> **Strategic move:** An action to influence beliefs or actions of other parties in a favorable way. To be effective, a strategic move must be credible.

The situation would still be as depicted in Figure 10.1. In particular, at node *C*, TV Delta would still choose 7:30 pm. So, at node *A*, Channel Z would still choose 8:00 pm.

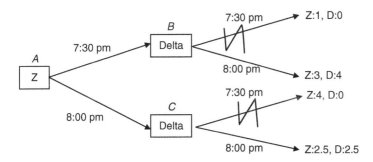

FIGURE 10.4 Scheduling the evening news: TV Delta outsources production facilities.

Notes: At node *B*, Delta will choose 8:00 pm. At node *C*, Delta will choose 8:00 pm. Looking forward from node *A*, Channel *Z* will choose 7:30 pm.

CSL: FREE TEXT MESSAGES

With over 6.2 million subscribers in a market of 17 million, Hong Kong Telecom CSL is the largest provider of mobile telecommunications services in Hong Kong. It skillfully uses discriminatory pricing to consolidate its market share and lock out competitors.

All CSL mobile service plans include 10,000 units of free on-network text messages. With its large market share, CSL's offer of free "on-net" text messages is a clever strategic move. This offer can draw customers away from smaller competitors, and help to entrench CSL's market position. Moreover, on the cost side, a carrier incurs lower costs for "on-net" communications, as compared with "off-net" communications that terminate on networks of other carriers.

Sources: www.hkcsl.com (accessed December 4, 2014); London Economics, "HKT's proposed acquisition of CSL," http://bit.ly/1F1CBEo, April 2014; "Keeping all in the family," *China Daily Asia*, May 16, 2014.

STRATEGIC MOVE IN WAR: DESTROY THE SHIPS

In 207 BC, Xiang Yu, Marquis of Lu, led a relatively small force to attack the Qin Dynasty's much larger army at Julu. Upon crossing the River Zhang, Xiang Yu famously gave the order to sink all the boats and destroy the cooking pots. He distributed just three days' rations to the soldiers.

In 1519, the Spanish conquistador, Hernando Cortés, led a small expedition from Cuba to conquer the Aztec Empire in Mexico. After landing at Veracruz, some members tried to return to Cuba. Cortes ordered his carpenters to dismantle the ships and use the timber and metal in the landward expedition.

By cutting off the means of retreat, both Xiang Yu and Cortés persuaded (or compelled) their soldiers to fight harder. Both generals succeeded despite their forces being vastly outnumbered. Xiang destroyed the Qin army and Cortés conquered Mexico.

Sources: "Battle of Julu," Wikipedia (accessed July 28, 2011); Bernal Díaz del Castillo, *The Discovery and Conquest of Mexico, 1517–21*, transl. A.P. Maudslay, New York: Harper & Brothers, 1928, pp. 168–169.

7. Conditional Strategic Move

Now suppose that, instead of outsourcing the news production facilities, TV Delta contracts with a fast food chain to broadcast advertisements during the 8:00 pm news. The advertising contract specifies that, if TV Delta fails to broadcast according to contract, it must compensate the fast food chain with $2 million a month. This means that if TV Delta schedules the news at 7:30 pm, it must pay compensation of $2 million a month.

By working out the game in extensive form, we can see that, with the advertising contract, the equilibrium is for Channel Z to broadcast at 7:30 pm, while TV Delta broadcasts at 8:00 pm. TV Delta's contract with the advertiser is a *conditional strategic move*. A **conditional strategic move** is an action under specified conditions to influence the beliefs or actions of other parties in a favorable way.

> **Conditional strategic move:** An action under specified conditions to influence the beliefs or actions of other parties in a favorable way.

To the extent that a promised or threatened action need not actually be carried out, the conditional strategic move has no cost. In equilibrium, TV Delta broadcasts news at 8:00 pm, and so it need not pay compensation to the fast food chain.

A more accurate name for an action like TV Delta outsourcing the production facilities is an *unconditional strategic move* because the action is not conditioned on any eventuality. An unconditional strategic move usually involves a cost under all circumstances. So, conditional strategic moves are more cost-effective than unconditional strategic moves.

Conditional strategic moves take two forms – promises, which convey benefits; and threats, which impose costs. TV Delta's advertising contract with the fast food chain is a promise. By the contract, TV Delta promises to pay $2 million a month in compensation if it does not broadcast the advertisements in the 8:00 pm news.

> **PROGRESS CHECK 10F**
> Revise Figure 10.1 to illustrate TV Delta's contract with the fast food chain. What is the equilibrium?

Promise

A **promise** conveys benefits, under specified conditions, to influence the beliefs or actions of other parties in a favorable way. TV Delta's advertising contract is a promise.

> **Promise:** Conveys benefits, under specified conditions, to change the beliefs or actions of other parties in favorable way.

To take another example, consider deposit insurance. Governments are concerned about the stability of their banking systems. Banks take deposits in checking and savings accounts and lend the funds to short- and long-term borrowers. So, generally, banks do not have enough cash at hand to repay all their depositors on short notice and are vulnerable to bank runs.

Consider a typical depositor. Referring to Figure 10.5, at node *A*, she must choose between maintaining her $100 savings with the bank or withdrawing the deposit to get cash. If she maintains the deposit, the outcome depends on the behavior of other depositors and is uncertain.

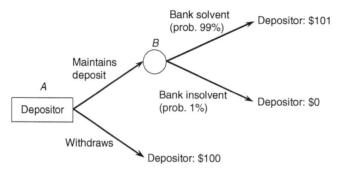

FIGURE 10.5 Bank deposit – without deposit insurance.

Note: Looking forward from node *A*, the consumer withdraws her deposit.

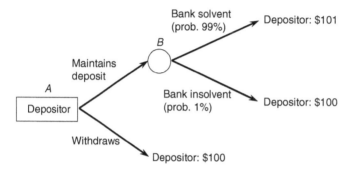

FIGURE 10.6 Bank deposit – with deposit insurance.

Note: Looking forward from node *A*, the consumer maintains her deposit.

We represent the uncertainty by a circular node. With 99% probability, the bank will remain solvent, and at the end of the year, the depositor will get $1 interest, thus a total of $101. With 1% probability, the bank will suffer a run and become insolvent, and at the end of the year, the depositor will get zero. Her expected wealth from maintaining the deposit is $101 × 0.99 + 0 = $99.99.

However, at node *A*, if the depositor withdraws her funds from the bank, she will get $100 with certainty, which is more than her wealth from maintaining the deposit. So, she would choose to withdraw.

Now suppose that the government offers deposit insurance. Then, if the bank cannot repay its customer's deposits, then the government will pay. Deposit insurance is a promise: the government pays only in the event that the bank cannot repay.

Figure 10.6 illustrates the strategic situation with deposit insurance. If the depositor maintains her deposit and the bank is insolvent, she would get $100. So, her expected wealth from maintaining the deposit is $101 × 0.99 + $100 × 0.01 = $100.99, which is more than she would get by withdrawing. Hence, at node *A*, the depositor would choose to maintain the deposit.

Accordingly, with deposit insurance, depositors will not withdraw their funds when they hear rumors that their bank is in difficulties. Deposit insurance can effectively prevent bank runs. If the government insures only solvent banks, then government need never pay out any compensation. That is the beauty of a conditional strategic move.

Threat

A **threat** imposes costs, under specified conditions, to influence the beliefs or actions of other parties in a favorable way. Threats are frequently used in negotiations. In bargaining with employers, unions may threaten to strike if their members' wages are not raised. Employers fear the disruption to operations resulting from a strike, so the threat of a strike may persuade an employer to concede on wages.

> **Threat:** Imposes costs, under specified conditions, to change the beliefs or actions of other parties in a favorable way.

The crucial issue is whether the union's threat of a strike is credible. Credibility is an issue because, during a strike, the workers must forgo part or all of their wages. Figure 10.7 is a game in extensive form that depicts a union demanding a $12 million increase in wages. The figure shows gains and losses for the workers relative to the status quo.

At node *B*, the union decides whether to strike. If they strike, then the workers would lose $4 million in current earnings and possibly gain $12 million in future earnings. If they do not strike, they will get the status quo. The strike will reduce the employer's profit by $3 million.

At node *A*, the employer decides whether to raise wages. If the employer raises wages, the higher wages would reduce its profit by $12 million. If it refuses to raise wages, it possibly faces a strike.

However, the union's threat to strike is only credible if, at node *B*, the workers are better off with a strike. This depends on the probability that the employer will eventually raise wages. Suppose that the probability that the employer will

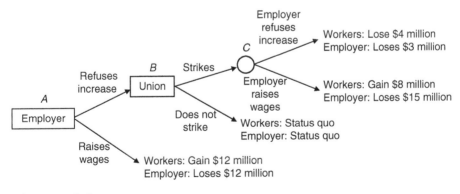

FIGURE 10.7 Strike.

Notes: At node *B*, the union will strike or not depending on the probability that the employer raises wages at node *C*. Looking forward from node *A*, the employer will raise or refuse to raise wages depending on whether the union will strike.

eventually raise wages is 20%. Then the probability that the employer will not raise wages is 80%. At node B, if the union strikes, the workers' expected earnings would be $8 \times 0.2 + (-4) \times 0.8 = -1.6$, which is a loss of \$1.6 million. So, the union's threat is not credible, and thus, the employer should refuse to raise wages.

The prevalence of strikes varies. In professional American football, strikes are rare. The career of a professional American football player is relatively short. If football players strike, they are trading off the loss of current earnings against higher earnings in the future. As football players have short careers, they are not so attracted by higher earnings in the future. Accordingly, football players are relatively less likely to strike than other players.

PROGRESS CHECK 10G

Referring to Figure 10.7, what is the minimum probability that the employer will eventually raise wages for the union's threat of a strike to be credible?

EMBRAER: WORRIED BY AIRBUS AND BOEING

As of the Paris Air Show in June 2011, Embraer had not yet decided to produce a narrow-body jet to compete with the Airbus A320 and Boeing 737. The Embraer CEO, Frederico Curado, remarked: "Going up against Boeing and Airbus in head-to-head competition is really tough . . . . They can have a very quick response and literally flood the market."

By contrast with Embraer, the incumbent manufacturers, Airbus and Boeing, had already established production, benefiting from the experience curve. Further, they could develop new versions of their existing planes at relatively low cost, taking advantage of economies of scope from existing models.

Indeed, both Airbus and Boeing raised the rates of production of their existing models. These increases in production possibly signaled further increases if new competitors such as Embraer should enter the market. Hence Curado's worry about "flood[ing] the market." If sufficiently credible, Airbus and Boeing might succeed in scaring off the competitors.

Source: "Airbus-Boeing duopoly holds narrow-body startups at bay at Paris Air Show," *Bloomberg*, June 23, 2011.

CLOROX: POISON PILL

The Clorox Company is famous for its eponymous bleach. In February 2011, the billionaire Carl Icahn announced that he had bought 12.5 million shares or 9.4% of Clorox's 133 million shares. Then, on July 15, he offered to buy the remaining shares for \$76.50 each.

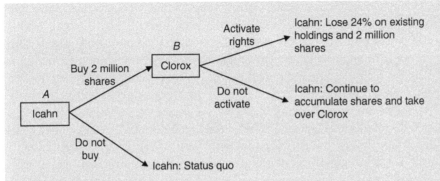

FIGURE 10.8 Poison pill.

Notes: At node *B*, Clorox will activate rights. Looking forward from node *A*, Icahn will not buy 2 million additional shares.

On July 18, Clorox's board of directors adopted a "shareholder rights plan" to ensure "fair and equal treatment" for all shareholders. The company issued to each holder of a common share one right to buy another share at half price. The rights could be exercised if any party acquired 10% or more of Clorox, except that the rights of the acquiring party would be void. Following the announcement, the price of Clorox's common shares fell by 2.0% to $73.04.

Figure 10.8 depicts the strategic situation between Icahn and Clorox. Suppose that, currently, the price of Clorox shares is $70.

At node *A*, Icahn must decide whether to acquire an additional 2 million shares. At node *B*, suppose that Clorox's board activates all rights except Icahn's, and all shareholders (except Icahn) buy additional shares at half price, or $35 each. With the increase in shares outstanding, the value of each share would fall to $53.37.[3]

Thus, the activation of the rights would reduce the value of Icahn's existing holding of 12.5 million shares and the additional 2 million shares by a whopping 24%. It is no wonder that such shareholder rights plans have been called *poison pills*. They hugely raise the cost of hostile takeovers. If the plans succeed in deterring bidders, the rights will never be activated.

Sources: "Icahn bids for Clorox, suggests others step up," *Reuters*, July 15, 2011; "The Clorox Company adopts stockholder rights plan," Clorox Company press release, July 18, 2011; Yahoo! Finance.

8. Repetition

So far, we have considered strategic interactions that take place only once. Many strategic interactions, however, are repeated. Generally, the range of possible strategies is much wider in repeated interactions than in one-shot scenarios. Specifically, a party may condition its action on the actions of the other party. Then the parties may be able to achieve better outcomes than in once-only interactions.

Let us see how such strategies can work in the cartel's dilemma. Referring to Table 10.1, both Jupiter and Saturn know that, if both maintain price, each would achieve higher profits than if both cut price. In a once-only situation, however, each station has an overwhelming incentive to cut price.

What if the situation is repeated? Then Jupiter can adopt a strategy under which it conditions its price on Saturn's previous price, and vice versa. One such strategy is "tit for tat" – I will begin by maintaining price and will continue until you cut price, in which case, I will cut price for one week and thereafter will follow your price.

A tit-for-tat strategy combines a promise with a threat. The promise is to maintain price if the other station maintains price. The threat is to cut price if the other station cuts price.

Is tit for tat an equilibrium strategy? Referring to Table 10.1, suppose that both Jupiter and Saturn adopt a tit-for-tat strategy. Each begins by maintaining price, with Jupiter and Saturn each earning $1,000. Suppose, however, that in some week, Saturn cuts price, while Jupiter maintains price. Then Saturn will earn $1,300 instead of $1,000, gaining $300.

In the following week, Jupiter would retaliate and cut price. What should Saturn do? It could continue cutting price, and then Jupiter would continue to retaliate. In this case, Saturn would earn $800 indefinitely. Alternatively, Saturn could go back to maintaining the price, and so restore cooperation thereafter. In this case, Saturn would earn $700 for one week and $1,000 afterward.

Tit for tat is an equilibrium strategy for Saturn if the one-time $300 gain is outweighed by the future losses due to Jupiter's retaliation. This depends on two factors. One is how Saturn values money in the future relative to the present, which is the concept of discounting introduced in Chapter 1. The less Saturn values money in the future, the more likely it is to cut price.

The other factor affecting whether tit for tat is an equilibrium strategy is the time horizon. The shorter the time horizon, due, for instance, to expiry of the leases of the stations and entry of new competitors, the more likely it is that Saturn would cut price.

Accordingly, under certain conditions, tit for tat is an equilibrium strategy in the repeated cartel's dilemma. When competing sellers interact over an extended period of time, they can maintain profit above the competitive level.

TIT FOR TAT WINS AGAIN

The political scientist, Robert Axelrod, invited various scholars to submit computer programs specifying strategies for a prisoners' dilemma (a game like the cartel's dilemma) repeated 200 times. Axelrod pitted each program against the others in a round-robin tournament.

Programs that were "nice" in the sense of not being first to cheat performed better than those that were not nice. The winning strategy was tit for tat. Axelrod announced these results and held a second tournament. Despite the opportunity to devise better strategies, no scholar could beat tit for tat, and the simple strategy also won the second tournament.

Based on the tournament results, Axelrod proposed four simple rules:

- Do not strike first.
- Reciprocate both good and bad.
- Act simply and clearly.
- Do not be envious.

Source: Robert Axelrod, *Evolution of Cooperation*, New York: Basic Books, 1984.

KEY TAKEAWAYS

- A situation is strategic if the parties consider interactions with one another in making decisions.
- Never use a dominated strategy.
- In a situation of simultaneous moves, a Nash equilibrium strategy is stable in the sense that, if other parties choose their Nash equilibrium strategies, each party prefers its own Nash equilibrium strategy.
- In competitive situations, it may help to randomize.
- Zero-sum games characterize extreme competition: one party can be better off only if another is worse off.
- In a situation of sequential moves, plan by looking forward to the final nodes and reasoning backward toward the initial node.
- Use strategic moves to influence the beliefs or actions of other parties in a favorable way. To be effective, they must be credible.
- If possible, use conditional strategic moves, both threats and promises, as they are more cost-effective than unconditional strategic moves.
- In repeated situations, get better outcomes through strategies that condition actions on the actions of others.

REVIEW QUESTIONS

1. In situations of (a) perfect competition and (b) monopoly, does it matter whether the seller acts strategically?
2. Explain why you should not use a dominated strategy.
3. Which of the following are reasons to adopt a Nash equilibrium strategy?
    (a) I can minimize my expected loss.
    (b) I can guarantee a minimum outcome.

(c) Even if the other party knows my strategy, it cannot take advantage of that information.

4. If others do not act strategically (for instance, they use a non-equilibrium strategy), should I follow?

5. Explain the meaning of a randomized strategy.

6. Some right-handed boxers also train themselves to box with their left hands. Which of the following strategies will be more effective? (a) Throw a left-hand punch after every three right-handers. (b) Box mainly with the right hand and throw a left-hand punch at random.

7. Explain the associations between: (a) zero-sum game and competition; and (b) positive-sum game and coordination.

8. In a game in strategic form, the consequences to the two players in every cell add up to –10. Is this a zero-sum game?

9. In a game in extensive form, what is wrong with planning by reasoning forward from the initial node?

10. In the Battle of the Bismarck Sea (Table 10.2), does the first mover have an advantage? Why or why not?

11. Why are conditional strategic moves better than unconditional strategic moves?

12. Suppose a bank offers deposit insurance to its depositors, with the compensation to be paid from its own funds. Why is this not credible?

13. In bargaining, a common tactic is to "walk away." Is this credible?

14. Loan sharks are not allowed to use the legal system to collect debts. Does this explain why they employ violence?

15. How do strategies in repeated strategic situations differ from those that occur only once?

DISCUSSION QUESTIONS

1. Susan and Greg stole a car and have been caught by the police. Detective Lenny Briscoe does not have sufficient evidence to convict them of auto theft. He ushers Susan and Greg into separate interview rooms and offers each a deal: "If the other suspect doesn't confess and you do, we'll give you a reward of $1,000." Each suspect knows that if neither confesses, they will be let off. If one confesses while the other does not, then the confessing suspect will receive the $1,000 reward, while the other will be jailed for one year. If both confess, each will be jailed for one year.

    (a) Construct a game in strategic form to analyze the choices of Susan and Greg between confessing and not confessing.

    (b) Identify the equilibrium/equilibria.

    (c) Compare this situation to the cartel's dilemma in Table 10.1.

2. The National Collegiate Athletic Association (NCAA) restricts the amount that colleges and universities may pay their student athletes. Suppose that there are just two colleges in the NCAA: Ivy and State. Each must choose between paying athletes according to NCAA rules and paying more. If both Ivy and

State follow the NCAA salaries, then each would earn $3 million. If one follows the NCAA salaries and the other pays more than NCAA salaries, then the college paying more can attract better players and would earn $5 million, while the college following NCAA would earn just $1 million. If both colleges pay more than NCAA salaries, they would increase their costs but not get better players, so both would earn $2 million.

   (a) Construct a game in strategic form to analyze the choices of Ivy and State, and identify the equilibrium/equilibria.

   (b) With government backing, the NCAA can punish colleges that pay more than the NCAA permitted salaries. How would this affect the equilibrium/equilibria?

   (c) Which of the following concepts best describes the NCAA rules on player salaries: (i) monopoly; (ii) monopsony; (iii) economies of scale; (iv) economies of scope. Explain your answer.

3. Launched in June 2007, Apple's iPhone quickly grabbed a substantial share of the global smart phone market. Competing mobile operating systems include Nokia's Symbian, Research-in-Motion's Blackberry, Google's Android, and Microsoft's Windows Mobile. In September 2010, soon after joining Nokia as CEO, Stephen Elop reviewed Nokia's strategy for smart phones.

   (a) Consider the strategic situation between Nokia and HTC, a Taiwanese manufacturer. If they both build phones on Symbian, HTC would earn $2 billion while Nokia would earn $4 billion. If they both build phones based on Windows Mobile, both HTC and Nokia would earn $2 billion. If HTC builds on Symbian while Nokia builds on Windows Mobile, each would earn zero. If HTC builds on Windows Mobile while Nokia builds on Symbian, HTC would earn zero and Nokia would earn $2 billion. Draw the game in strategic form and identify the equilibrium/ equilibria.

   (b) Use your answer in (a) to explain why Microsoft would offer to pay Nokia "billions of dollars" to build phones on Windows Mobile.

   (c) Which of the following apply to the game in (a): (i) zero-sum game; (ii) positive-sum game; (iii) economies of scale; (iv) economies of scope. Explain your answer.

4. On May 19, 2012, the UEFA Champions League final between Bayern Munich of Germany and Chelsea of England was decided by a penalty shoot-out. Manuel Neuer took Bayern's third kick. Chelsea goalkeeper Petr Čech guessed correctly that Neuer would kick to the left but the low shot crept past into the bottom left corner.

   (a) Construct a game in strategic form as follows. Neuer must choose between kicking to the left, center, or right. Čech must choose between moving to block on the left, center, or right. If Neuer scores, Bayern wins one point while Chelsea loses one point. If Čech succeeds in blocking, both teams get zero.

   (b) Is this a zero or positive-sum game?

   (c) Find the Nash equilibrium/equilibria in pure strategies, if they exist.

(d) Verify that the following is a Nash equilibrium in randomized strategies: each player plays left/centre/right with probability 1/3.

5. Pluto Limited is financed with $2 billion of debt at an interest rate of 10% and $8 billion of equity. If management works as usual, Pluto would earn revenues of $10 billion and incur operating expenses of $9.5 billion, and so operating income would be $0.5 billion. If management works hard to cut costs, operating expenses would be $9.0 billion.

   (a) Construct a game in extensive form with the following nodes. At the first node, a private-equity fund chooses between a leveraged buyout of Pluto and the status quo. At the subsequent node, management chooses between working as usual and cutting costs.

   (b) Suppose that the leveraged buyout recapitalizes Pluto to $8 billion of debt at an interest rate of 10% and $2 billion of equity. Calculate Pluto's profit if management: (i) works as usual; (ii) cuts costs.

   (c) Explain how the leveraged buyout serves as a strategic move to cut costs.

6. A major problem for China's state-controlled banks is loans to state-owned enterprises. Historically, many state-owned enterprises were financed with relatively little equity and large loans from state-controlled banks. On a strictly commercial basis, these loans should be classified as "non-performing." Banks should make provision for non-performing loans and, accordingly, reduce their profit and the book value of their assets. Banks are run by managers who care mainly about their job security.

   (a) Use a game in extensive form to depict the following scenario. Renmin Construction has borrowed 1 billion yuan at an interest rate of 5% from People's Bank. The loan is about to mature. The management of People's Bank must choose between rolling over the loan and demanding repayment. (i) If the bank rolls over the loan, Renmin Construction would continue in business and use part of the loan to pay the interest due to the bank. The loan is classified as performing and the bank management continues to be employed. (ii) If the bank demands repayment, Renmin Construction would default and the bank would have to write off 1 billion yuan. The government would replace the management.

   (b) Identify the equilibrium/equilibria of the game in (a).

   (c) Suppose that Renmin Construction is actually bankrupt and has no chance of ever making a profit. If the bank management aims to maximize profit, should it roll over the loan or demand repayment?

7. The government of Bulgaria has pegged its currency, the lev, at a rate of 1.95583 levs to one euro. The central bank is committed to exchanging euros for levs at this rate. In December 2014, the central bank had issued currency in circulation with face value of 10.17 billion levs, and Bulgaria's foreign exchange reserves totaled 35.0 billion levs. Other things being equal,

Bulgarians prefer to hold levs as they are more convenient for daily use than euros.

    (a) Construct a game in extensive form with the following nodes: at the first node, the typical Bulgarian chooses between redeeming levs for euros and not redeeming; at the following nodes, the central bank either has sufficient assets to meet the redemptions and remains solvent, or has insufficient assets and becomes insolvent.

    (b) As of December 2014, would the typical Bulgarian redeem her levs?

    (c) Suppose, however, that the central bank increases the amount of currency in circulation to 40 billion levs. Explain how the typical Bulgarian's decision whether to redeem depends on her beliefs about the decisions of other persons whether to redeem.

8. The German telecommunications provider Deutsche Telekom is rated Aa2 by Moody's on a scale ranging from the highest grade of Aaa through Aa, A, Baa, Ba, B, to the lowest grade of Caa. In its June 2000 bond issue worth $14.5 billion, Deutsche Telekom promised to increase the interest payment by 0.5 percentage points if its credit rating fell below A.

    (a) For simplicity, assume that the normal interest on the bonds is $870 million a year. Suppose that, some years later, Deutsche Telekom will choose between two investments. For the risky investment, it must issue new bonds with annual interest of $130 million. The risky investment will generate a cash flow of $1.5 billion with 50% probability, and $1 billion otherwise. The safe investment will not require additional borrowing and will yield $1.07 billion for sure. Using a game in extensive form, illustrate this choice, while ignoring the promise. At each final node, show the net cash flow (net of interest on all loans).

    (b) Now suppose that the additional borrowings for the risky investment would reduce Deutsche Telekom's credit rating below A and trigger its promise to raise the interest payment by 0.5% × $14.5 billion = $72.5 million. Suppose that banks will not lend if there is any possibility of negative net cash flow. How does Deutsche Telekom's promise affect the game in extensive form?

9. Bombardier, COMAC, Embraer, and Irkut have entered or are poised to enter the market for narrow-body jets. Focusing on COMAC and Embraer, Table 10.3 represents the strategies and corresponding profits of the two manufacturers if they act simultaneously.

    (a) Using suitable games in extensive form, show that this is a situation of first-mover advantage.

    (b) Suppose that the government of China guarantees COMAC that it would reimburse 110% of any losses on developing and producing the C919. How does that affect the equilibrium/equilibria in (a)?

    (c) How much should the Chinese government budget for the guarantee?

> **You are the consultant!**
>
> Consider some strategic situation – between your organization and a competitor, between your organization and a supplier or customer, or even between you and a rival at work. Apply a game in strategic form or extensive form to plan your strategy.

Appendix: Solving Nash Equilibrium in Randomized Strategies

This chapter has introduced the concept of randomization and showed its usefulness, especially in competitive contexts. There are two ways to solve for the Nash equilibrium with randomized strategies – graphical and algebraic. Let us apply the two methods to the (modified) situation of the gasoline stations described in Table 10.4.

Graphical

In Figure 10.9, the horizontal axis depicts the probability that Jupiter maintains price, and the vertical axis shows Saturn's expected profit. We draw two lines in Figure 10.9. One line shows Saturn's profit if it maintains price, as a function of the probability that Jupiter maintains price. By Table 10.4, if Jupiter maintains prices with certainty, Saturn's profit from maintaining price would be $900. However, if Jupiter maintains price with zero probability (cuts price), Saturn's profit from maintaining price would be $500.

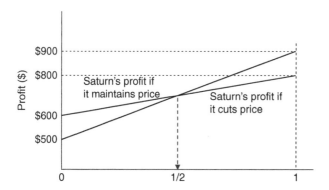

FIGURE 10.9 Solving Nash equilibrium in randomized strategies.

Notes: Saturn gets equal profit from maintaining price and cutting price if Jupiter maintains price with probability 1/2, and so Saturn is indifferent between maintaining and cutting price. Similarly for Jupiter. So, the Nash equilibrium in randomized strategies comprises Jupiter maintaining price with probability 1/2 and Saturn maintaining price with probability 1/2.

The other line shows Saturn's profit if it cuts price, as a function of the probability that Jupiter maintains price. By Table 10.4, if Jupiter maintains price with certainty, Saturn's profit from cutting price would be $800. However, if Jupiter maintains prices with zero probability (cuts price), Saturn's profit from cutting price would be $600.

The two lines cross at one point. At that point, Saturn's profit is the same whether it maintains or cuts price. That point marks Jupiter's Nash equilibrium probability, which turns out to be 1/2.

We can use a similar graph to determine Saturn's equilibrium probability, which also turns out to be 1/2.[4]

Algebraic

Another way to find the Nash equilibrium probabilities is to use algebra. In equilibrium, both Jupiter and Saturn must randomize. Suppose that Jupiter maintains price with probability q. For Saturn to be willing to randomize, it must be indifferent between the two pure strategies: maintain price and cut price. This means that Saturn must receive the same expected profit from the two pure strategies.

To calculate Saturn's expected profit from maintaining price, refer to Table 10.4. Saturn's profit would be $900 if Jupiter maintains price, which occurs with probability q, while Saturn's profit would be $500 if Jupiter cuts price, which occurs with probability $1 - q$. Hence, Saturn's expected profit from maintaining price would be $(900 \times q) + (500 \times (1 - q)) = 500 + 400q$.

Similarly, we can calculate Saturn's profit from cutting price, which would be $(800 \times q) + (600 \times (1 - q)) = 600 + 200q$. In randomized strategy equilibrium, Saturn must receive the same expected profit from pricing low and high. This means that $500 + 400q = 600 + 200q$, which implies that $q = 1/2$.

Likewise, we can determine Saturn's Nash equilibrium strategy. Suppose that Saturn maintains price with probability p. For Jupiter to be indifferent between its alternative pure strategies, it must earn the same expected profit from maintaining and cutting price. This means that $900p + 1,000(1 - p) = 1,300p + 600 (1 - p)$, or $p = 1/2$.

Notes

1   This discussion is based, in part, on Richard Tortoriello, "Aerospace & defense," *Standard & Poor's Industry Surveys*, February 10, 2011; "Airbus and Boeing call end to 'duopoly'," *Financial Times*, June 21, 2011; "Airbus-Boeing duopoly holds narrow-body startups at bay at Paris Air Show," *Bloomberg*, June 23, 2011.
2   This example is based on O. G. Haywood, "Military decision and game theory," *Journal of the Operations Research Society of America*, Vol. 2, No. 4, November 1954, pp. 365–385; and J. Rohwer and G. Hummelchen, *Chronology of the War at Sea, 1939–45*, Vol. 2, transl. Derek Masters, London: Ian Allan, 1974, p. 306.

3   After activation of the rights, the value of the company would be the prior market value, $70 × 133 million = $9.31 billion, plus the payment for the additional shares, $35 × (133 − 12.5) million = $4.22 billion, or a total of $13.53 billion. There would be 133 + (133 − 12.5) = 253.5 million shares, and so the value of each share would be $13,530/253.5 = $53.37.

4   This technique is based on Avinash Dixit and Barry Nalebuff, *Thinking Strategically: The Competitive Edge in Business, Politics, and Everyday Life*, New York: Norton, 1991, Chapter 7.

CHAPTER **11**

Oligopoly[1]

LEARNING OBJECTIVES

- For sellers competing on price to sell differentiated products, identify the price that maximizes profit and how to adjust the price.
- Appreciate that prices can be strategic complements.
- For sellers competing on capacity to sell a homogeneous product, identify the capacity that maximizes profit and how to adjust capacity.
- Appreciate that capacities can be strategic substitutes.
- Apply limit pricing to deter entry.
- Apply capacity leadership for first-mover advantage.
- Appreciate how to limit competition.

1. Introduction

Dynamic random-access memory (DRAM) provides high-speed storage and retrieval of data, and is a key component in computers. NAND flash memory is essential in devices, such as smart phones, that require a lot of space for data storage or fast recording. The demand for memory grows in tandem with sales of computers, smart phones, and other electronic devices. In 2010, global DRAM sales totaled $39.2 billion; NAND flash memory sales totaled $17.3 billion.[2]

Competition in the memory industry is intense, with relatively little product differentiation. However, the industry is not perfectly competitive. Samsung Electronics dominates the production of both DRAMs and NAND flash memory, with 38% and 40% shares, respectively (see Table 11.1). In both markets, the top four manufacturers have about a 90% share.

Table 11.1 Memory industry: share of production

Manufacturer	DRAM (%)	NAND (%)	Gross margin, recent average (%)
Elpida	16	–	5
Hynix	22	10	~40
Micron	13	10	~13
Samsung Electronics	38	40	>30
Toshiba	–	32	–

A major reason for the high concentration of the memory industry is large fixed costs. The cost of building a wafer fabrication plant has risen over time, and presently ranges from $3 billion to $8 billion.

Historically, with improvements in manufacturing technology and expansion of capacity, the price of memory has fallen by around 20–30% a year. Moreover, the industry must contend with volatile exchange rates. With prices set in US dollars, manufacturers outside the United States incur exchange rate risks.

Given the huge costs of investment and volatile prices and revenue, the memory industry is not for the faint-hearted. In 2006, Infineon spun off its DRAM manufacturing into Qimonda, which filed for insolvency protection three years later. Elpida, Japan's last manufacturer of memory, was sold to Micron in 2013.

With continued volatility in exchange rates, how should Samsung and other memory manufacturers adjust pricing and capacity to the fluctuation of the Korean won against the US dollar? How should they respond to the trend of consolidation as smaller competitors merge or exit completely? How would the consolidation of the memory industry affect buyers of memory such as manufacturers of computers and mobile phones?

The global semiconductor industry is obviously an *oligopoly*. An **oligopoly** is a market with a small number of sellers who behave strategically. Oligopoly is a market structure that lies between the two extremes of perfect competition and monopoly. Under perfect competition no seller has market power, while in a monopoly there is only one seller.

Oligopoly: A market with a small number of sellers who behave strategically.

To understand the impact of the fluctuation of the Korean won, we must understand how sellers decide capacity, production, and pricing under conditions of oligopoly. Since there are few sellers, it is likely that they would actively consider interactions with one another in business decisions. Hence, it is important to consider their strategic interaction. Accordingly, we apply the techniques of game theory developed in Chapter 10.

We distinguish between two time horizons – the short and long run. Generally, production capacity is less flexible than pricing, and hence businesses must decide on capacity (long run) before pricing (short run).

We first study oligopoly in the short run – how competing sellers set prices and how their pricing depends on whether the product is homogeneous or differentiated, and how each seller should adjust price in response to competitors' price changes. We then study oligopoly in the long run – how competing sellers decide on production capacity and how each seller should adjust capacity and production in response to competitors' changes in capacity and production.

Applying these models, we can explain how Samsung and other memory manufacturers should adjust capacity and pricing to changes in exchange rates and other costs. Further, we explain how memory manufacturers should adjust to consolidation of the industry.

Finally, we study how producers can benefit from restraining competition and the ways of accomplishing such restraint. The analysis suggests how consolidation of the memory industry would affect buyers such as computer manufacturers.

Managers in oligopolistic industries can apply the techniques and analysis of this chapter to plan more effective strategies in the face of competition.

2. Price Competition

Typically, in the short run, the strategic variable for oligopolistic sellers is price. The outcome of oligopolistic competition on price depends on whether the product is homogeneous or differentiated. Let us analyze the outcome in each of these two settings.

Homogeneous Product

Suppose that, in the market for wireless telecommunications, the market demand is represented as in Figure 11.1. The marginal cost of service is a constant $30 per subscriber per month.

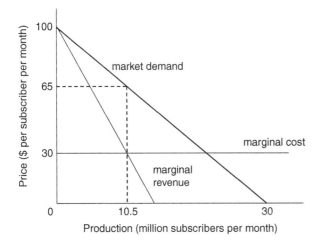

FIGURE 11.1 Monopoly.

Note: The monopoly maximizes profit at a scale of 10.5 million subscribers per month and a price of $65 per subscriber per month.

It will be useful to compare the market outcome in scenarios of monopoly and oligopoly. Referring to Figure 11.1, the scale at which marginal revenue equals marginal cost is 10.5 million subscribers and the corresponding price is $65 per subscriber per month. At that scale and price, the monopoly maximizes profit. The monopoly profit contribution is ($65 – $30) × 10.5 million = $367.5 million per month.

> **Duopoly:** A market with two sellers who behave strategically.

> **Bertrand oligopoly:** Sellers produce at constant marginal cost with unlimited capacity, and compete on price to sell a homogeneous product.

For simplicity, we consider a situation of **duopoly**. Suppose that there are just two sellers in the market, say, Luna Cellular and Mercury Wireless, and that they behave strategically. Each seller produces under conditions of constant marginal cost of $30 per subscriber per month with no capacity constraint. Luna and Mercury provide identical services, so the product is homogeneous. This describes the **Bertrand** model of oligopoly, named for the French mathematical economist who published it in 1883.

Under these conditions, the market equilibrium is perfectly competitive. Remarkably, even though the industry is a duopoly, the outcome is the same as with perfect competition. To see this, imagine that Luna Cellular charges some price above marginal cost, say $32.

Then Mercury has three choices: it can price above, at, or below $32. If Mercury charges above $32, all consumers would subscribe with Luna, and so Mercury will sell and earn nothing. If Mercury matches Luna's price $32, it would get half of the market demand and earn profit equal to the incremental margin, $32 – $30 = $2, per sale. However, if Mercury charges below $32, even slightly less, then it would get the entire market demand.

So, by marginally undercutting Luna's price of $32, Mercury can almost double its profit relative to matching the price. The reason is that its incremental margin is only slightly less than $2, but its sales would double. Indeed, Mercury faces a demand curve that is infinitely elastic with respect to a price cut below Luna's price.

The same reasoning applies to Luna. Accordingly, the Nash equilibrium in this duopoly is for both competitors to set prices equal to the marginal cost of $30. If either seller sets a price above $30, the other seller would undercut. The strategic logic is essentially the same as in the situation of the competing gasoline stations described in Table 10.1.

The result is quite dramatic. Even when there are only two competing sellers, each faces a demand curve that is so elastic that the market outcome is identical to that with perfect competition.

The same analysis applies even more strongly if there are more than two competitors. Every seller will prefer to undercut the others – its incremental margin would be only slightly lower, but its sales would increase in proportion to the number of competitors it undercuts. (As Chapter 10 shows, competing sellers can avoid ruinous price competition in repeated interaction. Using "tit-for-tat" strategies – price high and cut price only if the competitor cuts price – they might avoid price wars.)

Differentiated Products

What if the competing sellers offer differentiated products? With differentiation, if one seller undercuts the competitor's price, it would take away only part of the competitor's demand. Hence, the price-cutter's demand is not infinitely elastic. So, what is the equilibrium outcome?

Consider the following situation, which applies the **Hotelling** model of oligopoly. Suppose that consumers are located uniformly along a street one mile long, with the Luna and Mercury dealers at each end of the street. Each consumer is willing to pay up to $100 for the service but must incur a cost of $4 per mile to travel to a dealer to buy the service. So, a consumer located 0.25 mile from the Luna dealer would incur $4 \times 0.25 = \$1$ to travel to the Luna dealer, and $4 \times 0.75 = \$3$ to travel to the Mercury dealer.

> **Hotelling oligopoly:** Sellers compete on price to sell a product differentiated by distance from consumer.

In this situation, the differentiation is due to the difference in the consumer's distances from the two dealers. Luna and Mercury independently set prices simultaneously and incur a constant marginal cost of $30 per subscriber per month to provide the service.

Since Luna and Mercury set prices simultaneously, it is appropriate to apply the concept of Nash equilibrium. For simplicity, we assume that, in equilibrium, every consumer will buy. Let Luna set price p_L, and Mercury set price p_M. In the appendix to this chapter, we show that, given Mercury's

> **Residual demand curve:** Demand given the actions of competing sellers.

price, Luna's *residual demand* curve would be as shown in Figure 11.2. The **residual demand** is the demand given the actions of competing sellers.

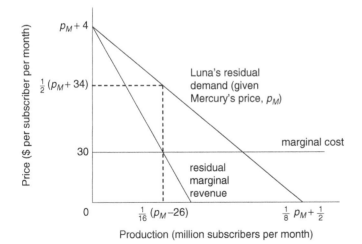

FIGURE 11.2 Price competition with differentiated products: residual demand.

Notes: Given Mercury's price, p_M, Luna's residual demand slopes downward from quantity 0 at price $p_M + 4$, to quantity $1/8\, p_M + 1/2$ at price 0. Luna maximizes profit at quantity $1/16(p_M - 26)$ and price $1/2(p_M + 34)$.

Given Mercury's price, p_M, and any possible price that it could set, consumers relatively closer to Luna would buy from Luna and those relatively closer to Mercury would buy from Mercury. The consumers' choices are relative to the prices set by Luna and Mercury. With information on the consumers' choices, Luna can calculate its sales. By repeating this procedure for every price that it could set, Luna can construct its residual demand curve.

The residual demand curve slopes downward. If Luna raises its price, some consumers (located relatively far from Luna) would switch to Mercury, and so Luna's sales would be lower. With the residual demand curve, Luna can construct its residual marginal revenue curve. Note that Luna's residual demand and marginal revenue curves depend on Mercury's price. Suppose that Mercury raises its price. Then some consumers (located relatively far from Mercury) would switch to Luna, and so Luna's residual demand and marginal revenue curves would be further to the right.

To maximize profit, Luna should produce at the scale where marginal revenue equals marginal cost. The profit-maximizing scale is $\frac{1}{16}(p_M - 26)$ and the corresponding price is $\frac{1}{2}(p_M + 34)$. Owing to the competition for consumers, Luna's profit-maximizing price depends on Mercury's price, p_M.

Figure 11.3 presents a graph of Luna's profit-maximizing price as a function of Mercury's price, p_M. It begins at a price of $30, which Luna would set if Mercury set a price of $26. Luna would never price below the marginal cost of $30. The graph then increases according to $\frac{1}{2}(p_M + 34)$.

| Best response function: A seller's best action as function of competing sellers' actions. | This graph of Luna's profit-maximizing price as a function of Mercury's price is Luna's *best response function*. The **best response function** represents the seller's best action as a function of the actions of competing sellers. Figure 11.3 |

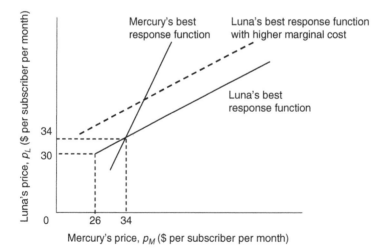

FIGURE 11.3 Price competition with differentiated products: best response functions.

Notes: Luna's best response function shows its profit-maximizing price, p_L, as a function of Mercury's price, p_M. Mercury's best response function shows its profit-maximizing price, p_M, as a function of Luna's price, p_L.

also depicts Mercury's best response function, which is its profit-maximizing price as a function of Luna's price, p_L.

Figure 11.3 is the graphical equivalent of the game in strategic form, where each party chooses from a continuum of strategies. (Chapter 10 considered strategic situations in which each party chose between two strategies, so could be represented by a table.) The Nash equilibrium is at the intersection of the best response functions. For both sellers, the Nash equilibrium strategy is to price at $34. By the properties of Nash equilibrium, if Mercury believes that Luna will price at $34, then it is best for Mercury to set price at $34, and vice versa.

In equilibrium, each seller earns an incremental margin of $34 − $30 = $4, and serves half of the consumers. Thus, in competition on price to sell differentiated products, the equilibrium price exceeds the marginal cost. Further, the equilibrium does not depend on fixed costs. Only the sellers' participation decisions – whether to produce at all – depend on fixed costs: specifically, each seller will produce only if the profit contribution exceeds its fixed cost.

Consumer Preferences

In the preceding example, the competing products were differentiated by location. Actually, the Hotelling model applies to differentiation in terms of any attribute on which consumers have differing preferences. The attribute could be taste (some prefer salty, others prefer sweet), design (some like functional, others like aesthetic), or membership of a customer loyalty program. Then the "transport cost" represents the consumer's disutility from consuming any attribute that differs from the ideal or most preferred.

What if the consumers' preferences are relatively stronger? Specifically, in the preceding example, what if the transport cost is $5 rather than $4 per mile? Referring to Luna's residual demand curve in Figure 11.2, the vertical intersection would be higher and the horizontal intersection would be further to the left. Luna's residual demand would be more inelastic, and so its profit-maximizing price would be higher.

Then, by Figure 11.3, Luna's best response function would be further up. Similarly, Mercury's best response function would be further to the right. Thus, the Nash equilibrium prices would be higher.

So, in the context of oligopoly, sellers can mitigate competition by differentiating their products. The stronger are the consumers' preferences over the differentiating attribute (the larger is the consumer's disutility from a less than ideal attribute), the less price elastic will be each seller's residual demand. With residual demand being less price elastic, the equilibrium prices would be higher.

Demand and Cost Changes

How should oligopolists competing on price respond to changes in demand and cost? Generally, the response comprises two steps. First, as in a monopoly, each seller should adjust price until its residual marginal revenue equals marginal cost. Second, in an oligopoly, the new price is a function of the other sellers' prices.

So, with the new demand or cost, the seller's best response function would shift and then establish a new equilibrium.

Consider an increase in market demand. In Figure 11.2, Luna's residual demand would shift to the right, and so the residual marginal revenue would shift to the right. So Luna's profit-maximizing price would be higher. Hence, in Figure 11.3, Luna's best response function would be higher. Similarly, Mercury's best response function would shift to the right. Thus, in the new equilibrium, each seller would set a higher price.

What about an increase in marginal cost? In Figure 11.2, with higher marginal cost, Luna's profit-maximizing price would be higher. Then, in Figure 11.3, Luna's best response function would be higher. If Mercury's marginal cost does not change, its best response function would remain the same. In the new equilibrium, both sellers raise price. However, Luna would raise price relatively more than Mercury.

So, in competition on price to sell differentiated products, if a seller incurs higher marginal cost, the competitors absorb part of the impact by raising their prices. The seller with higher cost loses consumers and profit contribution, but the loss is reduced to the extent that competitors respond with higher prices.

Strategic Complements[3]

Referring to Luna's best response function in Figure 11.3, if Mercury were to raise its price, then Luna should raise its price as well, while if Mercury were to cut its price, then Luna should also cut its price. Intuitively, if Mercury raises its price, some consumers would switch to Luna. So the marginal consumer (just indifferent between Luna and Mercury) would be relatively further from Luna. Hence, Luna's demand would become relatively inelastic, and so Luna would raise its price.

Likewise, if Mercury were to cut its price, some consumers would switch to Mercury. So the marginal consumer would be relatively closer to Luna's product. Hence, Luna's demand would become relatively elastic, and so Luna would cut its price.

Similarly, referring to Mercury' best response function, Mercury should always adjust its price in the same direction as Luna. Accordingly, in price competition between oligopolists with unlimited capacity that offer differentiated products (Hotelling model), prices are *strategic complements*. Actions are **strategic complements** if an adjustment by one party leads other parties to adjust in the same direction. In an oligopoly, if prices are strategic complements, then competitors would maximize profit by following each other's price moves in the same direction.

Strategic complements: An adjustment by one party leads others to adjust in same direction.

PROGRESS CHECK 11A

Suppose that the transport cost is less than $4 per mile. How would that affect the equilibrium prices?

VODAFONE: 4G PRICING

In the UK 4G mobile telecommunications market, EE has the largest market share with over 4 million subscribers, followed by O2 and Three with over 2 million each, and Vodafone with under 1 million.

The SIM-only market segment caters to subscribers with their own handset and who buy only the service. Among the entry-level plans, Three offers the cheapest at £7 a month, EE is next lowest at £9.99 a month, and O2's price is £11 a month, while Vodafone is the most expensive at £22 a month.

The competing providers differentiate by coverage (EE claims the largest network), quantity of included voice minutes and data, and prices for additional usage. Vodafone's plan includes 1GB of data, which is more than the others'. Nevertheless, Kester Mann, senior analyst at CCS Insight, remarked that Vodafone "will continue to lose share if it doesn't respond to the actions of its competitors, which have reduced tariffs."

Vodafone defended its pricing as offering good value especially considering sports and movies. Vodafone offers Sky Sports, Spotify, and Netflix in a 4G SIM-only plan for £27 a month.

Source: "Vodafone under pressure to cut its 4G SIM-only prices," *Mobile Magazine*, August 13, 2014.

3. Limit Pricing

So far, we have analyzed oligopoly strategy assuming that the competitors act simultaneously. Accordingly, we have applied the concept of Nash equilibrium. But what if one seller can act before others? Then it might be able to make strategic moves and exploit first-mover advantage. To develop strategy in such circumstances, we apply games in extensive form.

Consider the duopoly between Luna Cellular and Mercury Wireless, and allow Mercury to set price before Luna. Referring to Figure 11.4, at node A, Mercury sets its price, and then, at node B, Luna sets its price. Here, we allow a continuous choice of price, so it is not feasible to represent all of the possible choices in the extensive form.

In competition on price to sell differentiated products, if production involves a substantial fixed cost, one possible strategic move is to deter potential competitors from entering the industry. The strategy is to set such a low price that the potential competitor's residual demand is so low that the potential competitor cannot break even.

Referring to Figure 11.5, the lower is Mercury's price, p_M, the further to the left would be Luna's residual demand curve. If Mercury's price is low enough, Luna's residual demand curve would everywhere lie below its average cost curve. Note

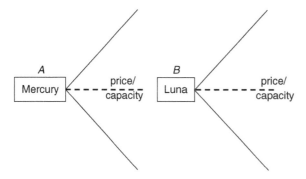

FIGURE 11.4 Strategic move.

Note: Mercury sets its price or capacity to influence Luna's choice of price or capacity in a favorable way.

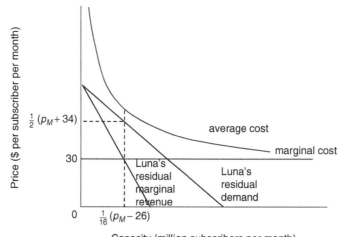

FIGURE 11.5 Limit pricing.

Notes: Mercury sets its price so low that Luna's residual demand falls below Luna's average cost curve. So, Luna will choose not to produce at all.

the shape of Luna's average cost curve: at low capacity, the average cost is high because of the fixed cost, and then the average cost declines with capacity as the fixed cost is divided by a larger scale of production.

Since Luna's residual demand curve is below the average cost curve at all scales of production, the price would be less than average cost at the profit-maximizing scale, $\frac{1}{16}(p_M - 26)$. Hence, Luna would incur a loss even at the "profit-maximizing" scale. Accordingly, its best strategy is not to produce at all.

The strategy of producing so much as to choke off potential entry is called **limit pricing**. It is so called because the leader sets a sufficiently low price that it takes away so much demand that a potential competitor cannot break even. Thus no other producer would enter the market.

> **Limit pricing:** The leader commits to pricing so low that a potential competitor cannot break even.

A strategy of limit pricing makes sense under two conditions. The first condition is that the leader's price is credible. Potential competitors must believe that the leader has committed to the entry-deterring level of price, and will not change if the potential competitor should enter. This means that, for the leader, it must be more profitable to produce at the entry-deterring price than to accommodate entry and produce an equal share with competitors.

The second condition is that production involves a substantial fixed cost. If there were no fixed cost, a potential competitor could break even at a very small scale of production. Referring to Figure 11.5, the average cost and marginal cost curves would be the same. So, at the profit-maximizing capacity, the price would exceed the average cost. So there is no way to deter the potential competitor from entry.

PROGRESS CHECK 11B

Suppose that Luna's fixed cost of production is higher. Referring to Figure 11.5, how would that affect Luna's cost curves and the price that Mercury must set to deter Luna from entry?

---

4. Capacity Competition

Typically, in the long run, the strategic variable for oligopolistic sellers is production capacity. We analyze the outcome of oligopolistic competition on capacity in the setting of a homogeneous product. For simplicity, we focus on a duopoly, and ignore utilization and inventories, and so capacity, production, and sales are all equal.

The market is as described in Figure 11.1, except that there are two providers. Luna and Mercury independently and simultaneously set production capacity, and then produce at a constant marginal cost of $30 per subscriber per month. The market price equates the demand with the total capacity offered by the two providers. This is the **Cournot** model of oligopoly, named for the French economist who published it in 1838.

> **Cournot oligopoly:** Sellers compete on production capacity to sell a homogeneous product.

Since Luna and Mercury set capacities simultaneously, it is appropriate to apply the concept of Nash equilibrium. Let Luna set capacity Q_L, and Mercury set capacity Q_M. Then, given Mercury's capacity, Luna's residual demand curve is as shown in Figure 11.6.

Recall that the residual demand is the demand given the actions of competing sellers. Here, the action of the competing seller is Mercury's capacity, Q_M. So, at every possible price, Luna's residual demand is the market demand less Mercury's production, Q_M.

To maximize profit, Luna should set production capacity at the scale where residual marginal revenue equals marginal cost. From the residual demand, Luna

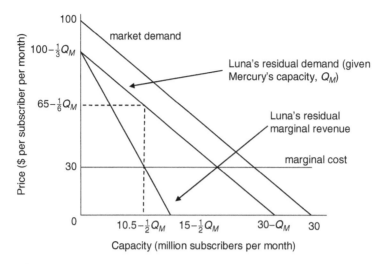

FIGURE 11.6 Capacity competition: residual demand.

Notes: Given Mercury's capacity, Luna's residual demand slopes downward to a quantity $300 - Q_M$ at price 0. Luna maximizes profit at a scale of $10.5 - 1/2Q_M$ and price $65 - 1/6Q_M$.

can calculate its residual marginal revenue. Referring to Figure 11.6, Luna's residual marginal revenue equals the marginal cost of $30, at the production capacity of $10.5 - \frac{1}{2}Q_M$. Owing to the competition for consumers, Luna's profit-maximizing capacity depends on Mercury's capacity, Q_M.

Figure 11.7 presents a graph of Luna's profit-maximizing capacity as a function of Mercury's capacity, Q_M. This graph is Luna's best response function. We can intuitively derive two extreme points on Luna's best response function. If Mercury sets capacity at zero, then Luna would effectively be a monopoly and should choose the profit-maximizing capacity of 10.5 million subscribers per month. If Mercury sets capacity at 21 million, then Luna's residual demand curve would be so far to the left that its residual marginal revenue would cross the marginal cost at a capacity of zero. Hence, Luna would choose zero capacity.

Figure 11.7 also depicts Mercury's best response function, which is its profit-maximizing capacity as a function of Luna's capacity, Q_L. Figure 11.7 is the graphical equivalent of the game in strategic form, where each party chooses from a continuum of strategies.

The Nash equilibrium is at the intersection of the two best response functions. For both sellers, the Nash equilibrium strategy is to set capacity at 7 million. By the properties of Nash equilibrium, if Mercury believes that Luna will choose capacity of 7 million, then it is best for Mercury to choose capacity of 7 million, and vice versa.

In equilibrium, the total capacity and production is $7 + 7 = 14$ million subscribers a month. Referring to the market demand, the market price is $\frac{10}{3} \times (30 - 14) = \$53.33$ per subscriber, so its profit contribution is $\$(53.33 - 30) \times 7 = \$163$ million a month. The equilibrium does not depend on fixed costs. Only the sellers' participation decisions – whether to produce at all – depend on fixed

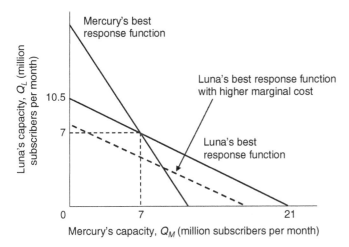

FIGURE 11.7 Capacity competition: best response functions.

Notes: Luna's best response function shows its profit-maximizing capacity, Q_L, as a function of Mercury's capacity, Q_M. Mercury's best response function shows its profit-maximizing capacity, Q_M, as a function of Luna's capacity, Q_L.

costs: specifically, each seller will produce only if the profit contribution exceed its fixed cost.

With a duopoly, the total capacity and production is 14 million subscribers a month, which exceeds the monopoly profit-maximizing capacity of 10.5 million. The duopoly price of $53.33 per subscriber is less than the monopoly price of $65 per subscriber. Finally, the combined profit contribution of the two duopolists, $326 million, is less than the monopoly profit contribution of $367.5 million.

Demand and Cost Changes

How should oligopolists competing on capacity respond to changes in demand and cost? Generally, the response comprises two steps. First, as in a monopoly, each seller should adjust capacity until its residual marginal revenue equals marginal cost. Second, in an oligopoly, the new capacity is a function of the other sellers' capacities. So, with the new demand or cost, the seller's best response function would shift and then establish a new equilibrium.

Consider an increase in market demand. In Figure 11.6, Luna's residual demand would shift to the right, and so the residual marginal revenue would shift to the right. So Luna's profit-maximizing capacity would be larger. Hence, in Figure 11.7, Luna's best response function would be higher. Similarly, Mercury's best response function would shift to the right. Thus, in the new equilibrium, each seller would choose larger capacity.

What about an increase in marginal cost? In Figure 11.6, with higher marginal cost, Luna's profit-maximizing capacity would be smaller. Hence, in Figure 11.7,

Luna's best response function would be lower. If Mercury's marginal cost does not change, its best response function would remain the same. In the new equilibrium, Luna reduces capacity while Mercury increases capacity.

So, in competition on capacity to sell a homogeneous product, if a seller incurs higher marginal cost, the competitors take advantage of the weakness to increase their capacities and grab market share. The seller with higher cost loses in two ways – by the higher cost itself and by the competitors' strategic adjustment.

PROGRESS CHECK 11C

In Figures 11.6 and 11.7, illustrate how Luna's choice of capacity and best response function would change if its marginal cost is lower.

Strategic Substitutes

Referring to Figure 11.6, if Mercury raises its production capacity, Luna's residual demand curve would shift to the left by the amount of Mercury's increase in capacity. Then Luna's profit-maximizing capacity (at which its residual marginal revenue equals marginal cost) would be lower. So, in Figure 11.7, Luna's best response function slopes downward: the larger is Mercury's capacity, the smaller the capacity that Luna chooses.

Similarly, Mercury's best response function slopes downward: the larger is Luna's capacity, the smaller the capacity that Mercury chooses. Among sellers producing at constant marginal cost and competing on production capacity, the

Strategic substitutes: An adjustment by one party leads others to adjust in the opposite direction.

capacity choices are *strategic substitutes*. Actions are **strategic substitutes** if an adjustment by one party leads other parties to adjust in the opposite direction. In an oligopoly, if production capacities are strategic substitutes, then competitors would maximize profit by adjusting capacity in the opposite direction to the adjustments of others.

A clear appreciation of whether business choices are strategic complements or strategic substitutes is very useful in strategic thinking. With this appreciation, managers can respond to competitor's actions even without knowing the best response functions or even the equilibrium.

Generally, whether business choices are strategic complements or strategic substitutes depends on the relevant demand and cost conditions. Among sellers producing at constant marginal cost with unlimited capacity, and competing on price to sell a differentiated product (Hotelling model), prices are strategic complements. Among sellers producing at constant marginal cost and competing on production capacity to sell a homogeneous product (Cournot model), capacities are strategic substitutes.

What about other business choices such as advertising and R&D expenditure? Generally, these may be either strategic complements or strategic substitutes depending on the relevant demand and cost conditions. For instance, increased R&D spending can have an effect similar to increased capacity. On the other hand, an increase in one seller's R&D expenditure may drive competitors to increase R&D as well, particularly when they compete for patents. So, R&D expenditures might be strategic complements or strategic substitutes, depending on the circumstances.

PROGRESS CHECK 11D

Suppose that R&D expenditures are strategic substitutes. On a graph like Figure 11.7, illustrate the best response functions.

MANUFACTURING MEMORY: NOT FOR THE FAINT-HEARTED

The DRAM and NAND flash memory industries are highly concentrated. Samsung Electronics dominates both industries, with shares of 38% and 40% shares, respectively. The top four manufacturers control around 90% of both markets.

The markets for memory are global with prices set in US dollars. Any depreciation of the Korean won against the US dollar would raise the US dollar cost of Korean manufacturers. In the short run, to the extent of product differentiation, Korean manufacturers should raise their prices. Since prices are strategic complements, competitors such as Micron would follow.

Given the high fixed costs and price volatility, the memory industries are consolidating through mergers and exits. Higher-cost manufacturers are likely to sell themselves or quit. With the consolidation, lower-cost producers such as Samsung and Hynix would earn larger margins and can further increase their production capacity and expand their market share.

Source: Clyde Montevirgen, "Semiconductors," *Standard & Poor's Industry Surveys*, May 12, 2011.

5. Capacity Leadership

So far, we have analyzed oligopolists' choice of capacity assuming that the competitors act simultaneously. Accordingly, we have applied the concept of Nash equilibrium. But what if one seller can act before others? Then it might be able to make strategic moves and gain first-mover advantage. To develop strategy in such circumstances, we apply games in extensive form, as we did in the analysis of limit pricing.

Consider the duopoly between Luna Cellular and Mercury Wireless, and allow Mercury to set capacity before Luna. Referring to Figure 11.4, at node A, Mercury sets capacity, and then, at node B, Luna sets capacity. A possible strategic move is to set larger capacity and push down the competitor's residual demand so that it chooses a smaller capacity. By grabbing a larger market share, the leader can raise its profit.

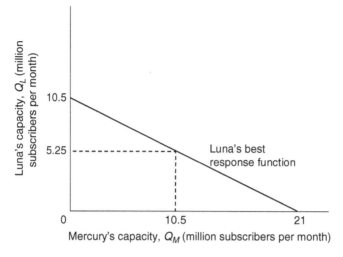

FIGURE 11.8 Capacity leadership.

Notes: Mercury sets capacity before Luna. It chooses capacity to maximize its profit, given that Luna would subsequently set capacity according to its best response function.

Figure 11.8 graphs Luna's best response function, which shows its choice of capacity as a function of Mercury's capacity, Q_M. Since Mercury sets capacity before Luna, Mercury can choose the capacity that maximizes its profit, given that Luna would subsequently set capacity according to its best response function. This is the **Stackelberg** model of oligopoly.

> **Stackelberg oligopoly:**
> Both leader and follower sell a homogeneous product, and the leader commits to some capacity to grab a larger share.

Through trial and error, Mercury can calculate the corresponding profit contribution from every level of capacity up to 21 million subscribers a month. The capacity which maximizes Mercury's profit, given that Luna would subsequently set capacity according to its best response function, is 10.5 million subscribers per month. Following its best response function, Luna would choose a capacity of 5.25 million. The market price would be $\frac{10}{3} \times (30 - 10.5 - 5.25) = \$47.50$ per subscriber per month.

As the industry leader, Mercury commits to twice the capacity of Luna, the industry follower. Since the product is homogeneous, both sell at the same market price. So Mercury enjoys first-mover advantage, earning double the profit contribution of Luna.

However, there is a downside to Mercury's commitment to large capacity. Taking into account Luna's capacity, the total capacity in the market is larger, and so the market price is lower. Indeed, in our example, the price with capacity leadership is $47.50 per subscriber per month, as compared with $53.33 if both sellers set capacity simultaneously.

A strategy of capacity leadership makes sense only if the leader's capacity is credible. Potential competitors must believe that the leader has committed to its capacity, and will not change if the potential competitor should enter. This means that, for the leader, it must be more profitable to produce at the pre-committed capacity (which implies a relatively low price) than to accommodate entry and produce an equal share with the competitor.

PROGRESS CHECK 11E

Referring to Figure 11.8, suppose that Mercury sets capacity at 21 million subscribers a month. How would Luna respond? What is bad about such a strategy for Mercury?

LAS VEGAS STRIP: EVOLUTION OF OLIGOPOLY

The Las Vegas Strip actually lies outside the city of Las Vegas, on the stretch of Las Vegas Boulevard between Sahara Avenue and Russell Road. Over time, Caesars Entertainment and MGM Resorts have consolidated the hotel industry on the Strip. In 2010, of a total of 67,000 rooms, Caesars Entertainment managed 22,880, while MGM managed over 12,000.

In the wake of the Great Recession, two new developments opened on the Strip. In late 2009, CityCenter, 50% owned and managed by MGM Resorts, added over 4,000 rooms. Then, in late 2010, Cosmopolitan, acquired by Deutsche Bank on foreclosure of a construction loan, added 2,000 rooms with another 1,000 in 2011.

The Moody's analyst Peggy Holloway described the outcome as a "perfect storm – visitor volume declined due to the recession at the same time significant new inventory entered the market." Between 2008 and 2010, MGM's hotel occupancy decreased from 92% to 89%, while its average daily rate fell from $148 to $108. The Sahara, with 1,720 rooms at the northern end of the Strip, closed in May 2011.

MGM's strategy in the Las Vegas Strip is consistent with capacity leadership. Together with Caesars Entertainment, it dominates the industry. By expanding capacity, it grabs market share. Weaker hotels like the Sahara shut down. MGM's room rates were hit by the Great Recession, but, in the longer term, it can reap the benefits of the larger share.

Sources: Caesars Entertainment Corp., Annual Report 2010; MGM Resorts, Annual Report 2010; "Sahara's closure on May 16 will mark 'the end of an era,'" *Las Vegas Sun*, March 11, 2011.

6. Restraining Competition

Generally, a monopoly is more profitable than an oligopoly – whether the sellers compete on price or capacity. Further, an oligopoly is more profitable than a perfectly competitive industry. Hence, a monopoly is the most profitable of all possible market structures.

Accordingly, rather than compete, sellers can raise profits by restraining competition among themselves. If sellers restrain competition to a sufficient degree, they can achieve the profit of a monopoly. Competing sellers can restrain competition through explicit agreement or by integration.

Cartels

A **cartel** is an agreement to restrain competition. A seller cartel is an agreement among sellers to restrain competition in supply, while a buyer cartel is an agreement among buyers to restrain competition in demand.

Typically, a seller cartel sets a maximum sales quota for each participant. By

> **Cartel:** An agreement to restrain competition.

limiting each participant's sales, the cartel restricts the quantity supplied and raises sellers' profit above the competitive level. The more effectively the cartel suppresses competition, the closer the cartel's profit will be to the monopoly level.

A seller cartel restrains sales to raise the market price above the competitive level. The higher the price, however, the more attractive it will be for an individual seller to sell more than its quota. To the extent that any one seller exceeds its quota, the quantity supplied will increase and the market price will fall. So, to be effective, a cartel must have some way to compel each participant to abide by its quota.

Further, if a cartel succeeds in raising the price above the competitive level, it will attract new sellers to enter the market. Hence, another issue for a cartel is how to keep out new entrants. Therefore, the key to an effective cartel, or, more generally, effective restriction of competition, is enforcement against existing sellers exceeding their quotas and against the entry of new competitors.

Enforcement

The laws of most developed countries seek to encourage competition and typically do not allow cartels except for specific exemptions. Cartels that are not legal must rely on informal enforcement. Generally, the effectiveness of informal enforcement depends on five factors.

*   *Number of sellers.* Enforcement is easier when there are fewer sellers to be monitored. So, a cartel will be more effective in a concentrated than in a fragmented industry.
*   *Excess capacity.* If all sellers are operating near capacity, then it will be difficult for them to expand; hence, there will be little incentive to exceed the specified quotas. By contrast, a seller with substantial excess capacity will have more incentive to exceed its quota.
*   *Sunk costs.* In the short run, competitive sellers are willing to operate so long as the price covers avoidable cost. Sellers with substantial sunk costs will be relatively more willing to cut price and exceed their quotas.

- *Barriers to entry and exit.* Recall from Chapter 8 that, in a perfectly contestable market, sellers can enter and exit at no cost. Suppose that all the sellers in a perfectly contestable market form a cartel. Despite their monopoly, they cannot raise the price above the long-run average cost, because that would draw new suppliers into the market, which would drive the market price back down.
- *Product.* If the product is homogeneous, then each individual seller faces a relatively elastic demand, so it can easily sell more than its quota. On the other hand, if the product is homogeneous, it is also easier for the cartel to monitor the various sellers. One way in which sellers circumvent a cartel is to sell more and claim that the additional items sold are not covered by the cartel agreement. Such cheating is difficult for a homogeneous product; hence, it is easier to enforce the cartel. Accordingly, whether it is easier or more difficult to enforce a cartel for a homogeneous or heterogeneous product is unclear.

Horizontal Integration

Cartels that are illegal must rely on private enforcement to prevent sellers from exceeding their quotas. However, competing sellers can restrain competition in a way that does not raise the difficulties of enforcement. The alternative is for the competing sellers to integrate.

Consider, for instance, a combination of two sellers, each of which has 50% of a market. The combined business will have a monopoly. While it may be illegal for two independent competitors to fix prices between themselves, it is certainly legal for the two parts of the same company to agree on prices. Hence, a combination that creates a monopoly will certainly be able to set price and sales at monopoly levels, subject, of course, to the entry of potential competitors.

> **Horizontal integration:** Combination of two entities, in the same or similar business, under a common ownership.

The combination of two entities, in the same or similar businesses, under a common ownership is called **horizontal integration**. By contrast, **vertical integration** is the combination of the assets for two successive stages of production under a common ownership. Chapter 14 analyzes vertical integration.

> **Vertical integration:** Combination of assets for successive stages of production under a common ownership.

The horizontal integration of any two businesses with market power will lead to a reduction in the quantity supplied, and hence raise the market price and increase profits. The increase in the market price will benefit competing sellers as they will enjoy higher profits.

PROGRESS CHECK 11F
Explain the difference between horizontal and vertical integration.

US MOBILE TELECOMMUNICATIONS: STILL FOUR

Verizon and AT&T dominate the US market for mobile telecommunications, with Sprint and T-Mobile in distant third and fourth places. With the aim of competing more effectively, Sprint proposed to merge with T-Mobile.

However, the federal government opposed a merger. The chairman of the Federal Communications Commission, Tom Wheeler, explained: "Four national wireless providers are good for American consumers."

In August 2014, Sprint bowed to the inevitable and withdrew from merger talks. Within weeks, Sprint and T-Mobile introduced new cheaper pricing plans. Sprint's new plan provided unlimited talk, text, and data for $60 a month, $20 cheaper than T-Mobile, and Sprint offered $350 to subscribers switching from other carriers. T-Mobile offered unlimited data service for 12 months to customers introducing new subscribers.

Sources: "No merger of Sprint and T-Mobile US, but plenty of taunts," *New York Times*, August 6, 2014; "T-Mobile, Sprint cut prices after merger talks," *Wall Street Journal*, August 21, 2014.

KEY TAKEAWAYS

- For sellers competing on price to sell differentiated products, to maximize profit, set price so that residual marginal revenue equals marginal cost.
- When demand or costs change, adjust price so that: (i) residual marginal revenue equals marginal cost; and (ii) the best response price is a Nash equilibrium.
- If prices are strategic complements, then adjust price in the same direction as competitors' prices.
- For sellers competing on capacity to sell a homogeneous product, to maximize profit, set capacity so that residual marginal revenue equals marginal cost.
- When demand or costs change, adjust capacity so that: (a) residual marginal revenue equals marginal cost; and (b) the best response capacity is a Nash equilibrium.
- If capacities are strategic substitutes, then adjust capacity in the opposite direction to competitors' capacities.
- To deter entry through limit pricing, set price so low that potential competitors cannot break even.
- To apply capacity leadership, choose capacity to maximize profit, given that competitors would choose capacity according to their best response functions.
- Limit competition through agreements and horizontal integration.

REVIEW QUESTIONS

1. Price will equal marginal cost only in a perfectly competitive industry. True or false? Explain your answer.

2. Explain the meaning of residual demand in the context of competition on: (a) price; (b) capacity.
3. Explain the meaning of best response function in the context of competition on: (a) price; (b) capacity.
4. If advertising expenditures are strategic complements, and your competitor raises advertising, how should you respond?
5. In an oligopoly, how does differentiation raise profit?
6. How is Figure 11.3 related to a game in strategic form?
7. In competition between sellers on capacity to sell a homogeneous product, how would an increase in fixed cost affect the equilibrium?
8. Explain the meaning of strategic substitutes.
9. Suppose that advertising expenditures are strategic substitutes. On a graph like Figure 11.7, illustrate the best response functions.
10. Explain why limit pricing does not make sense in an industry where production involves no fixed cost.
11. Suppose that your cost of capacity is sunk, once incurred. Does this help or hinder a strategy of limit pricing?
12. Suppose that you can commit to production capacity before other sellers set their capacity. Should you set a relatively larger or smaller capacity as compared to the situation where you commit to capacity simultaneously with other sellers?
13. In committing to production capacity before other sellers, why is it important to look forward and consider how the other sellers would set capacity?
14. What are the five factors that influence the effectiveness of a cartel?
15. Is a cartel easier or more difficult to enforce in a market with less heterogeneous products than in a market with more heterogeneous products?

DISCUSSION QUESTIONS

1. Major US carriers, including American and United Airlines, operate on a hub-and-spoke system, offering many frequent connections through their respective hubs. Travelers may prefer one airline to another depending on which hub is more convenient.
   (a) Suppose that American and United compete on price to sell differentiated products. If American cut fares on flights at its Dallas/Fort Worth airport hub, should United raise or reduce fares at that airport?
   (b) Compare competition between American and United at Chicago's O'Hare International Airport, which is a hub for both airlines, and at Dallas/Fort Worth Airport, which is a hub only for American. At which hub would price competition be more intense?
   (c) Suppose that the strength of traveler preferences over alternative hubs were to diminish. How should airlines adjust their prices?
2. Among the three major national newspapers in the USA, the *Wall Street Journal*, with average daily (Monday to Friday) circulation of 2.12 million, is

reputed to be conservative. By contrast, the *New York Times* is reputed to be liberal. Its average daily circulation is 916,900, of which 46% is sold in greater New York City. (Sources: "Wall Street Journal still first in daily circulation," mediadecoder.blogs.nytimes.com, May 3, 2011; New York Times Company, 2009 Annual Report.)

(a) Explain how a media industry analyst could apply the Hotelling model to competition between the *New York Times* and the *Wall Street Journal*.

(b) Suppose that the marginal cost of producing the *New York Times* increases by 20 cents. Using relevant diagrams, explain: (i) how the *New York Times* should adjust its price; and (ii) how the *Wall Street Journal* should respond.

(c) Suppose that people with more intense political preferences switch from reading newspapers to listening to radio talk shows, while a new generation of readers is more politically moderate. How should the *New York Times* and *Wall Street Journal* adjust their prices to these changes?

3. In the wake of expanding demand for their cars, Japanese manufacturers, Toyota and Honda, have expanded production at existing factories and established new plants in North America. In June 2006, Honda announced a new $550 million factory, creating 2,000 jobs, at Greensburg, Indiana. Meanwhile, US manufacturers, General Motors and Ford, facing declining demand, have offered incentives for workers to quit, so as to reduce production capacity.

(a) Suppose that, in the short run, Ford and General Motors compete on price to sell differentiated products. If GM increases price discounts, how should Ford adjust prices?

(b) Use the Cournot model to relate the expansion of capacity by Toyota and Honda to the contraction in capacity by Ford and General Motors.

(c) Suppose that Toyota exercises capacity leadership. How would that affect your explanation in (b)?

4. In February 2015, broadband and fixed line carrier BT (British Telecom) re-entered the UK mobile market by buying EE. BT will be able to sell bundles of service combining mobile, fixed line, broadband, and television. It will challenge Vodafone, which sells only mobile services. (Source: "BT unveils £1bn share placing to help fund EE takeover", *Telegraph*, February 12, 2015.)

(a) How will BT's purchase of EE affect the concentration of the UK mobile services market?

(b) Suppose that the competing mobile carriers set capacity by the Cournot model. If BT's purchase does not affect the marginal cost of EE, how would BT's entry affect the equilibrium capacities?

(c) Using a suitable figure, explain how BT's entry would affect the residual demand for Vodafone and how Vodafone should adjust its prices.

5. Emirates and other Middle East carriers have expanded aggressively into the "kangaroo" route between Britain and Australia. In 2013, Qantas and Emirates

agreed to coordinate schedules, advertising, and pricing, and share revenues. Qantas changed its kangaroo stopover from Singapore to Dubai. Subsequently, Virgin Atlantic withdrew from the kangaroo market. (Source: "Qantas-Emirates alliance receives full (draft) approval from Australia's competition authority," Centre for Aviation, December 20, 2012.)

(a) Suppose that airlines set capacity according to the Cournot model. If Emirates and Qantas reduce their marginal cost through the code-share agreement, how should other airlines adjust their capacity?

(b) Suppose that Emirates-Qantas exercises capacity leadership. How would other airlines adjust their capacity as compared with (a)?

(c) How will the agreement between Qantas and Emirates to share revenues affect their incentive to cut price?

(d) If Qantas and Emirates raise prices, how should other airlines respond?

6. In 2010, of a total of 67,000 rooms on the Las Vegas Strip, Caesars Entertainment managed 22,880, while MGM Resorts managed over 12,000. However, owing to the Great Recession and new hotel openings, between 2008 and 2010, MGM's hotel occupancy decreased from 92% to 89%, while its average daily room rate fell from $148 to $108. Meanwhile, CityCenter, managed by MGM Resorts, and the Cosmopolitan opened with 4,000 and 3,000 rooms respectively, and the 1,720-room Sahara closed. (Sources: Caesars Entertainment Corp., Annual Report 2010; MGM Resorts, Annual Report 2010; "Sahara's closure on May 16 will mark 'the end of an era,'" *Las Vegas Sun*, March 11, 2011.)

(a) Using a suitable figure, explain how the opening of CityCenter and the Cosmopolitan affects the residual demand for an existing hotel and how the existing hotel should adjust prices.

(b) If MGM Resorts had not reduced its room rates, what would have been the effect on occupancy?

(c) Use the Cournot model to explain MGM Resorts' opening a new hotel and Sahara's closing.

7. The OPEC cartel sets production quotas for each member country. As of May 2006, OPEC produced 33.33 million barrels per day (mbd), with an excess capacity of between 1.3 and 1.8 mbd. Virtually all of the excess capacity was in Saudi Arabia, while several OPEC members exceeded their production quotas. (Sources: US Energy Information Administration, *Short Term Energy Outlook*, June 6, 2006; *Energy Economist*, May 12, 2004; *BP Statistical Review of World Energy*, June 2006.)

(a) Explain why OPEC members individually would wish to produce more than their production quota. How would that affect the price of oil and producer profits?

(b) Suppose that Saudi Arabia enforces the cartel by threatening to increase production if any OPEC member exceeds its quota. Why is it important that Saudi Arabia has large excess capacity?

(c) Consider the production of oil by non-OPEC members. Suppose that they have no short-run excess capacity. How do they affect OPEC's ability to raise prices in the short and long run?

8. DRAM is used to store data in PCs and other consumer and industrial electronic products. DRAM manufacturing is a capital-intensive industry. In 2004, Elpida, Hynix, Infineon, Micron, and Samsung produced 80% of the world DRAM supply. In the early 2000s, executives of the five companies agreed to fix the prices of DRAMs for sale to computer manufacturers. They held meetings to discuss prices, and exchanged information on sales to particular customers.

   (a) How easy would it be to enforce the DRAM cartel?
   (b) Why did the DRAM cartel members provide sales information to each other?
   (c) Supposing that the DRAM cartel members wished to limit the exchange of information, which customers should they select to monitor?

9. Gesamtmetall is the federation of employers and IG Metall is the labor union in Germany's engineering industry. Under the German system of national collective bargaining, Gesamtmetall and IG Metall negotiate pay and working conditions for the entire industry.

   (a) With respect to labor, does Gesamtmetall serve as a buyer cartel or seller cartel? What about IG Metall?
   (b) Consider large employers such as Daimler Benz and Robert Bosch. Why might they prefer to negotiate separate deals with their own workers rather than comply with the national collective agreement?
   (c) If all large employers negotiate separate deals, how will this affect the wages and conditions that small companies must offer?

You are the consultant!

Suppose that your major competitor has increased production capacity. Write a memorandum to the board of directors explaining how your organization should respond.

Appendix: Solving Equilibria

Here, we derive the major results of this chapter with a linear demand curve, $Q = a - bp$, and constant marginal cost, c. To get the numerical results presented in the chapter, substitute $a = 30$, $b = 3/10$, and $c = 30$.

Monopoly

A monopolist facing a linear demand curve will produce at the scale where marginal revenue equals marginal cost. First, rewrite the demand curve for price as a function of quantity (the *inverse demand function*)

$$p = \frac{a}{b} - \frac{1}{b}Q. \qquad (11.1)$$

Then profit is total revenue minus total cost, or

$$\Pi(Q) = \left(\frac{a}{b} - \frac{1}{b}Q\right)Q - cQ = \frac{a}{b}Q - \frac{1}{b}Q^2 - cQ. \qquad (11.2)$$

To identify the profit-maximizing scale, differentiate (11.2) with respect to production, Q, and set the derivative equal to zero. After simplifying, we have

$$Q^* = \frac{1}{2}(a - bc). $$

Cournot Model: Capacity Competition with Homogeneous Product

In the Cournot model, the market price is the price at which the quantity demanded equals the capacity of the two sellers. By (11.1), with two sellers, Luna and Mercury, the inverse market demand is

$$p = \frac{a}{b} - \frac{1}{b}(Q_L + Q_M), \qquad (11.3)$$

where Q_L represents Luna's capacity and Q_M represents Mercury's capacity.
Each seller's profit depends on the other seller's capacity. Luna's profit is

$$\Pi_L = p \times Q_L - c \times Q_L = \left[\frac{a}{b} - \frac{1}{b}(Q_L + Q_M)\right]Q_L - cQ_L, $$

after substituting from (11.3). To identify the profit-maximizing capacity, differentiate the profit with respect to Luna's choice of capacity, Q_L, and set the derivative equal to zero. After simplifying, we have Luna's best response function,

$$Q_L = \frac{1}{2}(a - bc - Q_M). \qquad (11.4)$$

Similarly, we can derive Mercury's best response function,

$$Q_M = \frac{1}{2}(a - bc - Q_L). \qquad (11.5)$$

Figure 11.7 graphs the two best response functions.

In the Nash equilibrium, strategies Q_L and Q_M would satisfy both (11.4) and (11.5). Solving these two equations simultaneously, we have the equilibrium capacities,

$$Q_L^* = Q_M^* = \frac{1}{3}(a - bc).$$

Differing Costs

If the sellers have different marginal costs, c_L and c_M, then we can use the same procedure as above to solve for the Nash equilibrium,

$$Q_L^* = \frac{1}{3}[a - b(2c_L - c_M)]$$

and

$$Q_M^* = \frac{1}{3}[a - b(2c_M - c_L)].$$

Hotelling Model: Price Competition with Differentiated Products

The setting of the Hotelling model differs from the setting of the monopoly and Cournot duopoly. Here, we solve the equilibrium of a duopoly, where Luna and Mercury each produce at constant marginal cost, c, and consumers are willing to pay $100 for the service and incur a "transport cost" of t per mile to buy.

The key to calculating the demand for each seller is to identify the marginal consumer, located at some point, x^*, who is just indifferent between buying from the two sellers. Generally, for a consumer at location x, her expected utility from Luna's product would be

$$100 - p_L - t \times x. \tag{11.6}$$

That consumer would lie at a distance $1 - x$ from Mercury, so her expected utility from Mercury's product would be

$$100 - p_M - t \times (1 - x). \tag{11.7}$$

Hence, for the marginal consumer, the two expected utilities must be equal. Equating (11.6) and (11.7),

$$100 - p_L - tx^* = 100 - p_M - t(1 - x^*).$$

After simplifying, the location of the marginal consumer is

$$x^*(p_L, p_M) = \frac{1}{2t}(p_M - p_L + t). \tag{11.8}$$

Consumers located to the left of x^* would buy from Luna, while those to the right would buy from Mercury. So, x^* is the market share of Luna and $1 - x^*$ is the market share of Mercury.

Consider Luna. Its profit (as a function of Mercury's price) is

$$\Pi_L = (p_L - c) \times x^* = (p_L - c)\frac{1}{2t}(p_M - p_L + t),$$

after substituting from (11.8). To identify the profit-maximizing price, differentiate the profit with respect to Luna's price, p_L, and set the derivative equal to zero. After simplifying, we have Luna's best response function,

$$p_L = \frac{1}{2}(p_M + t + c). \tag{11.9}$$

Similarly, we can derive Mercury's best response function,

$$p_M = \frac{1}{2}(p_L + t + c). \tag{11.10}$$

Figure 11.3 graphs the two best response functions.

In the Nash equilibrium, strategies, p_L and p_M, would satisfy both (11.9) and (11.10). Solving these two equations simultaneously, we have the equilibrium prices,

$$p^*_L = p^*_M = c + t.$$

Notes

1   This chapter is more advanced. All but the section on capacity leadership (Section 5) may be omitted without loss of continuity. The section on capacity leadership provides background relevant to Chapter 15 on regulation.

2   The following discussion is based, in part, on Clyde Montevirgen, "Standard & Poor's Industry Surveys: Semiconductors," May 12, 2011; Elpida Memory, Inc., FY2010 Financial Review & Business Updates, May 12, 2011; "Qimonda," Wikipedia (accessed August 12, 2011).

3   This section is based on Jeremy Bulow, John Geanakoplos, and Paul Klemperer, "Multimarket oligopoly: strategic substitutes and complements," *Journal of Political Economy*, Vol. 93, No. 3, June 1985, pp. 488–511.

Imperfect Markets

CHAPTER 12

Externalities

LEARNING OBJECTIVES

- Understand positive and negative externalities.
- Appreciate economic efficiency as a benchmark and the opportunity to profit by resolving an externality.
- Appreciate how to resolve externalities and the corresponding barriers.
- Understand network effects and appreciate how to manage demand with network effects.
- Understand public goods.
- Appreciate how to provide public goods commercially.

1. Introduction

With over 1 million square feet of net leasable area, VivoCity is Singapore's largest mall. It is located on the western edge of the city, at the intersection of two subway lines, and attracts 40 million visitors annually.[1]

In 2010, 98.3% of VivoCity was leased to tenants, generating S$116.3 million in gross rental income. The mall's retail tenants pay a three-part rental: 86% is fixed, 13% is based on the retailer's sales revenue, while the remainder comprises service charges and contributions to advertising and promotion.

VivoCity's two largest retail tenants, renting 22.4% of the mall, are VivoMart, a combination of a hypermarket, upscale supermarket, and drug store, and Tangs Department Store. In 2010, VivoMart and Tangs paid an average rent of S$56 per square foot per year. By contrast, fashion stores paid almost three times as much, an average rent of S$157 per square foot per year.

Why does VivoCity charge systematically lower rentals to supermarkets and department stores than to specialty retailers? Why must VivoCity tenants contribute to a fund for advertising and promotion? Why do real estate developers build malls near transportation facilities such as subways?

We can address these questions through the concepts of *externality* and *public good*. An **externality** arises when one party directly conveys a benefit or cost to others (not through a market). An anchor store generates a positive externality for other stores. Department stores and cineplexes can serve as anchors. By drawing additional shoppers to the mall, they directly convey benefits to specialty stores.

> **Externality:** A benefit or cost directly conveyed to others.

Similarly, transport facilities generate externalities for retailers by moving consumers in large numbers. This explains why developers choose to locate shopping malls near subways and other transport facilities.

Here, we introduce the concept of an externality, characterize its economically efficient level (which maximizes value added), and then discuss how to achieve that level. Economic efficiency can be achieved through collective action of the parties involved or by merging the source and beneficiary of the externality. For instance, VivoCity charges lower rents to supermarkets and department stores. They attract shoppers who benefit fashion stores, which pay relatively higher rents to VivoCity.

A particular class of externalities is network externalities. These arise when a party directly conveys benefit or cost to everyone else in the same network. Network externalities underlie the rapid growth of the Internet. The same concept applies more widely to communications, media, and high-technology industries.

> **Public good:** One person's increase in consumption does not reduce the quantity available to others.

Finally, we introduce the concept of a public good, characterize its economically efficient level, and discuss how to achieve that level. An item is a **public good** if one person's increase in consumption does not reduce the quantity available to others.

Broadcast TV nicely illustrates a public good: one hour of TV can serve 100,000 or 1 million viewers with no difference in cost. In the provision of a public good, there is an extreme economy of scale with respect to the number of customers served (not with respect to volume of production). For tenants of a shopping mall, expenditures by the mall on advertising and promotion that attract more shoppers are a public good. The additional shoppers benefit all the stores in the mall.

In any market with externalities and public goods, managers can increase value added (and profit) by bringing provision closer to the economically efficient level. This chapter explains how to do so in a wide range of contexts.

2. Benchmark: Economic Efficiency

Externalities can be positive or negative. A **positive externality** arises when one party directly conveys a benefit to others. The additional customers that an anchor store generates for nearby specialty retailers constitute a positive externality. By contrast, a **negative externality** arises when one party directly imposes a cost on others. A betting shop imposes a negative externality on nearby toy stores by discouraging families with children from browsing nearby.

> **Positive externality:** A benefit directly conveyed to others.

> **Negative externality:** A cost directly imposed on others.

Positive Externality

To explain the benchmark level of a positive externality, consider the example of a department store on Main Street. It must decide how much to spend on advertising to attract shoppers. To attract more shoppers, it must spend more on advertising. The additional shoppers would increase the store's sales and profit contribution.

Table 12.1 presents the department store's revenues and costs at the various levels of customer traffic on a monthly basis. For instance, with 50,000 customers a month, the store's sales revenue would be $1.9 million, while the variable cost would be $1.0 million, and so the profit contribution would be $900,000. The cost of advertising to attract the 50,000 customers is $200,000. Accordingly, the overall profit would be $700,000.

The marginal profit contribution is the increase in profit contribution associated with the increase in customers. At 50,000 customers a month, the marginal profit contribution is $(900 – 800)/(50 – 40) = $10 per customer. The marginal customer cost is the increase in advertising expenditure associated with the increase in customers. At 50,000 customers a month, the marginal customer cost is $(200 – 160)/(50 – 40) = $4 per customer.

What level of customer traffic maximizes profit? Referring to Table 12.1, the department store maximizes profit at 60,000 customers a month. Its maximum

Table 12.1 Customer traffic and profit

Customers ('000)	Revenue ($ '000)	Variable cost ($ '000)	Profit contribution ($ '000)	Marginal profit contribution ($)	Advertising expenditure ($ '000)	Marginal customer cost ($)	Profit ($ '000)
0	0	0	0		0		0
10	460	200	260	26	40	4	220
20	880	400	480	22	80	4	400
30	1,260	600	660	18	120	4	540
40	1,600	800	800	14	160	4	640
50	1,900	1,000	900	10	200	4	700
60	2,160	1,200	960	4	240	4	720
70	2,380	1,400	980	2	280	4	700
80	2,560	1,600	960	-2	320	4	640
90	2,700	1,800	900	-6	360	4	540
100	2,800	2,000	800	-10	400	4	400
110	2,860	2,200	660	-14	440	4	220

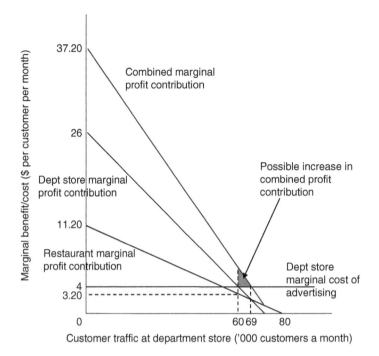

FIGURE 12.1 Positive externality.

Notes: The combined marginal benefit (profit contribution) is the vertical sum of the individual marginal benefits (profit contributions). The economically efficient level of customers is 69,000, where the combined marginal benefits equal the marginal cost. If the department store considers only its own benefit and cost, it would attract only 60,000 customers. By increasing to 69,000 customers, the department store and restaurant could gain the shaded area in additional profit.

profit is $720,000. At 60,000 customers a month, the marginal profit contribution and the marginal customer cost are both $4 per customer.

Figure 12.1 represents the same analysis graphically. The level of customer traffic that maximizes the department store's profit is that where the marginal profit contribution equals the marginal customer cost of $4 per customer.

The customers that the department store attracts would also shop at nearby specialty retailers selling fashion, lifestyle items, and food and beverages. However, there is no market through which specialty retailers pay the department store for the additional business. By definition, a positive externality conveys a benefit directly rather than through a market. Accordingly, the customers are an externality from the department store to the specialty retailers.

Consider a restaurant situated next to the department store. Table 12.2 presents the restaurant's revenues and costs at the various levels of the department store's customer traffic on a monthly basis. For instance, with 60,000 customers a month, the restaurant's sales revenue would be $1.392 million, while the variable cost would be $960,000, and so profit contribution and profit would be $432,000. The restaurant does not spend anything on advertising, so its profit contribution is the same as its profit.

Table 12.2 Customer traffic and externality

Customers ('000)	Revenue ($ '000)	Variable cost ($ '000)	Profit ($ '000)	Marginal profit ($)
10	272	160	112	11.20
20	528	320	208	9.60
30	768	480	288	8.00
40	992	640	352	6.40
50	1,200	800	400	4.80
60	1,392	960	432	3.20
70	1,568	1,120	448	1.60
80	1,728	1,280	448	0.00
90	1,872	1,440	432	-1.60
100	2,000	1,600	400	-3.20
110	2,112	1,760	352	-4.80

By the nature of an externality, the source of the externality considers only the benefits and costs to itself, while ignoring the benefits and costs to others. So, acting independently, the department store chooses to attract 60,000 customers a month. Referring to Figure 12.1, at that level of customer traffic, the restaurant's marginal profit is $3.20 per customer.

If the department store were to attract a 60,001st customer, that customer would raise the department store's profit contribution by a little less than $4, raise the department store's cost of advertising by $4, and raise the restaurant's profit by $3.20. So, the combination of the department store and restaurant would be better off by slightly less than $3.20.

Indeed, the department store could continue to raise the combined profit contribution of the department store and restaurant by increasing customer traffic up to the economically efficient level. Recall from Chapter 6 that, at the economically efficient level, the marginal benefit equals the marginal cost. In the present context, the department store's marginal benefit from customers is its marginal profit contribution, while the restaurant's marginal benefit from customers is its marginal profit contribution.

So, for economic efficiency in customer traffic, the number of customers should be such that the *combined* marginal benefit (department store's plus restaurant's marginal profit contribution) equals the marginal cost of attracting customers. Referring to Figure 12.1, the combined marginal benefit is the *vertical sum* of the department store's marginal profit contribution and the restaurant's marginal profit contribution. For instance, at 60,000 customers, the combined marginal benefit is $4+$3.20 = $7.20.

The economically efficient level of customer traffic is 69,000 customers. By increasing the number of customers from 60,000 to 69,000, the department store and restaurant can collectively gain the shaded area in additional profit contribution. So, if the department store could collect a fee from the restaurant for generating customer traffic, it would maximize total profit (from sales to customers and fee from restaurant) at 69,000 customers.

Another perspective is to suppose that the department store owns the restaurant. Then the department store would choose customer traffic to maximize the *combined* profit contribution of the store and restaurant. It would increase the number of customers up to the level that the combined marginal profit contribution equals the marginal cost of attracting customers, at 69,000 customers a month.

PROGRESS CHECK 12A

Suppose that the restaurant's marginal profit contribution is lower by $3.20 at all levels of customer traffic. Revise Figure 12.1 to show the economically efficient level of customer traffic.

Negative Externality

To explain the benchmark level of a negative externality, consider the example of a betting shop, located on Main Street next to the restaurant. The betting shop must decide how much to spend on advertising to attract gamblers.

Figure 12.2 represents the betting shop's marginal profit contribution and marginal cost of customers. The level of customer traffic that maximizes the betting

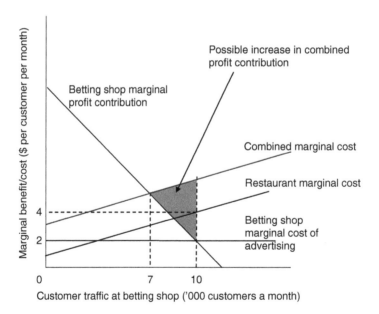

FIGURE 12.2 Negative externality.

Notes: The combined marginal cost is the vertical sum of the individual marginal costs. The economically efficient level of customers is 7,000, where the marginal benefit equals the combined marginal costs. If the betting shop considers only its own benefit and cost, it would attract 10,000 customers. By reducing to 7,000 customers, the betting shop and restaurant could gain the shaded area in additional profit.

shop's profit contribution is that where the marginal profit contribution equals the marginal customer cost of $2 per customer. That level is 10,000 customers a month.

However, the betting shop's customers discourage families with children from patronizing the next-door restaurant. So, the betting shop imposes a cost on the restaurant. Since it imposes the cost directly and not through a market, the cost is a negative externality.

Suppose that the greater the number of customers that the betting shop attracts, the higher is the restaurant's marginal cost, as measured by the restaurant's marginal loss of profit contribution. Figure 12.2 also shows the restaurant's marginal cost, as a function of the betting shop's customer traffic.

If the betting shop advertises to get 10,000 customers, the 10,000th customer imposes a marginal cost of $4 on the restaurant. If the betting shop were to reduce its customers by one, its profit contribution would be $2 lower, its advertising cost would be $2 lower, and the restaurant's cost would be $4 lower. So, the combination of the betting shop and restaurant would be better off by $4.

So, the reduction in customers would raise the combined profit contribution of the betting shop and restaurant. Indeed, the betting shop could increase the combined profit contribution by reducing customer traffic down to the economically efficient level. The economically efficient level is where the betting shop's marginal benefit (marginal profit contribution) equals the *combined* (betting shop's plus restaurant's) marginal cost of customers.

Referring to Figure 12.2, the combined marginal cost is the *vertical sum* of the betting shop's marginal cost of advertising and the restaurant's marginal cost (loss of profit contribution). For instance, at 10,000 customers a month, the vertical sum is $2 + $4 = $6.

The economically efficient level of customer traffic is 7,000 customers. By reducing the number of customers from 10,000 to 7,000, the betting shop and restaurant can collectively gain the shaded area in additional profit contribution. So if the betting shop could collect a fee from the restaurant for reducing customer traffic, it would maximize total profit (from sales to customers and fee from restaurant) at 7,000 customers.

Another perspective is to suppose that the betting shop owns the restaurant. Then the betting shop would choose customer traffic to maximize the *combined* profit contribution of the betting shop and restaurant. It would reduce the number of customers up to the level that the combined marginal profit contribution equals the marginal cost of attracting customers, at 7,000 customers a month.

PROGRESS CHECK 12B

Referring to Figure 12.2, suppose that the negative externality on the restaurant is stronger. How will this affect (a) the restaurant's marginal cost curve, and (b) the number of customers that maximizes the group profit contribution?

EXTERNALITIES IN TALENT: SILICON VALLEY

There is an exceptional concentration of information technology related businesses in the peninsula between the San Francisco Bay and the Pacific Ocean. The area, aptly nicknamed *Silicon Valley*, is home to high-technology leaders such as Apple, Hewlett-Packard, Intel, Google, and Facebook.

Stanford University and the Xerox Palo Alto Research Center (PARC) played key roles in the development of Silicon Valley. Basic and applied research at the two institutions has provided the foundation for many successful high-tech companies.

A local area network links separate personal computers over short distances. Robert Metcalfe and David Boggs invented the Ethernet local area network at Xerox PARC. In 1979, Metcalfe left Xerox PARC to found 3Com (the three "coms" being computer, communication, and compatibility), which commercialized the Ethernet technology.

Routers are devices that link computer networks that use different protocols. Sandy Lerner and Len Bosack started Cisco Systems while working at Stanford. In 1986, they left the university to run Cisco full-time. The company became the world's largest manufacturer of data-networking systems.

In 1996, two Stanford computer science graduate students, Sergey Brin and Lawrence Page, developed an algorithm for Internet search. Their research blossomed into Google, now a multi-billion-dollar company.

Sources: Douglas K. Smith and Robert C. Alexander, *Fumbling the Future*, New York: William Morrow, 1988, pp. 95–103; letter from Robert Metcalfe, July 16, 1996; letter from Cisco Systems, May 23, 1996; www.cisco.com and www.3com.com (accessed May 22, 1996), www.google.com (accessed August 9, 2011).

General Benchmark

We have separately discussed positive and negative externalities. Generally, in the presence of both positive and negative externalities, the affected parties maximize combined profit at the following benchmark: where the combined marginal benefits equal the combined marginal costs, which is the economically efficient level of the externality. An externality is **resolved** when the combined marginal benefits equal the combined marginal costs.

> **Externality resolved:**
> Combined marginal benefits equal combined marginal costs.

When the source of an externality considers only its own benefit and cost, it overlooks an opportunity for increasing profit. The source of a positive externality can raise profit by collecting a fee from the beneficiaries and increasing the level of externality. By contrast, the source of a negative externality can raise profit by collecting a fee from the sufferers and reducing the level of externality. There will be an opportunity for such a profit whenever the combined marginal benefits differ from the combined marginal cost.

The benchmark of economic efficiency applies whether or not the externalities are monetary. To take account of non-monetary externalities, just measure the benefits and costs in terms of money, and then apply the economic efficiency analysis.

ACADEMIC EXTERNALITIES: A FREE CAMPUS

In May 1995, the regents of the University of California met to choose the location for a new campus to become the tenth branch of the university. The regents considered two alternatives: a 2,000-acre site at Lake Yosemite offered free of charge by the Virginia Smith Trust and another site near the city of Fresno that had to be purchased. Swayed in part by the free land, the regents voted for Lake Yosemite.

The Virginia Smith Trust owned 7,000 acres of land by Lake Yosemite, used to graze cattle. The Trust projected that, with establishment of the new campus, it could earn $350 million from development of the remaining 5,000 acres of real estate. The positive externalities were sufficient to justify the "gift" to the University of California. UC Merced opened in 2005, and presently has over 6,000 students.

Source: "Lake Yosemite selected for proposed campus," *UC Focus* (Office of the President, University of California), Vol. 9, No. 5, June–July 1995, pp. 1 and 7.

3. Resolving Externalities

The benchmark for an externality is the economically efficient level, where the combined marginal benefits equal the combined marginal costs. Chapter 6 showed that, in a perfectly competitive market, the invisible hand ensures economic efficiency. By definition, however, externalities do not pass through markets. Hence, externalities will be resolved only through deliberate action.

Generally, externalities can be resolved in two ways – through common ownership of the source and recipient, or by agreement among the source and recipient. However, there are two obstacles to the resolution of externalities – the assignment of rights and possible free riding.

Common Ownership

In the example of the department store and restaurant, if the department store owned the restaurant, then the store would consider all the benefits and costs of additional customers. Hence, it would increase advertising to attract the economically efficient number of customers. Similarly, in the example of the betting shop and restaurant, if the betting shop owned the restaurant, then it would reduce advertising to attract the economically efficient number of customers.

These examples suggest one way to resolve an externality: combine the source and recipient of the externality under common ownership. The common owner would choose the economically efficient level of the externality, whether positive or negative.

Agreement

Besides common ownership, another way to resolve externalities is by agreement. The source and recipient of the externality could negotiate and agree on the level of the externality. For instance, the restaurant could offer to pay part of the department store's advertising cost. This would encourage the store to increase advertising. Similarly, the restaurant could pay the betting shop to reduce advertising.

An agreement to resolve an externality involves two steps. First, the affected parties must agree on how to resolve the externality. This step involves collecting information about the benefits and costs to the various parties, and then agreeing on the level of the externality.

The second step is to enforce compliance with the agreement. Enforcement includes monitoring the source of the externality and applying incentives to ensure that the source complies with the agreed level of the externality.

Assignment of Rights

One hurdle to resolution of externalities is unclear assignment of rights. In the example of the betting shop and restaurant, the externality might actually be resolved in two possible ways. The betting shop could reduce its advertising. Another way is for the restaurant to move away.

So does the betting shop have the right to impose an externality on the restaurant? Or does the restaurant have the right not to suffer an externality? If rights are not clearly assigned, then the two parties would have difficulty agreeing on common ownership or the level of the externality.

The assignment of rights is an acute issue in externalities from a common resource. Consider several oil producers drilling from the same oil field, multiple trawlers fishing the same stock, or various lumber producers cutting from the same forest. In these situations, without a clear assignment of property rights, the various competitors rush to grab production, ignoring the long-term impact on the resource.

Free Riding

The other hurdle is possible free riding. In the department store example, suppose that the department store customers also patronize nearby retailers that sell fashion, lifestyle items, and food and beverages. So, the department store provides positive externalities to all of these specialty retailers.

We have shown that the source and recipients of the externalities can resolve the externalities through common ownership or agreement. Now consider a florist that benefits from the department store's positive externalities. The florist might adopt a strategy of not paying the department store for advertising. The florist knows that the department store would still advertise, while other specialty retailers might still pay to increase the advertising. The department store and other specialty retailers cannot prevent their customers from patronizing the florist. So, the florist can benefit from the customers without paying anything.

In this strategy, the florist is taking a free ride on the advertising by the department store and fees paid by the other specialty retailers. Generally, a **free rider** pays less than its marginal benefit to resolution of the externality. At the extreme, the free rider pays nothing at all.

> **Free rider:** Contributes less than marginal benefit to resolution of externality.

Free riding arises whenever it is costly to exclude those who do not pay from benefiting from the externality. When it is easy to exclude those who do not pay, then all beneficiaries of the externality will pay for resolution, otherwise they would not benefit. Free riding is more serious when the externality affects many recipients. When an externality affects many recipients, the amount that any particular recipient must pay is relatively small. Hence, the other recipients may pay to resolve the externality even if some recipients take a free ride.

PROGRESS CHECK 12C

In the example of the betting shop and restaurant, what is the possible hurdle to resolving the externality?

VIVOCITY: RESOLVING EXTERNALITIES

With over 1 million square feet of net leasable area, VivoCity is Singapore's largest mall, attracting 40 million visitors a year. VivoCity's two largest retail tenants are VivoMart, a combination of a hypermarket, upscale supermarket, and drug store, and Tangs Department Store, which collectively occupy 22.4% of the mall.

VivoMart and Tangs, together with a cineplex and several medium-sized stores, what VivoCity management calls "mini anchors," pull customers into the mall. The customer traffic benefits smaller specialty stores, which occupy 33% of the mall.

In 2010, on a per square foot basis, the major and mini anchors achieved average sales of S$678 a year while paying rent of S$78 a year. By contrast, the specialty retailers achieved average sales of S$950 a year and paid an average rent of S$196 a year. So, the specialty retailers paid higher rent in both dollar terms and as a proportion of sales.

VivoCity resolves the externality between anchor tenants and other retailers by charging relatively lower rents to anchors and higher rents to other retailers. This is an established practice in the management of shopping malls. Through common management, retailers in a shopping mall can resolve externalities more effectively than retailers distributed on a public street.

Source: Mapletree Commercial Trust, Prospectus, April 18, 2011.

MICKEY MOUSE EXTERNALITIES

The Walt Disney Company owns and manages Disneyland in Anaheim, California. This theme park is surrounded by hundreds of businesses, including motels, restaurants, souvenir stores, and transportation services. Disneyland visitors are the major source of income for these neighboring businesses.

In the late 1980s, Disney decided to embark on a large program of investments to upgrade Disneyland. Before commencing construction, the company secretly bought much of the property around the theme park, including the Disneyland Hotel for $200 million. By purchasing the surrounding property, Disney ensured that it would capture the benefits from new attractions. Consequently, the company had a greater incentive to make the economically efficient level of investment in new attractions at the theme park.

Disney applied the same principle when developing its theme park on Lantau Island, Hong Kong. As a condition of the investment, the Hong Kong government awarded Disney a 20-year option to purchase an adjoining site. The government further agreed to restrict economic activity in the vicinity. It limited the height of nearby buildings, banned aircraft from flying over the park, and excluded ships from the seafront.

Hong Kong Tourism Commissioner Mike Rowse explained: "It is an essential element of a Disney theme park that people outside the park not be able to see in, and those inside not be able to see the 'real world' outside."

Sources: Gary Wilson, Chief Financial Officer, Disney Company, speech at the Anderson School, UCLA, March 15, 1989; "Disney given controls over area around park," *South China Morning Post*, November 20, 1999.

4. Network Effects and Externalities

Network effect: A benefit or cost that increases with the size of the network.

A **network effect** is a benefit or cost that increases with the size of the network. The adjective *network* emphasizes that the benefit or cost is generated by the entire network of users. An instant messaging service nicely illustrates a network effect. The benefit that one user derives from an instant messaging service increases with the number of other users.

The marginal benefit and demand from an item that exhibits network effects increases with the number of other users. For instance, when one more person subscribes to an instant messaging service, the marginal benefit and demand curves of all other users will shift up.

Related to the concept of a network effect is the *network externality*. A **network externality** is a benefit or cost directly conveyed to others that increases with the size of the network. Accordingly, a network externality is a network effect that is conveyed *directly*, and not through a market. As with externalities in general, the benchmark for a network externality is economic efficiency: the combined marginal benefits equal the combined marginal costs.

> **Network externality:**
> A benefit or cost directly conveyed to others that increases with the size of the network.

In markets with network effects, the character of demand and competition differs from that in conventional markets. We discuss each of these differences below.

Critical Mass

In a market with network effects, the demand may be zero unless the number of users exceeds critical mass. The **critical mass** is the number of users at which the demand becomes positive. Consider, for instance, instant messaging service. There is no demand if the number of users falls below some level. Who would want instant messaging if there is no one to communicate with?

> **Critical mass:** The number of users at which demand becomes positive.

Suppose that demand for instant messaging service is zero if there are fewer than 10,000 users. Then the critical mass is 10,000 users. The demand will be positive only if the price or other factors are sufficient to attract 10,000 users.

Technical standards play a key role in markets with network effects. Consider two incompatible instant messaging services. If each can attract at most 5,000 users, then neither will achieve critical mass. However, if both services conform to a common technical standard and interconnect, then they can collectively achieve the critical mass of 10,000.

The demand for some items depends on the presence of complementary hardware. For instance, the demand for web-based social media depends on consumer access to computers and smart phones. Similarly, the demand for Android apps depends on the number of Android smart phones and tablets. In this context, the **installed base** is the stock of the complementary hardware in service.

> **Installed base:**
> The quantity of complementary hardware in service.

Expectations

In a market with network effects, user expectations are important. Consider a situation where users simultaneously decide whether to subscribe to a new instant messaging service. There are two possible equilibria. In the good equilibrium, every potential user expects the others to subscribe, and accordingly subscribes. Then demand exceeds critical mass and the service succeeds as expected. By contrast, in the bad equilibrium, potential subscribers are pessimistic. Each one expects less than the critical mass to subscribe, and so does not subscribe. Then demand fails to reach critical mass and the service flops as expected.

Thus user expectations are very important. In equilibrium, expectations – whether pessimistic or optimistic – can be self-fulfilling. How to influence the expectations of potential users? One way is through commitments to ensure that demand will exceed critical mass. For instance, sellers of items with network effects may give away large quantities in order to establish a sufficient installed base.

Another way of influencing expectations is hype. For instance, a grand launch attended by famous athletes and movie stars may generate the self-fulfilling prophecy that demand for the item will attain critical mass.

Tipping

The demand in markets with network effects may be extremely sensitive to small differences among competitors. Suppose there are several competing products,

Tipping: The tendency for demand to shift toward a product with a small initial lead.

each of whose demand is close to critical mass. Then a small increase in the user base of one product can *tip* the market demand toward that product. **Tipping** is the tendency for demand to shift toward a product that has gained a small initial lead.

To illustrate tipping, consider two providers competing to introduce new instant messaging services. Each can guarantee 9,000 users. Then the market would tip toward the service which can get the additional 1,000 users and cross the threshold for critical mass. The other service would fail.

Accordingly, a market with network effects may "tip" toward one product. By contrast, in a conventional market, several competitors of similar size may continue profitably for a long time. Even if one seller gains an advantage in pricing or product quality, the entire market demand will not tip in its favor.

Price Elasticity

Chapter 3 introduced the concept of (own) price elasticity of demand, which is the percentage by which the quantity demanded changes if the price of the item rises by 1%. The presence of network effects influences the price elasticity in different ways, depending on whether the demand has reached critical mass.

For a product with network effects in demand, when the demand is below critical mass, the demand will be zero, and hence extremely price inelastic. Price reductions, however large, will not increase the demand at all.

The demand will be sensitive to price only when it exceeds critical mass. Then the network effect causes the market demand to be relatively more price elastic. Consider, for instance, a price increase. This would reduce the demand. The reduction would feed back through the network effect to further reduce the demand. The network effect tends to amplify the effect of a price increase on demand. Similarly, the network effect would amplify the effect of a price reduction.

Around the critical mass, the demand would be very price elastic. A slight price cut would pull demand above critical mass and further increase demand through the network effect. By contrast, a slight price increase would push demand below critical mass and then demand would collapse to zero.

PROGRESS CHECK 12D

How do conventional markets differ from markets with network effects?

HARNESSING NETWORK EXTERNALITIES: GOOGLE

Google harnesses network externalities in a very subtle way. Whenever a user submits a search to Google, the service uses its proprietary page-rank algorithm to display links to webpages in order of predicted relevance. Google tracks the links that people click on and updates its algorithm accordingly. Every search helps to refine Google's algorithm, and so, the more people search on Google, the better the quality of its service.

5. Public Goods

Open-air fireworks nicely illustrate the concept of a public good. An item is a public good if one person's increase in consumption does not reduce the quantity available to others. Equivalently, a public good provides *non-rival* consumption. Consumption is **non-rival** if one person's increase in consumption does not reduce the quantity available to others. If Mary watches a show of fireworks, she does not reduce the quantity that others can watch. Hence, fireworks provide non-rival consumption and are a public good.

> **Non-rival consumption:** One person's increase in consumption does not reduce the quantity available to others.

Another way of appreciating non-rival consumption is through the concept of economies of scale. Given that open-air fireworks are being provided to one viewer, the marginal cost of providing the same display to additional viewers is zero. There is an extreme economy of scale in providing a public good *with respect to the number of consumers*. The cost of provision is fixed with respect to the number of consumers and the marginal cost of serving an additional consumer is zero.

The economy of scale with respect to the number of consumers differs from an economy of scale with respect to the scale of provision. Increasing the length of a fireworks show does involve more costs and need not exhibit economies of scale.

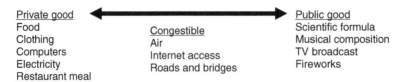

FIGURE 12.3 Rivalness.

Given the extreme economy of scale (with respect to the number of consumers), every additional customer brings in pure profit contribution. The business implication is to sell the public good to more customers (not quite to maximize the number of customers, but to maximize the revenue).

For instance, the content of movie is a public good. Thus movie producers increase their profit by selling the content through multiple formats – theaters, DVDs, cable TV, and free-to-air TV.

Rivalness

Public goods lie at one end of a spectrum of rivalness, with *private goods* at the other extreme (Figure 12.3). An item is a private good if one person's increase in consumption reduces the total available to others by the same quantity. Equivalently, a private good provides **rival consumption**, which means that one person's increase in consumption reduces the quantity available to others by the same amount.

> **Rival consumption:** One person's increase in consumption reduces the quantity available to others by the same amount.

Scientific formulas, musical compositions, TV broadcasts, and fireworks provide non-rival consumption. If one more person uses them, they do not reduce the quantity available for others.

By contrast, clothing and restaurant meals are private goods. If you wear a new polo shirt, no one else can wear it at the same time. If you eat an eight-ounce steak, then there will be eight ounces less for others.

> **Congestible consumption:** One person's increase in consumption partially reduces the total available to others.

Some items are neither public nor private, but provide **congestible consumption**. This means that one person's increase in consumption partially reduces the total quantity available to others. Congestible items are public goods when consumption is low but are private goods when consumption is high.

The Internet is congestible. At off-peak times, one person's increase in usage will not reduce the quality or speed of service to others. At peak times, however, the more people use the Internet, especially if they are downloading large files such as movies, the slower the service will be for others. The air around us is also congestible. The quality of the air is fine until the discharge of pollutants by drivers and factories is too high, whereupon the quality degrades.

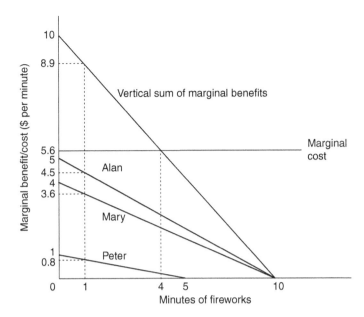

FIGURE 12.4 Economically efficient provision of public good.

Notes: At the economically efficient quantity of public good, the sum of the individual marginal benefits equals the marginal cost. Every individual marginal benefit curve lies below the marginal cost of $5.60; hence, no individual person would be willing to buy even one minute of fireworks. If each individual tries to get a free ride, it might not be possible to provide even one minute of fireworks on a commercial basis.

Benchmark: Economic Efficiency

We showed earlier that the economically efficient level of an externality is where the combined marginal benefits equal the combined marginal costs, and at that level there are no further opportunities to profit from adjusting the externality. Let us now show the same for a public good. Suppose that there are three viewers of open-air fireworks – Alan, Mary, and Peter – with marginal benefits as shown in Figure 12.4. The graph also shows the marginal cost of open-air fireworks, a constant $5.60 per minute.

Consider the provision of one minute of fireworks. Since fireworks are a public good, there will be one minute for each of the three viewers. Accordingly, each would be willing to pay their marginal benefit for that minute. By Figure 12.4, the sum of the marginal benefits to the three viewers is $0.80 + $3.60 + $4.50 = $8.90. The cost of one minute is $5.60, hence there is an opportunity to make a profit by providing one minute of fireworks. This same argument applies for additional quantities up to four minutes.

At four minutes of fireworks, the sum of the individual marginal benefits equals the marginal cost. Can someone make money by increasing provision to five minutes? By Figure 12.4, the fifth minute provides an additional benefit to Alan and Mary only. The sum of their marginal benefits is $2.00 + $2.50 = $4.50.

Since the cost of each minute is $5.60, providing the fifth minute would result in a loss.

So the opportunities for profit are exhausted at the point where the combined marginal benefits equal the marginal cost, which is the economically efficient quantity of the public good. Accordingly, at the economically efficient quantity, there are no further opportunities to profit from adjusting the provision of the public good.

Referring to Figure 12.4, notice that each of the individual marginal benefit curves lies below the marginal cost of $5.60. Hence, no individual person would be willing to buy even one minute of fireworks. The combined marginal benefit curve, however, lies above the marginal cost curve at quantities of between zero and four minutes.

Since a public good provides non-rival consumption, the three persons' willingness to pay is given by the combined marginal benefit, which is the vertical sum of the individual marginal benefit curves. While no single person would buy even one minute of fireworks, they collectively would be willing to pay for four minutes.

PROGRESS CHECK 12E

In Figure 12.4, include another marginal benefit curve and show the impact on the economically efficient quantity of fireworks.

VIVOCITY: ADVERTISING AND PROMOTION

With over 1 million square feet of net leasable area, VivoCity is Singapore's largest mall, attracting 40 million visitors a year. About 1% of the gross rental that VivoCity collects from tenants comprises service charges and contributions to advertising and promotion.

Advertising and promotion by the mall attract more customers to the mall. The additional customers could visit any of the retailers in the mall. Hence, the benefit of the advertising and promotion is non-rival among all the retailers. So, VivoCity finances the advertising and promotion from a charge to all retail tenants.

Source: Mapletree Commercial Trust, Prospectus, April 18, 2011.

6. Excludability

Having discussed the nature of public goods and their economically efficient quantity, we are now ready to discuss how public goods can actually be provided.

There is a fundamental condition for commercial provision of any product that is easy to overlook. That condition is that, in selling a product, the seller must be able to exclude those who do not pay. The condition is crucial in the commercial provision of public goods.

Consumption is **excludable** if the provider can exclude particular consumers. Typically, commercial provision of an item depends on excludability.

> **Excludable consumption:** The provider can exclude particular consumers.

When consumption of an item is not excludable, commercial provision will be difficult. To illustrate, let us suppose that Neptune Entertainment wants to provide one minute of open-air fireworks to Alan, Mary, and Peter. Referring to Figure 12.4, Neptune knows that, at that quantity, the individual marginal benefits of Alan, Mary, and Peter are $4.50, $3.60, and $0.80, respectively. If Neptune charges each person a price equal to their marginal benefit, then Neptune will collect $8.90 from these three people. Neptune's cost of providing one minute of fireworks is $5.60; hence, it will realize a profit of $3.30.

Peter, however, might reason that if he refuses to pay, while Alan and Mary do pay, then Neptune would collect $4.50 + $3.60 = $8.10, which would be enough to cover the cost of $5.60. Then Neptune would provide the one minute of fireworks and Peter would enjoy a free show. Alan and Mary, however, might also think in similar ways. If everyone tries to get a free show, Neptune will incur a loss. Hence, in the extreme, the free-rider problem prevents the provision of even one minute of fireworks on a commercial basis.

The basic problem is that, whenever consumption of some item is non-excludable, individual consumers will have an incentive to free-ride. Free riding will cut into the seller's revenues and thus reduce the seller's profit and hamper commercial provision of the item.

To understand the scope for commercial provision of public goods, we must first appreciate the distinction between content and delivery, and then the two factors that affect excludability, law and technology.

Content and Delivery

Television programming can be broadcast over the air or by cable. Regardless of the method of delivery, the content of broadcast TV is non-rival. If Nancy switches on her TV to watch the evening news, she does not affect the quantity of news available to other people. This is true whether the signal comes over the air or by cable.

The method of delivery, however, may be a public or private good. Delivery by free-to-air transmission is a public good. The same signal can serve any number of TV sets within the range of transmission. Delivery by cable, however, is a private good. Each cable serves only one TV set.

> A public good can be delivered in the form of a private good.

Scientific knowledge also illustrates the distinction between content and delivery. The formula for the drug atorvastatin is a public good. If one more manufacturer uses the formula, it does not reduce the quantity available to other manufacturers. However, the drug is delivered in the form of manufactured tablets. The tablet is a private good: if one person consumes a tablet, that tablet is unavailable to others.

Since private goods are excludable, a key way to provide public goods on a commercial basis is to deliver them in the form of private goods.

Law

The use of scientific formulas, musical compositions, and computer algorithms is non-rival. However, through the legal concept of *intellectual property*, the law has made their use legally excludable. The objective of intellectual property rights is to encourage innovation. The policy intent is that the profits from exclusive rights would encourage innovators to invest more in creative activities.

> **Patent:** A legal exclusive right to a product or process.

> **Copyright:** A legal exclusive right to artistic, literary, or musical expression.

Two particular forms of intellectual property rights are *patents* and *copyright*. A **patent** is a legal exclusive right to a product or process. It is illegal to manufacture a product or use a process covered by a patent without the permission of the patent owner. A **copyright** is a legal exclusive right to an artistic, literary, or musical expression. It is illegal to reproduce copyrighted material without the permission of the copyright owner.

Technology

In addition to the law, the other factor affecting excludability is technology. The content of TV programming is a public good. But the medium of delivery can be excludable. Free-to-air TV is not excludable. The station cannot prevent particular individuals from watching a broadcast. However, by using scrambling technology, the broadcast can be made excludable. Scrambling technology transforms the medium of delivery from being non-excludable to excludable.

Software provides another example. The algorithms and code underlying computer software are public goods. Users might copy software from one another. However, if the publisher includes in the software an activation code that it provides only to licensed users, then it can exclude those who do not pay.

PROGRESS CHECK 12F

Distinguish the content and delivery of a public good. How does this matter for commercial provision of a public good?

UNCLE SAM – PATENT INFRINGER?

"Cheap imitations are killing our business, and destroying thousands of good jobs." Who is complaining? Microsoft? Universal Studios? Bertelsmann? None of the above. It is Rosoboronexport, the Russian arms exporter.

During World War II, while being treated in hospital, Mikhail Timofeevich Kalashnikov conceived of a new assault rifle. In 1942, he was discharged from hospital and developed his concept. In 1949, following rigorous competitive trials, the Soviet Army adopted the new rifle as the AK-47. Kalashnikov was awarded the Stalin Prize First Class and Russian arms manufacturer Izhmash began production.

Fast forward 50 years. The US government is a leading buyer of AK-47s for supply to Afghanistan and Iraq. But not from Izhmash, which owns the relevant patents. Rather, the United States buys AK-47s from unlicensed manufacturers in Bulgaria, Hungary, and Romania. Somewhat helplessly, Rosoboronexport official Igor Sevastyanov declared: "We would like to inform everybody in the world that many countries, including the United States, have unfortunately violated recognized norms."

Source: "Russians take aim at AK-47 imitators," *International Herald Tribune*, July 26, 2004.

FREE-TO-AIR TV: COMMERCIAL PROVISION WITHOUT EXCLUSION?

Typically, commercial provision of a public good depends on excludability. Free-to-air TV is non-excludable. In America, however, four major networks provide free-to-air TV on a commercial basis. Far from limping along, the business has flourished. What is the networks' secret?

The primary source of revenues of free-to-air TV networks is advertising. While viewers do not directly pay for TV, they do pay indirectly. They pay by increasing their purchases of the advertised products and services. In the year 2013, 20th Century Fox's TV businesses earned operating income of $855 million on revenues of $4.86 billion.

Source: 20th Century Fox, Annual Report 2013.

KEY TAKEAWAYS

- Externalities are benefits or costs directly conveyed to others.
- The economically efficient level of an externality is where the combined marginal benefits equal the combined marginal costs.

- There is an opportunity to make a profit by resolving an externality up to the economically efficient level.
- Resolve an externality through merger or agreement.
- The two hurdles to resolution of an externality are unclear assignment of rights and possible free riding.
- Network effects are benefits or costs that increase with size of network.
- In the presence of network effects, manage user expectations to achieve critical mass.
- A public good provides non-rival consumption: One person's increase in consumption does not reduce the quantity available to others.
- Provide public goods on a commercial basis by excluding non-payers through law or technology.
- Increase profit by selling the public good to more consumers.

REVIEW QUESTIONS

1. What is the difference between a negative and a positive externality?
2. Luna and Neptune have both launched a new consumer electronic device. Luna's advertising is raising Neptune's demand. What is the economically efficient level of Luna's advertising?
3. Explain the relation between the combined marginal benefit curve from additional customers for all retailers in a mall and the retailers' individual marginal benefit curves.
4. When the sum of the marginal costs from a negative externality exceeds the marginal benefit to the source, what is the profit opportunity? Explain.
5. Explain how the following action will help to resolve the externalities generated by a new subway line: the subway system buys the property around the new stations.
6. What is the possible free-rider problem in the following context? Saturn City lies two miles off a busy highway. The city's major businesses have proposed to build an exit from the highway to draw traffic into the city.
7. Explain the possible network effects in the demand for spreadsheet software.
8. Give an example of a network externality, and in that context explain the concepts of critical mass and tipping.
9. Does the presence of network effects cause demand to be more or less price elastic?
10. Where are technical standards relatively more important: in markets with network effects or those without? Explain your answer.
11. Give an example of a public good. Explain how the use of the good is non-rival.
12. Which of the following are public goods? (a) Dental treatment at a public hospital. (b) Welfare payments to unemployed people. (c) National defense.
13. For a public good, why is the combined marginal benefit equal to the sum of the individual marginal benefits?
14. In what way does excludability depend on law and technology?
15. Why does it make sense to sell a public good to more consumers?

DISCUSSION QUESTIONS

1. VivoCity is Singapore's largest mall, attracting 40 million visitors a year. Its two largest retail tenants, occupying 22.4% of the mall, are VivoMart, a combination of a hypermarket, upscale supermarket, and drug store, and Tangs Department Store. In 2010, on a per square foot basis, VivoCity's major and mini anchors achieved average sales of S$678 a year while paying rent of S$78 a year. Specialty retailers achieved average sales of S$950 a year and paid an average rent of S$196 a year.
    (a) With a relevant diagram, illustrate a department store's marginal benefit from and marginal cost of attracting customers. Show the externality on a specialty retailer and identify the economically efficient number of customers.
    (b) Compare the ratio of rent to sales for major and mini anchors and for specialty retailers.
    (c) Explain why VivoCity charges lower rents to anchors than to specialty retailers.
    (d) Are externalities from a department store to nearby retailers more likely to be resolved for a store on a public street or in a shopping mall? Explain your answer.
2. One of the world's most abundant anchovy fisheries lies off the Pacific coast of Peru. Historically, Peruvian fisheries operated on an "Olympic system." The Managing Director of the fish producer Pacific Andes, Ng Joo Siang, remarked: "Nobody has time to preserve the fish because they want to catch as quickly as possible." Properly caught and processed for human consumption, anchovies could sell for 40–50 US cents per kilogram. The alternative is animal feed worth 10 cents per kilogram. (Source: "Fishery player Pacific Andes bets on regulatory changes, positions vessels in Peru," *The Edge Singapore*, August 18, 2008, p. 18.)
    (a) Explain the externalities under the "Olympic system." Compare production relative to the economically efficient level.
    (b) In 2008, the government of Peru changed the system and awarded each fish producer an individual quota of fish to catch. What would be the impact on economic efficiency?
    (c) The quotas were transferable. How would this help to achieve economic efficiency?
3. Choice International, a business-format franchisor of hotels, launched Cambria Suites to serve an upscale market segment. Choice International is concerned that franchisees maintain a consistent standard. It has contracted with a quality assurance specialist, LRA Worldwide, to conduct anonymous inspections of each Cambria Suites hotel twice yearly.
    (a) Using a relevant graph with 'effort' on the horizontal axis, illustrate a franchisee's marginal benefit and marginal cost of effort and explain its choice of effort.
    (b) How does the franchisee's effort benefit other franchisees? Explain in terms of an externality. On your graph for (a), identify the economically efficient effort.

(c) Why would one Cambria Suites franchisee want Choice International to inspect other franchisees?

    (d) Consider the deviation between the franchisee's choice of effort and the economically efficient effort. Would this be smaller or larger in a chain of hotels that are all in a single city than in an international chain?

4. BAA Airports Limited operates London's Heathrow Airport. Between 2008 and 2009, with the Great Recession, Heathrow passenger traffic fell by 1.5%. However, the proportion of long-haul traffic increased from 52.2% to 52.9% and the proportion of transfer passengers increased from 35.9% to 37.4%. (Source: BAA Airports Limited, Results for the year ended 31 December 2009.)

    (a) Explain how passenger traffic affects the demand for retail services such as restaurants and car rental at the airport.

    (b) Using relevant demand curves, compare airport expenditures on promoting passenger traffic at: (i) airports with retail facilities; and (ii) airports without retail facilities. Which airports would spend more on promoting passenger traffic? Assume that the airport maximizes the net benefit to all parts of the airport (including the retailers, if any).

    (c) BAA's financial report remarked that "strong in-terminal shopping performance reflected a higher proportion of intraterminal transfer passengers, providing longer departure lounge dwell times for such passengers." Would you advise BAA to extend the transfer times between flights, so that passengers must spend more time at the terminal?

5. In 2007, the computer manufacturer Dell spent $943 million on advertising. Many of Dell's advertisements feature "Intel inside." These advertisements boost the demand for other computer manufacturers using Intel microprocessors. Between 2007 and 2008, Dell's advertising expenditure fell from $943 to $811 million. The major reason was an increase in receipts for cooperative advertising. (Source: Dell Inc., Form 10K, 2010.)

    (a) With a relevant diagram, illustrate Dell's marginal benefit from and marginal cost of advertising. Show the externality on other computer manufacturers and identify the economically efficient level of advertising.

    (b) Explain why Intel makes cooperative advertising payments to Dell.

    (c) AMD competes with Intel to supply microprocessors to computer manufacturers. How should Intel take account of this competition in deciding payments for cooperative advertising?

6. With the growth of international trade and travel, more people are learning English. Major European companies have adopted English as a common language. English is also the standard language for communication among aircraft pilots and air-traffic controllers. Linguists estimate that, of 7,000 languages in use worldwide, nearly half will disappear within this century.

    (a) Compare the benefit of speaking a common language among: (i) truckers; (ii) pilots.

   (b) Does the growth of English generate a positive or negative externality for: (i) people who are already fluent in English; (ii) people who do not speak English?

   (c) Can the externalities in (b) be described as network externalities? Explain your answer.

   (d) How do critical mass and expectations apply to the survival of a language?

7. Microsoft's Excel dominates the market for spreadsheet software. Presently, its main competitor is Calc, a product of OpenOffice. OpenOffice emphasizes that Calc "looks and feels familiar and is instantly usable by anyone who has used a competitive product." (Source: OpenOffice.org.)

   (a) Explain the network effects in the demand for spreadsheet software.

   (b) Use the concept of critical mass and tipping to explain the demise of Lotus 1-2-3.

   (c) Why does OpenOffice stress that Calc is so similar to Excel?

   (d) Should Microsoft cooperate with OpenOffice in the further development of Calc?

8. Football, cricket, and other sports entertain thousands through live attendance and millions through TV. TV subscribers pay substantial fees to watch live sports. Others watch free but "pay" by consuming advertisements.

   (a) Alan, Mary, and Peter are sports fans. Using a suitable figure with quantity of sports (in hours per month) on the horizontal axis, explain the economically efficient production of sports for the three fans.

   (b) Use the figure to identify the marginal benefits of the three fans at the economically efficient level of production.

   (c) If a sports league were to broadcast only through subscription channels that charge a uniform price, can it achieve the efficient level of production?

   (d) What pricing policy are sports leagues applying? Does it help to achieve economic efficiency?

   (e) Some websites broadcast live sport without license from the sports league. How does this affect economically efficient production of sports?

9. Mikhail Kalashnikov conceived the AK-47 assault rifle while recuperating from wounds during World War II. Within 50 years, over 100 million AK-47s had been produced. Russian arms manufacturer Izhmash owns patents to the AK-47. However, the US government buys AK-47s from unlicensed manufacturers in Bulgaria, Hungary, and Romania for supply to its allies in Afghanistan and Iraq. (Sources: "Russians take aim at AK-47 imitators," *International Herald Tribune*, July 26, 2004; "AK-47's inventor peacefully retired," *Guardian*, October 26, 2003.)

   (a) Use the AK-47 to explain how engineering design is a public good.

   (b) Patents are only effective within the country in which they are granted. Explain how manufacturers in Bulgaria, Hungary, and Romania can free-ride on Kalashnikov's design.

(c) Maxim Piadiyshev, editor of *Arms Export Review*, explained the success of the rifle: "Compared to other automatic rifles at the time . . . it was very simple in production, use and maintenance, with eight moving parts." From Izhmash's viewpoint, does it help or hurt that the AK-47's design is simple yet effective?

You are the consultant!

Identify any externalities or network effects in your organization's activities. How should your organization take advantage of the profit opportunities?

Note

1   This discussion is based, in part, on Mapletree Commercial Trust, Prospectus, April 18, 2011.

Asymmetric Information

1. Introduction

In 2005, Countrywide Financial Corporation, the largest US mortgage lender, originated $490 billion of residential mortgages. Countrywide bundled the mortgages into pools and sold them completely or in part through mortgage-backed securities. Mortgage sales contributed $451.6 million, or 10.9% of the company's overall pre-tax earnings.[1]

Historically, Countrywide mostly lent through "prime conforming" mortgages, a standard set by the US federal government sponsored mortgage corporations, Fannie Mae and Freddie Mac. From 2004, faced with declining demand, Countrywide increased lending through prime non-conforming mortgages, subprime mortgages, and home equity loans from 40.2% to 64.1% of all mortgages.

Countrywide masked substantial risks in classifying loans. Banking regulators recommended that only loans to borrowers with a FICO (a credit score based on a system created by the Fair Isaac Company) score exceeding 620 be classified as "prime." However, Countrywide set no minimum FICO score for prime loans. Countrywide's "prime non-conforming" category included "Alt-A" mortgage loans with reduced or no documentation, no proof of income, or with loan to value ratios of 95% or more.

Other high-risk mortgages that Countrywide originated included 80/20 subprime loans and pay-option adjustable rate mortgages (ARMs). The 80/20 loan combined a first trust deed mortgage for 80% of the value of the home, and a second trust deed mortgage for the remaining 20% to provide a 100% loan. Pay-option ARMs did not require verification of the borrower's income.

Angelo Mozilo, Chairman and CEO of Countrywide, worried about the pay-option ARMs. In an email dated September 26, 2006, he directed the President and Chief Operating Officer, David Sambol, and the Chief Financial Officer, Eric Sieracki, to "sell all newly originated pay options and begin rolling off the bank balance sheet."

HSBC had purchased pools of 80/20 mortgages from Countrywide subject to the right to require Countrywide to buy back mortgages that did not meet specific conditions. In early 2006, HSBC exercised its right to require Countrywide to buy back the specific mortgages.

Countrywide's business and the market for mortgages present several questions. Why are mortgage borrowers subject to FICO scoring? Why did HSBC condition its purchase on the buyback right? Why did Mozilo ask senior management to sell the pay-option ARMs?

The relationship between borrowers and Countrywide, and that between Countrywide and investors such as HSBC, illustrate *asymmetric information*. In a situation of **asymmetric information**, one party has better information than another. Borrowers had better information about their income, assets, and willingness to repay (or default) than Countrywide.

> **Asymmetric information:** One party has better information than another.

In turn, Countrywide had better information about its mortgages than HSBC and other buyers of its mortgages and mortgage-backed securities. Mozilo's direction to sell all pay-option ARMs perfectly illustrates this asymmetry of information. Being particularly worried about the creditworthiness of the pay-option ARM borrowers, he decided to sell the mortgages to other investors.

Managers of financial institutions and investors are aware of the possible risks due to asymmetric information. Under such circumstances, they may refuse to engage in transactions and relationships which would increase value added unless the information asymmetry is resolved.

This chapter introduces four ways to resolve information asymmetry – appraisal, screening, signaling, and contingent contracts. FICO scores illustrate the technique of appraisal: originators of mortgages and buyers of mortgages use the scoring system to appraise the creditworthiness of borrowers. Through FICO scores, lenders try to gain more information about borrowers.

Less-informed parties use screening to discern the information of the better-informed parties. By limiting loans to borrowers who agree to credit checks (as Countrywide did not), lenders screen borrowers for their creditworthiness. In contrast, better-informed parties use signaling to communicate their information to less-informed parties. A contingent contract specifies actions under particular conditions. HSBC's right to require Countrywide to buy back specific mortgages illustrates a contingent contract.

The concept of information asymmetry and techniques to resolve asymmetries apply very broadly beyond finance, to commercial, non-commercial, and personal settings. Managers can use these methods to resolve information asymmetry and thus realize transactions and relationships to increase value added and profit.

2. Imperfect Information

Before analyzing situations of asymmetric information, we should understand the concept of *imperfect information*. To have **imperfect information** about something means not having certain knowledge about it. Most people have imperfect information about future events such as next Monday's Standard & Poor's 500 Index, the severity of the coming winter, and next

> **Imperfect information:** The absence of certain knowledge.

year's growth in employment. It is also possible to have imperfect information about things in the present or past. For instance, do you know precisely the height of K2 or the distance between Sydney and Tokyo?

Imperfect and Asymmetric Information

A single person can have imperfect information. By contrast, asymmetric information involves two or more parties, one of whom has better information than the other or others. Asymmetric information will always be associated with imperfect information, because the party with poorer information definitely will have imperfect information. For instance, if the seller knows the quality of a wine, but a potential buyer does not, then the buyer has imperfect information. The wine could be good or lousy, but the buyer does not know which for sure.

Although the concepts of asymmetric and imperfect information are related, it is important to appreciate the distinction. The reason is that a market can be perfectly competitive even when buyers and sellers have imperfect information, so long as their information is symmetric. Under perfect competition, the forces of demand and supply channel resources into economically efficient uses; hence, no further profitable transactions are possible.

For instance, the current demand for heating oil depends on expectations about temperatures in the coming winter. Buyers and sellers have equal access to meteorological forecasts. Based on these forecasts, each buyer determines its demand for heating oil. In a market equilibrium, the quantity demanded equals the quantity supplied and the marginal benefit equals the marginal cost. Hence, any further sales would be unprofitable.

By contrast, a market where information is asymmetric cannot be perfectly competitive. This means that, if buyers and sellers can resolve the information asymmetries, they can increase their benefits by more than their costs, and so add value.

Risk

When information is imperfect, there is risk. To understand the meaning of *risk*, let us consider the following example. Alice knows that, with probability 1.5%, someone will steal her $20,000 car within the next 12 months. If that were to happen, Alice would lose $20,000. If Alice's car is not stolen, however, Alice will lose nothing. The probability that her car will not be stolen is $100 - 1.5 = 98.5\%$.

Alice has imperfect information about her future losses, because she does not know for sure whether her car will be stolen. Alice bears a risk: either she will lose $20,000 with probability 1.5% or she will lose nothing with probability 98.5%. **Risk** is uncertainty about benefits or costs and arises whenever there is imperfect information about something that affects benefits or costs.

> **Risk:** Uncertainty about benefits or costs.

If Alice knew for sure that her car would not be stolen within the next 12 months, then she would not bear any risk. Similarly, if she knew for sure that her car would be stolen, she would also not bear any risk. It is because her information is imperfect that she faces risk.

To explain the distinction between risk and imperfect information, consider Bob, who is unrelated to Alice. Bob also has imperfect information about whether Alice's car will be stolen. But the fate of Alice's car does not affect Bob's benefits or costs. Hence, Bob does not bear any risk with regard to Alice's car.

Risk Aversion

> **Risk averse:** A person prefers a certain amount to risky amounts with the same expected value.

> **Risk neutral:** A person is indifferent between a certain amount and risky amounts with the same expected value.

How a person responds to situations involving risk depends on the extent to which he or she is *risk averse*. A person is **risk averse** if she or he prefers a certain amount to risky amounts with the same expected value. A person is **risk neutral** if she or he is indifferent between a certain amount and risky amounts with the same expected value.

Given Alice's possible losses and the probabilities, her expected loss is $(\$20,000 \times 0.015) + (\$0 \times 0.985) = \$300$. If Alice is risk averse, she will prefer to lose $300 for certain than to lose $20,000 with probability 1.5% or lose nothing with probability 98.5%. If Alice is risk neutral, she would be indifferent between the two scenarios.

Risk-averse persons will pay to avoid risk. *Insurance* is the business of taking certain payments in exchange for eliminating risk. Suppose that an insurer offers

Alice an insurance policy that pays her $20,000 if her car is stolen but pays nothing if her car is not stolen.

If Alice has the policy and her car is stolen, she loses the car but receives $20,000, so on balance, she gains and loses nothing. If her car is not stolen, the insurer will not pay her anything, so she gains and loses nothing. Thus, the insurance policy eliminates the risk that Alice must otherwise bear. Recall that, without insurance, Alice's expected loss is $300. Hence, if she is risk averse, she would pay at least $300 for the insurance policy.

How much risk-averse persons are willing to pay for insurance depends on their degree of risk aversion. A more risk-averse person will be willing to pay a larger amount to avoid risk. By contrast, a risk-neutral person will not pay more to avoid risk. For instance, suppose that Emily faces the same situation as Alice. If Emily is risk neutral, she would pay no more than $300 for the insurance policy.

It is important to understand the meaning of risk and risk aversion because, whenever information is asymmetric, the less-informed party has imperfect information. To the extent that this means uncertainty about benefits or costs, the less-informed party faces risk.

PROGRESS CHECK 13A

Suppose that Alice buys an insurance policy that pays her $20,000 if her car is stolen and nothing if her car is not stolen. Who of the following has imperfect information and who faces risk: (a) Alice; (b) the insurer?

---

3. Adverse Selection

The quality of wine depends on multiple factors, including the grapes used, location of the vineyard, weather, method of production, and age. Producers of wine have better information about these factors and the quality of the wine than consumers. So information is asymmetric.

Let us use the example of wine to analyze the nature of equilibrium and the effect of price changes on the quantity demanded and supplied in a market with asymmetric information. Consider a very basic setting where wine producers have no reputation and produce wine in plain bottles without labels.

Demand and Supply

Initially, suppose that producers offer only high-quality wine. Figure 13.1 shows the supply and demand for high-quality wine. In equilibrium at point b, the price would be $50 per bottle and production would be 300,000 bottles a month.

Now suppose that producers also produce 100,000 bottles of low-quality wine, at marginal cost ranging from zero to $1. In principle, two markets could exist: one

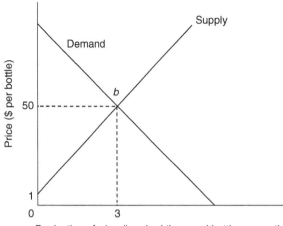

FIGURE 13.1 Market with symmetric information.

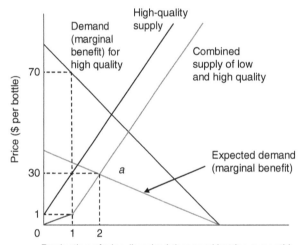

FIGURE 13.2 Market with adverse selection.

Notes: The combined supply of low- and high-quality wine begins with the supply of low-quality wine up to 100,000 bottles at $1 per bottle, then runs parallel to the supply of high-quality wine. The expected demand, which reflects the probability of getting wine of low quality, is the demand curve for wine of high quality shifted down by the proportion $1/Q$. The expected demand and combined supply cross at point a, where the price is $30 per bottle and production is 200,000 bottles a month.

for low-quality wine and another for high-quality wine. Suppose, however, that potential consumers cannot distinguish high from low quality. Then there can be only one market. In that single market, low-quality wine trades alongside high-quality wine, so the supply of high- and low-quality wine is combined.

Figure 13.2 illustrates the market with both low- and high-quality wine. The combined supply of low- and high-quality wine begins with the supply of low-quality wine from zero to 100,000 bottles at a marginal cost of $1 per bottle. Then the combined supply curve runs parallel to the supply of high-quality wine.[2]

What about the demand side of the market? Consumers do not know whether the wine is of low or high quality. Assume that they are risk neutral. Each consumer has a marginal benefit curve for high-quality wine. Suppose that their marginal benefit from low-quality wine is zero. So, each consumer's *expected marginal benefit* is the marginal benefit from high quality multiplied by the probability of getting high quality.

Suppose that consumers purchase a total of Q hundred thousand bottles, of which 100,000 are of low quality. Then each consumer has probability $1/Q$ of getting low-quality wine and probability $(Q - 1)/Q$ of getting high-quality wine. So, the consumer's expected marginal benefit is $(Q - 1)/Q$ of her marginal benefit for high-quality wine. The consumer's expected marginal benefit curve, which reflects the probability of getting low-quality wine, is her marginal benefit curve for high-quality wine, shifted down by the proportion $1/Q$ at every quantity.

Accordingly, the expected demand for wine, which reflects the probability of getting low-quality wine, is the demand curve for high-quality wine shifted down by the proportion $1/Q$. Equivalently, at every possible quantity, the consumers' actual willingness to pay is only a fraction $(Q - 1)/Q$ of their willingness to pay for the same of quantity of wine that is definitely of high quality.

Market Equilibrium

Having laid out the demand and the supply, we can identify the equilibrium. The expected demand and the combined supply cross at point a, where the price is $30 per bottle and the quantity Q is 200,000 units a month. Hence, the probability that a consumer gets low-quality wine is $100,000/200,000 = 50\%$. and the probability of getting high-quality wine is 50%.

Consumers cannot distinguish good from bad wines, and so they get an *adverse selection* – a mixture of bad and good wines. **Adverse selection** arises in situations of asymmetric information: the less-informed party draws a selection with relatively bad characteristics.

> **Adverse selection:** The less-informed party draws a selection with relatively bad characteristics.

What if the production of low-quality wine is lower or higher? If, for instance, there are 50,000 bottles of low-quality wine, then the expected demand would be higher and the combined supply of low- and high-quality wine would be further to the left. Then the equilibrium will have a higher price. The equilibrium production, however, might be lower or higher: the demand is higher, but supply is further to the left.

By contrast, if the production of low-quality wine is larger, then the expected demand would be lower and the combined supply would be further to the right. Hence, the market price would be lower. Again, production might be lower or higher, depending on the balance between demand and supply.

Economic Inefficiency

Referring to Figure 13.2, in the market equilibrium, the price is $30 per bottle and production is 200,000 bottles a month. Production comprises 100,000 bottles of low-quality wine and 100,000 bottles of high-quality wine. By the supply curve of high-quality wine, the marginal cost of producing the 100,000th bottle is $30.

Consumers buy up to the point that the expected marginal benefit (adjusted for the probability of getting low quality) equals the market price. Low-quality wine provides no marginal benefit, so, in equilibrium, the marginal benefit of consumers who get low-quality wine is less than the marginal cost.

By contrast, referring to the marginal benefit curve for high-quality wine, at 100,000 bottles a month, the marginal benefit is $70 per bottle. This exceeds the marginal cost of producing the high-quality wine, $30 per bottle. Accordingly, the equilibrium is not economically efficient.

If, somehow, another bottle of high-quality wine could be produced and sold, then there would be a consumer willing to pay a little less than $70, and it would cost a little more than $30 to produce. Accordingly, there is a potential value added of almost $40.

Essentially, sellers of low-quality wine impose a negative externality on consumers and producers of high-quality wine. By Chapter 12, we know that the negative externality would exceed the economically efficient level. This means that a profit can be made by resolving the externality, which, in this setting, means resolving the information asymmetry.

Market Failure

Before considering how to resolve an asymmetry of information, let us look at an extreme possibility. Suppose that wine producers produce F hundred thousand bottles of low-quality wine. Referring to Figure 13.3, the combined supply of low and high-quality wine has a kink at point c.

What if the quantity of low-quality wine is so large that the expected demand crosses the combined supply at some point d below the kink? In this case, there will be no supply of high-quality wine and the entire supply will be low-quality wine. Then a consumer's probability of getting high-quality wine would be zero. This means that the expected marginal benefit and the expected demand curve must coincide with the horizontal axis. Thus, the initial supposition that the expected demand crosses the combined supply at some point d is not valid.

So there cannot be a market equilibrium with the expected demand curve crossing the combined supply below the kink. Indeed, the same logic also shows that there

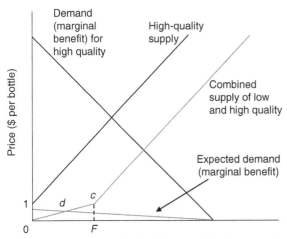

FIGURE 13.3 Market failure.

Notes: Supposing that the expected demand crosses the combined supply at point d, then the entire production will be of low quality. Then, the expected demand curve would coincide with the horizontal axis, and cannot cross the combined supply at point d. Generally, there cannot be an equilibrium with the expected demand curve crossing the combined supply above but close to the kink at point c.

cannot be an equilibrium with the expected demand curve crossing the combined supply above but close to the kink. If there cannot be an equilibrium, then consumers and sellers cannot trade. This means that the intrusion of low-quality wine has caused the entire market to fail!

Let us view the market failure from another perspective. A change in price has very different effects in a perfectly competitive market as compared to a market subject to adverse selection. Suppose that, in a perfectly competitive market, the quantity supplied exceeds the quantity demanded. Then a price reduction will reduce the quantity supplied and raise the quantity demanded. A sufficient reduction of the market price will restore equilibrium.

By contrast, suppose that the market for wine is out of equilibrium, with the quantity supplied exceeding the quantity demanded. Consider a reduction in the market price. The marginal cost of producing high-quality wine slopes upward from a minimum of $1 per bottle. So, when the market price is lower, high-quality wine producers produce less.

However, a reduction in the market price (so long as it remains above $1) does not affect the production of low-quality wine. Hence, the lower market price raises the proportion of low-quality wine, leaving consumers with a worse adverse selection. So their willingness to pay and the expected demand curve would fall.

Thus, in a market with adverse selection, a cut in price reduces both the quantity demanded and the quantity supplied, so it need not reduce the excess supply and restore equilibrium. At the extreme, if the price is cut very low, the expected demand curve would fall to zero and the market would fail completely.

PROGRESS CHECK 13C

Referring to Figure 13.3, suppose that the expected demand curve crosses the combined supply curve at point c. What would be the market equilibrium price and production?

LIFE INSURANCE: BETTING ON DEATH

Insurance is a market where buyers have better information (about themselves) than sellers. Life insurance is insurance against the event of death. It would be more accurate, but much less appealing, to call it *death insurance*. The probability of dying within a given period of time depends on the person's health and lifestyle.

The price that an insurer charges for an insurance policy is called a premium. Life insurers face an adverse selection problem: if an insurer charges a high premium, it is likely to draw applicants in relatively poor health or who maintain risky lifestyles.

Insurers collect information about applicants for life insurance – whether they smoke, their age and their medical history, and their employment, sports, and other activities. However, it is difficult for an insurer to obtain all the relevant information about an applicant's state of health and lifestyle. Hence, there remains asymmetric information between insurers and applicants for insurance.

VOLUNTARY RETIREMENT: DOWNSIZING THE HUMANE WAY

Given a mandate to reduce budgets and headcount, one appealing way is to encourage employees to quit or retire *voluntarily*. In the mid-2000s, under pressure to reduce middle management, the International Monetary Fund offered a generous voluntary separation program to all managers, regardless of age.

Among the professionals who left the IMF was Shang-jin Wei, Assistant Director in the Research Department. He took voluntary separation and became a professor at Columbia University.

Voluntary separation seems much more humane than forced retrenchment. But does it leave behind an adverse selection?

Sources: "Staff in black: IMF faces structural adjustment," Bretton Woods Project, January 31, 2008; Shang-jin Wei, curriculum vitae, October 12, 2010.

4. Appraisal

When information is asymmetric, the market outcome will not be economically efficient. Resolving the information asymmetry would raise benefits by more than costs, and so there is an opportunity to add value and make a profit.

The most obvious way to overcome asymmetric information is to obtain the information directly. Consumers and producers can engage experts to appraise the wine. Referring to Figure 13.2, in the equilibrium at point *a*, the marginal benefit of high-quality wine is $70, while the market price is $30. For the marginal consumer, there is a potential gain of almost $40 by identifying a high-quality wine. Similarly for the marginal producer of high-quality wine.

To the extent that appraisals are available, there will be a separate market for good wine. In that market, consumers and producers would have equal information, and so perfect competition will lead to economic efficiency.

An information asymmetry can be resolved by **appraisal** under two conditions. One is that the characteristic about which information is asymmetric must be objectively verifiable. If an expert cannot objectively distinguish high-quality from low-quality wine, then appraisals would not help. The appraisal must be objective: if different appraisers give different opinions, then information will still be asymmetric.

> **Appraisal:** Works if the characteristic about which information is asymmetric is objectively verifiable and if it is not too costly.

The other condition is that the potential gain from resolving the asymmetry must exceed the cost of appraisal. This, in turn, depends on two factors. One is the proportion of low quality relative to high quality. The other is the difference between the marginal benefit and marginal cost.

Who should procure the expert appraisal? A wine producer can obtain one appraisal and present it to many potential buyers. The appraisal is a public good: any number of potential buyers can use the same information. Hence, it is less costly for the seller to get an appraisal than for every potential buyer to procure an appraisal of the same item.

By contrast, if the buyer is the better-informed party and dealing with multiple sellers, it would be less costly for the buyer to procure the appraisal. Commercial borrowers are buyers of finance, while lenders and investors are suppliers of finance. Commercial borrowers typically pay credit rating agencies to appraise their creditworthiness and provide the credit rating to potential lenders and investors.

PROGRESS CHECK 13D

Will appraisals be more common in the market for cheap or more expensive wines?

COUNTRYWIDE: PAY-OPTION ARMS

In Countrywide's quest to generate income, pay-option ARM loans accounted for 17–21% of the mortgages that it originated. Typically, banks guard against adverse selection by appraising applicants for loans, and in particular, check the borrower's income.

Countrywide changed the lending model for the pay-option ARM by not requiring verification of the borrower's income. In June 2006, an audit revealed that over half of the borrowers had overstated their income by more than 10%, while over one-third had overstated by more than 50%.

By 2007, with interest rates rising and house prices falling, Countrywide began to incur large losses. The next year, Countrywide sold itself to the Bank of America.

Source: *Securities and Exchange Commission* v. *Angelo Mozilo, David Sambol, and Eric Sieracki*, US District Court for Central District of California, case no. CV09-03994, filed June 4, 2009.

5. Screening

Information asymmetries can be directly resolved through appraisal. However, appraisal is costly and not always feasible. So it is important to consider indirect alternatives. There are three ways to indirectly resolve asymmetric information. Here, we present *screening*, and discuss the two other methods – signaling and contingent contracts – in Sections 7 and 8. **Screening** is an initiative of a less-informed party to *indirectly* elicit the better-informed party's characteristics.

> **Screening:** An initiative of a less-informed party to indirectly elicit the better-informed party's characteristics.

Self-Selection

Screening exploits the sensitivity of the better-informed party to some variable that the less-informed party can control. The strategy is to design choices around that variable to induce **self-selection**, meaning that parties with different characteristics choose different alternatives.

> **Self-selection:** Parties with different characteristics choose different alternatives.

Consider the market where consumers cannot distinguish low- from high-quality wine. The unknown characteristic is the true quality of the wine. Suppose that consumers insist that they get the first bottle of wine free and pay double for the second bottle. Can this deal effectively screen low- from high-quality wine?

Suppose that consumers who get high-quality wine would buy the second bottle, while those who get low-quality wine would not buy the second bottle. So producers of low-quality wine would not get any revenue. They would not accept the deal. The deal makes sense only for producers of high-quality wine. Thus, it credibly screens the two types of producers.

Screening is possible only if the less-informed party can control some variable to which the better-informed parties are *differentially* sensitive. In the wine example, low-quality producers are more sensitive to the deal than high-quality producers.

By contrast with appraisal, screening reveals the information of the better-informed party indirectly. Screening is an indirect way of resolving an information asymmetry. Consumers do not directly determine whether wine is of high quality. Rather, they require producers to make a choice that indirectly communicates their characteristics.

A key business application of screening is to pricing. Chapter 9 on pricing presented *indirect segment discrimination*. Such discrimination applies screening to induce self-selection among buyers with different price elasticities of demand.

Differentiating Variables

In some instances, the less-informed party can choose between several differentiating variables. Ideally, the less-informed party should structure the choice that drives the biggest possible wedge between the better-informed parties with the different characteristics.

For instance, in pricing, airlines could use clothing as a differentiating variable, offering a lower fare to travelers wearing casual clothing and a higher fare to travelers in business attire. Business travelers could easily circumvent this differentiating variable; hence, it is not effective. By contrast, airlines have found advance booking and penalties for changes to be effective differentiating variables.

The most effective screening may involve a combination of the differentiating variables. For instance, airlines use a combination of advance booking, penalty for changes, and frequent flyer benefits to screen leisure from business travelers.

PROGRESS CHECK 13E

Collateral is property that a borrower provides to a lender as a security for a loan. If the borrower defaults on the loan, the lender can seize the collateral. Explain how a lender can use requirements for collateral to screen among borrowers with different willingness to repay.

SCREENING FOR LOVE: THE PRENUP

Human relationships are rife with information asymmetry. A particular concern among rich men and women entering into marriage is that their loving spouse might be marrying for the money. But they can sleep more easily with a prenuptial agreement. Typically, the prenuptial agreement specifies a minimum period of marriage before which the spouse can share a limited portion of the wealth and income. It is an effective way to screen gold-diggers from true life partners.

In October 2004, Tiger Woods married Elin Nordegren at the Sandy Lane resort, Barbados. Their prenuptial agreement specified that Ms Nordegren would receive $20 million after 10 years of marriage.

Fast forward five years. After Woods mysteriously crashed his car, a string of women came forward to reveal that they had had sex with him during his marriage. Woods reportedly renegotiated the prenuptial to pay Ms Nordegren $5 million immediately, shorten her vesting period to 7 years, and raise her maximum payout to $75 million.

Sources: "New details on Tiger's prenup," *Daily Beast*, December 3, 2009; "Tiger Woods mistress list rises to 11," go.com, December 9, 2009.

6. Auctions[3]

Sellers can apply indirect segment discrimination to screen among buyers who differ in their price sensitivity. Auctions are a particular form of indirect segment discrimination that exploits strategic interaction among the bidders.

Suppose that a wine grower wants to sell a vineyard. There are many potential buyers, and the seller wants to get the highest possible price. An auction applies competitive pressure to the participating bidders. Each bidder must act strategically since its best bid depends on the competing bids: if the other bids are low, then a bidder can win with a relatively low bid, while if the other bids are high, then a bidder must bid relatively high to win.

Each bidder faces a fundamental *tradeoff*. By bidding more aggressively, it will improve its chances of winning the auction. On the other hand, if it bids more aggressively, it will get a smaller profit from winning the auction.

The differentiating variable in an auction is the probability of winning. A bidder that values the item more will gain relatively more from winning the auction, and hence will bid higher. Thus, the auction induces self-selection among the participants according to their valuation of the item.

Auction Methods

Auctions may be conducted in various ways. The bidding can be open or sealed. In an auction for multiple items, each winning bidder can be required to pay the price that she bid, or the price bid by the marginal winning bidder. (The marginal winning bidder is the last bidder (in descending order of bids) to get an item.) The seller may specify a **reserve price**, below which it will not sell the item.

Reserve price: The price below which the seller will not sell the item.

- *Open/sealed bidding.* Auction houses such as Christie's and Sotheby's use open auctions. The auctioneer calls out prices in an ascending sequence, and the bidders indicate whether or not they wish to continue participating. By contrast, developers choosing a building contractor usually conduct sealed bid auctions.

- *Reserve price*. The seller may specify a reserve price, below which it will not sell the item. The reserve price forces bidders to bid higher. However, all the bids may fall below the reserve price and then the seller will get no revenue. So, in setting a reserve price, the seller must balance the increased revenue from a sale against the probability of no sale.

- *Prices for multiple units*. In a **discriminatory auction**, each winning bidder pays their bid. By contrast, in a **non-discriminatory auction**, each winning bidder pays the bid of the marginal winning bidder. Bidders at non-discriminatory auctions should bid relatively higher than at discriminatory auctions. Whether a seller gets higher revenue from a non-discriminatory auction depends on two factors. One is that bidders make relatively higher bids, but the other is that the seller collects only the bid of the marginal bidder for every item sold.

> **Discriminatory auction:** Each winning bidder pays their bid.

> **Non-discriminatory auction:** Each winning bidder pays the bid of the marginal winning bidder.

Winner's Curse

In addition to not knowing their competitors' strategies, the bidders participating in an auction may also be uncertain about the value of the item for sale. For instance, in the auction of the vineyard, the bidders may be unsure about the quantity of grapes that the land will yield. How will this uncertainty affect the bidding?

Consider the bidder who wins the auction of the vineyard. Then, by the fact of winning, the winning bidder can infer that it probably had the highest estimate of the yield. On the basis of all of the bidders' estimates, however, it may have overestimated the true yield and actually would incur a loss on the purchase.

The vineyard auction illustrates the *winner's curse*. The **winner's curse** arises in an auction where the various bidders are uncertain about some common element in the value of the item for sale. A bidder whose estimate of that common element is high is more likely to win. Hence, on average, the winning bidder is the one most likely to have overestimated the true value of the item.

> **Winner's curse:** The winning bidder overestimates the true value of the item.

A bidder should take account of the possibility of the winner's curse by bidding more conservatively, that is, aiming for a larger margin between its estimate of the value of the item and its bid. By bidding conservatively, the bidder can reduce the likelihood of overbidding for the item.

There are three circumstances in which the winner's curse is more severe and bidders should bid more conservatively:

- *If there are more bidders*. With 20 bidders, the winner will probably be one whose estimate is higher than 19 other estimates. By contrast, with four bidders, the winner's estimate is probably higher than three other estimates. An estimate that is higher than 19 others is more likely to exceed the true value than an estimate that is higher than three others.

- *If the true value of the item is more uncertain.* Consider, for instance, an auction for gold. There is no uncertainty about the true value of an ounce of gold. Every bidder would know the market price of gold, and hence all their estimates and bids would be the same. The winner's curse arises only when there is uncertainty about the true value of the item. If the true value of the item is more uncertain, then the probability that the highest estimate exceeds the true value will be higher, and so the extent of the winner's curse would be greater.

- *In a sealed-bid compared with an open auction.* In an open auction, bidders with relatively low values for the item will drop out progressively as the price ascends. Since the record of bidding is open, the remaining bidders can see the prices at which others drop out. The remaining bidders can then infer the dropping bidders' estimates of the true value. They can use this additional information to refine their estimate of the true value. Hence, open bidding mitigates the winner's curse.

PROGRESS CHECK 13F

The seller of a vineyard has procured an independent appraisal and provided it to bidders. How would this affect the extent of the winner's curse?

WINNER'S CURSE: TUAS SEWERS

Governments use auctions to procure goods and services. The principles of an auction to buy are exactly the same as for an auction to sell. In an auction where the bidders compete to supply an item with uncertain cost, the winner's curse is to overestimate the true cost.

In the construction industry, the cost of underground works is more difficult to estimate than above-ground works. In July 2014, the Public Utilities Board of Singapore invited tenders by sealed bid for a contract to build sewers in the Tuas area. Eight contractors submitted bids. Aik Leong Plumbing Construction bid the lowest, S$22.3 million, while Building Construction bid the highest, S$48.8 million. The average bid was S$32.4 million.

The Public Utilities Board awarded the contract to Aik Leong. It will be interesting to see whether Aik Leong underestimated the cost of construction.

Source: Government Electronic Business, www.gebiz.gov.sg (accessed December 9, 2014).

7. Signaling

Screening, an initiative of the less-informed party to elicit the characteristics of the better-informed party, is one indirect way to resolve asymmetric information. Another is **signaling**, an initiative of the better-informed party to communicate its characteristics to the less-informed party. The key is that the communication must be credible, that is, the parties with different characteristics choose different signaling policies.

> **Signaling:** An initiative of the better-informed party to communicate its characteristics to the less-informed party.

Recall the wine market where consumers cannot distinguish low- from high-quality wine. Suppose that a high-quality producer offers to give a full refund to any consumer who returns a partly-consumed bottle. Does the refund offer credibly signal that the wine is indeed of high quality?

Consider a producer of low-quality wine. If it offers the refund, all consumers would return their purchases for refund. So the low-quality producer will not offer the refund. Thus, only high-quality producers offer the refund, and the refund does induce self-selection and is a credible signal of high quality.

Signaling indirectly communicates the characteristics of the better-informed party and thereby resolves the information asymmetry. The producer of high-quality wine does not directly declare the product quality. Rather, the producer takes an action that indirectly and credibly communicates the high quality.

To be credible, a signal must induce self-selection among the better-informed parties. Specifically, the cost of the signal must be sufficiently lower for parties with superior characteristics than for parties with inferior characteristics. Then only those with superior characteristics will offer the signal.

Suppose that a wine producer labels its product "high quality." Would this be a credible signal? The answer depends on whether the action is relatively more costly for a low-quality producer. The cost of the "high quality" label is the same for producers of high and low-quality wine. Hence, such a label alone will not induce self-selection among producers and cannot be a credible signal.

PROGRESS CHECK 13G

Explain the difference between screening and signaling.

TOSHIBA: LEADING INNOVATION – SIGNALING THROUGH ADVERTISING AND REPUTATION

If labeling products as "high quality" is not a credible signal, why does Toshiba advertise "Leading Innovation"? Investment in advertising and building reputation can be a credible signal only if it induces self-selection – it must pay off for sellers of high quality and not pay off for sellers of low quality. Such signaling depends on three conditions:

- The investment must be *large and sunk*. If the advertising expenditure is reversible, then a seller of low quality can also make the same investment, pass on inferior products, and get its money back. A reversible investment will not be a credible signal.
- Buyers must be able to *detect poor quality fairly quickly*. If a seller can fool buyers for a long time, then even a seller offering poor quality can afford the sunk investment.
- Information about the poor quality must *cut the seller's future sales and quickly*. A one-time seller can afford to pass off poor quality because it will never face the punishment of losing repeat business.

8. Contingent Contracts

We have discussed two indirect ways to resolve an information asymmetry: screening and signaling. Another indirect approach is a *contingent contract*. A **contingent contract** specifies actions under particular conditions. Bets are contingent contracts: you get a dollar from me if the coin turns up heads, while I will get a dollar from you if it turns up tails. In this bet, the contingency is the side of the coin that faces up after the toss.

Contingent contract: Specifies actions under particular conditions.

To see how contingent contracts can resolve an information asymmetry, consider a wine producer selling a vineyard. Suppose that the seller knows that the vines will yield an exceptional quantity of grapes, say, 6,000 tons a year. However, it has no independent appraisal or other way to directly convince potential buyers.

What if the seller were to specify that it would sell the vineyard for a share of the grape production rather than a straight cash payment? By asking for a share, the seller is taking a payment that is contingent on the yield from the vines. If the yield is high, then the seller will get a larger payment, while if yield is low, then the seller will receive less.

By selling the vineyard for a share of the production, the seller can credibly convey its information to potential buyers. Sellers of average or relatively low-yielding vines would prefer to sell for cash. Hence, those selling relatively better vines can distinguish themselves by selling for a share of the production. The result is self-selection.

For a workplace example, suppose that an employer offers production-line workers a choice between a fixed wage and piece-rate wage. The piece-rate wage is essentially a contingent contract, with the wage contingent on the worker's productivity. The choice between fixed wage and piece-rate screens between workers of differing productivity.

RESOLVING INFORMATION ASYMMETRY: BUYBACK

As the originator of the mortgages, Countrywide had better information about the mortgages that it pooled for sale than buyers such as HSBC. Obviously aware of this asymmetry of information, HSBC bought 80/20 mortgages subject to a provision that it could require Countrywide to buy back mortgages that did not meet specific conditions.

The right to require buyback is a contingent contract. Indeed, in early 2006, HSBC exercised its right, and Countrywide had to repurchase the specified mortgages and incurred substantial losses.

Source: *Securities and Exchange Commission* v. *Angelo Mozilo, David Sambol, and Eric Sieracki*, US District Court for Central District of California, case no. CV09-03994, filed June 4, 2009.

HP: BUYING AUTONOMY WITHOUT CONTINGENT CONTRACT

In mergers and acquisitions, the buyer has less information about the value of the acquisition than the seller. One way to resolve the information asymmetry is a contingent contract that conditions payments on sales or profit targets. Another way is to pay in shares, so that the value of the payment depends on the value of the acquisition.

In August 2011, Hewlett-Packard (HP) announced that it would acquire British software producer Autonomy plc for £25.50 per share in cash without any conditions on future sales or profits. Analysts roundly criticized the $11.6 billion acquisition. However, HP CEO Leo Apotheker defended the deal, saying: "We have a pretty rigorous process inside H.P. that we follow for all our acquisitions, which is a D.C.F.-based model . . . . And we try to take a very conservative view."

Within a month, HP dismissed Mr Apotheker. Just over a year later, in November 2012, HP wrote down the acquisition by $8.8 billion, citing a "willful effort on behalf of certain former Autonomy employees to inflate the underlying financial metrics of the company in order to mislead investors and potential buyers".

Source: "From H.P., a blunder that seems to beat all," *New York Times*, November 30, 2012.

KEY TAKEAWAYS

- Risk is uncertainty about benefits or costs.
- A risk-averse person will pay to avoid risk.
- If information is asymmetric, the allocation of resources is not economically efficient, and there is an opportunity to add value and profit by resolving the asymmetry.

- If adverse selection is severe, the market will fail.
- Use appraisal if the characteristic about which information is asymmetric is objectively verifiable and if it is not too costly.
- Use screening to indirectly elicit the characteristics of the better-informed party if the screening induces self-selection.
- Adjust for the winner's curse in auction bidding.
- A better-informed party can use signaling to indirectly communicate its characteristics if the signaling induces self-selection.
- Use a contingent contract to screen or signal.

REVIEW QUESTIONS

1. Explain the difference between imperfect information and risk.
2. In the following situations, explain the asymmetry of information, if any: (a) Investors do not know the next day's Standard & Poor's 500 Index. (b) Acquirer is planning a takeover bid for Target at $50 a share, which is 25% above the current market price of $40, and is secretly buying shares of Target.
3. A bank has just rejected Ming's application for a car loan. Ming approaches the loan officer and offers to pay a higher interest rate. Why does the loan officer laugh?
4. If a borrower defaults on a secured loan, the creditor can seize and sell the item against which the loan is secured. Explain why the interest rate on secured loans is lower than that on unsecured loans.
5. A manufacturer of women's clothing pays production workers a piece rate. The human resources manager has proposed offering workers the alternative of a fixed salary. Explain the possible adverse selection.
6. Jill is about to buy a secondhand car at a below-market price. The seller assured Jill that the car is in perfect condition. Why should Jill get an expert to evaluate the car?
7. Young people do not have much driving history. Does this explain why insurers are reluctant to insure young drivers?
8. Give an example of screening. Explain: (a) the asymmetry of information; and (b) self-selection.
9. An automobile insurance policy with a $2,000 deductible only covers loss in excess of $2,000. Typically, automobile insurers offer policies with a choice between higher deductibles and higher premiums. Explain how this choice can screen among drivers with different probability of accident.
10. During peak hours, a tunnel is congested. From the standpoint of economic efficiency, the tunnel service should be allocated to the drivers who value time most highly. Explain how a toll can achieve economic efficiency.
11. This question relies on the auctions section. The seller of the rights to oil in a particular area has undertaken a geological study. Will the winner's curse be more serious if the seller (a) provides the study to all bidders, or (b) keeps the study secret?
12. How should a bidder adjust for the winner's curse in (a) an auction to sell, and (b) an auction to buy?

Table 13.1 Southwest Airlines

	2010	2009	2008
Operating revenues ($ million)	12,104	10,350	11,023
Operating expenses ($ million)	11,116	10,088	10,574
Operating income ($ million)	988	262	449
Net income ($ million)	459	99	178
Available seat miles (millions)	98,437	98,001	103,271
Average fuel cost ($ per gallon)	2.51	2.12	2.44
Fuel consumed (million gallons)	1,437	1,428	1,511

13. Give an example of signaling. Explain: (a) the asymmetry of information; and (b) self-selection.
14. A producer of financial management software offers full refunds to any dissatisfied purchaser. Is the refund policy a credible signal of product quality?
15. How does the following contract help to resolve asymmetric information? Acquirer buys all of Target's shares and pays partly in cash and partly in Acquirer shares.

DISCUSSION QUESTIONS

1. Southwest Airlines pioneered the concept of the low-cost airline, operating from secondary airports with short hops and quick turnarounds. In 2010, Southwest increased net income by 4.6 times to $459 million. In 2008–2009, as the price of oil fell sharply, Southwest decided to reduce its hedging, and so realized hedging-related losses that reduced net income. Table 13.1 reports selected financial and operating information.
    (a) Referring to Southwest's fuel consumption in 2010, explain how a 10-cent increase in the price of jet fuel would affect Southwest's costs and income.
    (b) Southwest is averse to risk. Explain why it buys crude oil derivatives to hedge the price of jet fuel.
    (c) Suppose that the actual price of crude oil turns out to be *lower* than the price at which Southwest hedged. Was Southwest wrong to have hedged?
2. Some Chinese dairy producers add melamine to raw milk, which raises the apparent protein content in testing. In 2008, melamine contamination caused six babies to die and harmed hundreds of thousands of others. As Chinese parents flocked to buy baby formula in Hong Kong, supermarkets had to ration sales.
    (a) Using a relevant diagram, illustrate the equilibrium price and production in the following market. The supply curve of contaminated milk is a straight line from zero production at zero marginal cost to production of 1 million kilograms a month at 10 yuan per kilogram. The supply curve of pure milk is a straight line from zero production at 10 yuan per kilogram to 3 million kilograms a month at 25 yuan per kilogram. Consumers

cannot distinguish pure and contaminated milk. Their demand for pure milk is zero at 50 yuan per kilogram and 10 million kilograms a month at zero price. The demand for contaminated milk is zero at all prices.

(b) Using your diagram in (a), illustrate how the market can fail if farmers increase the production of contaminated milk.

3. Hong Kong University of Science and Technology has contracted with HSBC Insurance to provide medical insurance to all university employees. Medical insurance covers the cost of the treatment and prescriptions necessary for the insured party to recover from an illness or accident.

(a) Explain the asymmetry of information between the insurer and the University employees.

(b) How does a group policy, covering *all* employees of an organization, mitigate adverse selection for the insurer?

(c) Unlike falling sick or meeting with accidents, in many cases, women voluntarily enter into pregnancy. Explain why HSBC covers pregnancy as part of the basic coverage, rather than as an option.

4. Corporations borrow by issuing commercial paper and bonds. They may commission ratings by credit rating agencies and provide the ratings to investors. Moody's ratings correlate well with actual defaults. Between 2005 and 2010, the average five-year default rate was 0.81% among investment-grade (Baa and higher) issuers, and 22.38% among speculative-grade (Caa and lower) issuers. (Source: Moody's Investors Service, "The performance of Moody's corporate debt ratings," March 2010 quarterly update.)

(a) Explain the asymmetry of information between issuers of securities (borrowers) and potential investors (lenders).

(b) Why do issuers of securities rather than potential investors commission credit ratings?

(c) Why is it important that ratings have correlated well with actual defaults?

(d) By issuing more debt, a corporation may raise the probability of default. Should ratings be fixed or adjusted over time?

5. Historically, credit rating agencies rated issuers, i.e., companies and governments. A new and fast-growing business is to rate structured products such as mortgage-backed securities. A single investment bank may issue tens or hundreds of structured products. Ray McDaniel, CEO of Moody's, acknowledged that issuers negotiate and redesign structured products to achieve particular credit ratings, and that issuers shop around the competing credit rating agencies for the best rating. (Source: "Ray McDaniel, Moody's," *FT View from the Top*, video, October 11, 2007.)

(a) Explain the asymmetry of information between issuers of structured products and potential investors.

(b) Compare the degree of asymmetry of information about issuers *vis-à-vis* structured products.

(c) In light of McDaniel's disclosures, how effective is appraisal in resolving asymmetries of information over structured products?

(d) Legislators have proposed to require issuers of mortgage-backed securities to retain a minimum fraction of the securities that they issue. How would this help to resolve the asymmetry of information?

6. In October 2004, Tiger Woods married Elin Nordegren at the Sandy Lane resort, Barbados. Their prenuptial agreement specified that Ms Nordegren would receive $20 million after 10 years of marriage. (Source: "New details on Tiger's prenup," *Daily Beast*, December 3, 2009.)

   (a) Explain the asymmetry of information in a marriage between a wealthy man or woman and a relatively poorer spouse.
   (b) Explain the prenuptial agreement in terms of a contingent contract.
   (c) How can the prenuptial agreement screen gold-diggers from true life partners?
   (d) Can the relatively poorer person use the prenuptial agreement to signal his or her true quality?

7. This question relies on the auctions section. In 2001, Singapore's Land Transport Authority shortlisted three contractors to build a section of the Marina Line subway: Nishimatsu-Lum Chang Joint Venture (NLC), S$275 million; Impregilo SPA-Hua Kok Realty Joint Venture, S$343 million; and Samsung Corporation Engineering and Construction, S$345 million. Three years later, in May 2004, the lowest three bids for contract 855 of the Circle Line were much closer: NLC, S$376–389 million; Woh Hup-Shanghai Tunnel Engineering Co.–Alpine Mayreder consortium, S$390–398 million; and Obayashi, S$400.3 million.

   (a) Explain the winner's curse in the context of the bidding for the Marina Line.
   (b) Explain how a contractor's degree of risk aversion would affect the amount that it bids.
   (c) What experience from the Marina Line bidding did NLC apply in bidding for contract 855?
   (d) Explain why the Authority should provide all available information about the soil conditions to the bidders.
   (e) In tunneling projects, should the Authority offer to share part of the contractor's cost overrun? How would such sharing affect the contractors' bids?

8. Tesla Motors, pioneer of high-performance electric automobiles, launched a sports car, the Roadster, in 2008, followed by the luxury Model S, in 2012. In early 2014, Tesla announced an eight-year warranty on the battery pack and drive unit with no mileage limit. CEO Elon Musk emphasized: "If we truly believe that electric motors are fundamentally more reliable than gasoline engines, with far fewer moving parts and no oily residue or combustion by-products to gum up the works, then our warranty policy should reflect that." (Source: "Do warranty extensions make sense?" *The Star (Toronto)*, November 21, 2014.)

   (a) Explain the asymmetry of information between Tesla and its potential customers.
   (b) Explain the extended warranty in terms of a contingent contract.

(c) Under what conditions will an extended warranty be a credible signal of superior quality?

    (d) How does Tesla's financial condition affect the credibility of the warranty as a signal?

9. Genzyme manufactures "orphan drugs" that target rare genetic diseases. In July 2010, Sanofi-aventis offered to acquire Genzyme at $69 a share. Genzyme's board rejected the offer and sought $75 a share. Sanofi disagreed with Genzyme about the future sales of its new multiple sclerosis drug, Lemtrada. Eventually, in February 2011, Genzyme accepted a revised offer of $74 per share in cash plus a contingent value right (CVR) worth up to $14 per share depending on the sales of Lemtrada and other milestones. (Sources: "Sanofi steps up Genzyme pursuit," *Financial Times*, August 29, 2010; Genzyme Corporation media release, "Sanofi-aventis to acquire Genzyme for $74.00 in cash per share plus contingent value right," February 16, 2011.)

    (a) Explain the asymmetry of information between Sanofi and Genzyme.

    (b) How could the CVR resolve the asymmetry of information? Compare Sanofi's valuation of the CVR with Genzyme's valuation.

    (c) Could the asymmetry be resolved directly by Sanofi inspecting Genzyme's accounts and facilities?

You are the consultant!

Identify any asymmetry of information in your organization's activities. Write a memo to the board of directors explaining how your organization could exploit the profit opportunities.

Notes

1   This discussion is based, in part, on *Securities and Exchange Commission* v. *Angelo Mozilo, David Sambol, and Eric Sieracki*, US District Court for Central District of California, case no. CV09-03994, filed June 4, 2009.

2   This model is adapted from B. Peter Pashigan, *Price Theory and Applications*, New York: McGraw-Hill, 1995, pp. 520–526.

3   This section is more advanced. It may be omitted without loss of continuity.

Incentives and Organization

1. Introduction

In April 2004, Boeing launched development of the 787 Dreamliner with an order of 50 planes from All Nippon Airways. The Boeing 787 is a twin-engine medium- to long-range wide-body jet with capacity of 200–300 passengers. With extensive use of composite materials in construction, the 787 is designed to consume 20% less fuel than the similar-sized Boeing 767.[1]

Traditionally, Boeing designed and built the major parts, and then assembled the planes at its Everett and Renton, Washington, factories. In a major departure, the then Chairman and CEO, Harry Stonecipher, and the then head of Commercial Airplanes, Alan Mulally, decided to subcontract the design and construction of major parts of the 787, including the wing, fuselage, and tail. Boeing would then need only a relatively small workforce at the Everett factory to carry out final assembly.

By radically outsourcing the production work, Boeing aimed to substantially reduce the assets required to support production, and so boost the return on net assets. Mr Stonecipher had applied the same outsourcing strategy as President and CEO of military contractor McDonnell Douglas, which merged with Boeing in 1997.

Boeing had planned the first flight of the 787 Dreamliner for August 2007 and deliveries to All Nippon Airways by late 2008. However, by mid-2007, construction was behind schedule. The Chairman and CEO, James McNerney (successor to Stonecipher, who was dismissed in March 2005 for a "personal relationship" with another employee) acknowledged that subcontractors had not delivered according to specification: "We were surprised on the physical reality of some of the things that we received from suppliers versus the documentation."

After repeated delays, the first flight actually took place only in December 2009. Meanwhile, Boeing was forced to buy a factory in Charleston, South Carolina, from Vought Aircraft Industries at a cost of $1 billion. Vought had contracted to design and build the 787's rear fuselage. However, facing technical and financial challenges, Vought's owner, the private-equity investor Carlyle Group, would not increase its investment and instead sought to sell the business. The Vought CEO, Elmer Doty, explained that "the financial demands of this program are clearly growing beyond what a company our size can support."

How was Boeing's outsourcing related to supplier delays and its surprise at the quality of supplier performance? Why did the outsourcing lead Boeing to buy the Charleston factory from Vought? How would Boeing's purchase affect the performance of the Charleston factory?

| | **Organizational architecture** comprises the distribution of ownership, incentive schemes, and monitoring systems. Boeing's experience with production of the Dreamliner clearly demonstrates the importance of organizational architecture. Far from increasing the company's return on net assets, the outsourcing strategy inflated development costs by an estimated 50–80% over the original plan of $8–10 billion. |

Organizational architecture: The distribution of ownership, incentive schemes, and monitoring systems.

This chapter presents a framework for analyzing organizational architecture. An efficient organizational architecture resolves four issues of internal management – holdup, moral hazard, monopoly power, and economies of scale and scope. Holdup is an action to exploit the dependence of another party. For instance, Vought Aircraft Industries refused to increase investment despite challenges in producing the rear fuselage sections. Vought's holdup forced Boeing to buy the Charleston plant.

Moral hazard arises when one party's actions affect but are not observed by another party. It results from asymmetry of information about actions. The Boeing CEO James McNerney expressed surprise at the subcontractors' quality of work. Evidently, Boeing suffered from the moral hazard of its subcontractors. The moral hazard was further manifest in the systematic delays to the Dreamliner program.

The architecture of an organization, particularly vertical integration, affects the degree of moral hazard and potential for holdup. Vertical integration is the opposite of outsourcing. When an organization outsources a particular input, it is vertically disintegrating out of the production of that input. By acquiring the Charleston factory, Boeing reversed its outsourcing strategy, and vertically integrated into the manufacturing of the rear fuselage and so avoided further holdup.

Besides moral hazard and holdup, the architecture of an organization also influences the extent of internal monopoly power and economies of scale and scope. Together, all of these determine the economic efficiency of the organization. To the extent that there is any economic inefficiency, there will be an opportunity for managers to add value and increase the profit.

2. Moral Hazard

Marie is a salesperson. By the very nature of her job, a salesperson operates independently. Hence, it is difficult for Marie's employer to monitor her work. Marie alone decides how many customers to visit and how much effort to spend on selling. Her employer wants her to exert the maximum effort – to be patient and persuasive, yet persistent.

In this example, the salesperson is subject to *moral hazard* relative to her employer. A party is subject to **moral hazard** if its actions affect but are not observed by another party.

> **Moral hazard:** One party's actions affect but are not observed by another party.

Asymmetric Information about Actions

If the employer can freely monitor the salesperson at all times, then it can directly specify her effort – how many customers to visit, how to persuade them, etc. Then the salesperson would not be subject to moral hazard. Moral hazard arises because information is asymmetric. The employer depends on the salesperson's effort but cannot observe it.

Chapter 13 discussed asymmetric information in markets such as life insurance where the applicant has better information about her health, and lending where the borrower has better information about her ability to repay. In those situations, the asymmetry of information concerned some characteristic(s) of the better-informed party.

By contrast, in the case of the salesperson, Marie has better information about her effort than her employer. In this case, the asymmetry of information concerns some action of the better-informed party. This information asymmetry is a necessary condition for moral hazard.

Economic Inefficiency

The salesperson acts independently. She chooses her effort to maximize her personal net benefit. The salesperson's net benefit is her compensation less her cost of effort. The level of effort that maximizes her net benefit is that where her marginal compensation equals her marginal cost. Referring to Figure 14.1, the salesperson will choose 120 units of effort. At that level of effort, the salesperson's marginal compensation and marginal cost are $10 per unit of effort.

What if the salesperson were to increase her effort by one unit? Figure 14.1 also shows the employer's marginal profit contribution. The salesperson's effort increases her employer's profit contribution. When the salesperson exerts 120 units of effort, the employer's marginal profit contribution is $25. So, the salesperson's additional unit of effort would increase the employer's profit contribution by a little less than $25 (a little less because the marginal profit contribution curve slopes downward).

The cost to the salesperson of the additional unit would be a little more than $10 (a little more because the marginal cost curve slopes upward). So, the additional unit of effort would add value by increasing the employer's marginal profit contribution by more than the salesperson's marginal cost. Indeed, the salesperson could continue adding value by raising effort up to 250 units. The additional value (the excess of profit contribution over cost) to the employer and salesperson would be the shaded area *abc*.

Essentially, the salesperson is generating a positive externality for her employer. So, as with any positive externality, if it is not resolved, then the situation is not economically efficient. So there is an opportunity to add value and raise profit by resolving the externality.

In the sales context, resolving the externality means resolving the moral hazard between the salesperson and her employer. The shaded area *abc* represents the

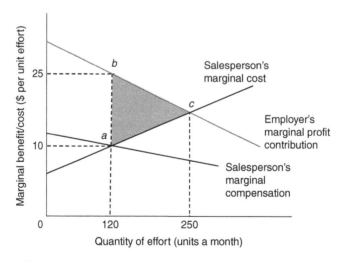

FIGURE 14.1 Economically efficient effort.

Notes: The salesperson chooses 120 units of effort, which balances her marginal compensation with her marginal cost. The economically efficient level of effort, 250 units, balances the employer's marginal profit contribution with the salesperson's marginal cost.

amount of profit that can be earned by resolving the moral hazard. The challenge then is how to do so.

Degree of Moral Hazard

Suppose that the salesperson's marginal compensation coincides exactly with the employer's marginal profit contribution. Then the salesperson would choose the economically efficient level of effort. Under these conditions, there will be no moral hazard.

Referring to Figure 14.1, the lower the salesperson's marginal compensation is relative to the employer's marginal profit contribution, the lower will be the effort that the salesperson chooses relative to the economically efficient level.

We can measure the degree of moral hazard by the difference between the economically efficient action and the action chosen by the party subject to moral hazard. The larger this difference is, the greater are the degree of moral hazard and the added value that can be realized by resolving the moral hazard.

PROGRESS CHECK 14A

Suppose that the salesperson's marginal cost of effort in Figure 14.1 is higher. Draw the new marginal cost curve. How does this affect: (a) the economically efficient level of effort; (b) the effort that the salesperson actually chooses?

MORAL HAZARD AT THE TOP

Top executives in large publicly listed corporations are subject to moral hazard relative to shareholders. Publicly listed companies have many diverse shareholders ranging from pension funds with million-dollar holdings to individuals with several hundred shares. It is not worthwhile for small shareholders to monitor the managers of the company. They can instead free-ride on the monitoring efforts of other shareholders.

Shareholders are primarily concerned about the value of their shares. By contrast, CEOs and other senior managers may have different objectives.

On April 20, 2010, British Petroleum's oil rig, Deepwater Horizon, located in the Gulf of Mexico, exploded. BP's CEO, Tony Hayward, downplayed the incident, describing the Gulf as a "big ocean" and claiming that the environmental impact would be "very very modest."

During the ensuing crisis, Hayward took time off to sail his yacht. Facing mounting criticism, he decided to resign. The price of BP shares rose by 4.85%, increasing the market value of the company by $5.6 billion.

Source: "BP chief Hayward 'negotiating exit deal,'" *BBC News*, July 25, 2010; "BP oil spill: the rise and fall of Tony Hayward," *Telegraph*, July 27, 2010.

BOEING 787: A NEW WAY TO BUILD PLANES

Traditionally, Boeing designed and built the major parts, and then assembled planes at its Everett and Renton, Washington, factories. In a major departure, the then Chairman and CEO, Harry Stonecipher, and the then head of Commercial Airplanes, Alan Mulally, decided to subcontract design and construction of major parts of the 787, including the wing, fuselage, and tail. Boeing would then need only a relatively small workforce at the Everett factory to carry out final assembly. By extensive outsourcing, Boeing hoped to reduce its production assets, and so boost its return on net assets.

Boeing had planned the first flight of the 787 Dreamliner for August 2007 and deliveries to All Nippon Airways by late 2008. However, by mid-2007, construction was behind schedule. The Chairman and CEO, James McNerney (successor to Stonecipher), acknowledged that subcontractors had not delivered according to specification: "We were surprised on the physical reality of some of the things that we received from suppliers versus the documentation."

The outsourcing strategy had placed Boeing in a position of asymmetric information relative to its subcontractors. The result was severe moral hazard, to the extent that Boeing had to despatch hundreds of manufacturing engineers and procurement staff to assist major subcontractors. Boeing had to provide almost $1 billion for just the first six-month delay in production.

Source: "787 delay could wind up costing Boeing $1 billion," *Seattle Times*, October 25, 2007.

3. Incentives

We have identified the potential gains from resolving moral hazard. Generally, there are two complementary approaches. One is to invest in monitoring, surveillance, and other methods of collecting information about the actions of the party subject to moral hazard. The other approach is to align the incentives of the party subject to moral hazard with those of the less-informed party.

Monitoring systems and incentive schemes are two elements of organizational architecture. They are complementary because all incentives must be based on actions that can be observed, so the better the available information, the wider will be the choice of incentive schemes. Ideally, the relevant parties would like to completely resolve the moral hazard, so that the better-informed party will make the economically efficient choice. Let us now discuss how to resolve the moral hazard of a salesperson relative to her employer.

Monitoring

The simplest monitoring system focuses on objective measures of performance such as hours on the job. However, hours on the job and effort are not the same thing. A salesperson can start at 8:00 am and finish at 5:00 pm, but do nothing during that time. Accordingly, employers need monitoring systems that provide more than basic objective information.

One method that employers frequently use to collect information is supervision. It is not cost-effective for supervisors to monitor subordinates all the time, however. So supervisors make random checks. Chapter 10 discussed the advantages of randomization. The same principle applies to supervision: the supervisor should check staff at random, rather than according to some regular pattern.

Employers can also enlist customers to monitor the performance of employees. Customers have a natural advantage in monitoring salespersons, as salespersons spend more time with customers than at the employer's office. Employers can encourage customers to report salespersons' performance.

Performance Pay

The counterpart to monitoring systems is incentive schemes. Incentive schemes resolve moral hazard by linking compensation to some measure of performance. The schemes depend on a link between the *unobservable* action and some *observable* measure of performance. Generally, the scope of incentive schemes depends on what indicators of the unobservable action are available.

An employer can use the information provided by monitoring systems to structure incentives for its workers. While Marie's employer cannot observe her effort, it can observe the value of her sales. So, it can base incentives on Marie's sales revenue.

One common incentive scheme is **performance pay**, which bases pay on some measure of performance. Let us consider performance pay for the salesperson. Suppose first that Marie receives a fixed wage of $4,000 a month and that her employer does not monitor her at all, not even requiring her to keep a diary of sales calls.

> **Performance pay:** An incentive scheme that bases pay on some measure of performance.

With a fixed wage and no monitoring, Marie cannot affect her earnings in any way, however hard she works. Her marginal compensation from effort will be zero. In Figure 14.2, the salesperson's marginal compensation with a fixed wage is the horizontal axis. This is lower than the salesperson's marginal cost at all levels of effort. Hence, she would choose zero effort.

Now suppose that the employer pays Marie a 10% commission on sales revenue. This is an example of payment based on performance. The more Marie sells, the more she will earn. With this incentive scheme, her marginal compensation from effort will be positive. The height and slope of her marginal compensation curve depend on how her effort affects sales revenue.

Figure 14.2 also shows the marginal compensation with a 10% commission. This crosses her marginal cost at an effort of 30 units. With a 10% commission, the salesperson chooses 30 units of effort. Accordingly, the commission partly resolves the salesperson's moral hazard.

An incentive scheme is relatively stronger if it provides a higher marginal compensation for effort. Suppose that the employer strengthens the incentive scheme by raising the commission to 15%. Then the marginal compensation curve would

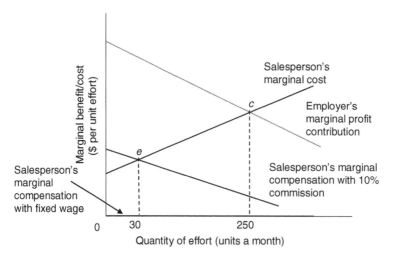

FIGURE 14.2 Performance pay.

Notes: With a fixed wage, the salesperson's marginal compensation is the horizontal axis, and she chooses zero effort. With a 10% commission, she chooses 30 units of effort.

be higher, and it would cross the marginal cost curve at a higher level of effort. This shows that a stronger incentive scheme induces the salesperson to increase effort.

PROGRESS CHECK 14B

Using Figure 14.2, draw a marginal compensation curve such that the salesperson would choose the economically efficient level of effort.

Performance Quota

If the employer pays a 100% commission, Marie's marginal compensation would align with the employer's marginal revenue and she would choose the economically efficient 250 units of effort. But then her employer would make no profit.

| **Performance quota:** A minimum standard of performance, below which penalties apply. | Another way to induce the salesperson to choose the economically efficient level of effort is a *performance quota*. A **performance quota** is a minimum standard of performance, below which penalties apply. The penalties could include deferral of promotion, reduction in pay, or even dismissal. |

To apply a performance quota, the employer must identify the sales revenue that would result if the salesperson chose the economically efficient 250 units of effort. Suppose that 250 units of effort would generate sales revenue of $30,000. Then the employer should set the performance quota at $30,000 a month. Figure 14.3 shows the salesperson's marginal compensation curve with such a quota.

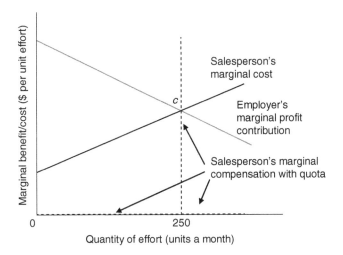

FIGURE 14.3 Performance quota.

Note: With a performance quota, the salesperson chooses 250 units of effort, which balances her marginal compensation with her marginal cost.

The salesperson's marginal compensation curve has three parts. Recall that the employer pays the salesperson a fixed monthly wage provided that she meets the quota; otherwise the salesperson will be dismissed. At 249 units of effort and below, the salesperson will be dismissed. Additional effort does not affect her earnings; hence, her marginal compensation is zero.

The incentive scheme pays the salesperson no extra for additional effort above 250 units. Accordingly, at 251 units of effort and above, the salesperson's marginal compensation also is zero. The marginal compensation, however, is very high at exactly 250 units of effort. An increase in effort from 249 to 250 units is just enough to satisfy the quota and hence allows the salesperson to retain her job.

Thus, the salesperson's marginal compensation curve follows the horizontal axis from 0 to 249 units of effort, spikes up at 250 units, and then follows the horizontal axis again at 251 units of effort and above. Therefore, the marginal compensation curve crosses the marginal cost at 250 units of effort. Accordingly, the salesperson chooses 250 units of effort.

A performance quota is a cost-effective way of inducing the salesperson to choose the economically efficient level of effort. It is cost-effective because it does not reward effort below or above the economically efficient level. It focuses the incentive at the economically efficient level of effort.

PROGRESS CHECK 14C

Suppose that 200 units of effort would generate $25,000 worth of sales. Using Figure 14.3, illustrate the salesperson's marginal compensation if the employer specifies a sales quota of $25,000 a month.

MONITORING TRUCK DRIVERS: ONBOARD COMPUTERS

Truck drivers operate independently and may travel far from base. The management of a trucking business may equip trucks with onboard computers to monitor drivers.

A study of the US trucking industry found significant patterns in the adoption of onboard computers. Only 7% of owner-operated trucks were equipped with onboard computers, as compared to 19% of employee-operated trucks. An owner-operator would not need to monitor himself, hence derives less benefit from an onboard computer.

Only 6% of trucks that operated at less than 50 miles from base were equipped with an onboard computer. By contrast, 19% of trucks that operated at distances of 100–200 miles had onboard computers. Truckers who operate at greater distance will be more difficult to monitor through personal supervision. Hence, management derives a greater benefit from installing an onboard computer to monitor such drivers.

Source: Thomas N. Hubbard, "The demand for monitoring technologies: the case of trucking," *Quarterly Journal of Economics*, Vol. 115, No. 2, May 2000, pp. 533–560.

WHEN INCENTIVES ARE TOO WEAK: REAL ESTATE AGENTS

Real estate agents are paid a percentage commission on the sales price. So both the agent and home seller would like to get a higher price. However, the agent incurs effort in selling, which the seller might not observe. So the agent is subject to moral hazard.

Consider, for instance, a $300,000 house. Assume that the brokerage fee is 6%, split equally between the seller's and buyer's agents. The seller's agent must split half of her fee with her agency, so she actual receives 1.5%.

Suppose that the agent could sell the house for $310,000 with more effort. The seller would get 94% of the additional $10,000, or $9,400. The agent would get 1.5% of the additional $10,000, or $150. Would the agent consider the extra effort worth $150?

Professor Steven Levitt studied the sales of 100,000 Chicago houses, some of which were owned and sold by the agents themselves. On average, the agent-owned homes were marketed for 10 days longer and achieved a 3% higher price. Not surprising, since an agent selling her own house would not be subject to moral hazard.

Source: Steven D. Levitt and Stephen J. Dubner, *Freakonomics*, London: HarperCollins, 2005, pp. 8–9.

4. Risk and Multiple Responsibilities

The combination of incentives and monitoring can help to resolve moral hazard. Here, we expand on the analysis of incentives to consider two serious side-effects of incentives. One is risk and the other is worse performance on other responsibilities.

Risk

Incentive schemes resolve moral hazard by linking compensation to some observable measure of the unobservable action. But what if the measure is affected by factors other than the unobservable action? Then the payments will depend on these other factors. A party who is subject to moral hazard and has imperfect information about these factors will face risk.

Consider, for instance, the salesperson's commission on monthly sales revenue. Besides the salesperson's effort, the actual sales may depend on the general state of the economy, competition and other factors. The salesperson may be uncertain about these other factors. So the commission scheme imposes risk on her. Risk will arise if the party subject to moral hazard is uncertain about her compensation.

To achieve economic efficiency, the incentive scheme must balance the incentive for effort with the cost of risk. The cost of risk depends on three factors:

*   *Impact of extraneous factors.* The extent of risk depends on the degree to which the extraneous factors affect the measure on which incentives are based. If the measure is sensitive to these extraneous factors and the factors are subject to wide swings, then the risk would be relatively large.
*   *Risk aversion.* If the party subject to moral hazard is risk neutral, then the risk imposes no cost. The cost of risk increases with the degree of risk aversion.
*   *Strength of incentive scheme.* Stronger incentives would induce the salesperson to increase her effort. However, stronger incentives would also impose a heavier burden of risk. For instance, with a higher commission, a larger part of the salesperson's income would depend on sales and vary with uncertain factors.

Generally, the incentive scheme should be stronger if the extraneous factors are weaker and the party subject to moral hazard is relatively less risk averse. Conversely, the incentives should be weaker if the extraneous factors have a stronger influence and risk aversion is higher.

> **Cost of risk** depends on:
> *   impact of extraneous factors;
> *   risk aversion;
> *   strength of incentive scheme.

Relative Performance Incentives

One way to resolve moral hazard without imposing risk is to use *relative performance incentives*. In the sales context, Marie's employer could pay each salesperson a fixed monthly wage plus a commission for sales revenue in excess of the average for all salespersons.

This incentive scheme would not penalize salespersons for extraneous factors like a bad economy. If the economy weakens, this would affect all the sales of all salespersons. If Marie exerts relatively more effort, she will still achieve higher sales than the average and hence will earn a larger commission.

By gauging performance on a relative basis, the incentive scheme cancels out the effect of extraneous factors to the extent that they affect all salespersons equally. This reduces the risk due to extraneous factors. Relative incentive schemes are most useful where common extraneous factors are important.

Multiple Responsibilities

In many situations, the party subject to moral hazard has multiple responsibilities. For instance, a sales representative may be responsible for initial sales as well as providing post-sales service. In a factory, production supervisors may be responsible for meeting output targets as well as maintaining quality.

Ideally, in these situations, an incentive scheme should resolve a balance of the multiple responsibilities. This means that there should be some investment in monitoring each of the unobservable actions and incentives based on the corresponding indicators.

Balancing multiple responsibilities becomes harder when it is more difficult to measure performance on some responsibilities than others. An incentive scheme may focus on a particular responsibility because that dimension is relatively easier to monitor. Recall that the scope of an incentive scheme depends on the available indicators of the unobservable action.

Suppose that the incentive scheme focuses on just one responsibility. Then it will induce better performance on that dimension but have the side-effect of aggravating the moral hazard with regard to the other responsibilities.

For instance, a factory wants its production supervisors to meet output targets as well as maintain product quality. Output is easy to measure. However, product quality may be difficult to measure. If the factory adopts a strong incentive scheme for output, the supervisors would tend to focus on output, and quality would fall.

Incentive schemes focus on actions for which there are reliable measures of performance. If, however, there are important responsibilities for which it is difficult to measure performance, then it may be better to adopt relatively weak performance incentives in general. A deliberate use of *weak incentives* is a way to achieve a balance among multiple responsibilities.

PROGRESS CHECK 14D

Suppose that a department store has switched its sales clerks from a fixed salary to a salary plus a commission on sales. How will this affect the sales clerks' incentive to process returns?

EVALUATING MANAGERIAL PERFORMANCE: MEDTRONIC

Headquartered in Minneapolis, Medtronic manufactures medical devices for a wide range of conditions, including cardiac rhythm disease, coronary artery and peripheral vascular disease, diabetes, and neurological illnesses. In 2010–2011, Medtronic earned net income of $3.10 billion (or $2.86 per share) on revenue of $15.93 billion.

One measure of the performance of a company is total shareholder return, which includes dividends and appreciation in the share price. Between 2006 and 2011, Medtronic yielded total shareholder return of −9.4%. If that were not bad enough, during the same period, the total shareholder return on the S&P 500 Health Care Equipment Index was 15%.

This example suggests that a reasonable way of evaluating companies is to measure their performance against that of other companies in the same industry. Relative performance evaluation cancels out background factors over which managers have no control and provides a more accurate measure of management's performance.

Indeed, Medtronic links incentive pay for senior managers to three measures: growth of earnings per share, and return on capital and growth of revenue relative to a peer group of manufacturers of pharmaceuticals and medical instruments.

Sources: Medtronic, Inc., proxy statement, July 15, 2011; Form 10K, 2011.

5. Holdup

Moral hazard arises when one party's actions affect but are not observed by another party. A related managerial issue is *holdup*. To explain holdup, suppose that Luna Supermarket engaged Mercury Logistics to deliver grocery orders. Their contract specified that Mercury should make two rounds of deliveries a day, at 12:00 noon and 4:00 pm. One day, however, Luna received so many orders that it asked Mercury to make a third round of deliveries. Mercury took the opportunity to demand twice the usual fee.

In this example, Mercury took advantage of Luna's special need to *hold up* the supermarket. A **holdup** is an action to exploit another party's dependence. Holdup is distinct from moral hazard in that it does not require asymmetric information. For example, when Luna requested the extra delivery, Mercury openly demanded a higher fee. Luna could clearly observe Mercury's action – there was no asymmetry of information.

> **Holdup:** An action to exploit another party's dependence.

Mercury's holdup has implications beyond the exceptional fee that Luna paid on one occasion. The potential for holdup in the future would lead Luna to take precautions. For instance, Luna might limit the number of delivery orders that it accepts, or it might even establish its own delivery service. These precautions would either reduce Luna's revenues or increase its costs.

Generally, whenever there is the potential for holdup, other parties will take precautions to avoid dependence. These precautions either reduce benefits or increase costs. So, the potential for holdup reduces overall value and economic efficiency. This means that there is an opportunity to add value and increase profit by resolving the holdup.

Specific Investments

One particular type of precaution against holdup is worth emphasizing. It is to reduce specific investments. Suppose that, to optimize delivery time and fuel, Mercury has installed a computerized route planning system. Clients must prepare delivery orders using specialized software.

Specificity: The percentage of an investment that will be lost if the asset is switched to another use.

In this example, acquiring, installing, and learning to use the delivery system is an investment by Luna that is specific to its relationship with Mercury. The **specificity** of an investment in an asset is the percentage that will be lost if the asset is switched to another use.

For instance, suppose that Luna must spend $4,500 to acquire the delivery system, comprising software and a computer, and $500 on training. If Luna switches to another logistics provider, it can reuse only the computer, worth $1,000. It would have to write off the software and training. So, the specificity of the investment in the delivery system is $(4,500 + 500 - 1,000)/(4,500 + 500) = 80\%$.

Any asset, whether physical or human, can be specific. Learning to use an organization's systems is a specific human investment by the employee. The training that organizations provide to employees is a specific investment. If the employees quit, the organization will have to write off the investment.

The potential for holdup will deter all forms of specific investments. If holdup could be prevented, the relevant parties would increase specific investments and so add value and increase profit.

Incomplete Contracts

Suppose that the contract between Luna and Mercury had specified conditions under which Luna could request an additional delivery and the corresponding fee. Then Mercury would not have been able to hold up Luna. Generally, the scope for a holdup depends on the extent to which the contract between the parties is *incomplete*.

Complete contract: Specifies the actions of all parties under every possible contingency.

A **complete contract** specifies the actions of all parties under every possible contingency. By contrast, a contract is incomplete if it does not specify the actions of the parties in some contingency. The actions specified by the contract possibly include payments.

It would be extremely costly for Luna and Mercury to agree and prepare a complete contract. A huge number of contingencies must be covered: the need for a fourth delivery, the possibility that Mercury's truck may break down, and the possibility of an earthquake are just a few. Rather than consider every such detail, the two parties will probably agree on an incomplete contract.

So, in practice, all contracts are incomplete, and deliberately so. The issue is then how incomplete the contract should be. Generally, the appropriate degree of incompleteness depends on two factors:

- *Potential benefits and costs.* The larger the stakes, the more the parties should invest in preparing the contract. Luna Supermarket sells dairy products and small stationery items. Dairy products account for a large part of Luna's sales and are much more important than small stationery items. Accordingly, Luna should write a more detailed contract with its supplier of dairy products than its supplier of stationery.

> A contract should be more detailed if:
> - potential benefits and costs are larger;
> - possible contingencies are more serious.

- *Possible contingencies.* Dairy products are perishable and sold in high volume, hence Luna needs frequent supply. Moreover, the supply of dairy products is relatively more vulnerable to disruptions by bad weather, transportation problems, and labor disputes. So, Luna needs more assurance about the supply of dairy products, and so will write a more detailed contract.

PROGRESS CHECK 14E

What factors should the parties consider in deciding how detailed a contract to prepare?

AVOIDING SPECIFICITY IN ELECTRIC POWER INVESTMENTS: FLOATING POWER PLANTS

Plagued by violence and instability, Iraq faces many challenges, one of which is to provide a reliable supply of electricity. Many Iraqi businesses and families have bought generators to provide a necessary but costly backup supply.

In 2007, the Turkish energy group, Karadeniz Holding AŞ, initiated the "Power of Friendship" project to supply 615 megawatts (MW) of electricity to Iraq. Karadeniz bought secondhand generating sets in China and Dubai. It then arranged to overhaul the generators and install them on four vessels at shipyards in Turkey and Singapore.

The *Doğan Bey*, with a capacity of 126.4 MW, and *Kaya Bey*, with a capacity of 216.4 MW, are moored at the ports of Um Qasr and Al Zubayr, and supply electricity to the Basra region in south-eastern Iraq.

Source: "Wärtsilä receives O&M agreement for Iraqi floating power plants," Wärtsilä Corporation, trade and technical press release, May 12, 2010.

6. Ownership

Ownership: Rights to residual control, which are those rights that have not been contracted away.

Holdup can be resolved by changing the *ownership* of the relevant assets. **Ownership** means the rights to *residual control*, which are those rights that have not been contracted away.

To explain the meaning of residual control, suppose that Saturn Properties borrowed $5 million from a bank to develop a supermarket, which it has rented to Luna on a five-year lease. The bank has a mortgage against the building. This means that, if Saturn fails to make the loan payments on time, the bank will have the legal right to take possession of the building. This is a right that Saturn contracted away to get the loan.

Saturn has also entered into a five-year lease with Luna Supermarket. Through the lease, Luna has the right to use the property for five years. This is another right that Saturn has contracted away.

As owner, Saturn has residual control. This means that it has all rights except those contracted away. For instance, it may have the right to enter into a second mortgage on the building, and it has the right to use the building after the expiration of Luna's lease.

A transfer of ownership means shifting the rights of residual control to another party. Suppose that Luna buys ownership of the supermarket building from Saturn. Then Luna would have all the rights that previously belonged to Saturn.

Residual Income

Residual income: Income remaining after payment of all other claims.

One dimension of residual control is particularly worth emphasizing. The owner of an asset also has the right to receive the **residual income** from the asset, which is the income remaining after payment of all other claims.

To illustrate, suppose that Saturn collects $100,000 a month in rent from Luna. Saturn's expenses include $50,000 in interest and principal to the bank as well as $20,000 in taxes and other expenses. As owner of the building, Saturn receives the residual income of $100,000 − $50,0000 − $20,000 = $30,000.

The important implication is that, as the recipient of the residual income, the owner gets the full benefit of changes in income and costs. For instance, if Saturn can raise the rent by $5,000 to $105,000, then its profit would increase by $5,000 to $35,000. Similarly, if Saturn can reduce expenses by $2,000, then its profit would increase by $2,000 to $32,000.

So the owner has the full incentive to maximize the value of the asset. Other parties would not have the same incentive. If information about their actions is asymmetric, they would be subject to moral hazard relative to the owner. Even in the absence of asymmetric information, they may hold up the owner and exploit the owner's dependence.

Vertical Integration

As introduced in Chapter 11, **vertical integration** is the combination of the assets for two successive stages of production under a common ownership. With common ownership, the owner would have full incentive to maximize the value of the combined assets. By contrast, with separate ownership, the owner of each asset would only maximize the value of its asset, and possibly at the expense of the owner of the other asset.

> **Vertical integration:** The combination of assets for two successive stages of production under common ownership.

Vertical integration is downstream or upstream, depending on whether it involves the acquisition of assets for a stage of production nearer to or further from the final consumer. Suppose, for instance, that a food manufacturer acquires a supermarket. Since the supermarket operates a stage of production nearer to the final consumer, this is an example of downstream vertical integration. By contrast, if the food manufacturer were to acquire a dairy farm, it would be vertically integrating upstream.

The decision to vertically integrate upstream is often characterized as the choice of whether to "make or buy." The food manufacturer can either *buy* milk from farmers or establish its own farm to *make* the input for its production.

Similarly, the decision to vertically integrate downstream may be characterized as the choice of whether to "sell or use." The dairy farmer can either *sell* its products to food manufacturers or establish its own factory and *use* its milk as input into production of processed foods.

Vertical integration or disintegration changes the ownership of assets, and hence alters the distribution of the rights to residual control and residual income. As we explain in the next section, these in turn affect the degree of moral hazard and the potential for holdup.

PROGRESS CHECK 14F

Explain the difference between upstream and downstream vertical integration.

CONTRACT AND OWNERSHIP: THE NORTH EUROPEAN GAS PIPELINE

Gazprom, one of the world's largest energy producers, initiated the North European Gas Pipeline to transport gas from central Russia under the Baltic Sea to western Europe. The total investment is €4.6 billion. Of course, once the pipeline is completed, the costs of construction are sunk. So, Gazprom is vulnerable to holdup by the customers for its gas.

Before construction, in December 2005, Gazprom established the North European Gas Pipeline Company with two German companies, Wintershall, a unit of BASF, and E.ON Ruhrgas, as minority shareholders to build the pipeline. Subsequently, the company was renamed Nord Stream, and the German shareholders sold part of their shares to the leading gas suppliers, Gasunie of the Netherlands and GDF/Suez of France.

Soon afterward, Gazprom locked in the key German customers with long-term contracts. In January 2006, Wintershall signed a 20-year contract to buy 8 billion cubic meters of gas a year from 2010 to 2030. Then, in August 2006, E.ON signed a 15-year contract to buy 4 billion cubic meters a year from 2020 to 2035.

Sources: Nord Stream AG; "Like it or not, many countries are locked in to Gazprom," *New York Times*, January 5, 2006.

7. Organizational Architecture

Chapter 1 discussed the vertical and horizontal boundaries of an organization. An oil company that produces crude, refines it, and markets gasoline is more vertically integrated than one that only produces crude. A media organization that publishes newspapers and provides cable television and broadband service has wider horizontal boundaries than one that specializes in cable television service.

Vertical and horizontal boundaries are just two aspects of the organizational architecture, which comprises the distribution of ownership, incentive schemes, and monitoring systems. From the viewpoint of managerial economics, the design of organizational architecture depends on a balance among four issues:

> Organizational architecture depends on a balance among:
>
> - holdup;
> - moral hazard;
> - internal market power;
> - economies of scale, scope, and experience.

- holdup,
- moral hazard,
- internal market power, and
- economies of scale, scope, and experience,

and the mechanisms by which these issues may be resolved.

We have already discussed specific ways of resolving holdup and moral hazard. Here, we consider how ownership will affect holdup, moral hazard, internal market power, and economies of scale, scope, and experience.

Holdup

How would changing the ownership of the relevant assets resolve holdup? Recall that when Luna requested an additional delivery at short notice, Mercury extracted a higher fee. What if Luna had an in-house delivery service? To make the additional delivery, it might have to order a driver to work overtime. The driver could demand a special overtime payment. By doing so, however, the driver runs the risk that Luna may replace her with another worker.

If the driver strikes, the cost imposed on Luna is the cost of replacing the driver at short notice. This is less costly than replacing the truck and driver which would be necessary if an outsourced delivery service should withhold its services.

As this example suggests, even an employee can engage in holdup. However, an employee is less likely than an external contractor to engage in holdup and would impose lower costs if she did so. The reason is that the external contractor owns the assets necessary to provide the service. Residual control of an asset includes the right to withhold its services. Hence, an external contractor has the power to withhold the services of its assets.

By contrast, an employee has no such power since the assets on which she works belong to the employer. With less power, the employee is less likely to behave opportunistically and engage in holdup and would impose lower cost if she did so. Accordingly, vertical integration can mitigate the potential for holdup.

Moral Hazard

Changes in ownership also affect the degree of moral hazard. If Luna Supermarket vertically integrates into the delivery business, it must engage drivers. Then it would change from dealing with an owner who supplies a service to dealing with an employee. As we showed above, employees are subject to moral hazard.

Generally, the employer's marginal profit contribution exceeds the worker's marginal compensation. Since the worker chooses effort according to her marginal compensation, she chooses less than the economically efficient level of effort.

By contrast, suppose that the employee owns the business. Then the worker receives the residual income. Hence, if the worker exerts an additional unit of effort, she will receive the entire marginal profit contribution. If she reduces effort by one unit, she will suffer the entire reduction in the profit contribution. Thus, when balancing her marginal benefit with the marginal cost, the worker will choose the economically efficient level of effort. Giving ownership to the worker will resolve the moral hazard.

This explains why many businesses pay senior managers through shares and stock options. To the extent that these managers have a share of ownership, their interests will be more closely aligned with those of the business, which reduces the degree of the moral hazard.

Vertical integration changes ownership. Since an employee is subject to relatively greater moral hazard than an owner, vertical integration increases the degree of moral hazard.

Internal Market Power

Changes in ownership will affect the monopoly power of internal sources of inputs and monopsony power of internal users of outputs. If Luna establishes its own delivery service, it will prefer using its own delivery service to engaging an external contractor. This is a reasonable policy to the extent that some of the costs of the in-house delivery service are sunk.

The preference in favor of an internal provider, however, means creating an internal monopoly. Chapter 8 showed that a seller with market power would restrict production and raise price. An internal provider may also use its market power to raise its price. Then the organization as a whole will find that the cost of internal provision may rise above the price charged by external contractors. This higher cost must be borne by the organization.

One way of resolving an internal monopoly is a policy to outsource whenever the internal provider's cost exceeds that of external sources. *Outsourcing* is the purchase of services or supplies from external sources. It subjects internal providers to the discipline of market competition, and so limits the extent to which the cost of internal provision diverges from the competitive level.

Similarly, if a business produces an input that it uses internally for downstream production, the downstream user may acquire monopsony power. Chapter 8 showed that a buyer with market power would restrict purchases to depress the price. A policy to sell externally whenever the external price is higher than the internal transfer price can resolve the internal monopsony power.

Economies of Scale, Scope, and Experience

Finally, changes in ownership affect the extent of economies of scale, scope, and experience. Recall from Chapter 7 that, if there are economies of scale, then the average cost of provision will be lower with a larger scale. Typically, an internal provider will operate at a smaller scale than an external contractor. It then is necessary to consider how the average cost varies with the scale of production.

For instance, Luna Supermarket's deliveries may occupy a truck and driver for only four hours a day. If Luna were to set up its own delivery service, its utilization of the assets and human resources would be relatively low. By contrast, an external delivery contractor may get 10 or 12 hours of work per day from its equipment and personnel. The external contractor would have better capacity utilization and hence a lower average cost. To this extent, it would be less costly to purchase the service from the external contractor.

We can also illustrate the significance of scale economies by comparing a supermarket's need for delivery service with that for armored truck service to convey cash and checks. While some supermarkets own a delivery service, they are not likely to own an armored truck service. It would hardly be efficient for a supermarket to buy an armored truck that makes one daily trip to the bank.

The analysis of ownership and the experience curve are similar to those for economies of scale. If the business expects a relatively low cumulative volume, it would be high up on the experience curve. By contrast, a specialized provider might consolidate sufficient orders from multiple users that it can push further down the experience curve and realize lower average cost.

From Chapter 7, if there are economies of scope across two products, then the total cost of production will be lower when the two products are produced together than when they are produced separately. Economies of scope are a key reason for the growth of supermarkets at the expense of traditional stores. A supermarket can supply items at a relatively lower cost than more specialized stores such as bakeries, groceries, and newsstands.

Economies of scope are the major factor in favor of wide horizontal organizational boundaries. However, for an individual organization, economies of scope have countervailing effects. If it already produces one item, then it can reduce total cost by producing the other one as well. However, if it does not already produce either item, then economies of scope imply that it should outsource both.

Balance

The appropriate organizational architecture depends on a balance among the four issues – the scope for holdup, the degree of moral hazard, internal market power, and the extent of economies of scale, scope, and experience – and on other ways to resolve these issues.

Specifically, holdup can be resolved through more detailed contracts, moral hazard can be resolved through incentives and monitoring, and internal market power can be resolved through outsourcing and external sales. Generally, the economically efficient solution will involve a mix of all policies.

Let us illustrate the application of this framework with two examples. One concerns the vertical boundaries of the organization, while the other concerns its horizontal boundaries. The two examples show that the same framework can be applied to address both vertical and horizontal dimensions of organizational architecture.

A function that many organizations consider whether to "make or buy" is information technology services. As Figure 14.4 shows, this decision resolves into a balance among four issues. Two factors favor the decision to "make." One is

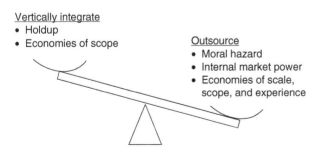

FIGURE 14.4 Vertical integration.

Notes: In favor of vertical integration: holdup and economies of scope. In favor of outsourcing: moral hazard, internal market power, and economies of scale, scope, and experience.

the extent to which the potential for holdup cannot be cost-effectively reduced through more detailed contracts. The other is the extent to which the internal provider enjoys economies of scope in information technology services.

There are three factors in favor of deciding to "buy." One is the extent to which the moral hazard of the internal information technology group cannot be cost-effectively resolved through incentive schemes and monitoring systems. Another is the extent to which internal monopoly power cannot be cost-effectively redressed through outsourcing. A third is the extent to which the internal unit will lack economies of scale, scope, or experience in providing information technology services.

Decisions whether to "make or buy" concern the vertical boundaries of the organization. An organization must also consider its horizontal boundaries. For instance, should a bus operator also be in the trucking business? As the businesses are not vertically related, holdup and internal market power are not major issues. The key factor in favor of owning both businesses is economies of scope, while the factor against is the extent to which moral hazard in the trucking unit cannot be cost-effectively resolved through incentive schemes and monitoring systems.

PROGRESS CHECK 14G

What are the four issues to consider in the decision whether to "make or buy"?

NISSAN: SECOND-SOURCING BATTERIES

Projecting huge growth in the demand for electric cars, Nissan set up plants at Zama (Japan), Sunderland (Britain), and Smyrna (Tennessee) with capacity to manufacture up to 500,000 batteries a year.

In late 2014, Nissan reportedly reviewed its strategy for batteries. The demand for electric cars had grown much less than projected. The previous year, Nissan and strategic partner, Renault, sold only 67,000 electric cars.

Another problem was Nissan's cost of producing batteries. A company executive remarked: "We set out to be a leader in battery manufacturing but it turned out to be less competitive than we'd wanted . . . . We're still between six months and a year behind LG in price-performance terms."

In the strategic review, one option was for Nissan to concentrate production in Japan and sell the British and American facilities to LG Chem (South Korea). Renault pressed Nissan to adopt dual sourcing and buy batteries from LG Chem.

Source: "Nissan faces battery plant cuts as electric car hopes fade," *Reuters*, September 15, 2014.

BOEING'S CHARLESTON PURCHASE: NOT ACCORDING TO PLAN

In a major departure from previous strategy, the then Chairman and CEO, Harry Stonecipher, and the then head of Commercial Airplanes, Alan Mulally, decided to radically outsource design and construction of the 787. Boeing would focus on final assembly. The new strategy would reduce the assets required to support production, and so boost Boeing's return on net assets.

Boeing contracted with Vought Aircraft Industries to design and build two sections of the 787's rear fuselage at Vought's factory in Charleston, South Carolina. It also contracted with an adjacent joint venture between Vought and Alenia of Italy to join the various fuselage sections – the two rear sections built by Vought, two mid-sections built in Italy by Alenia, and a section built by Kawasaki in Japan. The joint venture would then send the assembled fuselage to Everett for final assembly.

However, Vought faced technical and financial difficulties. Vought's owner, the private-equity investor Carlyle Group, refused to increase its investment and instead sought to sell the company. Vought's CEO, Elmer Doty, explained that "the financial demands of this program are clearly growing beyond what a company our size can support."

In 2008, Boeing bought Vought's share of the joint venture with Alenia. Finally, in July 2009, to resolve the holdup, Boeing again resorted to vertical integration and bought the Charleston factory from Vought at a cost of $1 billion.

Source: "Boeing's buy of 787 plant will cost $1B," *Seattle Times*, July 7, 2009.

KEY TAKEAWAYS

- Moral hazard arises if one party's actions affect but are not observed by another party.
- Resolve moral hazard through monitoring and incentives.
- Incentives create risk, the cost of which increases with the impact of the extraneous factors, risk aversion, and strength of the incentives.
- For better performance on multiple responsibilities which vary in their ease of measurement, use weaker incentives.
- Holdup is action to exploit another party's dependence.
- Resolve holdup through detailed contracts, with more detail if potential benefits and costs are larger, and if contingencies have larger impact.
- Ownership is the rights to residual control, which are those rights that have not been contracted away.
- Vertical integration is the combination of the assets for two successive stages of production under a common ownership.
- Apply organizational architecture to balance holdup, moral hazard, internal market power, and economies of scale, scope, and experience.

REVIEW QUESTIONS

1. In the context of your business or organization, explain the meaning of organizational architecture.
2. Explain the moral hazard in the following situation. Leah has just bought comprehensive insurance on her car that covers loss and damage for any reason, including theft. Her insurer is concerned that she may take fewer precautions against theft.
3. By considering benefits and costs to the various parties, explain why resolving moral hazard can be profitable.
4. Why is it better to pay a real estate broker by commission, whereby she receives a percentage of the selling price of the property, rather than an hourly rate?
5. Your compensation package includes shares of the company, which vest after three years. Explain the risk that you bear.
6. Explain how a taxi company can structure incentives based on relative performance to motivate its drivers to maintain their taxis carefully and avoid breakdowns.
7. A secretary's job includes typing letters and other responsibilities. Comment on a proposal to pay a secretary according to the number of letters that he types.
8. Maria is a pilot. Which of the following investments by her is relatively more specific to the airline that she works for? (a) An executive MBA program. (b) Training on the airline's flight management system.
9. Why do businesses enter into contracts that are deliberately incomplete?
10. In the context of an incorporated business, explain the meaning of: (a) residual control; (b) residual income.
11. Give an example of a holdup. Explain how this will induce the affected parties to avoid specific investments.
12. How does the potential for holdup reduce the value of transactions and relationships?
13. A car manufacturer has experienced holdup by its supplier of electronics. Should the car manufacturer produce the electronics internally?
14. How can outsourcing resolve the monopoly power of an internal supplier?
15. Explain the roles of economies of scope in decisions about horizontal integration.

DISCUSSION QUESTIONS

1. The National University of Singapore provides outpatient medical insurance to faculty and staff. The plan covers the entire bill for treatment and medicine at an approved general practitioner subject to a copayment of S$5.
   (a) Construct a diagram with quantity of healthcare (including treatment and medicines) on the horizontal axis and marginal benefit and marginal cost of healthcare on the vertical axis. Draw the patient's marginal benefit and marginal cost, and the insurer's marginal cost.

(b) Compare the level of healthcare that the patient would choose with the level that maximizes the patient's benefit less the insurer's cost.

(c) How does the S$5 copayment affect the patient's choice between (i) a generic drug that costs $5 and (ii) a branded drug that costs $50?

(d) Suppose that the University replaces the S$5 copayment with a 10% copayment. Use your diagram to illustrate how that would affect the patient's choice of healthcare.

2. Mapletree Commercial Trust owns Singapore's largest mall, VivoCity. The Trust has contracted with Mapletree Investments to manage the mall. The manager is responsible for the carpark, as well as cleaning, security, and other common services. The mall's retail tenants pay a three-part rental: in 2010, 86% was fixed, and 13% was based on the retailer's sales revenue, while the remainder comprised service charges and contributions to advertising and promotion. (Source: Mapletree Commercial Trust, Prospectus, April 18, 2011.)

(a) How is the manager of VivoCity subject to moral hazard relative to its tenants?

(b) How does the variable payment align the interests of landlord and tenant?

(c) Ideally, should the variable payment be based on the tenant's gross revenue or net revenue (gross revenue less cost of goods sold)?

(d) Mapletree Investments is a developer of commercial and industrial real estate. It sells completed projects to Mapletree Commercial Trust. Discuss the asymmetry of information between the two entities.

3. Pension funds and trusts may be limited to investing in securities of particular credit rating, e.g., AAA. To appeal to such investors, investment banks that issue structured products need to meet the required credit rating. The credit rating agencies, Fitch Ratings, Moody's Investor Services, and Standard & Poor's Ratings Services, will rate a security and, after issuance, continue to update the rating over the life of the security. The agency charges the issuer a fee for rating as well as a fee for updating.

(a) Consider the managers of an investment bank which plans to issue a structured product. Would they be more concerned about the initial rating or updating?

(b) How does your answer to (a) depend on the turnover of investment bank managers?

(c) What is the incentive for the rating agency to rate a structured product as AAA?

(d) Who would be more affected by inaccuracy in updating: the issuer or the rating agency?

4. Mayo Clinic, a non-profit provider of healthcare, whose motto is "the needs of the patient come first," pays doctors a salary rather than a fee for service. Dr John C. Lewin, chief executive of the American College of Cardiology, argues that salaried doctors can provide better healthcare and lamented that most US healthcare is "divided between small practices and community hospitals that aren't linked together with incentives to coordinate care." (Source: "A new way to pay physicians," *NYTimes.com*, September 23, 2009.)

(a) Consider the conventional model of healthcare which pays doctors according to the amount of treatment that they provide. Using a relevant figure (with hypothetical demand and marginal cost), explain how the doctor will over-treat the patient.

(b) If doctors are paid a fixed salary, how would that affect their incentive to over-treat?

(c) Dr Lewin believes that a vertically integrated system provides better healthcare. Suppose that a hospital integrates with a group of heart specialists. Explain the moral hazard of the doctors relative to the hospital.

(d) Following the integration in (c), how should the hospital motivate the doctors?

5. Alibaba, which operates Taobao and Tmall, is the world's largest online marketplace. In the 15 months before its initial public offering, it awarded employees 68.5 million units of restricted shares and options for 21.8 million shares, with a total value exceeding $5 billion. (Source: "Alibaba and the kingdom of sumptuous stock grants," *Fortune*, September 12, 2014.)

(a) Using a relevant diagram, illustrate the company's marginal profit contribution, and a senior executive's marginal compensation and marginal cost as a function of the senior executive's effort.

(b) Use the diagram to explain how the stock options are intended to motivate senior executives of Alibaba.

(c) The Alibaba executives also receive a salary from the company. How do the stock options affect the risk that they bear?

(d) Explain why Alibaba should condition incentive compensation on Alibaba's performance relative to competitors.

6. Boeing contracted with Vought Aircraft Industries to design and build two sections of the 787's rear fuselage at Charleston, South Carolina. Boeing also contracted with an adjacent joint venture between Vought and Alenia of Italy to assemble fuselage sections. Facing technical and financial difficulties, Vought's owner, the Carlyle Group, refused to increase its investment and instead sought to sell the company. In 2008, Boeing bought Vought's share of the joint venture with Alenia, and then, in July 2009, Boeing bought the Charleston factory from Vought at a cost of $1 billion. (Source: "Boeing's buy of 787 plant will cost $1B," *Seattle Times*, July 7, 2009.)

(a) Explain the mutual dependence between Boeing and Vought.

(b) Explain Carlyle Group's refusal to increase investment in terms of holdup.

(c) The potential for holdup by a subcontractor may lead a manufacturer to contract with two subcontractors, a practice called "second-sourcing." Explain why second-sourcing may be inefficient in terms of the experience curve.

(d) Suppose that the Carlyle Group had a higher discount rate (shorter time horizon) than Alenia. Would that explain why the Carlyle Group but not Alenia tried to exit their Boeing contracts?

(e) The Carlyle Group approached various potential buyers. Why would Boeing be willing to pay more than other potential buyers?

7. The €4.6 billion North European Gas Pipeline transports natural gas from central Russia to Germany. Gazprom first conceived of the project in 1997. In January 2006, Gazprom signed a 20-year contract with Wintershall, a unit of BASF, to sell 8 billion cubic meters of gas a year from 2010 to 2030. Then, in August 2006, Gazprom signed a 15-year contract with E.ON to sell 4 billion cubic meters a year from 2020 to 2035.

    (a) Why was it important for Gazprom to sign these contracts before commencing construction of the pipeline?

    (b) Would it be just as good for Gazprom to sign an initial five-year contract with the German customers and then renew the contract later on?

    (c) Should the contracts specify the price of the gas or leave it for later negotiation?

    (d) The German companies also bought shares in the pipeline. How would this help to resolve the potential for holdup?

8. Wärtsilä, with headquarters in Helsinki, Finland, advertises the operating flexibility of its electric power generating plants: "If you need to relocate, modular construction will make the move easier. Or you can choose a Wärtsilä floating power plant or a Wärtsilä Power Module and become truly mobile."

    (a) How is the specificity of an investment related to sunk costs?

    (b) Explain the concept of specific investments in relation to building an electric power generation facility.

    (c) Is the problem of holdup more or less serious for investments with a longer payback period?

    (d) Do you expect the demand among investors for floating power plants to be greater or less in countries with high political risk? Explain why.

9. Nissan and NEC jointly established Automotive Energy Supply Corporation (AESC) to manufacture high-performance lithium-ion batteries. AESC invested over $1 billion in new plants at Zama (Japan), Sunderland (Britain), and Smyrna (Tennessee) with capacity to manufacture up to 500,000 batteries a year. The Sunderland and Smyrna plants are co-located with Nissan car manufacturing. Nissan contracted with NEC to buy electrodes for 220,000 units of 24 kWh batteries a year. However, the demand for electric cars grew less than projected. In 2013, Nissan and strategic partner, Renault, sold just 67,000 electric cars. Further, AESC's cost of production was higher than that of external competitor LG Chem of South Korea. (Source: "Nissan faces battery plant cuts as electric car hopes fade," *Reuters*, September 15, 2014.)

    (a) Evaluate the specificity of AESC's investment in the Sunderland and Smyrna plants.

    (b) What holdup problem does NEC face?

    (c) Why would Nissan contract to buy a minimum number of electrodes each year from NEC?

    (d) How do (i) economies of scale; and (ii) the experience curve explain why AESC cannot produce as cheaply as LG Chem?

    (e) In light of (d), explain the costs and benefits of vertical integration.

You are the consultant!

Consider the architecture of your organization. How can your organization add value by:

(a) outsourcing/insourcing,
(b) revising incentive schemes,
(c) adjusting ownership?

Notes

1   The following discussion is based, in part, on "The affair that grounded Stonecipher," *Business Week*, March 8, 2005; "787 delay could wind up costing Boeing $1 billion," *Seattle Times*, October 25, 2007; "Boeing's buy of 787 plant will cost $1B," *Seattle Times*, July 7, 2009; "A 'prescient' warning to Boeing on 787 trouble," *Seattle Times*, February 5, 2011; "Boeing 787 Dreamliner," Wikipedia (accessed August 21, 2011).

15

Regulation

1. Introduction

North Delhi Power Limited (NDPL), a joint venture of the Tata Power Company (51%) and Government of Delhi (49%), has the monopoly franchise to distribute electricity in the north and northwest areas of India's capital. It serves 1.2 million customers in a population of 5 million. In 2010, NDPL earned net profit after tax of 3.5 billion Indian rupees on revenue of 34.0 billion rupees.[1]

Between 2002 and 2011, NDPL reduced losses of electricity due to theft and technical reasons from 74% to just 14%. Under the terms of its franchise, NDPL splits the additional revenue from reduction in losses between its shareholders and customers.

Historically, NDPL specialized in distribution of electricity. It buys over 1,100 megawatts (MW) of electricity on long-term contracts from Pragati Power Corporation and other generators of electricity. In a new initiative toward vertical integration, NDPL is building a 108 MW gas-based combined cycle power generation plant at Rithala in North Delhi. NDPL justified the new plant as "obviat[ing] the need for an equivalent amount of expensive bilateral power."

The Delhi Electricity Regulatory Commission regulates the electricity industry and limits profits to a maximum return on equity of 14% or 16%. The maximum allowed return differs by the provider's function (generation, distribution, or transmission) and has varied over time. In 2007, Pragati Power petitioned the Commission to increase its approved equity. However, NDPL challenged the proposed increase and the Commission rejected the petition.

Why did the Delhi government award NDPL a monopoly franchise to distribute electricity? Should the government allow NDPL's move toward vertical integration? Why does the Delhi Electricity Regulatory Commission limit the return on equity of electricity providers? Why did NDPL challenge Pragati Power's petition to increase its approved equity?

This chapter addresses the role of the government in situations where buyers and sellers, acting independently and selfishly, do not equalize marginal benefit and marginal cost. So, the invisible hand fails – the allocation of resources is not economically efficient.

If private action fails to resolve the economic inefficiency, then there may be a role for government regulation. If the government can resolve the divergence between marginal benefit and marginal cost, then it will increase net benefit for society.

To understand the role of government regulation, we consider the various possible sources of economic inefficiency: market power, externalities, and asymmetric information. For each source of economic inefficiency, we analyze the conditions under which the government should intervene and the appropriate form of regulation.

In businesses with significant economies of scale or scope relative to demand, it may be economically efficient to award a monopoly franchise. Then the government must regulate the monopoly's exercise of market power. The Delhi government chose to regulate NDPL's profits according to a maximum return on equity.

Under regulation of return on equity, the regulated business would seek to increase its approved equity. The larger its approved equity, then the higher will be its allowed profit. This explains why Pragati Power petitioned to increase its approved equity, and why NDPL, which buys electricity from Pragati, opposed the petition.

Besides market power, the invisible hand may also fail because of information asymmetries and externalities. This chapter also discusses how the government can resolve asymmetric information through regulation of disclosure, conduct, and business structure, and resolve externalities through standards and user fees.

Regulated industries serve both businesses and consumers. Hence, as NDPL's opposition to Pragati's petition illustrates, it is important for businesses as well as consumers to understand the basis and methods of government regulation.

2. Natural Monopoly

A market is a **natural monopoly** if the average cost of production is minimized with a single supplier. Essentially, economies of scale or scope are large relative to the market demand. For instance, electricity is distributed through a network of cables. Consider a town with two competing electricity distributors with separate infrastructure. Then two sets of cables would run into every home, office, and factory. In the electricity distribution industry, allowing competition would result in wasteful duplication.

> **Natural monopoly:**
> A market where
> the average cost of
> production is minimized
> with a single supplier.

Other examples of natural monopolies include broadband service, distribution of gas and water, and sewage collection. In all of these markets, the economies of scale may be large relative to the market demand. So, the average cost of production is lowest when there is only one supplier.

If a market is a natural monopoly, the government should prohibit competition and allow only a single supplier. This would establish the conditions for production at the lowest average cost.

The monopoly, however, might exploit its exclusive right to raise its price at the expense of its customers. The increase in the price would force the marginal benefit above the marginal cost. Accordingly, to ensure economic efficiency, the government must control the monopoly. The government can do this in two ways:

* The government itself can own the business, and operate at the economically efficient level.
* Award a monopoly franchise to a commercial enterprise and subject the monopoly to regulation.

Government Ownership

In principle, government ownership and operation is the simplest and most direct way to ensure economic efficiency. However, in practice, government-owned enterprises tend to be relatively inefficient, and so government ownership and operation fails to achieve economic efficiency.

> Controlling monopoly:
> * government ownership and operation; or
> * regulate commercial enterprise.

One source of inefficiency is that government-owned enterprises are prone to be coopted by employees, so that the enterprise serves its employees rather than its customers. Some symptoms of employee control are high wages and overstaffing, both of which inflate the cost of production.

Another source of inefficiency is that government-owned enterprises depend on the government for investment funds. The government budget must finance everything from social welfare to military equipment. A government-owned enterprise must compete with other priorities for an allocation from the budget and may not be able to secure the economically efficient level of investment.

Owing to the limitations of government ownership and operation, a worldwide trend has been to *privatize* government-owned enterprises. **Privatization** means transferring ownership from the government to the private sector. It does not necessarily mean allowing competition. Indeed, many privatized enterprises are monopolies in their markets.

> **Privatization:** Transfer of ownership from government to private sector.

Price Regulation

Recall from Chapter 6 that the provision of a good or service will be economically efficient at the level where marginal benefit equals marginal cost. Suppose that the government awards an exclusive franchise for electricity distribution to Jupiter Power. Jupiter's costs include a fixed cost and a constant marginal cost of $40 per megawatt-hour (MWh). Figure 15.1 shows the cost of distribution and the demand for electricity.

Suppose that the government requires the provider to set its price equal to its marginal cost and to meet the quantity demanded. Then, referring to Figure 15.1, at every possible quantity, the price will be the marginal cost. In effect, the government's policy forces the provider to behave like a perfectly competitive supplier. This policy is called **marginal cost pricing**.

> **Marginal cost pricing:** The provider must set the price equal to the marginal cost and supply the quantity demanded.

The demand curve crosses the marginal cost curve at point *a*. If Jupiter sets a price of $40 per megawatt-hour, the market would demand a quantity of 10,000 MWh. Under marginal cost pricing regulation, Jupiter must supply the quantity demanded; hence, it must produce 10,000 MWh. Now, each customer buys the quantity that balances its marginal benefit with the

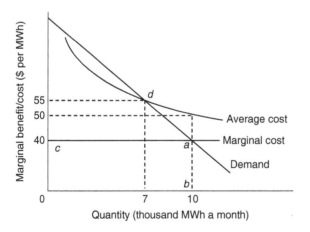

FIGURE 15.1 Price regulation.

Notes: The demand curve crosses the marginal cost curve at *a*. Under marginal cost pricing, the provider sets a price of $40 per MWh and the market quantity demanded is 10,000 MWh a month. The demand curve crosses the average cost curve at *d*. Under average cost pricing, the provider sets a price of per $55 MWh and the market quantity demanded is 7,000 MWh.

price. Hence, marginal benefit equals marginal cost, which is the condition for economic efficiency.

Price regulation presents two challenges. One is that, under marginal cost pricing, the provider may incur a loss. Jupiter's revenue is represented by the area 0*bac*, which is $40 × 10,000 = $400,000 a month. The average cost at 10,000 MWh is $50 per MWh, which means that the total cost is $50 × 10,000 = $500,000. With marginal cost pricing, the provider would incur a loss of $500,000 − $400,000 = $100,000 a month.

Accordingly, the government must provide a subsidy of $100,000 a month to ensure that the provider is financially viable. The subsidy is necessary to achieve economic efficiency. However, the regulator must then raise funds to provide the subsidy.

How should the government regulate Jupiter if it does not wish to provide a subsidy? The policy that most closely approaches economic efficiency while allowing the provider to break even is *average cost pricing*. Under **average cost pricing**, the provider must set the price equal to average cost and supply the quantity demanded. With average cost pricing, the provider would exactly cover its costs. Applying average cost pricing to Jupiter, the price would be $55 per megawatt-hour and the quantity demanded would be 7,000 MWh a month.

> **Average cost pricing:** The provider must set the price equal to the average cost and supply the quantity demanded.

The other challenge in price regulation is to acquire information about the provider's costs. The franchise holder has a strong incentive to overreport its costs. Then the regulator will allow a higher price, which would enable the provider to increase its profit. Indeed, the situation of the regulator and franchise holder is one of asymmetric information. As Chapter 13 shows, the information asymmetry, if not resolved, would result in economic inefficiency.

PROGRESS CHECK 15A

Referring to Figure 15.1, suppose that the demand is higher. How would that affect the optimal price?

Rate-of-Return Regulation

Under price regulation, the franchise holder may exaggerate its reported costs and so inflate the regulated price. The alternative to price regulation is rate-of-return regulation. This avoids the issue of costs by focusing on the franchise holder's profit. The regulator allows the franchise holder to set prices freely, provided that it does not exceed the maximum allowed profit.

Under rate-of-return regulation, the regulator stipulates the franchise holder's maximum allowed profit in terms of a maximum rate of return on the value of the **rate base**. The rate base may be specified by assets or equity. Whenever

> **Rate base:** Assets or equity on which the franchise holder may earn the allowed rate of return.

the franchise holder's rate of return exceeds the specified maximum, it will be required to reduce its prices.

Suppose, for instance, that Jupiter Power is regulated to a maximum 12% rate of return on allowed assets of $5 million. Then the maximum allowed profit would be $0.12 \times \$5$ million = $600,000 a year.

Rate-of-return regulation presents three challenges in implementation:

- *Rate of return*. One challenge is to set the allowed rate of return. Typically, the rate base is large, so a small difference in the allowed rate of return will translate into a large sum of money. Since the franchise holder is a monopoly, there would be few comparable businesses, so it would be difficult to determine the appropriate rate of return.
- *Rate base*. Another challenge is to determine what assets are needed to provide the regulated service and, hence, should be counted in the rate base. The franchise holder will seek the widest possible definition to increase its profit.
- *Overinvestment*. Finally, the franchise holder has an incentive to invest beyond the economically efficient level. By enlarging the rate base, the allowed rate of return will be applied to a larger base, and so the franchise holder can increase its profit.

AUSTRALIA: PRICE REGULATION OF TRUNK TELECOMMUNICATIONS

The Australian Competition and Consumer Commission (ACCC) subjects telecommunications with bandwidth of 2 megabits per second or greater to regulation. The ACCC regulates price according to total service long-run incremental cost (TSLRIC), which is essentially the marginal cost of service based on commercially available efficient technology, and taking account of economies of scale and scope.

The ACCC has justified regulating by TSLRIC for four reasons:

- If the service provider faced effective competition, its prices would approximate TSLRIC.
- TSLRIC provides a risk-adjusted return on investment, and so encourages efficient investment in infrastructure.
- TSLRIC encourages the efficient use of existing infrastructure.
- TSLRIC allows the service provider to fully recover its efficient costs of providing service.

Source: Australian Competition and Consumer Commission, *Domestic Transmission Capacity Service: Final Report*, March 2009, pp. 36–37.

3. Potentially Competitive Market

By contrast with a natural monopoly, a **potentially competitive market** is one where economies of scale and scope are small relative to market demand. So having two or more competing suppliers would not raise average costs. In a potentially competitive market, with perfect competition, the invisible hand will ensure economic efficiency. Hence, in any potentially competitive market, the government should promote competition.

> **Potentially competitive market:** Economies of scale and scope are small relative to market demand.

Competition Law

The basic way in which governments promote competition is through competition law (also called "antimonopoly" or "antitrust" law). However, industries that are subject to specific regulation may also be required to comply with competition law specific to the industry.

Table 15.1 lists the key laws regarding competition in various jurisdictions. In addition to these laws, individual countries within the European Union and

Table 15.1 Competition laws

Jurisdiction	Law	Enforcement agency
Australia	Competition and Consumer Act 2010	Australian Competition and Consumer Commission
Canada	Competition Act 1985	Competition Bureau
China	Anti-Monopoly Law 2007	National Development and Reform Commission; State Administration for Industry and Commerce; Ministry of Commerce
European Union	Treaty on the Functioning of the European Union, 2009: Articles 101–106	Directorate General for Competition, European Commission
Japan	Anti-Monopoly Act 1947	Fair Trade Commission
Korea	Monopoly Regulation and Fair Trade Act 1980	Fair Trade Commission
New Zealand	Commerce Act 1986	Commerce Commission
Taiwan	Fair Trade Act 1991	Fair Trade Commission
United Kingdom	Competition Act 1998; Enterprise Act 2002	Competition and Markets Authority
United States of America	Sherman Act 1890; Clayton Act 1914; Federal Trade Commission Act 1914; Robinson–Patman Act 1938; Hart–Scott Rodino Antitrust Improvement Act 1976	Department of Justice; Federal Trade Commission

individual US states may have their own competition laws. Table 15.1 also lists the agencies responsible for enforcing competition laws in the various jurisdictions.

Generally, competition laws prohibit the following:

- competitors from colluding on price or other aspects of purchases or sales;
- businesses with market power from abusing their market power;
- mergers or acquisitions that would create substantial market power.

Competition laws prohibit:

- collusion;
- abuse of market power;
- harmful mergers.

In addition, competition laws may prohibit or restrict specific business practices such as control over resale prices and exclusive agreements. What exactly is prohibited varies from one jurisdiction to another.

The mission of the competition agency is to enforce competition laws. One role is to prosecute competitors that engage in collusion and businesses that abuse market power. The other role is to review proposals for mergers and acquisitions. The competition agency must ensure that any proposed merger or acquisition complies with the law. The agency may approve the proposed combination subject to specific conditions such as the divestment of particular businesses to mitigate the anticompetitive impact of the combination.

Besides government enforcement, the competition laws may also provide for persons harmed by anticompetitive behavior to take legal action in civil law. Under US federal antitrust laws, for instance, plaintiffs in civil actions can recover damages of three times the harm that they suffered. Further, civil plaintiffs can petition courts for an injunction against anticompetitive conduct.

Structural Regulation

The fact that one market is a natural monopoly does not necessarily mean that related upstream or downstream markets are also natural monopolies. In electricity, for instance, production may be potentially competitive even while transmission and distribution are natural monopolies. Likewise, distribution of water may be a natural monopoly, while production is potentially competitive.

Under such circumstances, the government must consider how to preserve the benefits of monopoly in one market while fostering competition in the other. A special challenge to the regulator arises when the monopoly franchise holder also participates in the potentially competitive market.

To illustrate the issues, suppose that the government awards a monopoly franchise for distribution of electricity, while allowing competition in generation. Jupiter Power has the monopoly franchise over distribution. So, it also has a monopsony over the purchase of electricity from generators. Hence, the government must regulate Jupiter's monopoly over distribution of electricity as well as its monopsony over purchases of electricity.

Now suppose that Jupiter has vertically integrated upstream into the generation of electricity. Then Jupiter may have an incentive to favor its internal generator of electricity and discriminate against competing generators. The regulator should intervene to ensure fair competition. However, Jupiter might exploit its superior information about technical and other issues to confound the regulator. So competing generators of electricity may be at a disadvantage in supplying the distribution monopoly.

One solution to this challenge is *structural regulation* to separate the natural monopoly from the potentially competitive market. Under **structural regulation**, the regulator stipulates the conditions under which a business may produce vertically related goods and services.

> **Structural regulation:**
> Stipulating conditions for a business to produce vertically related goods and services.

In the electricity case, the regulator could require Jupiter to separate its electricity distribution and generation businesses. In the extreme, it could simply disallow Jupiter from generating electricity. With Jupiter purely distributing electricity, it would have no incentive to discriminate among generators of electricity.

PROGRESS CHECK 15B

Explain the meaning of structural regulation to promote competition.

EXECUTING A GLOBAL MERGER

In May 2011, the German automobile group, Volkswagen, owned 72% of Swedish truck maker, Scania, and 30% of German truck maker, MAN. Ferdinand Piech, the Chairman of Volkswagen's Supervisory Board and also Chairman of MAN, aimed to strengthen the collaboration between Scania and MAN.

Volkswagen commenced a tender offer for MAN at €95 per ordinary share and €59.90 per preference share. However, Volkswagen anticipated that "[a]ntitrust restrictions [would] pose high hurdles for a more in-depth co-operation, as MAN on the one hand and Scania and Volkswagen on the other hand are regarded as competitors."

To complete the merger with MAN, Volkswagen had to seek the approval of the European Commission as well as competition and regulatory authorities in Australia, Brazil, Canada, China, France, Germany, Italy, Japan, Mexico, Turkey, and the USA.

Sources: Volkswagen AG, offer document, May 30, 2011; "Volkswagen submits merger control application to EU Commission," Press Release 282/2011, August 23, 2011.

ELECTRICITY IN NORTH DELHI

In the electricity industry, transmission and distribution exhibit strong economies of scale, while generation does not. In 2001, the government of India's capital, Delhi, restructured and privatized its electricity agency into seven companies – two for generation, one for transmission, and four for distribution.

The Delhi government awarded each of four companies a monopoly franchise for distribution of electricity in designated areas. NDPL holds the franchise for the north and northwest areas. It buys over 1,100 MW of electricity on long-term contracts from generators of electricity.

In a new initiative toward vertical integration, NDPL is building a 108 MW gas-based combined cycle power generation plant at Rithala in North Delhi. NDPL justified the new plant as "obviat[ing] the need for an equivalent amount of expensive bilateral power." But what does that portend for competition in the market for generation of electricity?

Source: North Delhi Power Limited, Annual Report, 2009–10.

4. Asymmetric Information

Another situation in which the invisible hand may fail is where information about some characteristic or future action is asymmetric. Chapters 13 and 14 show that, if the information asymmetry is not resolved, the marginal benefit will diverge from marginal cost, and the allocation of resources will not be economically efficient.

Consider, for instance, the market for medical services. Patients rely on surgeons for advice as well as treatment. Owing to the asymmetry of information between surgeon and patient, the surgeons are subject to moral hazard. Surgeons may overprescribe treatment to increase their incomes.

Figure 15.2 illustrates the market equilibrium. The true demand is the patients' marginal benefit if they had the same information as their surgeons. The inflated demand results from asymmetry of information and exceeds the true demand to the extent that surgeons induce patients to get excessive treatment.

The inflated demand crosses the supply of medical services at point a. In the market equilibrium, the price is $140 per hour and the quantity of treatment is 210,000 hours a month. At that quantity, the true marginal benefit of medical services is $50, which is the height of the true demand curve. The marginal cost of medical services is $140, the height of the supply curve at the equilibrium quantity. In equilibrium, the marginal cost exceeds the true marginal benefit by $90. This economic inefficiency results from the asymmetry of information between surgeons and patients.

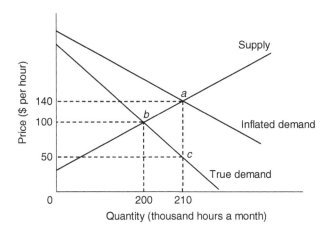

FIGURE 15.2 Moral hazard in medical services.

Notes: The inflated demand is higher than the true demand. The market equilibrium lies at *a*, where the inflated demand crosses the supply. The price is $140 per hour and the quantity is 210,000 hours a month. If the moral hazard can be resolved, the inflated demand would shift down to the true demand and the equilibrium would be at *b*, where the true demand (marginal benefit) equals the supply (marginal cost).

In situations of asymmetric information, the regulator might possibly resolve the asymmetry by regulating the better-informed party's

* disclosure of information,
* conduct, and
* business structure.

> Regulate information asymmetry through:
> * information disclosure;
> * conduct;
> * business structure.

In medical services, to the extent that the regulation is effective, the inflated demand in Figure 15.2 would shift down toward the true demand. Then the equilibrium would be closer to point *b*, where the true marginal benefit equals the marginal cost.

Disclosure

The most obvious way to resolve asymmetric information is to require the better-informed party to disclose its information truthfully. However, disclosure will resolve the asymmetry only if the information can be objectively verified. In the case of surgery, the patient's need is a matter of professional judgment, hence disclosure may not resolve the information asymmetry.

> Disclosure resolves asymmetry if information can be objectively verified.

Consider another situation of asymmetric information: financial advisors hard-selling risky investments. The regulator can require financial advisors to disclose the riskiness of investments. This might help to resolve the information asymmetry if the client understands the disclosure.

Conduct Regulation

Instead of directly resolving an information asymmetry, an alternative is to regulate the *conduct* of the better-informed party and so limit the extent to which it can exploit informational advantage. If parties with better information cannot exploit their advantage, then the outcome would be closer to the economically efficient level.

For example, the regulator of financial services can stipulate that financial advisors must evaluate their clients' risk profile before marketing any investment products. The regulator can also stipulate a minimum "cooling-off period" during which an investor may withdraw from the purchase of any investment without penalty. Such regulations of conduct restrict the scope for a financial advisor to pressure investors into buying unsuitable investments.

Structural Regulation

Another way to limit the extent to which a better-informed party can exploit an informational advantage is to regulate the *structure* of the industry. By enforcing separation of different businesses, a regulator may reduce the opportunities for exploiting superior information.

The market for medical services illustrates structural regulation. In some countries, doctors are limited to providing advice and treatment, and are prohibited from selling medicines and medical supplies. This regulation effectively dissuades doctors from excessive prescription of medicines.

The market for financial services also illustrates structural regulation. Following the subprime financial crisis, various regulators have proposed that commercial banks, which take deposits from retail customers, should not be allowed to engage in trading of derivatives and other securities. This structural regulation limits the exposure of commercial banks to risk.

PROGRESS CHECK 15C

How can the government regulate asymmetries of information?

STRUCTURAL REGULATION IN REAL ESTATE BROKERAGE

In real estate brokerage, a dual agent represents both the buyer and seller. A dual agent is inherently conflicted. The agent may tell the seller how much the buyer is willing to pay, or tell the buyer how much the seller is willing to accept.

Does dual agency favor the buyer or seller? The empirical evidence is mixed. In a study of over 21,000 residential transactions in central Virginia between 2000 and 2009, dual agency was associated with 1.7% lower prices.

By contrast, among over 18,000 residential transactions in Johnson County, Indiana, between 2000 and 2010, dual agency was associated with prices that were 4.8% higher for property owned by the agent. However, there was no significant difference in prices for properties owned by unrelated individuals.

The government of Singapore prohibits dual agency and requires that the buyer and seller be represented by different agents.

Sources: Raymond T. Brastow and Bennie D. Waller, "Dual agency representation: incentive conflicts or efficiencies," *Journal of Real Estate Research*, Vol. 35, No. 2, 2013; Ken Johnson, Zhenguo Lin, and Jia Xie, "Dual agent distortions in real estate transactions," *Real Estate Economics*, 29 March 2015, DOI: 10.1111/1540-6229.12073.

5. Externalities

The invisible hand may fail in situations of externalities, that is, when some benefit or cost passes directly from source to recipient and not through a market. In the absence of a market, the invisible hand cannot work. There are no markets for factory emissions or discharge of contaminated water. Furthermore, pollution affects so many entities that private action would probably not resolve the externality. Government regulation may be the only solution.

Chapter 12 showed that, for economic efficiency, the level of an externality should be such that marginal benefit equals marginal cost. The benefit of emissions is in allowing the sources to avoid the cost of clean disposal. The cost of emissions is the harm to the health of the victims.

As depicted in Figure 15.3, the economically efficient rate of emissions is 800,000 tons a year, where the marginal benefit equals the marginal cost to society. How can this be achieved? Generally, there are two ways of regulating externalities:

- user fees or taxes;
- standards or quotas.

> **Regulation of externalities:**
> - user fees or taxes;
> - standards or quotas.

User Fee/Tax

One method of regulation aims to mimic Adam Smith's invisible hand: allow all sources to emit as much as they like provided that they pay the appropriate user fee or tax. Referring to Figure 15.3, at the economically efficient rate of emissions, the marginal cost to society is $35 per ton. Suppose that the regulator sets a user fee for emissions of $35 per ton and allows every source (user) to buy as large an amount of emissions as it would like at that price.

Consider an oil refinery that emits pollutants. To maximize profits, the refinery should buy emissions up to the rate where the marginal benefit of emissions

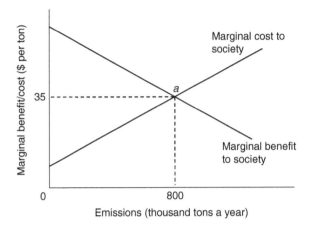

FIGURE 15.3 Economic efficiency in emissions.

Note: The economically efficient rate of emissions is 800,000 tons a year, where the marginal benefit and the marginal cost to society are both equal to $35 per ton.

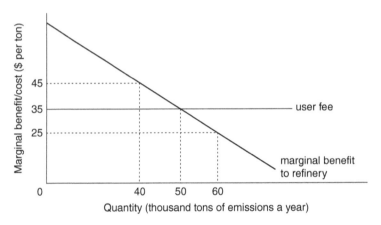

FIGURE 15.4 User fee.

Notes: The refinery's marginal benefit equals the $35 fee, at an emissions rate of 50,000 tons a year. If the refinery emitted 40,000 tons, the marginal benefit would be $45, which exceeds the $35 fee, so by increasing emissions, the refinery could increase profits. If the refinery emitted 60,000 tons, then the marginal benefit would be $25, which is less than the $35 fee, so the refinery should cut back on emissions.

balances the $35 fee. Suppose that, as shown in Figure 15.4, the refinery's marginal benefit balances the $35 fee at an emissions rate of 50,000 tons a year.

To see why 50,000 tons maximizes profit, consider emissions of less than 50,000 tons a year – say, 40,000 tons. Then the refinery's marginal benefit from more emissions would be $45, which exceeds the $35 fee. So it should increase emissions and raise profit. If it emits more than 50,000 tons a year, then its marginal benefit would be less than the $35 fee. So it should reduce emissions.

All sources would emit up to the level that their marginal benefit equals $35. Since the regulator charges the same $35 fee to all sources, the marginal benefits of all sources would be equal.

Furthermore, the regulator sets the fee according to the social marginal cost of emissions, $35. Thus, the marginal benefits equal the user fee which equals the social marginal cost of emissions. So, the user fee implements the economically efficient rate of emissions.

Quota/Standard

The other method of regulation is directly through standards or quotas. From Figure 15.3, the economically efficient rate of emissions is 800,000 tons a year. So the regulator could simply stipulate a maximum quota of 800,000 tons a year. However, there are many sources of emissions. How should the regulator allocate the quota among the various sources?

One way is to issue licenses for 800,000 tons of emissions a year and sell the licenses through public auction. Each source would demand licenses according to its marginal benefit from emissions. The market demand would be the social marginal benefit curve in Figure 15.3.

The supply of licenses would be perfectly inelastic at 800,000 tons a year. By Figure 15.3, the marginal benefit of the 800,000th ton of emissions is $35. Thus, the equilibrium price of a license – where quantity demanded equals quantity supplied – would be $35.

Each source would buy licenses up to the level that its marginal benefit equals the price of $35. Hence, the quantity of emissions would be economically efficient. By selling emissions licenses, the regulator is effectively charging a user fee that is determined by a competitive market.

PROGRESS CHECK 15D

Referring to Figure 15.3, compare the social benefit and cost with user fees of $25 per ton and $45 per ton.

Congestion

The demand for facilities such as bridges and tunnels varies with time. Outside peak hours, the facilities provide non-rival use. By contrast, during peak hours, each additional user generates congestion, the costs of which include delays and more accidents. Congestion is a negative externality.

Consider a tunnel that can smoothly convey up to 30 vehicles a minute. From the standpoint of economic efficiency, traffic through the tunnel should be managed so that the marginal benefit of each user balances the marginal cost. When there are fewer than 30 vehicles a minute, the marginal cost of a crossing is nothing. So the tunnel should not exclude any driver.

When, however, 30 vehicles per minute are in the tunnel, the marginal cost becomes positive. For economic efficiency, the tunnel should set a toll equal to the marginal cost. This will ensure that the only drivers who enter the tunnel are those whose benefit exceeds the marginal cost.

What if the tunnel does not charge a toll? Consider the decision of a marginal driver (the 31st) whether to enter the tunnel or wait until there is less traffic. If the driver enters immediately, she will save some time. In making the decision, that driver compares her private benefit from crossing at that time with her private cost, and ignores the additional costs on other drivers. Owing to this negative externality, too many drivers enter the tunnel relative to the economically efficient number.

Generally, for economic efficiency, congestible facilities should levy a user fee equal to the marginal cost of use, where the cost includes the externalities imposed on other users. As the marginal cost varies with the time of day, so should the price. This pricing would ensure economically efficient usage of facilities such as bridges, tunnels, roads, and subways.

Congestion illustrates an externality that varies over time. A similar principle applies to externalities that vary geographically. With differences in marginal benefit and marginal cost, the economically efficient level of the externality would vary. And so would the appropriate user fee or tax.

Accidents

Accidents are a specific class of externalities which are probabilistic. For instance, the possibility of automobile accidents means that every driver imposes a possible negative externality on others. The likelihood and severity of the externality depend on the care with which she drives.

As Figure 15.5 illustrates, the driver chooses the level of care where her marginal benefit (in terms of the reduced expected harm from accidents) equals marginal cost. However, the economically efficient degree of care balances the marginal benefit to society with the driver's marginal cost of care. The marginal benefit to society includes the reduction in expected harm to *other drivers*, so exceeds the marginal benefit to the driver herself.

Accidents possibly involve so many people that private action will not resolve the externality. Then government intervention is necessary. Typically, however, the government does not intervene directly. Rather, the government assigns rights which then establish the basis for the relevant parties to resolve the externality. Specifically, the law specifies the *liability* of the parties to an accident. **Liability** is the set of conditions under which one party must pay compensation for causing harm to another.

> **Liability:** The conditions under which one party must pay compensation for causing harm to another.

In effect, by specifying liability and compensation, the law implicitly sets a price for causing an accident or, equivalently, a price for failing to take care. Unlike prices in conventional markets, the price for an accident is paid only after the event.

So, given the law, each driver chooses the level of care to balance her marginal benefit of care (in terms of the reduced expected liability for compensation and

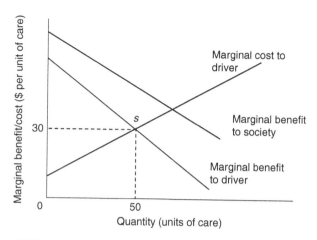

FIGURE 15.5 Accidents.

Notes: The driver would choose the level of care where her marginal benefit equals marginal cost. This is lower than the economically efficient level of care, where the marginal benefit to society equals the marginal cost of care to the driver.

reduced harm from accidents) against her marginal cost. With the appropriate liability and compensation, the driver would choose the economically efficient level of care. Referring to Figure 15.5, this will happen if the marginal benefit of care to the driver balances the marginal cost at the economically efficient level.

PROGRESS CHECK 15E

Suppose that, relative to the situation in Figure 15.5, the courts double the compensation that injurers must pay accident victims. How will this affect a driver's choice of care?

AUSTRALIA: REDUCING CARBON

Australia generates about 80% of its electricity from coal. Among economically advanced countries, it emits the greatest amount of greenhouse gases per capita. Prime Minister Kevin Rudd was overthrown by his deputy, Julia Gillard, after he failed to pass legislation to reduce carbon emissions.

In July 2011, the new government of Prime Minister Julia Gillard committed to reducing Australia's carbon emissions by 80% from 2000 levels by 2050. From July 2012, the government would impose a tax of A$23 per ton of carbon emissions on the top 500 polluters. From 2015, it would replace the tax with a market-based emissions trading scheme. Meanwhile, the government would provide financial incentives to close the country's most polluting power stations.

Source: "Breaching the brick wall," *The Economist*, July 11, 2011.

KEY TAKEAWAYS

- A market is a natural monopoly if the average cost of production is minimized with a single supplier.
- Governments can regulate monopolies by either rate of return or price.
- In a potentially competitive market, economies of scale and scope are small relative to market demand.
- Governments can foster competition through competition law and structural regulation.
- Governments can regulate markets with asymmetric information through disclosure, conduct, and structure.
- Governments can regulate externalities through user fees/taxes or quotas/standards.
- Governments can regulate accidents by establishing legal rights.

REVIEW QUESTIONS

1. Explain the concept of a natural monopoly.
2. What are the challenges for the efficiency of businesses owned and operated by government?
3. Explain marginal cost pricing.
4. What are the problems with price regulation?
5. Explain rate-of-return regulation.
6. What are the problems with rate-of-return regulation?
7. Does privatization necessarily increase competition? Explain why or why not.
8. Generally, what does competition law seek to prohibit?
9. Mandatory disclosure is always the best way to resolve asymmetric information. True or false?
10. Explain how to resolve asymmetric information by regulating conduct and business structure.
11. Explain how to regulate construction site noise with a user fee.
12. Explain how to regulate automobile emissions by a standard.
13. Why should the government charge a toll for use of a tunnel?
14. Why should the charge for using a bridge vary by the time of day?
15. How does the government regulate accidents?

DISCUSSION QUESTIONS

1. The Delhi electricity industry is vertically separated into generation, transmission, and distribution. The government awarded monopoly franchises for transmission and distribution to various companies. The Delhi Electricity Regulatory Commission regulates the monopolies to a maximum 14% rate of return on equity. Between 2005 and 2011, the Commission refused increases in prices, although two of the distribution companies incurred losses. (Source: "Delhiites to

pay 22% more for power as regulator clears hike," *Financial Express*, August 27, 2011.)

    (a) Why did the Delhi government separate the industry into generation, transmission, and distribution? Why did it award monopolies for transmission and distribution?

    (b) What challenges would the Commission face in administering rate-of-return regulation?

    (c) Explain the Commission's refusal to allow price increases in terms of holdup.

    (d) Three of the distribution companies are joint ventures between the private sector and the Delhi government. How does the government shareholding affect the potential for holdup by the government?

2. The Independent Pricing and Regulatory Tribunal regulates the prices set by the Office of Water, the monopoly supplier of water in New South Wales, Australia. In 2010, the Office of Water sought higher prices to cover an A$186 million increase in costs. The Tribunal approved only 41% of the cost increase. It also implemented a two-part tariff for users with meters. The fixed part of the tariff would yield 70% of revenue, with the remaining 30% coming from the usage charge. (Source: Independent Pricing and Regulatory Tribunal, *Review of Prices for the Water Administration Ministerial Corporation*, October 2010.)

    (a) Explain natural monopoly in the context of water distribution.

    (b) Using a relevant diagram, explain average cost pricing of water.

    (c) If the monopoly's costs increase, use your diagram in (b) to explain how the regulator should adjust price.

    (d) Why would the Office of Water inflate its reported costs?

    (e) Explain how the two-part tariff would encourage users to economize on water.

3. In Hong Kong, the supply of electric power is monopolized by two vertically integrated companies. Hong Kong Electric supplies Hong Kong Island, while China Light and Power supplies Kowloon and the New Territories. The Hong Kong government regulates each company to a maximum 9.99% rate of return on net fixed assets. Although the two companies' networks are just a few kilometers apart, they do not interconnect.

    (a) Discuss whether vertical integration of the Hong Kong electricity industry is economically efficient.

    (b) Given differences in the demand for electricity between Hong Kong Island and Kowloon and the New Territories, how would interconnection increase economic efficiency?

    (c) Why do the two electricity companies oppose interconnection?

4. In the United States, all stockbrokers must insure customer accounts up to $500,000 with the Securities Investor Protection Corporation (SIPC). SIPC insurance covers customers for losses on cash, stocks, and bonds due to default by the broker. The SIPC does not cover losses on other investments such as commodity futures.

    (a) Can you explain the government requirement for SIPC insurance in terms of asymmetric information between brokers and investors?

(b) Some brokers purchase private insurance to cover losses that exceed the minimum SIPC insurance coverage. Explain this practice as a way in which brokers can signal their financial reliability.

(c) Commodity futures are more complex than stocks and bonds. Why is it reasonable for SIPC not to insure losses on futures?

5. With a fast-growing population, India's economy would boom if young people were sufficiently educated. Many parents appreciate the value of education and send their children to school. However, some private schools fail to educate their pupils, and illiterate parents do not know that they are being cheated.

(a) Using a relevant figure, explain the effect of asymmetry of information in the market for education.

(b) Discuss how regulation of (i) disclosure, (ii) conduct, and (iii) structure might help to resolve the asymmetry of information.

(c) How can charities and social enterprise help?

6. In India, many poor parents prefer their children to work rather than attend school. In 2014, Akshaya Patra provided free lunches to 1.4 million children in over 10,600 government and government-aided schools across ten states to encourage attendance at school.

(a) Suppose that some parents have a very high discount rate. How would that affect their choice between sending their children to school and work?

(b) Does education of children generate an externality? Does that justify a subsidy to education?

(c) To what extent does your analysis in (b) apply to tertiary as compared to primary and secondary education?

(d) Generally, economists argue that giving cash is more efficient than gifts in kind. Discuss whether Akshaya Patra should give students an equivalent cash subsidy instead of the free lunch.

7. The US Federal Aviation Administration (FAA) classifies all civil transport aircraft according to noise. The categories range from Stage 1, which is the noisiest, to Stage 4, which is the quietest category. In 2013, the FAA prohibited the operation of Stage 2 jet aircraft weighing less than 75,000 pounds. Some of the jets can be retro-fitted to meet Stage 3 standards. (Source: "FAA Stage 2 noise ban rule bars older jets in U.S.," *ainonline.com*, August 4, 2013.)

(a) Who should regulate aircraft noise: the federal government or local airport authorities?

(b) Consider an airport that has specified standards for aircraft noise. Should the airport create permits for aircraft noise and allow airlines to trade these permits?

(c) Using a relevant diagram, explain how the airport should determine the level of noise to allow. Should the level vary with the time of day?

8. Among economically advanced countries, Australia emits the largest amount of greenhouse gases per capita. In July 2011, the government of Prime Minister Julia Gillard committed to reducing Australia's carbon emissions. From July 2012, the government would impose a tax of A$23 per ton of carbon emissions

on the top 500 polluters. From 2015, it would replace the tax with a market-based emissions trading scheme.

    (a) Using a relevant diagram, explain how the government should determine the tax on carbon emissions.

    (b) Using the same diagram, explain how the government should determine the quota for total emissions.

    (c) How would emissions trading establish a price for emissions?

9. With rental rates exceeding $3,000 per square foot per year, retail space in Causeway Bay, Hong Kong, is among the world's most expensive. In 2011, the Town Planning Board limited the height of future buildings in the area to between 130 and 200 meters. Real estate developer Hysan Group, which owns nine properties in the area, asked the Board to relax the limits, but the Board denied the application. (Source: "Long hours didn't cloud our judgment on Causeway Bay building restrictions, town planners say," *South China Morning Post*, December 1, 2014.)

    (a) What externality does the height restrictions resolve?

    (b) How would the Hysan Group benefit from relaxing the height restrictions?

    (c) Using a relevant diagram, explain how the Town Planning Board should determine the restrictions on height.

    (d) Should the restrictions on height be the same throughout Hong Kong?

You are the consultant!

How does government regulation affect your organization? Write a memorandum to the government explaining how to improve the administration of regulation.

Note

1   This discussion is based, in part, on Delhi Electricity Regulatory Commission, Petition for Approval of Aggregate Revenue Requirement and Multi Year Generation Tariff for Pragati Power Corporation Limited for the FY 2007–08 to FY 2010–11, Petition No. 39/2007; North Delhi Power Limited, Annual Report, 2009–10.

16

CHAPTER

Answers to Selected Progress Check and Review Questions

Chapter 1. Introduction to Managerial Economics

1A. Value added = Buyer benefit − Seller cost = Buyer surplus + Seller economic profit.

1B. 0, 0, …, 0, 300.

1C. Max's NPV from the MBA would be

$$-\$50,000 - \frac{50,000}{1.10} + \frac{95,000}{1.10^2} + \frac{95,000}{1.10^3} + \frac{95,000}{1.10^4} = \$119,319.$$

He should continue in his current job, which gives a higher NPV.

1D. [Omitted.]

1E. The three branches are: (i) competitive markets; (ii) market power; and (iii) imperfect markets. Competitive markets have large numbers of buyers and sellers, none of which can influence market conditions. By contrast, a buyer or seller with market power can influence market conditions. A market is imperfect if one party directly conveys benefits or costs to others, or if one party has better information than another.

1. Value added is the difference between buyer benefit and seller cost. Economic profit is the difference between seller revenue and seller cost.

2. Value added is the difference between buyer benefit and seller cost. So, even though the charity receives no revenue, it need not be destroying value. For the free mosquito nets to create value, the buyer's benefit must exceed the seller's cost.

3. [Omitted.]

4. [Omitted.]

5. People act with bounded rationality because they have limited cognitive ability and lack self-control.

6. The employer could invest the $1 million today, which would yield a positive return, and so the pension fund would have more than required to pay out $1 million in the future.
7. If the inflows exceed the outflows after accounting for the timing of the inflows and outflows, then the NPV will be positive.
8. With regard to vertical boundaries, a local cable TV provider that produces TV series is more vertically integrated than a local cable TV provider that buys TV series from others.
9. A university merging with a hospital is expanding its horizontal boundaries. A university shutting some faculty is shrinking its horizontal boundaries.
10. When Apple outsources the manufacturing of iPhones to a contractor in China, it is vertically disintegrating.
11. (a) The electricity market includes buyers and sellers. (b) The electricity industry consists of sellers only.
12. (a) False. (b) False.
13. Demand and supply model.
14. A manufacturer with market power can influence conditions of demand and/or supply.
15. (b).

Chapter 2. Demand

2A. The theater must cut its price by $3 from $11 to $8.
2B. (a) It slopes downward because of diminishing marginal benefit. (b) Assuming that all-in-one stereos are an inferior product, the drop in the consumer's income will cause the demand curve to shift to the right.
2C. Online movies are a substitute for seeing movies in the theater. A fall in the price of online movies will cause the demand curve for theater movies to shift to the left.
2D. If the price of movies is $8, Joy's buyer surplus would be the area under her demand curve above the horizontal line at the price of $8.

1. [Omitted.]
2. [Omitted.]
3. [Omitted.]
4. [Omitted.]
5. Introduction of the new birth-control device will: (a) reduce the demand for male condoms; (b) reduce the demand for birth-control pills.
6. Pepsi advertising will: (a) increase the demand for Pepsi; and (b) decrease the demand for Coca-Cola.
7. Changes in consumer incomes would affect consumer demand for Apple iPhones, and so affect Apple's demand for microprocessors.
8. ATMs are a substitute for bank clerks. The higher labor costs will increase the demand for ATMs.

9. Buyer surplus is the difference between buyer's total benefit from consumption and the buyer's actual expenditure.

10. False. Whether the buyer is a consumer or business, buyer surplus is the difference between buyer's total benefit from consumption and the buyer's actual expenditure.

11. Each person has a different marginal benefit for the flight. The market demand curve shows the marginal benefits of the various consumers, arranged from the consumer with highest marginal benefit to the consumer with lowest marginal benefit.

12. Draw any straight line which includes the point at 200 minutes and 10 cents. Antonella's buyer surplus is the area between the demand curve and the 10 cents line.

13. Not true. Each additional item provides lower marginal benefit. Actual savings are the difference between total benefit and the price paid.

14. A package deal provides a fixed level of consumption at a lump-sum price. A broadband service provider can design a package deal providing a fixed level of consumption at a price just a little less than the consumer's total benefit.

15. Two part pricing is a pricing scheme comprising a fixed payment and a charge based on usage. A broadband service provider can design a two-part price such that the fixed charge extracts the consumers' buyer surplus.

Chapter 3. Elasticity

3A. The proportionate change in quantity demanded is $(1.5 - 1.44)/1.44 = 0.06/1.44 = 0.042$. The proportionate change in price is $(1 - 1.10)/1.10 = -0.10/1.10 = -0.091$. The own-price elasticity is $0.042/(-0.091) = -0.46$.

3B. The intuitive factors that influence the own-price elasticity of demand are: (a) availability of direct or indirect substitutes; (b) the buyer's prior commitments; (c) the benefits/costs of economizing.

3C. The proportionate change in quantity demanded would be $-2.5 \times 7\% = -17.5\%$. The proportionate change in expenditure would be $7\% - 17.5\% = -10.5\%$.

3D. The own-price elasticity is always a negative number. But the income elasticity could be negative or positive, depending on whether the item is a normal or inferior good.

3E. For a non-durable good, the longer the time that buyers have to adjust, the bigger will be the response to a price change.

1. [Omitted.]

2. The demand curve slopes downward, hence the own-price elasticity is negative. The proportionate changes in quantity demanded and price of an item are pure numbers. Hence, the own-price elasticity is a pure number with no units.

3. If a 1% price increase causes less than a 1% drop in quantity demanded, then the demand is price inelastic. If a 1% price increase causes more than a 1% drop in quantity demanded, then the demand is price elastic.

4. The demand of executives traveling at the expense of their employers will be less elastic. They incur the costs of economizing but their employers receive the benefit.

5. Rise. The proportionate change in expenditure would be $10\% \times (1 - 0.7) = 3\%$.

6. The volume of sales would change by $-1.5 \times (-5\%) = 7.5\%$.

7. [Omitted.]

8. True.

9. Complements.

10. Advertising by one product brand will draw customers from customers of other brands as well as increase the demand for beer in general. Advertising of beer in general can only increase the market demand.

11. The change in quantity demanded would be $1.3 \times 5\% = 6.5\%$.

12. More elastic in the long run.

13. The increase in quantity demanded would be 2.85% in the short run and 3.91% in the long run.

14. If consumers are influenced by sunk costs, they will be less responsive to changes in price, and so their demand will be less elastic.

15. (a) More elastic. (b) Less elastic.

Chapter 4. Supply

4A. If the fixed cost were higher, the variable cost curve would not be affected, while the total cost curve would be shifted up by the extent of the increase in fixed cost.

4B. If the fixed cost were higher, the average variable cost and marginal cost curves would not be affected, while the average cost curve would be shifted up.

4C. Luna should produce at the rate where marginal cost is $7.50 per sheet.

4D. It should produce 6,000 sheets a week.

4E. The new seller surplus would be the area between the new price line of $9 per sheet and Luna's supply curve. The seller surplus would increase by the area between the $9 and $7 price lines.

4F. Supply would be inelastic if production capacity is fully used and the adjustment time is short.

1. The short run is a time horizon within which a seller cannot adjust at least one input. By contrast, the long run is a time horizon long enough that the seller can adjust all inputs. Assuming that all fixed costs are also sunk, while all variable costs are not sunk, then there are fixed costs only in the short run, while all costs are variable in the long run.

2. The average cost of $5 includes the average fixed cost. But, in the short run, the fixed cost is unavoidable. In the short run, the factory should accept orders so long as the price of a shirt covers the average *variable* cost.

3. Nothing. Marginal costs are not necessarily related to fixed costs.

4. The marginal product of advertising for a manufacturer of shampoos is the increase in sales arising from an additional dollar of advertising. With more of the advertising inputs, there will be a diminishing marginal product.

5. If the seller is so small that it can sell as much as it would like at the market price.

6. Since the price is less than the marginal cost, the producer can raise profit by reducing production.

7. The analysis underestimates the increase in profit. It considers only the increase in profit on the existing production, and ignores the increase in profit resulting from an increase in production.

8. Price is revenue divided by sales (or production), while average variable cost is variable cost divided by sales (or production).

9. Not necessarily. In the short run, it depends on whether or not the revenue covers the variable cost. If not, then they should shut down. In the long run, it depends on whether or not the revenue covers average cost.

10. Price is revenue divided by sales (or production), while average cost is total cost divided by sales (or production).

11. In the short run, the business should continue in production so long as its revenue covers the variable cost. In the long run, the business should continue in production so long as its revenue covers the total cost.

12. (a) The supply of furniture will be lower (shift to the left). (b) The supply of furniture will be higher (shift to the right).

13. For a given increase in price, if the supply curve is more elastic, the increase in seller surplus will be larger.

14. True.

15. The supply will be relatively more elastic in the long run.

Chapter 5. Market Equilibrium

5A. The conditions for a market to be in perfect competition are as follows. (a) The product is homogeneous. (b) There are many buyers, none of whom has market power. (c) There are many sellers, none of whom has market power. (d) New buyers and sellers can enter freely, and existing buyers and sellers can exit freely. (e) All buyers and all sellers have symmetric information about market conditions.

5B. See Figure 5.1. If price drops to $160 per ton-mile, the quantity demanded will exceed the quantity supplied.

5C. (a) False. (b) True.

5D. In Figure 5.4, the entire demand curve would shift to the left by 2 billion ton-miles. The supply curve would not shift. The equilibrium price would fall below $200 per ton-mile and production would fall below 10 billion ton-miles a year.

5E. The short-run price would be higher and the long-run price would be lower. Hence, the difference between the short- and long-run prices would be greater.

1. (a) The service is close to homogeneous. (b) There are many consumers in the market, each of whom buys a small quantity. (c) There may be few dry

cleaners, depending on the density of population. (d) Entry and exit are relatively free. (e) Consumers and dry cleaners probably have symmetric information about market conditions.

2. (a) The good is close to homogeneous. (b) There are many buyers in the market, each of whom buys a small quantity. (c) There may be few manufacturers. (d) Entry and exit are relatively free. (e) Buyers and manufacturers probably have symmetric information about market conditions.

3. This regulation presents a barrier to entry, and hence reduces the degree of competition.

4. The price will tend to fall.

5. The price will tend to rise.

6. The increase in consumer incomes would shift the demand for clothing upward (consumers are willing to pay more) and to the right (at every price, consumers want to buy more). The effect on the market price depends on the price elasticity of supply. If supply is completely inelastic, the price would increase the most. If supply is completely elastic, the price would not increase at all.

7. The effect of any upward shift in demand depends on the price elasticities of demand and supply. The impact on price will be greater if demand is more elastic, and supply is more inelastic.

8. The effect of any upward shift in demand depends on the price elasticities of demand and supply. The impact on quantity consumed will be greater if demand is more elastic, and supply is more elastic.

9. If demand is completely inelastic, consumers would pay a lot for additional cars, and production would increase the most. However, if demand is completely elastic, consumers would not be willing to pay more for additional cars, and production would not increase at all.

10. The effect of any shift in supply depends on the price elasticities of demand and supply. The impact on the price will be greater if demand is more inelastic, and supply is more inelastic.

11. The effect of any shift in supply depends on the price elasticities of demand and supply. The impact on the quantity produced will be greater if demand is more elastic, and supply is more inelastic.

12. An increase in wages would shift upward the supply of restaurant meals. The effect of any change in supply depends, in part, on the price elasticity of demand. If the demand is very elastic, a reduction in supply would not affect the price. By contrast, if demand is very inelastic, a reduction in supply would reduce the price.

13. The supply curve is more elastic in the long run than in the short run. Accordingly, the price increases more in the short run than in the long run.

14. The supply curve is more elastic in the long run than in the short run. Accordingly, the production increases more in the long run than in the short run.

15. The effects of an increase in demand depend on the elasticities of demand and supply. Hence, the difference in short- and long-run effects of an increase in demand depends on the difference between short- and long-run price elasticities.

Chapter 6. Economic Efficiency

6A. The concept of economic efficiency extends beyond technical efficiency. For economic efficiency, the production of the item must be such that the marginal benefit equals the marginal cost. Technical efficiency means providing an item at the minimum possible cost. It does not imply that scarce resources are being well used.

6B. The price in a market system has two roles. First, the price communicates necessary information. It tells buyers how much to purchase and tells sellers how much to supply. Second, the price provides a concrete incentive for each buyer to buy that quantity and maximize net benefit, and for each seller to supply that quantity and maximize its profit.

6C. With decentralization, Jupiter should set the transfer price equal to the market price of semiconductors. Then the electronics division will use semiconductors up to the point where marginal benefit equals the transfer price. This will ensure economic efficiency.

6D. It does not affect the difference between freight-inclusive and free on board pricing.

6E. The buyer's price increases relatively more. Hence, the incidence of the tax on travelers will be relatively higher.

1. Children were using bread (in sport) up to the point that the marginal benefit equaled the very low price. This price was less than the marginal cost. Hence, the marginal benefit of use was less than the marginal cost and not economically efficient.

2. The condition that all users receive the same marginal benefit.

3. Each prisoner of war received the parcel for free. Prisoners vary in their preferences for cigarettes and chocolate. If each prisoner gets the same quantity of each item, then their marginal benefits will be different.

4. The self-employed workers would get a higher wage (because they need not pay tax), so they would work up to a level of hours where their marginal cost would be higher than that of the employed workers. Hence, the allocation of labor is not economically efficient.

5. In a competitive finance market, all buyers (investors) purchase up to the quantity where the marginal benefit equals the market price of the funds, and all sellers (banks) supply up to the quantity where the marginal cost equals the market price of the funds. Buyers and sellers face the same market price; hence, the allocation of investment funds is economically efficient.

6. Suppose that the price control forces the price to below the marginal cost. Consumers would buy to the quantity such that their marginal benefit equals the price. This would be less than the marginal cost, causing economic inefficiency in the allocation of rice.

7. Outsourcing is the purchase of services or supplies from external sources. The opposite of outsourcing is vertical integration.

8. The transfer price is the price charged for the sale of crude oil from the crude oil division to the refining division.
9. To ensure that the department store uses the economically efficient quantity of retail space.
10. A price that includes freight is called cost including freight. A free on board price does not include the freight cost.
11. Payment refers to who conveys the money to the agent. Incidence refers to the impact in terms of price – buyer's price and seller's price.
12. With free shipping, the retail supply curve would be lower and the demand curve would be higher. If vendors charge for shipping, the retail supply curve would be higher and the demand curve would be lower. The total price (good plus shipping) to consumers would be the same.
13. If the demand is perfectly elastic, the tax will be incident completely on the supply side and there would no incidence on consumers.
14. Both demand and supply increase. The incidence on airlines and consumers depends on the price elasticities of supply and demand.
15. If the demand is inelastic relative to supply, the tax will be incident mostly on the demand side. The difference between the pre-tax prices at the airport and in the city would be larger.

Chapter 7. Costs

7A. The opportunity cost is $8 million. So, if Luna commences R&D, its profit would be the profit contribution minus the R&D expense minus the opportunity cost, $20 - 10 - 8 = 2 million. So, the correct decision is to commence R&D.
7B. (a) Set the transfer price equal to the market price. (b) Set the transfer price equal to the opportunity cost of the input (which is the consuming division's marginal benefit from that input).
7C. The avoidable cost of R&D is $10 - 1 = 9 million. Hence, if Luna continues R&D, the cost would be $9 million, and the profit would be the profit contribution minus the avoidable cost of R&D, $8 - 9 = -$1$ million, that is, a loss of $1 million. So, the correct decision is to cancel the R&D.
7D. [Omitted.]
7E. Total cost = $26,900 + $3,500 = $30,400. There are neither economies nor diseconomies of scope.
7F. The new experience curve is higher at every level of cumulative production than the experience curve with 20% cost reduction.

1. The client could have used the time spent with the salesman on other activities. In addition, the salesman buys lunch for his client with the objective of increasing sales.
2. Value added = Buyer benefit − Seller cost = Buyer surplus + Economic profit. The social enterprise does not receive any revenue. However, it does create value to the extent that the benefit (of education) exceeds the cost.

Since the enterprise does not earn any revenue, its EBITDA is the negative of its costs.

3. The residential development group should pay the market price of lumber to the building materials division.

4. Luna Biotech's manufacturing division should set its price equal to the opportunity cost of the process.

5. Jupiter (loan-financed) looks like it is less profitable than Mercury (an identical business, but equity-financed) because conventional accounting requires interest payments to be expensed, but not expected dividends. In terms of EBITDA, Mercury must account for the cost of equity, so the performance of the two companies would be more similar.

6. No. The pensions of retired employees are sunk costs. Once the business commits to hire the employees, it must pay its retired employees their pensions. The pensions are already committed and unavoidable. In forward-looking business decisions, managers should only consider avoidable costs.

7. Sunk costs are more significant in situation (a). The business depends on permanent staff rather than part-time workers. The employment of permanent staff is a long-term commitment.

8. No. Although the average fixed costs will fall with the scale of the production, the variable cost will most probably increase with the scale of production due to nurses working inefficiently (for example, too many nurses will get in each other's way). Since the fixed costs are not substantial, the increase in average variable cost will outweigh the decrease in average fixed cost.

9. Fixed costs can be either sunk or avoidable. Fixed costs that are sunk are those fixed costs that are committed and can never be recovered. Fixed costs that are avoidable are those fixed costs that can be avoided with a change of plan. Sunk costs need not be fixed in the sense of supporting any scale of production.

10. In an industry with economies of scale, businesses operating on a larger scale will be able to achieve a lower average cost. Therefore, businesses should aim to produce on a large scale. This means mass marketing and low prices.

11. Economies of scale pertain to a single product. Economies of scope pertain to multiple products. With economies of scale, increasing the scale of production would reduce average costs. With economies of scope, increasing the scope of production would reduce average costs.

12. When there are economies of scope for two products, it is cheaper to produce them together. Therefore, companies should produce both products to achieve lower cost than competitors which specialize in producing one of the products.

13. An experience curve with a learning percentage of 100% is horizontal (no reduction in average cost with increase in cumulative production).

14. With an experience curve, average cost falls with cumulative production. So, it is essential to forecast cumulative production accurately. This forecast is crucial for planning investments and setting prices.

15. Production of a newspaper involves a substantial fixed cost. Decision-makers subject to the fixed-cost fallacy include part of the fixed cost in variable cost. Hence, they overestimate the average variable (and marginal) cost.

Chapter 8. Monopoly

8A. Barriers to competition and the elasticity of demand or supply.
8B. If the demand is very elastic, then the marginal revenue will be close to the price.
8C. It should raise price, so reducing sales to the production where its marginal cost equals its marginal revenue.
8D. The new marginal cost will cross the (unchanged) marginal revenue at a smaller quantity of production. Hence, Venus should set a higher price to induce that quantity of sales.
8E. Advertising expenditure equals $(135 - 71) \times 0.14 \times 1.3 = \$11.65$ million.
8F. With a higher price and lower marginal cost, the incremental margin will be higher, and so R&D expenditure should be higher.
8G. Venus's total expenditure is represented by either the area $u0vx$ under the marginal expenditure curve from a quantity of 0 to 6,000 tons or the rectangle $t0vz$.

1. [Omitted.]
2. Patents, copyright, trademarks, and trade secrets.
3. With economies of scale, a producer that produces on a larger scale will have a cost advantage over other producers. So, it can price lower and dominate its market.
4. To sell additional units, a seller must reduce its price. So, when increasing sales by one unit, the seller will gain the price of the marginal unit but lose revenue on the inframarginal units. Hence, the marginal revenue is less than or equal to the price.
5. True.
6. The publisher should reduce its price and sell additional units. For these units, the marginal revenue is greater than marginal cost, thereby increasing total profit. It should reduce price until the marginal revenue equals the marginal cost.
7. The profit-maximizing quantity is such that the marginal revenue equals the marginal cost. Hence, after a change in costs, the seller should look for the quantity where the marginal revenue equals the new marginal cost. So it must consider both the marginal revenue and the marginal cost.
8. The profit-maximizing quantity is such that the marginal revenue equals the marginal cost. Hence, after a change in demand, the seller should look for the quantity where the new marginal revenue equals the marginal cost. So it must consider both the marginal revenue and the marginal cost.
9. Advertising expenditure equals $(100 - 40) \times 0.01 \times 500,000 = \$0.3$ million.

10. Reduce advertising expenditure until the advertising–sales ratio equals the incremental margin multiplied by the advertising elasticity of demand.

11. The R&D elasticity of demand depends on two factors: one is the effectiveness of R&D in generating new products and enhancing existing products; and the other is the effect of new and enhanced products on demand.

12. Raise R&D expenditure until the R&D–sales ratio equals the incremental margin multiplied by the R&D elasticity of demand. Intuitively, the higher is the incremental margin and the more sensitive is demand to R&D expenditure, the more the business should spend on R&D.

13. False.

14. True.

15. In a perfectly competitive market, every buyer purchases at a scale where its marginal expenditure equals the market price; hence, its incremental margin percentage is zero. By contrast, a monopsony restricts purchases to get a lower price and increase its net benefit above the competitive level. The more inelastic is the market expenditure, the more the buyer can reduce price below its marginal expenditure.

Chapter 9. Pricing

9A. $(p - 70)/p = 1/2$, so price equals $140.

9B. It does not extract the entire buyer surplus, and it does not provide the economically efficient quantity.

9C. Area $adb = 0.5 \times 2{,}500 \times (400 - 240) = \$200{,}000$. Area $bec = 0.5 \times 2{,}500 \times (240 - 80) = \$200{,}000$.

9D. Adults: With the marginal cost of $100, the marginal cost is equal to marginal revenue at a smaller quantity. At the new quantity, the price would be higher. Seniors: With the marginal cost of $100, the marginal cost is equal to marginal revenue at a smaller quantity. At the new quantity, the price would be higher.

9E. The CF price in Japan is

$$\frac{p - 30{,}000}{p} = -\frac{1}{-2.5},$$

or $p = ¥50{,}000$. The domestic price is $350 = ¥35{,}000$. So the difference is ¥15,000.

9F. Buyer surplus of business traveler: unrestricted $= \$501 - \$500 = \$1$; restricted $= \$401 - \$180 = \$221$. Buyer surplus of leisure traveler: unrestricted $= \$201 - \$500 = -\$299$; restricted $= \$101 - \$180 = -\$79$. The leisure traveler will not buy either the unrestricted fare or the restricted fare. So indirect segment discrimination will not work.

9G. Indirect segment discrimination is less profitable than direct segment discrimination for two reasons. (a) Buyer benefit: to induce buyers with different attributes to choose different products, sellers may have to resort to designing low-end products in a less appealing way. (b) Cost: implementing indirect discrimination may involve relatively higher costs.

1. With uniform pricing, the price of a product depends on both the price elasticity of demand and marginal cost. Whether to set a higher price for the own-label merchandise depends on two factors. (a) Since the demand for the own-label good is less elastic than for the branded good, the incremental margin percentage should be higher for the own-label good. (b) However, the marginal cost of the own-label good would be lower than that of the branded good.
2. By the formula for uniform pricing,

$$\frac{p-2}{p} = -\frac{1}{-1.25},$$

so the price is $10.
3. No. It should adjust price so that the incremental margin percentage, $(p-40)/p$, equals the absolute value of the reciprocal of the price elasticity of demand.
4. The pricing method used by the book publishers is cost-plus pricing. It ignores the price elasticity of demand.
5. Complete price discrimination increases profit by resolving two shortcomings of uniform pricing. Complete price discrimination extracts the entire buyer surplus by pricing each unit at the buyer's benefit. In addition, it provides the economically efficient quantity, where marginal benefit equals the marginal cost.
6. The two conditions that are necessary to implement complete price discrimination are as follows: (a) the seller must know each potential buyer's individual demand curve; (b) the seller must be able to prevent customers from buying at a low price and reselling to others at a higher price (arbitrage).
7. [Omitted.]
8. FOB pricing considers only the difference in the cost of delivery to the different markets, and it ignores the difference in the price elasticity of demand. CF pricing takes into consideration both the different price elasticities and the different marginal costs.
9. Newspapers. To discriminate by the buyer's location, buyers must not adjust location to take advantage of the price differences. Buyers will not shift location to save on the price of a newspaper. Also, the value of newspaper content depreciates fast, so no buyer would wait for resale of a newspaper from a cheaper location.
10. [Omitted.]
11. Those who rent at the expense of others will be less sensitive to the higher gasoline prices at the car rental agencies and will not make the additional effort to look for cheaper gasoline. The person who makes the buying decision does not pay the bill.

12. Coupons can be used to discriminate on price because it takes time and effort to redeem a coupon. To the extent that consumers whose demand is more price elastic are also those whose time is less valuable, they will redeem the coupon and get a lower price.

13. From highest profit to lowest: complete price discrimination, direct segment discrimination, indirect segment discrimination, uniform pricing.

14. Information technology both assists and hinders the seller's ability to discriminate on price. Through the Internet, marketers can collect detailed information on consumer preferences. Furthermore, technology helps to reduce the cost of storing, analyzing and applying this information, enabling sellers to offer products that better suit customer demand. However, technology has enabled the growth of search services. So, consumers can more easily compare products and prices.

15. Cannibalization occurs when high-benefit segments buy the item aimed at low-benefit segments. First, sellers can make the differences between the high-margin item and low-marginal item more salient by upgrading the high-margin item and degrading the low-marginal item. Second, products can be designed with multiple discriminating variables. Lastly, cannibalization can be mitigated by controlling the availability of the low-margin item.

Chapter 10. Strategic Thinking

10A. In perfect competition, there are so many producers that decisions made by a single producer do not affect others. The increase in the production of nails (made by your company) will not affect the market price, so this decision is not strategic.

10B. The Nash equilibrium is for both Jupiter and Saturn to cut price.

10C. (a) If Saturn maintains price, the expected consequence is

$$\frac{2}{5} \times 900 + \frac{3}{5} \times 500 = 660.$$

(b) If Saturn cuts price, the expected consequence is

$$\frac{2}{5} \times 800 + \frac{3}{5} \times 600 = 680.$$

10D. (a) Positive-sum game. The sums of the outcomes for the parties are different (between −3 and 2) in the various cells of the game in strategic form.
(b) Positive-sum game. The sums of the outcomes for the parties are different (between 1,200 and 1,800) in the various cells of the game in strategic form.

10E. There is no first-mover advantage because the equilibrium is the same – both cut price – whether Jupiter or Saturn moves first.

10F. The new game in extensive form begins at a node where TV Delta chooses between contracting and not contracting with the fast food chain. Each possible action leads to nodes where Channel Z chooses between 7:30 pm and 8:00 pm. In turn, each of Channel Z's actions leads to nodes where TV Delta chooses between 7:30 pm and 8:00 pm. In equilibrium, TV Delta chooses to advertise, Channel Z chooses 7:30 pm, and TV Delta chooses 8:00 pm.

10G. Let the minimum probability that the employer will eventually raise wages be R. Then the expected increase in earnings from a strike would be $(-4 + 12) \times R + (-4) \times (1 - R)$. For the threat of strike to be credible, the expected increase in earnings from a strike must be at least zero, $(-4 + 12) \times R + (-4) \times (1 - R) \geq 0$, or $8R - 4 + 4R \geq 0$, or $R \geq 1/3$. So, the minimum probability is 1/3.

1. (a) In perfect competition, there are so many sellers that decisions made by a single player do not affect others. So, it does not matter whether the seller acts strategically. (b) In a monopoly, there is only one seller. However, it must consider potential entrants to its market. Therefore, it has to act strategically.

2. A dominated strategy generates worse consequences than some other strategy, *regardless* of the other parties' choices. Therefore, you should not adopt a dominated strategy.

3. Only (c).

4. If others do not act strategically, I should choose the best strategy, even if it is not a Nash equilibrium strategy. But, I should never use a dominated strategy.

5. In a randomized strategy, the party specifies a probability for each of the alternative pure strategies. Then it adopts each pure strategy randomly according to the probabilities. The probabilities must add up to 1.

6. Strategy (b) is more effective. It is random and unpredictable, and so the boxer's opponent will not be able to anticipate the move and counter it.

7. In a zero-sum game, the outcomes for the parties add up to the same number in every cell of the game in strategic form. Therefore, one party can become better off only if another is made worse off – which is the essence of competition. By contrast, in a positive-sum game, the outcomes for the parties add up to different numbers in the various cells. Hence, one party can become better off without another being made worse off. By coordinating, one party can become better off without another being made worse off.

8. Yes. The outcomes for the parties add up to the same number in every cell of the game in strategic form.

9. By reasoning forward from the initial node, the party will not be able to anticipate the other parties' responses and adjust its own response to maximize its expected outcome.

10. The equilibrium is the same – both US and Japan head north – whether the US moves first or second. So there is no first-mover advantage.

11. If the conditional strategic move (promised or threatened action) need not actually be carried out, the conditional strategic move has no cost. On the other hand, an unconditional strategic move will involve a cost under all circumstances. Therefore, conditional strategic moves are more cost-effective than unconditional strategic moves.

12. Deposit insurance pays compensation to depositors if the bank becomes insolvent. The deposit insurance funded by the bank itself may not be credible because, if the bank becomes insolvent, it may not have funds to pay the compensation.

13. The "walk away" tactic is credible only if the person has a better offer elsewhere and is better off by walking away. So the credibility of "walking away" depends on the probability that the person has a better offer elsewhere.

14. Both the legal system and violence are threats to persuade borrowers to repay their loans. Since loan sharks are not allowed to use the legal system to collect debts, they employ violent threats (costs) to persuade borrowers to repay.

15. There are many more possible strategies in repeated interactions than in once-only scenarios. In particular, a party can choose a strategy in which it conditions its action on the actions of the other party.

Chapter 11. Oligopoly

11A. Luna's residual demand curve would be more elastic, so its profit-maximizing price would be lower. Then its best response function would be further to the left. Similarly, Mercury's best response function would be lower. The equilibrium prices would be lower.

11B. The average cost would be higher (the fixed cost does not affect the marginal cost). The limit price (the lowest price that Mercury can set and deter Luna from entry) would be higher.

11C. In Figure 11.6, if Luna's marginal cost is lower, its profit-maximizing price would be lower and production would be higher. So, in Figure 11.7, Luna's best response function would be further to the right.

11D. The graph would be like Figure 11.7, with the downward-sloping best response functions.

11E. If Mercury sets capacity at 21 million subscribers a month, Luna's best response is capacity of zero. This strategy is bad for Mercury because it would depress the market price and reduce its profit.

11F. Horizontal integration is the combination of two entities, in the same or similar business, under a common ownership. Vertical integration is the combination of assets for two successive stages of production under a common ownership.

1. False. In a Bertrand oligopoly, price equals marginal cost.

2. (a) The residual demand curve of one seller is the demand given the prices of competing sellers. (b) The residual demand curve of one seller is the demand given the capacities of competing sellers.

3. (a) The best response function of one seller is the seller's profit-maximizing price as a function of the prices of competing sellers. (b) The best response function of one seller is the seller's profit-maximizing capacity as a function of the capacities of competing sellers.

4. You should adjust in the same direction as your competitor, which is to raise your advertising.

5. With differentiation, if one seller undercuts the competitor's price, it would take away only part (and not all) of the competitor's demand. So, differentiation softens competition.

6. A strategic form shows the strategies of the various parties and the corresponding consequences.

7. The increase in fixed cost does not affect the equilibrium (provided that it is not so large as to cause the producer to cease production).

8. Actions are strategic substitutes if one party's adjustment of action leads others to adjust in the opposite direction.

9. The graph would be like Figure 11.7, with the downward-sloping best response functions.

10. If the fixed cost of production is zero, the average cost and marginal cost curves would be the same and a seller can break even at small scale. So the price leader must set a price below its own average and marginal cost (and incur a loss) to deter the potential competitor from entering the market.

11. Sunk cost of capacity helps to implement a strategy of limit pricing. Looking forward, unavoidable costs would be lower, and so a strategy of maintaining a low price would be more credible.

12. Relatively larger. Your commitment to a larger capacity would push your competitors to smaller capacity.

13. Because the production committed will affect the capacity set by other sellers. This will in turn affect the price and profits.

14. Number of sellers, excess capacity, sunk costs, barriers to entry and exit, and product homogeneity.

15. It depends. If the product is more homogeneous (less heterogeneous), each seller will have a relatively elastic demand, therefore, it easily can sell more than its quota. However, having a homogeneous product enables the cartel to monitor the various sellers more easily.

Chapter 12. Externalities

12A. The new combined marginal profit contribution is lower by $3.20. The new economically efficient level of customer traffic would be 60,000 customers a month.

12B. (a) The restaurant's marginal cost curve will be higher. (b) The number of customers that maximizes the group profit contribution will be lower.

12C. The possible hurdle to resolving the externality is the assignment of rights. Does the betting shop have the right to attract customers or does the restaurant have the right not to be bothered by gamblers? (This situation involves only two parties, betting shop and restaurant, so free riding is not a problem.)

12D. There are four differences: (a) Critical mass: in markets with network effects, the demand may be zero unless the number of users exceeds critical mass. (b) Expectations: in markets with network effects, user expectations are important in demand. (c) Tipping: in markets with network effects, the demand may be extremely sensitive to small differences among competitors. (d) Price elasticity: in markets with network effects, the price elasticity may differ according to whether the demand has reached critical mass.

12E. An additional marginal benefit curve would increase the vertical sum of marginal benefits, and so possibly increase the economically efficient quantity of fireworks.

12F. Consider, for instance, a musical composition. It is a public good. However, it can be delivered in the form of a private good through copyright. The ability to deliver a public good in the form of a private good enables the commercial provision of the public good.

1. A positive externality directly conveys benefits to others. A negative externality directly imposes costs on others.

2. Luna's economically efficient level of advertising is where the combined marginal profit contribution equals the combined marginal cost of advertising.

3. The combined marginal benefit curve from additional customers for all retailers is the vertical sum of the retailers' individual marginal benefit curves.

4. When the sum of the marginal costs from a negative externality exceeds the marginal benefit to the source, there is an opportunity for profit by reducing the externality. The amount that the victims would be willing to pay to reduce the externality would exceed the amount that the source would require in compensation to reduce the externality.

5. The new subway will generate positive externalities for the property around the new stations as people benefit from convenient transportation. Therefore, by purchasing the properties around the new stations, the subway company will capture the benefits that the new stations will generate.

6. Once the highway exit is built, it would be difficult to exclude any particular business from benefiting from the additional traffic. The free-rider problem is that each individual business would try to avoid contributing to the cost of building the highway exit (knowing that it can still enjoy the benefit).

7. The benefit that one person obtains from using a particular spreadsheet program increases with the number of other users. The more widespread is the usage of that spreadsheet software, the more convenient it will be for users to share their data and work.

8. [Omitted.]
9. It depends on whether the demand is below or above critical mass. If demand is below critical mass, the demand will be zero and extremely price inelastic. On the other hand, if demand is above critical mass, if there is a price reduction, this will increase the demand, so the demand would be elastic. If demand far exceeds critical mass, any increase in demand will feed back through the network effect to further increase the demand. Then the demand would be inelastic to price.
10. Technical standards are relatively more important in markets with network effects. Having common technical standards for different suppliers helps those suppliers to jointly achieve critical mass in demand.
11. [Omitted.]
12. Only (c) is a public good.
13. The quantity of the public good available to each user does not decrease with additional users.
14. Laws such as patents and copyright enable owners of scientific formulas or artistic, literary, or musical expression (examples of public goods) to exclude those who do not pay for using them. Technology may enable the delivery of the public good to be excludable.
15. If the public good is being provided to one person, the marginal cost of providing the same public good to additional users is zero. The cost of provision is fixed with respect to the number of consumers, and the marginal cost of serving additional users is zero.

Chapter 13. Asymmetric Information

13A. Alice has imperfect information but does not face risk. The insurer has imperfect information and faces risk.
13B. Relative to the market with 100,000 bottles of low-quality wine, the combined supply would be closer to the supply curve of high-quality wine, and the market price and quantity produced would be higher.
13C. If the expected demand curve crosses the combined supply curve at point c, in the market equilibrium, all wine would be low quality. Hence, the expected demand would drop to zero, and the market would fail.
13D. Appraisals will be more common in the market for more expensive wine. The price of the wine would be more likely to cover the cost of appraisal.
13E. Borrowers who are more willing to repay will be relatively more likely to post collateral.
13F. This information would reduce every bidder's uncertainty about the true value of the vineyard. Hence, it would reduce the extent of the winner's curse.
13G. Screening is an initiative of the less-informed party, while signaling is an initiative of the better-informed party.

1. Imperfect information is the absence of certain knowledge. Risk is uncertainty about benefits or costs. A person can have imperfect information about some possibility, but if that possibility does not affect her/his benefits or costs, it does not impose any risk on her/him.

2. (a) No asymmetry. (b) The directors of Acquirer have better information than the general investor.

3. Ming's offer to pay a higher interest rate indicates that he is less likely to repay the loan.

4. Two reasons: (a) Less risk. If a borrower defaults on a secured loan, the creditor can seize and sell the item against which the loan is secured. (b) Less adverse selection. The security serves to screen good from bad borrowers.

5. The fixed salary will draw relatively less hardworking workers than a piece rate.

6. It is in the seller's interest to conceal negative information about the car.

7. With less information about the younger drivers, the insurers would be less able to screen between good and bad drivers among them. So insurers are more vulnerable to adverse selection.

8. [Omitted.]

9. Drivers with a lower probability of accident will prefer a higher deductible as they are less likely to make a claim.

10. Drivers whose value of time is less than the toll will not pay, and hence will be screened away in favor of those whose value of time exceeds the toll.

11. The winner's curse would be more serious in (b). By contrast, in (a), the study would reduce the uncertainty of every bidder, and so reduce the winner's curse.

12. In all auctions, the bidder should bid more conservatively. (a) In an auction to sell, this means bidding higher. (b) In an auction to buy, this means bidding lower.

13. [Omitted.]

14. Yes. It is relatively more costly for producers of poorer-quality software to offer the full refund, because their customers are more likely to demand the refund.

15. By accepting payment in Acquirer's shares, the actual amount that target receives will depend on Target's true value (which Target knows but Acquirer does not).

Chapter 14. Incentives and Organization

14A. (a) The economically efficient effort will be lower. (b) The effort that the worker actually chooses will be lower at e.

14B. Draw any salesperson's marginal compensation curve that crosses the salesperson's marginal cost curve at 250 units of effort a month.

14C. The salesperson's marginal compensation curve is zero up to just below 200 units of effort a month, vertical at 200 units, and zero above 200 units.

14D. The commission on sales will reduce the sales clerks' incentive to process returns.

14E. Potential benefits and costs, and possible contingencies.

14F. Upstream vertical integration is the acquisition of assets for a stage of production further from the final consumer. Downstream vertical integration is the acquisition of assets for a stage of production closer to the final consumer.

14G. The potential to reduce holdup through detailed contracting; the potential to resolve moral hazard through incentives and monitoring; the potential for outsourcing to reduce internal monopoly power; and the extent of economies of scale, scope, and experience.

1. [Omitted.]
2. It is costly for the insurer to monitor Leah's precautions, so information is asymmetric. Leah bears the cost of precautions but receives only part of the benefit.
3. The party subject to moral hazard will choose the activity at the level where their own marginal benefit equals own marginal cost. At that level, the sum of marginal benefits to all parties differs from the sum of marginal costs to all parties. So a profit can be made by adjusting the activity to the level where the sum of marginal benefits equals the sum of marginal costs.
4. It can help to resolve moral hazard by linking compensation to some measure of performance.
5. Your compensation will be affected by factors other than your performance, such as the general state of the economy and competition.
6. Reward the drivers for repair and breakdown expenses below the average for all drivers, and penalize them for expenses above the average.
7. The scheme will reduce the secretary's incentive for effort in the other tasks.
8. (b) Training on the airline's flight management system is more specific.
9. Because the additional cost of preparing a complete contract outweighs the potential benefit in avoidance of holdup.
10. (a) Shareholders have residual control (rights that have not been contracted away). For instance, they may dismiss the current board of directors and management. (b) Shareholders also have the rights to residual income (income remaining after the payment of all other claims). They receive dividends only after all other claims, such as interest and debts, have been paid.
11. [Omitted.]
12. The potential for holdup in the future would lead one party to take precautions such as writing more detailed contracts and avoiding specific investments. The precautions would increase its costs and reduce its revenues.
13. It should consider the disadvantages of internal production – moral hazard, internal monopoly, and inefficient scale, scope and experience.
14. Outsourcing constrains the monopoly power of the internal supplier.
15. Economies of scope are one reason for horizontal integration: the organization can produce a variety of products at lower cost than if each item were

produced separately. However, if the organization produces none of the items for which there are economies of scope, then it should outsource all of them rather than producing a subset.

Chapter 15. Regulation

15A. The optimal price would be the same (equal to the marginal cost). However, the consumption would be larger.

15B. Under structural regulation, the regulator stipulates the conditions under which a business may produce vertically related goods and services (to separate the natural monopoly from the potentially competitive market).

15C. In situations of asymmetric information, the regulator may be able to resolve the asymmetry by regulating the disclosure of information, conduct, and business structure of the better-informed party.

15D. If the user fee is $25 per ton, polluters would emit to a level where the marginal benefit of emissions is less than the marginal cost. If the user fee is $45 per ton, polluters would emit to a level where the marginal benefit of emissions exceeds the marginal cost.

15E. The driver would choose a new level of care where her marginal benefit equals marginal cost. It would be higher than the original level.

1. A market is a natural monopoly if the average cost of production is minimized with a single supplier.

2. One source of inefficiency is that government-owned enterprises are prone to be coopted by employees, so that the enterprise serves its employees rather than its customers. Another source of inefficiency is that government-owned enterprises may not get the optimal quantity of investment funds.

3. Marginal cost pricing means that a provider must set its price equal to marginal cost and supply the quantity demanded.

4. Price regulation gives the regulated entity an incentive to exaggerate its reported costs and so increase its actual profit.

5. Under rate-of-return regulation, the regulator stipulates the franchise holder's maximum allowed profit in terms of a maximum rate of return on the value of the rate base.

6. Under rate-of-return regulation, the regulated entity has little incentive to minimize costs and has an incentive to inflate the rate base.

7. Privatization means transferring ownership from the public to the private sector. Allowing competition means removing an exclusive (monopoly) right. A government-owned monopoly may be privatized without allowing competition.

8. To increase economic efficiency, competition law prohibits: (a) collusion; (b) abuse of monopoly power; and (c) mergers that create substantial market power.

9. False. If the information cannot be objectively verified, disclosure will not resolve the asymmetry.
10. Regulation of conduct and structure may prevent the party with superior information from exploiting that advantage, and so resolve the information asymmetry.
11. (a) The regulator could charge a user fee for noise generated by the construction equipment. (b) The regulator could set a standard and make it illegal for noise from construction equipment to exceed the standard.
12. Set a standard for engines in terms of emissions (quantity per hour).
13. The toll can induce the user to balance the marginal cost of congestion against her/his marginal benefit, achieving economic efficiency and resolving congestion.
14. Because the marginal cost of congestion varies by the time of day.
15. The government specifies the liability and compensation for accidents through law. The potential source of harm will take care to reduce liability.

Index